THE
WORD OF THE LORD
IS UPON ME

THE
WORD OF THE LORD
IS UPON ME

The Righteous Performance of

Martin Luther King, Jr.

JONATHAN RIEDER

The Belknap Press of
Harvard University Press

Cambridge, Massachusetts, and London, England

2008

Library of Congress Cataloging-in-Publication Data
Rieder, Jonathan.
The word of the Lord is upon me : the righteous performance of
Martin Luther King, Jr. / Jonathan Rieder.
p.   cm.
Includes bibliographical references and index.
ISBN 978-0-674-02822-7 (alk. paper)
1. King, Martin Luther, Jr., 1929–1968—Oratory.
2. King, Martin Luther, Jr., 1929–1968—Language.   I. Title.

E185.97.K5R54   2008
323.092—dc22   2007047272

Acknowledgments

I've acquired a lot of debts in writing this book. My discoveries in various archives would not have been possible without the skilled assistance of personnel at many collections. Over the years, the staff at the Howard University Divinity School library provided access to King tapes from their sermon collection as well as a comfortable environment in which to listen to them. Jim Baggett, Head of the Archives at the Birmingham Public Library, got me oriented in the Bull Connor Papers Collection, provided tapes of Selma and Birmingham mass meetings, and gave me important insights into that period. I thank the Birmingham Civil Rights Institute, Wayne Coleman, Head of Archives, and Dr. Horace Huntley, director of its Oral History Project, for their openness to scholars; the Assistant Archivist there, Laura Anderson, graciously pointed me toward recently acquired recordings of King in Birmingham mass meetings and other materials. At the King Center Library and Archives in Atlanta, Cynthia Patterson Lewis, Archives Director, and Elaine Hall, Archival Assistant, were wonderful guides to the vast King storehouse and donated their own considerable wisdom about King. In serving as stewards of not so distant collective memories of injustice, these institutions and the people who staff them affirm a collective resolve never to forget.

At Emory University, Randall K. Burkett, Curator of African American Collections, and Naomi Nelson, Coordinator for Research Services, helped me navigate through the David Garrow papers as well as other sources. Cyma Horowitz, Chief Librarian of the Blaustein Library of the American Jewish Committee, tracked down copies of King's speeches before Jewish audiences as well as information relevant to those appearances. Kerry Williams at the Auburn Avenue Research Library made available materials relevant to King's childhood.

It is impossible to overstate the generosity of so many of King's remarkable intimates and associates who enriched my understanding of the man and the movement of which he was only one part. Interviews with Juanita Abernathy, Rev. Willie Bolden, Rev. Walter Fauntroy, Tom Houck, J. T. Johnson, Rev. Bernard Lafayette, Andrew Levison, Congressman John Lewis, Rev. Joseph Lowery, Andrew Marrissett, Terrie Randolph, Rev. C. T. Vivian, Rev. Wyatt Tee Walker, Ambassador Andrew Young, and others who prefer to go unnamed were crucial to grasping King in all his nuance. I also thank Susannah Heschel for taking the time to share her reflections of her father, Rabbi Abraham Joshua Heschel, and his relationship with King.

The work of three King historians provided the indispensable chronicle and insight upon which my sociological analysis builds: David Garrow and his magisterial starting point, *Bearing the Cross;* Taylor Branch's three-book epic (*Parting the Waters, Pillar of Fire, At Canaan's Edge*); and the gargantuan efforts of Clayborne Carson and the King Papers project at Stanford University. Suffice it to say that the spines of my copies of their books have long since broken. *The Word of the Lord Is Upon Me* could not have been written without those pathbreaking efforts.

I have also learned much from a special subset of other King scholars: Lewis Baldwin, James Cone, Adam Fairclough, David Levering Lewis, Richard Lischer, and Keith Miller. At times I part company with each of them on this or that count, but I could never have arrived at the parting without having been engaged by their arguments and grappling with them. Their contribution exceeds a particular fact or insight; it extends to the less tangible realm of ways of seeing and hearing King without which I might not have even noticed features that have become important to me over the years.

This project has been almost two decades in the making. During that time, colleagues and commentators have offered important suggestions, observations, and reservations. But a number of people contributed so directly that I must mention them here. Although I thought I had a handle on the project from the outset, a fellowship at the Institute for Advanced Study at Princeton in 1991–92 propelled me on a line of inquiry that five years later would lead me to conclude that my take on King was wrong and that I had to dig deeper. I am especially grateful to Michael Walzer, both for the group of people he assembled that year (including Luc Boltanski, the late Franco Ferraresi, Elisabetta Galeotti, Jennifer Hochschild, and Georgia Warnke) and for his writings about Exodus and "connected critics" which clearly inform this work.

David Garrow helped in ways beyond his scholarship; I thank him for his generous response to queries. On my trips to and through Atlanta, Tom Remington of the Emory University Political Science Department and Nancy Roth Remington offered, along with their enthusiasm for the project and sharp observation, food, friendship, and a bed. Russell Adams, the long-standing chair of the Howard University Afro-American Studies Department, shared historical context and evocative vignettes of Benjamin Mays and Morehouse College to illuminate King's early years. I owe special thanks for the immense generosity of David Chappell, author of the fascinating *No Stone of Hope: Prophetic Religion and the Death of Jim Crow.* He offered a flood of cautions and critiques, and I heeded a vast number of them. Devra Ferst served splendidly as a research assistant when she was an undergraduate at Barnard.

Harvard University Press deserves more than polite mention. My work with my editor Mike Aronson, who also edited my book *Canarsie,* proves you can get the band back together again. In the present case, Mike was a decisive influence on the book that ultimately emerged. His line-by-line reading of the final manuscript was a display of erudition, sharp stylistic instincts, and common sense. Who else could have spotted a misphrasing of free rider theory, a misspelling of Rabbi Maurice Eisendrath's name, and a missing "t" in Wilson Pickett? I'm also grateful for the contribution of Mary Ellen Geer, the manuscript editor at Harvard Press, to the entire production process. With her perfect aesthetic and intellectual pitch, she improved almost every page of the manuscript.

I am equally lucky to have in my life a number of people who are lovers of words; virtually all of them spend their lives writing, editing, and illustrating them. Many friends were drafted into the title search, but Nancy Miller and Steve Kling responded to the call far more often than I had a right to expect. Lee Caspar, Jim Davidson, and Andrew Glassman read through the manuscript and enriched it with their searching comments and good sense. My brothers Eric Rieder and Rem Rieder applied their extraordinary editorial powers to the book; they did yeoman and repeat service in all matters, and the book is much better for their efforts. *The Word of the Lord Is Upon Me* was also improved by Daniel Ross-Rieder, who brought his literary acuity and swashbuckling intellectual style to discussions of many aspects of the book. Above all, Catherine J. Ross, my partner in the most cosmic sense, has been my partner in the writing endeavor. Mainly, I'm grateful for her; here I'm grateful for her intellectual clarity. She critiqued more drafts, caught more interpretive nuances in such phrases as "My dear fellow clergymen," and excised more inelegant phrases than anyone.

The final acknowledgment is the most primal: to my father and mother, Rick and Dolly Rieder, lifelong liberals in the best sense. Their actions as much as their words taught us that we should care passionately about the civil rights movement. I dedicate the book to their memories.

Contents

ONE   The Artistry of Argument   *1*

Part I   INSIDE THE CIRCLE OF THE TRIBE

TWO   The Geometry of Belonging   *21*

THREE   Brotherhood and *Brother*hood   *32*

FOUR   Backstage and Blackstage   *50*

FIVE   Race Men and Real Men   *64*

SIX   The Prophetic Backstage   *75*

Part II   SON OF A (BLACK) PREACHER MAN

SEVEN   Flight from the Folk?   *91*

EIGHT   Homilies of Black Liberation   *110*

NINE   Raw and Refined   *131*

Contents

Part III   KING IN THE MASS MEETINGS

TEN   Beloved Black Community   158

ELEVEN   The Physics of Deliverance   179

TWELVE   The Rationality of Defiance   199

THIRTEEN   The Courage to Be   219

FOURTEEN   Free Riders and Freedom Riders   237

Part IV   CROSSING OVER INTO BELOVED COMMUNITY

FIFTEEN   Artifice and Authenticity   254

SIXTEEN   Practicing What You Preach   267

SEVENTEEN   Validating the Movement   286

EIGHTEEN   The Allure of Rudeness   302

NINETEEN   Black Interludes in the Crossover Moment   318

Notes   339

Index   383

Illustrations

"I've Been to the Mountaintop," Martin Luther King's last speech, Memphis, April 3, 1968. © Bettmann / CORBIS.   *frontispiece*

Martin Luther King in the study of Ebenezer Baptist Church, 1961. Photograph by Henri Cartier-Bresson. Magnum Photos.   *xiv*

Bernard Lee, Andrew Young, Robert Green, Martin Luther King, Lawrence Guyot, Harry Bowie, and Stokely Carmichael at a meeting during the Meredith March, June 1966. Photograph by Bob Fitch, © Bob Fitch Photo.   *17*

Reverend King at Ebenezer Baptist Church, November 8, 1964. © Flip Schulke / CORBIS.   *87*

Martin Luther King speaking at a rally in Jackson, Mississippi, June 1966. © Flip Schulke / CORBIS.   *151*

Martin Luther King with Rabbi Abraham Joshua Heschel on the Selma to Montgomery march, March 1965. Photograph by Bruce Davidson. Magnum Photos.   *249*

THE
WORD OF THE LORD
IS UPON ME

ONE

The Artistry of Argument

"I'm sorry, you don't know me," Martin Luther King, Jr., once declared from the pulpit, recounting his reply to a journalist who had questioned his denunciations of the Vietnam War. King was livid because both black and white critics wanted to confine him to the ghetto of "black" issues. Around that time, President Lyndon Johnson, smarting himself from King's criticism, was heard muttering, "That goddamn nigger preacher!" It wasn't just that they didn't get the man; they misjudged the character of his vocation. King's ministry would not be bounded. A number of years earlier, he had written: "Just as the eighth century prophets left their little villages and carried their 'thus saith the Lord' far beyond the boundaries of their hometowns . . . I too am compelled to carry the gospel of freedom beyond my particular hometown."[1]

Forty years after an assassin's bullet felled King, it is still not so easy to know the man. Was he the apostle of agape, that Greek word for selfless love he favored so much? An angry prophet who chastised America, "You got a lot of repenting to do"? A fierce Moses leading a black liberation

1

army modeled on Joshua's pounding feet? An Uncle Tom who zealously turned the other cheek? A silky smooth ambassador to whites, decorously translating black experience into familiar terms that might gently stir their conscience? Or the black preacher whose intensities could not be masked by the refinements of white theology? In truth, King was a little bit of all those things, and still others: exhorter, guide, translator, therapist, emissary, gadfly, scold. Maybe it's best to say that King had an uncommon ability to glide in and out of black, white, and other idioms and identities in an elaborate dance of empathy. Straddling audiences, he blurred not just the lines between them but their very meaning.

This chameleon King lies at the center of my story. In the redeemed nation prefigured in King's oratory, the identities that composed the American nation were more fluid and mixed, the borders between groups more permeable than ever. King's faith in mankind coexisted with a primal love of black people that did not impede his leaps into the imagination of others. He made himself Moses. He seized the words of Keats, Harry Emerson Fosdick, and James Weldon Johnson. He sidled into the dialect of beloved slave ancestors. He assumed the sensibility of angry black nationalists. His relentless sympathy extended to white racists, whose words of vitriol he dramatically pronounced to more fully inhabit them. "I am an untouchable," King affirmed after returning from India. If he'd been a German during the rising Nazi tide, he said, he would have worn a Jewish star.

This book explores the extraordinary performances through which King played with these possibilities before white and black audiences, in down-home moments and refined ones, as he joshed and justified. Part I examines the special talk—from rowdy teasing to spiritual intimacy—that emerged when King was with black colleagues, and the rival pulls of black identity and mankind as a whole that accompanied it. Part II delves into the tension between raw and refined, race and "all God's children," that marked King's preaching. Part III looks at King's rousing oratory in mass meetings, which mixed black preaching and civil religion, race rapture and the universal tasks of every insurgency. Part IV explores the crossover King who roused whites with lofty appeals to "amazing universalism" and "beloved community"; in those addresses to the nation, mainstream Protestant churches, Jewish organizations, labor unions, and readers of his trade books, King's "rude" censure of whites and displays of irrepressible, at times even bitter, blackness were a counterpoint to his sublime voice, reassuring images of black nobility, and deference to white moral notions.

As this organization suggests, this book is not biography, history, or theology. It is mainly an interpretive effort to understand a complex man—not the deep thinker or the inspiring doer, but the fluent speaker who did inspiring things with his words. My aim is to look at Martin Luther King in light of the wide range of situations in which he dwelled and the full range of talk he uttered in them: jokes, eulogies, sermons, speeches, chats, storytelling, exhortations, jeremiads, taunts, repartee, confessions, lamentation, complaints, and gallows humor. In this effort, I owe much to several extraordinary works that have sharpened our sense of King's complexity.[2] Ultimately, however, my portrait of King has emerged from a close reading of his writings, recordings of his speeches and sermons, and in-depth interviews with some of the people who knew him best.

Inevitably, this approach risks the impression that there was no "real" King—only a succession of fleeting personae evoked by particular occasions. The common association of performance with the scripted, the unreal, and the mendacious only fortifies that risk. So does the fact that I attend more to King's language and the way he deployed it than to the rich complexities of his beliefs. So it's important to say this flat out and up front: while it is true that King revealed different aspects of himself in these various settings, they were not entirely self-enclosed, and the man who spoke in them exhibited a remarkable constancy. As for the charge of fakery, "performance" as used here mainly reflects this truism: we know other people mainly through the way they display their inner states. Such displays tend to be channeled in ways at once conventional and idiosyncratic, which means the observer needs to know how to read them. In this sense, performance provides a way to grasp the real as much as to veil it. Uncovering the nuances of King's displays makes the nuances of the man readily accessible.

Such fathoming entails vigilance. As the great anthropologist of talk Dell Hymes warned, you assume at your peril that words simply mean what they say and say what they mean.[3] An act of speaking is often full of tension and ambiguity. As a result, a focus on any single feature of King's talk, such as idiom, obscures other features of talk—voice, rhythm, content, tone, ground, context, even silence—through which he communicated with his various audiences. Any one—or combination—of those features might carry the primary message of identity. The favored channel could even vary from setting to setting, and King was agile enough to convey different aspects of his identity in different channels at the same time. Often small departures carry more clues than his boilerplate—the time, say, when his veneration of the slaves took on a momentary tone of resentment, evoking the pain of black exile that can't be forgotten, even if it can be forgiven in the interest of "loving your enemies."

As that flash of indignation indicates, such subtleties suggest a more complex figure than the one revered by the nation on his birthday. It is no surprise that the avatar of American dreaming is the King who entered the pantheon of civil religion. From "all God's children" to beloved community, King ranged across humanistic, Christian, and Jeffersonian idioms to express his faith in "amazing universalism." That high-flown note struck a chord with many whites who thrilled to the words, "We will be able to speed up that day when all of God's children, black men and white men, Jews and Gentiles, Protestants and Catholics will be able to join hands."[4] The vision of one humanity is especially beguiling after so many years of separatist effusions, of queer nations and hip-hop nations, of hijab and yarmulke worn if not on the sleeve at least with panache, of aroused evangelicals who want their crèches in the public square. One should not forget that less cherished pioneer of identity politics back in the 1960s, Alabama Governor George Wallace, with his Confederate flag dwarfing the American one over the Alabama state house and the unapologetic way he wore cracker ethnicity on *his* sleeve—and in your face and on his bad-boy snarl of a grin.

But no matter how appealing this vision of mankind may be, the idolatry of King has come at a cost: it has sifted out the unsettlement that King inflicted, and meant to inflict, on a nonchalant, often clueless nation. The mantra "I Have a Dream," ripped out of the context of King's subversive gospel, has become the ambient noise of a society eager for good news—at least once a year, during the King holiday. The man Vincent Harding dubbed "the inconvenient hero" has been transformed into a marker of smugness, enlisted to show how far the nation has traveled from the ancient racist order to the lush freedoms of today. The proponent of a tough-minded theology who harbored few illusions about the strength of racism or of the insurgency required to fight it has become a sappy version of Rodney King bleating, "Can we all get along?"

This treacly icon has come at another cost: the skewed reading of King's relationship to blackness. In a bit of chicanery around the time of his Contract with America, Newt Gingrich parroted King's celebration of "the content of character"[5] as if King's dream were some leave-me-alone faith in moxie and property rights, shorn of its race pride and righteous edge. But King's America was less a redeemer nation than a nation in need of redemption, whose killing in Vietnam and indifference to the poor he deemed sinfully in line with its history of racism and genocide against the Indians.

Such trivializing pushed some members of King's prophetic band of colleagues over the top in Selma, Alabama, in the spring of 2005 at the Jubilee celebration of Bloody Sunday, the 1965 rampage in which state troopers on horseback greeted civil rights marchers on the Pettus Bridge with flailing truncheons and bullwhips. Up on the podium of Brown Chapel AME not far from the bridge, now-Congressman John Lewis, the gracious impresario of the event and a casualty of that massacre, a disquieted-looking Jesse Jackson, and the ever regally handsome Harry Belafonte looked on as then-leader of the Senate Bill Frist presented the church with an American flag that had flown over the capitol. Up there as well, Virginia Senator George Allen, who had yet to hurl his "macaca" insult, seemed to squirm as speakers called for the renewal of the Voting Rights Act. It took Rev. C. T. Vivian, a graduate of the circle of Nashville nonviolence and a close King colleague on the executive staff of the organization King headed (the Southern Christian Leadership Conference), to truly summon King's fire—invoking Exodus, declaiming against the Iraq war, and calling for beating swords into plowshares. "America," one could almost hear King saying once again, "you got a lot of repenting to do."

Exactly four decades earlier, following a march to Montgomery that began in that very chapel, it was no convenient King who opposed the sorry normality of American life to the more redemptive kind that judged it harshly. "For we know that it was normalcy in Marion (*Yes sir*) that led to the brutal murder of Jimmie Lee Jackson. (*Speak*) It was normalcy in Birmingham (*Yes*) that led to the murder on Sunday morning of four beautiful, unoffending, innocent girls. It was normalcy on Highway 80 (*Yes sir*) that led state troopers to use tear gas and horses and billy clubs against unarmed human beings who were simply marching for justice. (*Speak sir*) . . . The only normalcy that we will settle for (*Yes sir*) is the normalcy that recognizes the dignity and worth of all of God's children. The only normalcy that we will settle for is the normalcy that allows judgment to run down like waters, and righteousness like a mighty stream. (*Yes sir*)."[6]

Oddly, the hip-hop generation's seeming indifference to King's vision is in one respect consonant with the mainstream view of the comforting King. It's not that they warmed to King as they did to Malcolm X. In a culture that prized a rougher idea of masculinity, how else to respond to King's invitation, "Hurt us and we will win you with our capacity to suffer." Hip-hop coolness seemed a reprise of that older barb offered up by younger militants to repudiate the flawed exchange at the heart of Christian nonviolence, as if "De Lawd," as they ragged on King, was not so much noble as a chump. Other send-ups implied still more serious claims—that King and his crew weren't tough enough, weren't black enough. But despite any differences between those who exalted beloved community and those who disdained it, they shared something fundamental. Both tended to view integration as an either/or proposition; they parted company only in the evaluation of it. Yet for King such oppositions of integration and nationalism, race and nation, were incomparably simplistic. And they were beside the point. His vision of America was marked by the rich mix of civil and ethnic identities he managed to infuse into it.

The problem with the image of the universalistic King is not that it's wrong but that it is partial. It obscures too many other vital aspects of the man. The more pedestrian ones involved his devotion to soul food and love of spirituals. More revealing was his concession, "Ohhh, I know it's hard to love the white man"; the copious anger that at times spilled into racial bitterness; and his zeal for extolling black hair and skin. King was also a wicked practitioner of the "dozens"—that black game of ritual insult—who could "crack on" his sidekicks, and crackers too, with an imitative precision that would have been acidly mean if not for the affection that drove his jokes about fried chicken and raunchier ones as well. "You and King were some down-to-earth street brothers!" was Andrew Young's daughter's surprised reaction when she discovered the less sanitized reality of her father's years with King.

These aspects resonate with more recent scholarly efforts to rescue King from the portraits that featured him parsing white texts—there he goes ruminating Rauschenbusch—in favor of the race-man heir of Daddy

6

King and the genealogical line of the black folk preacher. In a sense, this revisiting was trying to recover the King that his audience of ordinary black people already took for granted. As Hortense Spillers noted early on, "Dr. King knew the oral tradition intimately, being himself a son of a preaching father. Though he was trained in the universities and academies, his sermons were infused and enlightened by the interpretation of the gospel message as he heard it while young and growing in the southern hill-soil of Georgia." That was the source of the shared response that "fired the response of black people by the thousands who heard him." Spillers grants that the audience "may have understood the historical-political analyses, but to be sure, the heart will long remember and take joy in the emotional achievement of the Word as King delivered it."[7]

The ample truth of this rendering explains why three of the four parts of this book are devoted to King's "black" talk. At times his oratory to whites really was a "performance" in the more cannily deceptive sense of the word. King vigilantly crafted his March on Washington speech, at least the one he intended to give, as a "white" speech for white consumption and maximum payoff. Even when King delivered similar set pieces before white and black audiences, the renditions had different twists to them. There was a vibrant backstage of black talk—with his rambunctious friends, before his home congregation at Ebenezer Baptist Church, in the black communion he fashioned in the mass meetings. It materialized as much in absence as in presence: the things King tended to expunge from his talk in white venues were often significant.

We could stop with this easy calibration—black audience, black talk; white audience, white talk—and fill an entire book with this theme. But stopping there would be stopping short and selling King short. The most obvious danger in this pairing comes from pushing racial thinking too far, equating "black" (whatever that might mean) with authenticity. If the "black" King was the "real" King, then who was the other King? At least some of the ethnic reclamation implies that the white sources and fancy theology were, in the charitable rendering, a bowing to necessity required by the crossover enterprise. But one quickly sinks into the quicksand of eternal regression: was King's borrowing from the Jews and their story of Exodus—"Wade in the water, children," the "Promised Land"—really "blacker" than his sampling from white liberal Protestants, to whom he was so viscerally drawn? If so, why did he venture outside the Afro-Baptist tradition to borrow the Exodus rendering of a nineteenth-century New England white preacher like Phillips Brooks? To put the problem more generally, to place such emphasis on King's vernacular sources and idioms as the sign of his genuine self risks falling into a highbrow version of the ghetto taboo on "talking white."

This equation of blackness and the genuine gets more tangled. To say that King's talk to whites was a "performance" while his black talk was not strains any proper understanding of rhetorical acts. Even Black Power rhetoric was a good deal less self-sufficient than its street braggadocio implied. Malcolm X, fishing for converts on the street corner, was as much a prisoner of the badass expectations of *his* audience as King was of the elevated expectations of his. Malcolm X too shifted idioms as he careened between street corner and mosque. Nor did the white audience vanish as a relevant category in black nationalist polemic. In its mode of honky-baiting, a political variant of trash-talk, black nationalism endowed the white audience with heightened power, if only as sacrificial victims, cabalistic enemies, and objects of denunciations. To complicate matters, King had his own Christian equivalent of "telling the man," in which he catered to whites not to save their faces but as a prelude to savaging them.

It can't even be said that King's "black" talk was always less stylized than his "white" talk. In fact, as we will discover, there was no such thing as pure unadulterated blackness. Race—and the very notions of "black talk" and "white talk" if taken as anything more than handy but loose categories—founders on all manner of variation. There was no single black backstage, and there were diverse black front stages too, and white equivalents of each. Discussing his "socialist" economic ideas, King once asked the Caribbean writer C. L. R. James, "'You don't hear that from me in the pulpit, do you?' . . . King leaned over to me saying, 'I don't say such things from the pulpit, James, but that is what I really believe.'"[8]

Ultimately, then, we will run up against this paradox. As we pursue the blackness in King's joking, preaching, and exhorting, we will find not only that "blackness" disguises other dynamics (black talk or a kind of masculine cutting up with friends who happened to be black?) but also that the ethnic has a curious way of circling back to the universal. King once described blackness as an interim state, a temporary adjustment to the nation's failure to implement the ideal of "all God's children." That was also true in a less grand sense: King's blackness waxed and waned even during so-called black talk.

King was not just a crossover artist but a code switcher who switched in and out of idioms as he moved between black and white audiences. But he also made such moves *within* his black talk and his white talk. He did not refrain from invoking agape, Keats, and Buber in churches across the Black Belt. Indeed, this reveals the true significance of King's performance at the March on Washington. At the very moment King was fashioning what was destined to become one of the nation's most profound moments, he abandoned his prepared text and took off on a flying bout of preaching that was as exultant a display of blackness before the nation as one could imagine at the time.

These quirks and swerves lie at the heart of the King who prevails here, a man who blended all sorts of oppositions. The key crossings were not just between black and white but between raw and refined, sacred and secular, prophetic and pragmatic. This mixing suggests a distinctly more modern image of King than we have fully absorbed—neither ethereal integrationist nor vernacular black man, not even a "rooted universalist," but, precociously enough, a "postethnic" man who could articulate his complex sense of self by drawing from a rich repertoire of rhetorics and identities.[9] He could express his deepest longings through Afro-Baptist idioms as well as all sorts of others—one more reason why the distinction between the universalistic King and the Afro-Baptist one, between white refinement and vernacular intensity, can never be hard and fast.

Thus the circle was squared when some maverick hip-hop artists finally came to consecrate King in the 1990s, relishing the beats and flow of the great sampler himself. For King was a turntablist in two senses. He turned the tables on whites, throwing their moral precepts back at them like a lance. But he was a turntablist in a more technical sense, always mixing and matching sounds and idioms. If the prophet was a performer, his endeavor was aesthetic as well as ethical.

As in any artistic enterprise, sensibility was key, and King was singularly equipped for the task of appealing to diverse audiences. In different realms, King was drawn to contrasts—poetically, midnight and morning; organizationally, the wildness of such preacher colleagues as James Bevel and the equipoise of Andrew Young; in his sermons, form and fervency.

King's special gift, his undeniable charisma, added another personal aspect to the equation. Born "Mike," he became Martin Luther and the King. He was a Christian warrior and a prince of peace. Charging words with prophetic power, he made the word of freedom flesh.

It was not the grandeur of the task alone that conferred the epic aura. King encouraged it. In Memphis the night before his death, he cast himself as Moses and peered over into Canaan. Even King's knack for lifting black people into biblical stories was double-edged, as when he painted word pictures of the flying dust kicked up by Joshua's army and hurled the Negro insurgents of Selma into the battle of Jericho. But as a kind of magician who served as the agent of their transfiguration, he was participating in his own elevation as the nexus between mundane chronicle and sacred story.

Clearly, the accolades credit King too much. Neither King's iconic individuality nor his majestic language was the entire story of even the King endeavor, let alone the Christian portion of the civil rights movement. The image of Joshua's army reminds us of the limits of the image of the charismatic performer who works his magic alone. Countless comrades, a division of labor that included a field staff of rougher race men who mobilized the people in Black Belt towns and got them in the spirit for a King appearance, the rich inheritance of the black church that offered expressive means and resonant stories, the cultural building blocks that composed a mass meeting, a resource-rich network of Jewish, liberal Protestant, and other white friends, the venues they provided and the mutual affection that issued from the whole endeavor—all these things went into a King performance. Accordingly, getting King right will require side excursions from time to time—they are not really tangents—into the broader field of social force in which King was embedded and the people who embodied it.

A King performance was a collective act in a more tangible sense: his words were not entirely his. Often the case with public speakers, this applied with special force to King, whose sermons and speeches were collage compositions. King was forever weaving bits from Amos and Isaiah, hymns and spirituals, Keats and Carlyle, black theologian Howard Thurman and white Presbyterian minister George Buttrick, Paul Tillich and Thomas Jefferson, into mosaics of sound. But these were only the literal debts. King owed his proficiency to the institutions through which he acquired his craft. If he was able to provoke assorted audiences, it was because his life lay at the junction of diverse lines of affiliation that taught him to speak in many tongues. Those networks formed a transmission belt through which the raw materials of song, argument, homily, citation, inflection, philosophy, sermon, rhythm, examples, authors, theology, and ideas flowed.[10]

In this respect, King's vocation was not so unique. Becoming a moral virtuoso, like becoming an auto mechanic, a ballet dancer, or a surgeon, requires an unsentimental education. As with Jerry Falwell lying in bed at night listening to radio preachers or Jesse Jackson scrutinizing King's every phrase and move, King had to absorb tradition, perfect technique, and learn to navigate the oddities of audience. A better comparison may be with Malcolm X, who mastered a wider range of idioms: the jive talk of his hipster days, his prison self-tutorial in the Western canon, the esoteric language of the mosque, street-corner diatribes against devils, and the secular radicalism of his Audubon Ballroom stint. The angry nationalist even developed his own version of outreach to whites, the outrageous address to college students, the stylized pleasures of which George Wallace and Louis Farrakhan would mine as well.

The crossover King, then, was made as much as born. His artistry was the outcome of intensive training that began in the black worlds of his family, Atlanta's Sweet Auburn Avenue, and his father's Ebenezer Baptist Church. Here King acquired his grasp of the sanctified character of the word from a community that prized charismatic speaking and cultivated it too. King's father, Daddy King, was an old-school preacher who could hoop and holler. His internship in country Baptist practice had begun in boyhood: "So many of the old-time preachers, who could recite Scriptures for hours on end, provided me with a great sense of the gestures, the cadences, the deeply emotive quality of their styles of ministry. And when I was alone, I would try to duplicate the things I heard them do."[11]

Flowing down the chain of generations, these verbal skills were handed over to King. "Watching his father and other ministers dominate audiences with artfully chosen words, the young boy tingled with excitement," King's Morehouse classmate, Lerone Bennett, observed, "and the urge to speak, to express himself, to turn and twist and lift audiences, seized him and never afterwards left him." There is a premonition of the powerful crescendos of the preacher in the boy who moved audiences with his soulful rendition of "I Want to Be More and More Like Jesus." "At six, he began singing hymns at church groups and conventions, accompanied by Mother Dear on the piano. Now he belted out a rollicking gospel song, now groaned through a slow and sobbing hymn. He sang his favorite with 'a blues fervor.' . . . They often wept and 'rocked with joy' when he performed for them." Ebenezer Baptist Church was on the circuit of revivals that drew gospel singers like Mahalia Jackson, a friend of Daddy King, and James Cleveland. Through the long reach of his father's connections, King was exposed to extraordinary preachers like C. L. Franklin and a raft of others. Although King never had a public born-again experience, he followed his sister up the aisle when she was called. By the time of his trial ordination sermon at Ebenezer, he had mastered the basics. The consummate showman made a show of putting away his notes before starting to preach.[12]

King acquired cultural capital as well as inherited it. As he moved out into the world of white institutions after he graduated from Morehouse College, a renowned historically black institution, King expanded his repertoire of the idioms and ideas that would help him reach broader audiences. At Crozer Theological Seminary, he took course after course in preaching and honed his command of the formal structures of white homily to such grand effect that his classmates crowded around when King was preaching. Boston University Divinity School, where he subordinated the craft of oral performance to the study of texts by the likes of Paul Tillich, provided a theological topping off. He also earned the prized designation of "Doctor," which would be converted to a less imposing "Doc" among his friends and colleagues. All along, he devoured the sermons of the finest exemplars of white liberal Protestant preaching. He took in their forms, copied their titles, absorbed their quotes. At their invitation, he would come to cross over into their world.

It might be tempting to attribute the raw to the black world, the refined to the white, but one should avoid the lazy romance of primitivism this implies. Elegance, polish, and refinement were black ideals no less than white ones. The letters King wrote his father as a boy suggest the early allure of a formal epistolary style. As a teenager, King was already recoiling from the pyrotechnics of the folk pulpit. At Morehouse King found a model of sophisticated preaching in its president, Benjamin

Mays, who embodied the same synthesis of intellect and passion that drew King to such masters of the craft as Gardner Taylor, Sandy Ray, Mordecai Johnson, Howard Thurman, Vernon Johns, and many others. Committed to a professional identity as a preacher by his late teenage years, King did not discriminate. He listened to the radio sermons of that luminary of white liberal Protestant homily, Harry Emerson Fosdick, even as he dashed across Auburn Avenue on the sly to Wheat Street Baptist Church to catch the words of Rev. William Borders, his father's rival and author of the sermon "I am Somebody."

That dash might seem like the attempt of an "alert striver," to use David Levering Lewis's apt phrase for King, to flee from his father. And it's true that Daddy King was straight out of the Georgia woods. In his own telling, he was "a backwoods Bible thumper with a gift for a lot of hollering" who did not realize he was "mangling the language" when he arrived in Atlanta, where his "rag tag" speech inspired derision and correction. His rooming-house mates needled him: "Seems to me that a young man named King would know just a small amount of the King's English." Upon meeting his future wife, the daughter of prominent minister A. D. Williams, Daddy King was struck by the fact that she "spoke so well, so clearly, and she put so many words together so well in one sentence." He told her, "Well, I'se preachin' in two places . . . Ain't been here but a short while."[13]

Yet one can't ignore the contexts which give meaning to contrasts like coarse and polished. King may have been more urbane than his Daddy, but he owed that urbanity to the cultural capital that his father had painfully amassed over decades. A self-improver hungry for respect in the world of Afro-Brahmin Atlanta, Daddy King worked hard to shed his country mien and prove himself worthy of belonging. King Jr.'s attraction to fancy words thus paid homage to his father's striving. "It was true that I had a lot of rough edges, but to my mind they were only temporary," Daddy King recalled. "I planned to be as smooth as the most polished people in town." Surviving the humiliation of being placed in the fifth grade when he was years older than his classmates, he worked hard; and during his delivery job, he remembered, "All along the way I'd be reciting my lessons to myself. I'd walk down the street practicing my rules of English grammar, tangling them all up at times, yelling at myself for being so slow." Eventually, that grit would pay off with admission to a distinguished college. Daddy King was a Morehouse man, the junior King a legacy.[14]

In 1953, Martin Luther King, Jr., left Boston to return to the South to serve as the pastor of Dexter Avenue Baptist Church in Montgomery, Alabama. He had acquired most of the resources he would need for the remarkable career that stretched before him. But this was all promise and preamble. Inciting an insurgency, leading a movement, waging the battles of Birmingham and Selma, gracing the cover of *Time* magazine, winning the Nobel Prize, meeting with presidents, delivering the "I Have a Dream" speech—if these loomed surprisingly close in time, they were the farthest thing from his mind. He was fixed on finishing his dissertation and revamping the Dexter church budget. Happenstance would determine what King would do with his capacious fluency; starting with the Montgomery bus boycott, the rising up of ordinary black people gave King a chance to discover new possibilities, in himself as much as in those words he loved so much.

As we sort through the phases of King's life, and the phrases too, one theme seems inescapable: King constantly evinced delight in language. Never just a means of displaying status (though he had a show-off streak) or signaling membership (racial or otherwise), the delight was sensuous, the pleasure of the play of words and the act of speaking. "His mother has said that she cannot recall a time when he was not fascinated by the sound and power of words. 'You just wait and see,' he told his mother at the age of six, 'I'm going to get me some *big* words.' The idea of using words as weapons of defense and offense was thus early implanted and seems to have grown in King as naturally as a flower."[15]

Sitting in his Morehouse elocution class, King played the cutup: called on by the professor, who asked him how he was doing, King replied, "I surmise that my physical equilibrium is organically quiescent."[16] The exhorter who exultantly drew out that folksy exclamation in a Mississippi rally, "Oh, we goin' to have a tiiime in Washington," was the same King who savored the sound of "Aristophanes," distending it long enough to create sprung rhythm and dramatic sibilance.

At the same time, for a man whose daily round consisted of giving hundreds of speeches and sermons a year, there's a sense in which language wasn't all that important. His feelings of blackness were too abiding to be vested in any particular way of speaking. More important, his Christian faith and love of mankind were too abiding to be similarly limited. Despite all the efforts to grasp "the real King," that King was never reducible to this or that idiom, source, or inflection. The key lay in the substance of his argument and the commitments that animated it.

Ultimately, words were not as important as the Word. In his sermon "Paul's Letter to American Christians," using the ventriloquism he indulged in recurrently, King let Paul speak this interpretive warning: "So American Christians, you may master the intricacies of the English language. You may possess all of the eloquence of articulate speech. But even if you 'speak with the tongues of men and angels, and have not love, you are become as sounding brass, or a tinkling cymbal.'"[17]

The constant for King lay beyond language, beyond performance, beyond race. The core of the man was the power of his faith, his love of humanity, and an irrepressible resolve to free black people, and other people too. This was the basic truth that no fancy scholarship can improve on. The best we can do is plumb that truth in its artful intricacy. King himself said it best countless times. His own reply to any unease implied by the accusation "you don't know me" trumpeted the unity that drove his civil rights ministry no less than his religious one, his "black" talk and his "white" talk: "But when God speaks, who can but prophesy? *(Amen)* The word of God is upon me like *fire* shut up in my bones, *(Yes. That's right)* and when God's word gets upon me, I've got to say it, I've got to tell it all over everywhere. [Shouting] *(Yes)* And God has called me *(Yes)* to deliver those that are in captivity. *(Sir)*."[18]

Part I

INSIDE THE CIRCLE OF THE TRIBE

"Let's talk black"

The adult life of Martin Luther King amounted to a long venture in leaping across the borders of race, religion, and talk. Even as the ferocity of white backlash and the war in Vietnam tested his optimism about the American experiment, he still envisioned a movement toward "a world-wide fellowship that lifts neighborly concern beyond one's tribe, race, class and nation."[1] Yet until 1948, when he graduated from college and left Atlanta for Crozer Theological Seminary in Chester, Pennsylvania, he lived a life nestled in the nurturing black worlds of his family, Atlanta's Auburn Avenue neighborhood, Ebenezer Baptist Church, and Morehouse College. He was also a member of the NAACP, Alpha Phi Alpha (the national black fraternity), and the National Baptist Convention, the nation's largest black organization. Even as his networks branched out after the Montgomery bus boycott to include new relationships with whites, as well as assorted Ghanaians and Gandhians from India, he spent most of his intimate life in the company of other blacks.

No matter how much King celebrated the idea of "amazing universalism," he lived a life steeped in "blackness," which took many forms: primal, pondered, and political. It was a given of his everyday life, the social circles in which he traveled, the cultural forms he had absorbed by osmosis and training, and even the shifting meaning of words like "we" and "our." It's not that King reserved the vision of beloved community for mixed and white audiences on formal occasions. He was genuinely fond of white friends and colleagues, and his condemnations of black separatism were equally heartfelt. Still, this separation between the moral vision of beloved community and King's lived experience sustained dual notions of brotherhood reflected in King's "black" talk and his "white" talk.

18

"Let's talk black" was what Jesse Jackson said to a group of black reporters in 1984 right before he referred to Jews as "Hymies" and New York City as "Hymie Town." That proposal was more than an invitation to switch to a franker kind of chatting. It envisioned candor in racial terms, defining the occasion as a tribal moment among those sharing racial or ethnic identity. The significance of the gaffe was heightened by the fact that Jackson did not need to mention race to achieve this frank kind of talk and safeguard anonymity. He only had to invoke the convention of "background," in which reporters and their sources routinely agree to chat without attribution. In a further complication, Milton Coleman, the reporter who broke the story, cited Jackson's failure to invoke that rule as justification for his revealing the conversation. Coleman, a black man himself, was reviled by some blacks as a traitor to his race for putting the norms of his profession above those of racial loyalty.

What could be more different from the idea of loyalty to one's race than King's vision of beloved community? One of King's favorite hymns was "In God there is no East or West," and he often quoted the words of the Apostle Paul that inspired it: "There is neither Jew nor Greek, there is neither bond nor free, there is neither male nor female: For ye are all one in Christ Jesus." The existence of separate white and black churches in King's sermon "Paul's Letter to American Christians" loomed as an affront to the sacred notion of "all God's children." Another favorite phrase of King's, "single garment of destiny," expressed that same ideal in a more secular idiom. King liked to juxtapose "brotherhood" and "neighborhood," but whatever the auditory joys of that contrast, it was the thematic one that mattered. "The real problem," he emphasized, "is that through our scientific genius we've made of the world a neighborhood, but through our moral and spiritual genius we've failed to make of it a brotherhood (*Lord have mercy*)."[2]

Yet King's use of the phrase "white brothers" points to an ambiguity at the heart of brotherhood. Despite its seemingly race-free aspect as a status open to all, the "white" coming right before "brothers" suggests that it was almost impossible not to think about race in a society that enforced all kinds of racial division. Its very presence highlighted the effort needed to open the category of brothers to all. In this sense, brotherhood was as much a moral ideal to strive toward as a reality experienced in everyday life.

As the 1960s revealed the continuing brutality of white racism and King succumbed to a rising lack of confidence in the white capacity for moral transformation, greater ambiguity crept into King's use of the word "brothers" even as his references to "white brothers" diminished. Only a few years after his 1963 "I Have a Dream" speech at the March on Washington, King spoke the following words in a Christmas sermon at Ebenezer Baptist Church: "I must confess to you today that not long after talking about that dream I started seeing it turn into a nightmare. . . . I watched that dream turn into a nightmare as I moved through the ghettos of the nation and saw my black brothers and sisters perishing on a lonely island of poverty."[3]

The dual meaning of "brothers" introduces the theme of Part I, which explores King's personal relationships and his more general views of black and white relations. Although not a separatist, in many respects King lived a separate black life, with its own ideals and identities, idioms and institutions. In a pattern of doubling, an ethnic version of *brother*hood co-existed with the appeals to brotherhood that King paraded especially but not exclusively before whites. And yet the key word here is "coexisted"; it never supplanted them. Over and over, we will run up against this para-doxical truth: King's most intense moments of black identity often re-vealed the limits of blackness in his life as much as its power. There were all kinds of black audiences, which differed from each other almost as much as they did from white audiences. Some of King's "black talk" was actually southern preacher talk or male boisterousness. Most important, blackness never vanquished passions and preoccupations of a more uni-versal sort.

TWO

The Geometry of Belonging

"[Jesus was] a gifted Jewish prophet with a lot of personal problems"

In leaving black Atlanta to attend seminary in the North, King was moving forward into uncharted territory. Only then did King encounter the white world in a sustained fashion. A brief look at his life in predominantly white institutions only underscores the power of blackness in his everyday life.

Martin Luther King's socially privileged childhood provided much shelter from racial insult, but he did not escape all contact with whites. He had a white playmate whose father ran a grocery store in the neighborhood. He interacted with whites during the summer he spent picking tobacco in Connecticut, and joined an interracial religious group while in college. Still, King was no stranger to racial wounds. The shock and hurt that surfaced in his initial forays across the border of race underscore the density of his black ties, the immunity from racist slight they provided, and the power of race as a source of trust and knowledge.

In his father King had a model of the defiant race man who went through a lengthy period of hatred of whites and remained suspicious of them. Having witnessed as a boy a bloodthirsty racist beating that turned into a lynching, Daddy King told his mother that "I'd carry a hatred in me for white people until the day I died. I would hate every one of them and fight them day and night, trying my best to destroy any of them I had a chance to." "I don't like it, M.L.,'" was Daddy King's response when the younger King broached the subject of the interracial college venture. "I said to him, 'You don't need to risk any betrayals from them, and that's mainly what you'll get."[1]

King's experience of racism wasn't only vicarious. When he was seven, his white playmate's father forbade them to play together, and the reason was King's race. According to Daddy King, his wife Bunch, as King's mother was known, "was hardly able to console him. His heart, he said, was broken. How could anybody refuse to be a friend with somebody else because they were not the same color? 'Why?' he asked his mother. 'Why don't white people like us, Mother dear?'"[2]

A pointed encounter with white meanness came in 1944 on the occasion of an oratory contest sponsored by the black Elks in Dublin, Georgia, where King delivered a speech titled "The Negro and the Constitution." "Black America still wears chains," the thirteen-year-old King pronounced. "The finest Negro is at the mercy of the meanest white man." He referred to the plight of Marian Anderson, whose musical invocations of race and nation at the Lincoln Memorial on Easter Sunday in 1939 foreshadowed his own at the March on Washington. "When the words of 'America' and 'Nobody Knows De Trouble I Seen' rang out over that great gathering, there was a hush on the sea of uplifted faces, black and white, and a new baptism of liberty, equality and fraternity." Having lifted the audience as Marian Anderson had lifted her own, King sent them crashing back to earth, noting that Anderson could not find a decent hotel in America that would have her. White racists loomed as perverse tormentors as King intoned, "So, with their right hand they raise to high places the great who have dark skins, and with their left, they slap us down to keep us in 'our places.'"

Nicknamed "tweed" for his sartorial flash, King charged, "Yes, America you have stripped me of my garments." The brotherhood he envisioned here was the more primordial one of skin and species. "And I with my brother of blackest hue possessing at last my rightful heritage and holding my head erect, may stand beside the Saxon—a Negro—and yet a man!"[3]

King did not know "they" were about to slap him down (back to Atlanta. When whites boarded the segregated pub which King and his mates were traveling, the bus driver ordered tant blacks to give up their seats and cursed them as "niggers" sons of bitches." "M.L. resisted at first, but his teacher finally encouraged him to get up and the young man had to stand for several hours as the bus made its way to Atlanta. 'It was,' King recalled twenty years later, 'the angriest I have ever been in my life.'"[4] King proclaimed his hatred for all white people, a feeling that lingered for years.

Such encounters offered certain compensations, providing a fund of experiences that King could draw on to forge racial communion. The hurt they left could help take a bit of the aura off the exalted Mosaic leader, revealing King as a black everyman who had suffered as all members of his race did. The work King had to do to get beyond his anger and the role of his parents' cautions not to hate set up a creative tension between raw feeling and its sublimation that was always present in King's black and white talk. Ironically, even before Malcolm X embraced the doctrine of white devils, young King had succumbed to and transcended racial hatred.

More vibrant relations with whites began in the white northern settings of Crozer Theological Seminary outside Philadelphia and then at Boston University. During high school, King's curiosity about whites had been whetted during that summer in Connecticut. His experience of his return to the South as "a curtain dropping over me" as he left his integrated train car at the Mason-Dixon line contrasted with the freedom that excited him in the North. Back at Morehouse, he defied his father's warnings about whites and participated in fledgling student efforts at interracial connection that reinforced his idealistic belief in the possibilities of integration.

At Crozer, the lackadaisical playboy gave way to the engaged student who flourished on the intellectual terms of the new world. Yet the fit between King and his new environment was hardly perfect, which underscored the practical limits to beloved community. Of that initial venture in crossing over, King would write, "I was well aware of the typical white stereotype of the Negro, that he is always late, that he's loud and always laughing, that he's dirty and messy, and for a while I was terribly conscious of trying to avoid identification with it. If I were a minute late to class, I was almost morbidly conscious of it and sure that everyone else noticed it."[5]

That self-consciousness about black laughter led to a severe repression of King's natural talent for teasing, mimicry, and general hilarity. "Rather than be thought of as always laughing, I'm afraid I was grimly serious for a time. I had a tendency to overdress, to keep my room spotless, my shoes perfectly shined and my clothes immaculately pressed." The most poignant expression of the need he felt to step gingerly through life with a watchful eye—on himself as much as on others—came at a picnic where watermelon was served. "I didn't want to be seen eating it because of the association in many people's minds between Negroes and watermelon. It was silly, I know, but it shows how white prejudices can affect the Negro."[6]

The racial voice in King's chronicle reflected tension between the natural sense of ease he felt back in Atlanta and his new feelings of standing out and being observed. In this white world, there was always a lurking danger of a misstep that would impugn his entire race. But there was another layer of tension in those musings that surfaced throughout his life. As revealed by his words "it was silly, I know" and "grimly serious," King had a heightened awareness, even of his own self-consciousness. That additional twist attested to the sensitivity of King's radar—a drawback of sorts but also an asset to draw on for the future crossover artist. It presaged the splitting that we will encounter in some of King's most revealing moments between "black" feelings and the idealized self that did not always welcome them.

If King's radar was especially fine-tuned, his concern with deportment reflected a racial vigilance and the ideal of refinement that were pervasive in elite black settings of the time. That vintage cultural milieu has been lovingly captured by Russell Adams, who was a member of the Morehouse class that arrived on campus just months after King departed for Crozer. The decades-long chair of the Howard University Afro-American Studies Department, Adams received his doctorate in political science at the University of Chicago, thereby following in the footsteps of Mays, whose admonitions on how to conduct oneself in white settings were simple: "Be your best self at all times and don't bring dishonor to the race." This was the period, Adams recalls, "when the *Pittsburgh Courier* carried Marcus Boulware's weekly column on standard English usage on the same page with Mays' column on education and public issues."

King likely underwent the same rigorous training in manners that Adams had to tackle during his years at "the House." "Mays' office underwrote a six-person training table on 'Proper Dining,' presided over by a Mrs. Stewart, a quadroon grande dame more New England than Abigail Adams. Amy Vanderbilt was the national expert on fine dining etiquette and we had to learn the Vanderbilt basics in the use of china, cutlery, stemware, finger bowls, and of course assorted napkins while dressed in suits and ties. When Mrs. Stewart peered over her pince nez glasses and said, 'Mr. Adams we will miss you next Sunday,' she meant that you had passed the Vanderbilt dining test. I dined there at least twice before Mrs. Stewart dismissed me."[7]

The transformation of scrutiny into self-scrutiny also reflected the geometry of King's divided relationships. Both at Crozer and at Boston University, the ethnic and the universal endured in the very design of his daily round. Long before King was shuttling between black audiences in Selma and white ones at the National Cathedral in Washington, D.C., the American Jewish Congress, and the White House, he did the same thing at Crozer and Boston University, where he studied for his doctorate in theology after seminary. During the whole time he was studying formal sermon structures, he was preaching to responsive black congregations at Ebenezer, Twelfth Street Baptist Church in Boston, and other black churches in Michigan, South Carolina, and Pennsylvania.

In February 1954, on a B.U. qualifying exam, King observed, "There is something quite sublime about this ethical system of [the philosopher] Fichte. To see that the external world exists for persons and as an outlet for their fulfillment of duty is quite lofty."[8] Later that same month, he spoke about a less arcane ethical quandary before a black Detroit congregation that bucked him up with cries of "Come on," "That's right," and "Lord help him." King played with the sensuous possibilities of the word "slick," its hissing sound and ghetto resonance, to create a street aura. Despite the fancier echo of "survival of the fittest" on which he was riffing, it was mainly a foil to his gleefully enunciated "survival of the slickest"—with the accent on that last word: "Whoever can be the slickest is the one who's right. It's all right to lie, but lie with dignity. [Laughter] It's all right to steal and to rob and extort, but do it with a bit of finesse. (*Yes*)." The churchgoers broke into laughter as King said it was all right to violate the

Ten Commandments as long as one glimpsed an inviolable eleventh: "Thou shalt not get caught." By the end of the sermon, King was nearly shouting along with the congregation.[9]

King may have carried off the balancing act with panache, but straddling worlds also had practical consequences. Because white institutions did not claim all of King's time, he was under the influence of rival pressures, teachings, and warnings. Parallel worlds also created a buffer between the intimate black world and the less intimate white one. The primacy of King's black core played out in his membership in a range of black sanctuaries within or near the white world—local black churches, intellectual salons, the national connections that channeled King's religious and romantic interests, and black friendships. Analogues to today's "black table" in school cafeterias, these were safe havens in which King and his colleagues could indulge in various kinds of ironic, skeptical, joyful, sardonic, and romantic practices that affirmed separateness.

Instead of being utterly swallowed up in the life of Crozer, King was absorbed into the coterie around Rev. J. Pius Barbour, a Morehouse man and an old friend of Daddy King. As it would in Boston, here the long reach of the senior King linked King Jr. to a local black pastor and his congregation, just as a national black circuit linked King to suitable potential brides at Columbia University and New England Conservatory. But King didn't need Daddy King to entice him into the Barbour orbit. The pastor of Calvary Baptist Church in Chester, Barbour sustained a lively rival universe for Crozer blacks, a counterpoint to the predominantly white seminary they dubbed "Barbour University."

The first black graduate of Crozer, Barbour was a learned man, well versed in philosophy and literature, who once gave a Men's Day sermon entitled "'Dirt-Men; Meat-Men; Spirit Men': . . . Naturalism, Existentialism, and Theism," in which, as he would tell it, "I gave the Bourgeoisie hell especially the Negro Bourgeoisie and their Ranch homes and installment plans."[10] He was also active in the National Baptist Convention and would join forces in the failed palace coup against its politically conservative leadership that later allied King with major progressive preachers—King's hero, Gardner Taylor; his favorite preacher, C. L. Franklin; the stalwart Sandy Ray.

The Duke professor of preaching Richard Lischer has reconstructed this second track at "Barbour University," which offered black students a collective independent study in modern black preaching. After the Sunday sermon at Calvary, the students came to Barbour's home where he "would painstakingly lead the group through each movement of that morning's sermon, pausing over transitions, phrasing, and imagery. He encouraged them to be logical in their delineation of ideas but imaginative and evangelical in their elaboration."[11] In tune with the black preaching tradition, Barbour did not stint on rhythm despite his ample learning. This synthesis of performance and theology, sound and substance, was very much in the spirit of many of King's models and mentors.

The black students who gathered around Barbour received more than instruction. They brought their dates to his home, listened to prize fights, feasted on soul food. Barbour served as a relay station to Calvary Baptist Church and the black community of Chester, where King established quite a presence. Sara Richardson, who worked with King on the Calvary youth group, recalled, "He could tell jokes so dry and then burst out laughing himself, and then you had to laugh." He spent hours drinking in the Calvary choir's rendition of old time spirituals. Like many others who crossed paths with King, Richardson remembered his love of chitterlings, fried chicken, and black-eyed peas. "He loved anything that was 'soul,'" said Emma Anderson, another Calvary member, whose sweet potato pie was a King favorite. In Boston, King found a similar black world in Roxbury around Twelfth Street Baptist Church. Its pastor, an old King family friend, was glad to watch out for and over King. It was the pastor's secretary, with links to the Atlanta world through marriage into the family of Benjamin Mays, who plotted to bring Coretta and King together.[12]

The personal clique from Morehouse days, partially reconstituted at Crozer with the arrival of King's friend Walter McCall, provided another kind of sanctuary. He and "Mac" went on the prowl for women together, shared their sexual rating system, and double-dated. With one exception, King's erotic and romantic interests were confined to black women. King was with McCall when they and their dates were denied service at a New Jersey restaurant. When they refused to leave, the owner threatened them with a gun.

The McCall-King duo was part of a larger crew of black students who socialized around the campus pool table and enjoyed the impish, at times riotous moments when they were distanced from the official reality. Ever alert to the subtleties of performance, King biographer Taylor Branch brings alive the black backstage in all its vibrancy: "The Negro students shared much merriment in contrasting [Crozer homiletics professor Robert] Keighton's archly formal structure with their own homemade preaching formulas. Keighton might have his Ladder Sermon, they joked, but they had Rabbit in the Bushes, by which they meant that if they felt the crowd stir, they should repeat the theme, just as a hunter shoots into the shaking bush on the assumption that a rabbit might be there. . . . King and Walter McCall liked nothing better than sneaking in to hear their Negro classmates preach in real churches off campus. Both of them were accomplished mimics. To the mortification of the classmate, McCall would shout out a countrified parody of what they had heard, full of emotional fireworks about Jesus as the Holy Spirit incarnate, and then King would deliver the 'correct' versions in equally exaggerated spiels of Enslin's rational historicism, speaking of Jesus as a gifted Jewish prophet with a lot of personal problems."[13]

Such contests of code offered more than cathartic release; they allowed King, McCall, and the others to try on new modes and scoff at old ones. At the same time, their over-the-top lampoons of each acknowledged the vexations of straddling social worlds. For these black students who were enrolled in a predominantly white seminary, the rituals hinted at a pressing need for black space and relief from the white world.

The "Dialectical Society" that King formed at Boston University offered a more complex case of black sanctuary. Certainly its racial character was more oblique than that of "Barbour University." A secular intellectual salon more than an Afro-Baptist brotherhood, the Boston group on its surface had a more universalist cast. If anything, it seemed to reproduce academic pretensions in exaggerated form. Some of King's philosophizing, despite its earnestness, bordered on self-parody in its pomposity, sounding close to the gibberish he once spouted at Morehouse in his elocution class. Its imitative character and the affectations it encouraged—King started smoking a pipe—may have evinced an insecure desire to belong. In any case, the more politically minded black students soon abandoned these cerebral pursuits as racially irrelevant. And yet the basic form of this group, with black students meeting at King's apartment, once more suggested a desire for black communion. Even the group's efforts to expunge race as superficially topical had a racial inflection: it could be taken less as a denial of race than a hard-headed calculation about what black philosophers had to do to prove their mettle in a segregated society.

Can we say that the philosophical, high-styling King was surface gloss, while the King of Calvary Baptist and of banter with McCall was the genuine article?[14] This verdict suggests a sharper line between the genuine and the spurious than the evidence warrants or King experienced. If the "white" world was not the primary one for King, it was nonetheless a source of inspiration, enjoyment, and intimacy. Despite all the satires of the official reality, King was no internal migrant. The sanctuary for him was not an alienated redoubt. King's adept handling of a number of racial incidents earned him the respect of his white colleagues at Crozer, where he was elected class president and served as valedictorian. King reciprocated, forming friendships with white students and professors that continued after he returned to the South. At Boston University, the Dialectical Society eventually drew occasional whites, and King invited his dissertation director, Harold DeWolfe, to present a paper there. In 1966, an ailing DeWolfe joined King in Mississippi when King continued the march of James Meredith, the first student to integrate the University of Mississippi, after Meredith was shot. King asked DeWolfe to offer the closing prayer.

Nor did King find the cultural content at Crozer and Boston University alienating or inimical. To reduce the curriculum to "white" sources imposes categories that did not capture King's own taste. By all accounts, his grappling with the ideas of the theologian Reinhold Niebuhr, whose doubts about the perfectibility of man tempered social gospel zeal with hard-boiled skepticism, was neither dutiful nor driven solely by the motive of vindicating the race. If King "almost never spoke of Gandhi personally, . . . he confessed that he became 'enamored' of Niebuhr, who 'left me in a state of confusion'"; King privately called him a critical influence. Niebuhr "touched him on all his tender points, from pacifism and race to sin."[15]

Maybe the sermon forms taught in homiletics class did not square with the fervent preaching that many of Crozer's black students had known, but King had long rejected the "carnival" atmosphere of the black folk pulpit. Nothing forced him to take ten preaching classes at Crozer, except his zeal for the white Protestant preachers who inspired him so. King had been exposed to liberal Protestantism and the social gospel in a black institution by beloved black mentors like Benjamin Mays, as well as George Kelsey, his theology professor at Morehouse. So he never regarded them as white impositions. Anticipating the hybrid confections he would serve up to black and white audiences alike, King not only savored the preaching of Harry Emerson Fosdick like an aficionado but also, in an act of reverse crossover, borrowed a Fosdick homily for his own trial sermon at Ebenezer Baptist Church.

It is significant that King had no qualms about expressing his deepest feelings about race in his crossover rhetoric. In a paper that he wrote for a course taught by his favorite Crozer professor, George Davis, titled "Autobiography of Religious Development," King exposed a childhood racial wound. With a comfort born of confidence, King set the scene at his parents' dining table, bringing Davis right into the family sanctum as he recycled his parents' advice. "As my parents discussed some of the tragedies that had resulted from this problem [of racism] and some of the insults they themselves had confronted on account of it I was greatly shocked, and from that moment on I was determined to hate every white person," he wrote in the paper. "As I grew older and older this feeling continued to grow. My parents would always tell me that I should not hate the white [man], but that it was my duty as a Christian to love him."

That strategy did not immediately take, King disclosed to Davis. "The question arose in my mind, how could I love a race of people [who] hated me and who had been responsible for breaking me up with one of my best childhood friends? . . . I did not conquer this anti White feeling until I entered college."[16] In the context of a segregated society, this sharing represented a moment of genuine communion between the races, even if it was a different sort of intimacy than the one King achieved with Mac in their various exploits or the camaraderie with Barbour down the road.

The riskiest form of race mixing in the late 1940s was inevitably erotic. King's love affair with a white woman, apparently his only one, pushed up against that taboo. King's desire to marry Betty, whose German immigrant mother was the Crozer cook, was as revealing as the efforts of blacks to quash the relationship. A titanic struggle ensued between the moral power of beloved community and the institutional power of racial community. As word of King's serious intentions toward his white lover circulated through the circuits of black gossip, his friends mobilized against

the marriage. A friend tried to dissuade him: "I told him it was a dangerous situation and it could get out of hand and if it did get out of
hand it would affect his career." Ed Whitaker, another friend, "seconded
Barbour's stern advice. If King wanted to return south to pastor, as he often said, an interracial marriage would create severe problems in the black
community as well as the white."[17] Whitaker "listened as King resolved
several times over the next few months to marry Betty, railing out in anger
at the cruel and silly forces in life that were keeping two people from doing what they most wanted to do."[18] In the end, King deferred to the on-
slaught, unable to face the pain that he knew "marrying white" would
cause his mother. He was, in Barbour's reckoning, "a man of a broken
heart—he never recovered."[19]

THREE

Brotherhood and *Brother*hood

"I know a lot of white people have a lot of devil in them"

"I am here because there are twenty million Negroes in the United States and I love every one of them," Martin Luther King exulted at an Albany, Georgia, mass meeting in 1962.[1] King's love of mankind could never obscure the intensity of his affection for "my people," as he often addressed them. Throughout his life, there was always a creative interplay between King's deepest spiritual convictions and the primal bonds of blackness.

Some of King's admirers judged his talk of beloved community naïve and sappy, but for his detractors, the call to black people to love those who reviled them was absurd. That was the gist of the black nationalists' rebuke of what they deemed the foolish sentimentality of turning the other cheek: "Too much love, too much love, nothing hurts a nigger like too much love." The very rawness of the word "nigger" was itself a challenge to gauzy illusions. And it's true, King's musings on the subject, in which he habitually reached for the Greek words *eros, philea,* and *agape,* sound incredibly ethereal.

If Bayard Rustin was startled to discover that King bandied about terms like "agape" before unlettered church audiences, it should not be surprising that King did not hold back when he was addressing the elite women at Spelman, the historically black college that was Morehouse's sister school. Describing eros as "aesthetic love," King observed that "Plato talked about it a great deal in his Dialogue, 'the yearning of the soul for the realm of the divine.' . . . In a sense Shakespeare was talking about Eros when he said, . . . 'It is an everfixed mark that looks on tempests and is never shaken. It is a star to every wandering bark.'" King didn't soar quite as much in describing philea, or "intimate affection between personal friends." "You love because you are loved. It is a reciprocal love."[2]

But neither of these warm and tangible sentiments applied as precisely to the love King had in mind for the white man as agape, a spiritualized love that in his telling seemed like an act of will. This kind of love is God-like, "the love of God operating in the human heart," and thus almost inhuman: "It is understanding, creative, redemptive goodwill for all men. It is spontaneous love which seeks nothing in return. . . . You love men not because you like them, not because their ways appeal to you, not because they have any particular meaning to you at the moment, but you love them because God loves them."[3]

Not because you like them. As all those things that loving the white man did not entail indicate, a strain of hard-boiled realism swirled around the edges of King's love talk. Over and over, he said that such love was not based on affection; over and over, he said it was not "sentimental bosh." These disclaimers may have reassured those blacks for whom the idea of loving some generic white man was hard to swallow. "What do you mean about this love thing?" King asked the Spelman women in a preemptive strike at skepticism. "You are talking about people who oppose you, loving people who are trying to misuse you, . . . That is impossible!'" Moments later, King confessed, "I am very happy [Jesus] did not say like your enemies, because it is very hard to like some people. It is hard to like some senator who waters down the civil rights bill in Congress."[4]

To stress such difficulties was less than a gushing endorsement of whites as a whole. On the contrary, suggesting that racial bitterness was natural and perhaps even inevitable granted a certain permission to feel such feelings. From his own experience King knew how the sting of the word "nigger" could transform all whites into enemies. Racial vengeance was the easy part, which was why so much "emotion work" was required to overcome it. Often when he reflected on that "difficulty," King would sigh, "Ohhh, I know it's not easy [to love the white man]."[5]

King's reflections on loving enemies carried an even ruder implication: If loving the white man was hard, maybe the white man wasn't so lovable. That could slide into the backhanded compliment King voiced in a mass meeting as he inverted the hierarchy of white power and black dependency: "Now we say in this nonviolent movement that you got to love this white man. And God knows he needs our love."[6] As if that didn't quite convey the troubled condition of the Caucasian, King repeated immediately, "He needs our love." At the same time, King's references to "our white brothers who have not yet been redeemed" conferred virtue on the black people who embodied redemptive love, just as he elevated blacks when he urged them not to let white barbarians pull them down to their level. Recurrently, King translated the redemptive theme into a more therapeutic idiom as "our white brothers" evolved into "sick white brothers." The boast that blacks could "heal our sick white brothers" not only named and nailed white people for their sinfulness but also reversed the standard terms of white normality and black deficiency. So did King's diagnosis, in mass meetings and sermons alike, that racist whites were in thrall to demonic fears, self-delusion, and guilt. Here was the ultimate counter to racist imagery of black animality; racist whites were the true primitives.

A similar interplay of high principle and ethnic affection was at work in King's musings on intermarriage. "Individuals marry, not races," King often reminded listeners. From his own break-up with Betty back at Crozer, he knew the heartbreak that enforcers of racial purity, no matter what their color, could inflict on innocent lovers. There was apparently some low-level black grumbling when Cornish Rogers, a fellow black graduate student at Boston University, brought a Japanese theology student with whom he was romantically involved to the Dialectical Society. "But," as Rogers remembered, "King went out of his way to register his approval of the relationship and commented that our relationship was what the movement for integration was all about." As King observed while preaching at Ebenezer, "Nobody talks about intermarriage in Jamaica or South America. You don't get the discussion anywhere much but in America and South Africa."[7]

Despite the seemingly cool register of comparative observation, King was capable of denouncing taboos on human affection with great passion. "The fact that the discussion even comes up in a country," King preached, "means that society is sick"—bringing down all the emphatic weight of judgment on that last word. (He also decried such doubts as "white supremacy sneaking down.") "The minute you say that, you are saying in substance you don't want your daughter to marry a Negro because you think there is something inherently wrong with the very being of the Negro."[8]

Yet despite his cavorting, King did not stray with white women. Although Ralph Abernathy, King's closest friend, never divulged King's explanation for his infidelity, he did confirm that King was exclusively attracted to black women, and it seems not for lack of willing partners. One amazed King staffer described the erotic energy flowing at a suburban New York City fundraiser: "I watched women making passes at Martin Luther King. I *could not believe* what I was seeing in white Westchester [New York] women. . . . It was unbelievable. . . . They would walk up to him and they would sort of lick their lips and hint, and [hand him] notes."[9]

As a Morehouse student, King had confronted "the scarecrow of social mingling" in a letter of reproach to the *Atlanta Constitution*. "Remember that almost the total of race mixture in America has come, not at Negro initiative, but by the acts of those very white men who talk loudest of race purity. We aren't eager to marry white girls, and we would like to have our own girls left alone by both white toughs and white aristocrats." The phrase King used repeatedly in connection with intermarriage, "It's really not a problem for me," certified his credentials as an erotic race man, a point he sometimes accentuated by adding, "because I'm more concerned about being the white man's brother than his brother-in-law (*Amen*)."[10]

King once regaled the Ebenezer congregation with the story of a white woman seated next to him on a plane who was crowing about "how liberal she was." There was a tinge of sarcasm in his singsong voice as he recounted, "She believes that we should have the right to vote and have access to public accommodations." But then she had added, "Now I must honestly say, Doctor King, that I wouldn't want a Negro to marry my daughter." Typically, King did not blast her as a cracker. Instead, he accused her of "unconscious racism." But the high point of King's rejoinder, at least as measured by the audience's laughter, came when King, slipping a bit further into a drawl, explained that he had fired back: "I wouldn't want my daughter to marry [the segregationist Alabama governor] George Wallace." If that riposte defined the problem as one of racism rather than race, King deepened the ethnic repartee when he bragged, "And, ah, secondly, I don't have that problem because I'm already married to a mighty beautiful Negro. And I have no desire to marry nobody else!"[11]

King's primal identity as a black man found expression in his special sensitivity to criticism. Here the alignment between the universal and the particular was as intricate as ever. On the one hand, King's sensitivity applied equally to criticism from whites and from blacks. On the other, the special quality of his bristling was racially specific in each case. King angrily complained to his white friend Stanley Levison in April 1967 that whites were displeased he had wandered off the plantation of race to criticize the Vietnam War. "The thing is I am to stay in my place and I am a Negro leader, and I should not stray from a position of moderation. I can't do that."[12] He was convinced that the *Washington Post* and *New York Times* editorials criticizing him for his Vietnam stance were nothing but blatant racism. Was he entitled to opinions only on black issues? A sarcastic King preached at Ebenezer, "Oh, the press was so noble in its applause and so noble in its praise that I was saying be nonviolent toward Bull Connor," referring to his racist adversary in Birmingham. Meanwhile, "There is something strangely inconsistent about a nation and a press that will praise you when you say be nonviolent toward [Selma sheriff] Jim Clark, but will curse you and damn you when you say be nonviolent toward little brown Vietnamese children!"[13]

With the not-so-gratuitous "brown" before "Vietnamese children" sharpening the racial edge, King's grievance drew force from the hypocrisy of whites and their transgression of color-blind universalism. By contrast, his response to black criticism was driven less by formal principle than by ethnic feelings for "my own people" and his hurt and disappointment that they were not bucking him up. "Even Negroes," King complained at a Los Angeles church, were criticizing him; and he voiced that lament almost word for word at Ebenezer in the sermon "Unfulfilled Dreams." He repeated the gist of the complaint in Memphis, the night before he was killed: "Sometimes I feel discouraged, having to take so much abuse and criticism, sometimes from my own people."

King was so sensitive to black criticism that a streetwalker's barb in-

duced a jarring swerve in his daily round. King and two of his closest colleagues, Bernard Lee and Andrew Young, were stopped at a light in the
Cleveland black ghetto when prostitutes recognized King and yelled at
him, "There's that Uncle Tom, Martin Luther King. What *he* doing
here?" King was so upset that he insisted, "'Bernard, turn this car around.
I want to talk with that woman.' Bernard moaned, 'Oh, Doc, don't pay
any attention to those women. They're just ignorant.' He just kept driving straight ahead. 'TURN THE CAR AROUND, BERNARD!' Martin
shouted." Young underscored the depth of King's distress: "He hardly ever
raised his voice like that."[14]

In the increasingly volatile 1960s, as black militant groups were threatening to kill him, King confessed to a nagging feeling of guilty regret. "I
shouldn't feel any different," he said about black militant groups threatening his life as opposed to threats from whites, but the truth was irrepressible: "I do feel differently . . . I am really annoyed at myself. I can't believe
that these black groups are people who really want my death." As Stewart
Burns astutely comments, "After all of his years of battling white racism, it
had come to this: black people mattered to him more than whites."[15]

"Was there really a bit of Malcolm X in every black man?" Peter
Goldman asks in his fine book on Malcolm X. "Martin Luther King is
said to have confessed to a friend once that, yes, even he felt an empathetic twinge of hatred when he saw Malcolm railing at white folks on
television." Usually, King's grace, Christian faith, and propensity for saving face restrained his rude and bitter feelings, but they still leaked out occasionally. After President Kennedy was assassinated, "Jacqueline Kennedy knelt prayerfully with her children against the late President's coffin.
'Look at her,' the [federal] agents heard King say, 'Sucking him off one
last time.'"[16]

It's hard to fathom such meanness unless it is placed in the context of
King's fierce disappointment in Kennedy for his appeasement of the white
South, appointment of segregationist judges, and tendency to cast the
race problem in terms of realpolitik. Kennedy's dealings with Governor
Ross Barnett over the integration of the University of Mississippi, King
said, "made Negroes feel like pawns in a white man's political game."[17]
One of the bitterest pills to swallow came in 1965 when President Lyndon
Johnson, in his otherwise stirring "We Shall Overcome" speech right after
the Selma march, acknowledged the killing by racists of a white minister,

Rev. James Reeb, who had come to join the protest in Selma, but failed to mention the death of Jimmie Lee Jackson, a young black activist who was killed by the police in nearby Marion. As Andrew Young described it, "We couldn't help but feel bitter about the fact that it took the murder of a white minister to cause the federal government to become concerned about the safety of demonstrators and serious about ensuring our right to vote."[18]

King's own experience enhanced his empathy for the bitterness of fellow blacks. True, in his public pronouncements King was resolute in his rejection of ethnocentrism as an un-Christian affront. He insisted that "black supremacy is as dangerous as white supremacy. . . . God isn't interested merely in the freedom of black men and brown men and yellow men, but God is interested in the freedom of the whole human race." But the more subtle sign of King's sense of identity was the quality of the rejection as much as the fact of it. His censure was marked not by chastisement but by his emphasis on the racist conditions that produced the rioting. After the Watts riots in 1965, King refused to separate himself from the outburst of black rage. He did not brand rioters as sinful or sick—all qualities he attributed to racist whites. Preaching to the Ebenezer congregation, he referred to rioters as "my black brothers and sisters" and situated them in an exonerating context: "In the midst of anger and understandable outrage, in the midst of their hurt, in the midst of their disappointment, [they] turn to misguided riots to solve that problem."[19]

Before a black congregation in Los Angeles, King momentarily placed himself inside the community of black rage with a confession. His phrase "I know the temptation" laid down an empathetic beat; both the knowing and the tempting derived from the wounding history shared by "all of us." The "we" and the "us" throughout this passage are unapologetically racial, not human: "Now I know the temptation. I know the temptation which comes to all of us. We've been trampled over so long. I know the temptation that comes to all of us, we've seen the viciousness of lynching mobs with our own eyes. We've seen police brutality in our own lives. We are still the last hired and the first fired. So many doors are closed in our faces. And there is a temptation for us to end up with bitterness."

King specifically reached out to those nationalist brothers and sisters with a grant of recognition, scored by a new repetition: "And I understand these people who have ended up in despair. I understand why there are some who have been a little misguided and they've ended up feeling that the problem can't be solved within and so they talk about racial separation rather than racial integration. I understand their response. I have analyzed it psychologically and I understand it. But in spite of the fact that I understand it I must say to them in patient terms that that isn't the way."

I understand. I know the temptation. It comes to *all of us.* This was more than a confection tossed to the audience; it was the avowal of shared history and the feelings it generated. Only after one more nod to the sensibility of the bitter ("I must say to you in patient terms") did King elevate them to the higher plane of Jesus of Nazareth with his declarative syncopation:

> No, we need not hate,
> We need not use violence,
> There is another way,
> The way as old as the insights of Jesus of Nazareth,
> As modern as the techniques of Mohandas K. Gandhi,
> There is another way.
> A way as old as Jesus saying "love your enemies,
> Bless them that curse you,
> Pray for them that spitefully use you, . . ."
> There is another way,
> A way as old as Jesus saying,
> "Turn the other cheek . . ."
> This is what we've got to see.
> Ohhh, there is a power in this way.[20]

King's love of black people, his confession that "I know the temptation," and his boast of being married "to a fine Negro woman" defined his powerful sense of blackness. But King's sense of unity was political as much as primal, and was rooted in his hard-boiled analysis of what black deliverance required. No matter how mixed the sources, that solidarity was reflected in his concrete dealings with black skeptics who rejected the idea of beloved community—black nationalists, ethnocentric provincials, and street toughs. In such encounters, King revealed his great ability to imaginatively enter worlds other than his own and to express his faith in nonviolence as a kind of Christian witness—gifts he deployed before black and white audiences alike. In this sense, the various roles of guide, translator, and exegete that King adopted in his overtures to whites were never absent from his black talk either.

As early as 1962, after a flurry of bottle-throwing threatened the nonviolent aura of the SCLC campaign in Albany, Georgia, King visited the poolrooms and juke joints that provided a cynical counterpoint to the church-based mass meeting. Accompanied by his colleague and closest friend Ralph Abernathy and another civil rights worker, Charles Jones, King made the rounds of the dives. His forays into such alien terrain were usually prompted by the aims of recruiting field staff or quelling violence. Jones opened by saying, "We want to talk to you" [about the violence last night]. "The man made his shot, the balls clicking. 'Who wants to?'" and Jones replied, "Doctor King. This is Doctor King." "They looked at him with interest. He smiled at them, almost timidly." There was something a bit off-key in King's stilted overture to the pool players, "How're you, gents?" He then apologized, "I hate to hold up your pool game. I used to be a pool shark myself."[21]

These awkward nods to the vernacular were not the only prelude to his main objective of preempting violence. King also prefaced his pacifist plea with a subtle nod to indomitable will: "We have had our demonstrations saying we will no longer accept segregation." After having established his masculine credentials, he now moved to his main point. "One thing about the movement is that it is non-violent. As you know, there was some violence last night. Nothing could hurt our movement more. It's exactly what our opposition likes to see. In order that we can continue on a Christian basis with love and non-violence, I wanted to talk to you all and urge you to be non-violent, not to throw bottles. I know if you do this, we are destined to win." He told another group of men, "We don't need guns and ammunition—just the power of souls."[22]

The tensions between beloved community and black nationalism on the southern front came to a head most famously in 1966 during the Meredith March. James Meredith, the first black to enter the University of Mississippi in 1962, had begun his own quixotic protest march through Mississippi. When he was shot by racists along the route, the Southern Christian Leadership Conference (SCLC), the organization King headed, was drawn into continuing the march along with more radical civil rights groups like the Student Nonviolent Coordinating Committee (SNCC).

In a heated contest in a Greenwood mass meeting, representatives of the two rival organizations squared off against each other: Willie Ricks, one of SNCC's most powerful exhorters, and Hosea Williams, an executive staffer in the SCLC. Ricks's cries of "Black Power" were met by Williams's counter-cry, "freedom now." The media effort to frame the throw-down in high contrast obscured the more ambiguous reality.

Black Power celebrated both the importance of racial identity and the visibility of its display. It thereby threatened to undermine the postwar conventions of civil religion, which did not repress identities of race, ethnicity, and religion so much as consign them to private life. To the extent that black power made race the primary source of loyalty and value, it defied King's religious faith. Nor could he abide the degeneration of black pride into braggadocio, honky-baiting, and the rhetoric of menace. He rebuffed the SNCC efforts to ban whites from the march and recoiled from the contempt for nonviolence contained in the SNCC riff on a freedom song, "I'm gonna bomb when the spirit say bomb . . . shoot when the spirit say shoot."

King invited Stokely Carmichael, the leader of SNCC, and others to join him in a Yazoo City, Mississippi, parish house for a "frank discussion" of their differences. King urged the younger militants to give up "Black Power" as a polarizing slogan that could only hurt the movement, frighten sympathetic whites, and give racist ones a cover for their hatred. Carmichael did not dispute King's reading of white reception; he simply disputed its relevance to black strategy. As Clayborne Carson chronicled, a 1964 SNCC position paper observed that "a single white person who participated in a meeting of black people could change the tone of that meeting: 'People would immediately start talking about "brotherhood," "love," etc.; race would not be discussed.'" Two years later, Carmichael was acting on behalf of their view that what truly mattered was how the phrase "Black Power" made blacks feel. As Carmichael put it, "For once, black people are going to use the words they want to use—not just the words whites want to hear."[23]

King never denied the legitimacy of black power. Instead, he sought alternatives that might avoid the more florid association of the words "black" and "power." His relentless parsing suggested that the substantive divide between the parties was less than it appeared. If King's ability to step out of the black perspective to weigh the impact of black words on others betrayed his crossover radar and universalistic empathy, these were deployed against certain forms of black power and not others.

Clearly King did not balk at making forceful assertions of identity, before mixed audiences as well as black ones. Around the time of the Meredith March, he told a racially mixed audience of thousands at Chicago's Soldier Field, "We must not be ashamed of being black. We must believe with all of our hearts that black is as beautiful as any other color." The following year in a speech to the SCLC board, King castigated "the white man's crimes" and "cultural homicide." "Yes," he told the audience, "I was a slave through my foreparents, and yes, I'm not ashamed of that. I'm ashamed of the people who were so sinful to make me a slave *(Yes sir)* . . . I'm black, but I'm black and beautiful *(Yes)*."[24]

King was also quite capable of boasting with gritty naturalism, "Now, I don't know if you like your hair. But I have good hair. I don't know where the illusion came into being that straight hair is the only good hair . . . And my hair is as good as anybody's hair." If King came to the point of adopting the modish phrase "I'm black and beautiful," his celebration of black hair predated that slogan by years. As a thirteen-year-old boy, he had already reached out in solidarity to his brothers of "blackest hue." In a typical formulation that did not hesitate to affirm blackness with the words of a nineteenth-century British abolitionist, King recited these favorite lines from the poet William Cowper in the most diverse settings: "Every Negro . . . must come to the point that he will believe with the eloquent poet: 'Fleecy locks and black complexion, / Cannot forfeit nature's claim. / Skin may differ, but affection, / Dwells in black and white the same.' *(All right, Yeah)*."[25]

This was the backdrop against which King forged racial communion with Carmichael during the Meredith March. Huddling together out of the spotlight, King made clear to Carmichael that he had no problem with blacks amassing power just as the Jews, Italians, and other ethnic groups had done. As they sparred over alternatives to the phrase "Black Power," King—in a concession to this "blackening" strategy—offered "black equality." At one point on the march, King did not object when Carmichael demanded that a white SCLC staffer leave the room because he didn't want white people there. When alone with his own colleagues,

King expressed his admiration for the SNCC freedom fighters. If some of them had turned against the sustaining faith of "beloved community," King saw it as a "cry of pain."

All this helps to explain why King did not speak out publicly as pressure to revile Carmichael mounted. The NAACP condemned the inflammatory idiom, but King refused to join in. Beyond any practical effort to maintain black solidarity, King's relationship with Carmichael and other SNCC leaders was full of warmth and respect. As Andrew Young witnessed, when Carmichael was gassed in Canton, Mississippi, and his hysterical crying and screaming would not relent, "Martin just took him by the hand and said, 'Stokely, let's go somewhere and sit down and talk.'" After Willie Ricks had let loose with his nationalist chant, King affectionately dubbed him "Black Power." When King told Ricks that "he lacked only clothes to make a fine minister, Ricks boldly asked to borrow some, and King surprised him with an invitation to take freely from his closet in Atlanta." About to take off with Carmichael for a concert at Tougaloo College, a nearby black college, King told his SCLC staff, "I'm sorry, y'all. James Brown is on. I'm gone."[26]

The early sparring with Black Power was a portent of collisions to come. Turning northward in the mid-1960s, King and the SCLC discovered a devastating ghetto cynicism about Christian forbearance and beloved community. On urban street corners where Malcolm X's reviling of "white devils" excited a secular form of call and response, appeals to "white brothers" did not go down as well as they did in southern churches. In Harlem people threw eggs at King in 1963, and when he returned to New York City the next year in an effort to quell rioting, he was greeted with cries of "Uncle Tom." "Martin Luther King's primary concern is in defending the white man," Malcolm X pronounced, "and if he can elevate the black man's condition at the same time, then the black man will be elevated . . . Martin Luther King isn't preaching love—he's preaching love the white man."[27]

Things came to a head in Chicago in 1966 when King tried to calm a volatile Chicago crowd with a disquisition on the sacred value of nonviolence. Ralph Abernathy observed it firsthand: "They grew sullen and rebellious and either walked away in disgust or else began shouting obscenities and other insults at him." Minutes later, the street erupted in rioting.

For the very first time, Abernathy recalled, King had met up with "a crowd of blacks that he could neither reason with nor overpower with his rhetoric."[28]

Yet King did not flinch at the idea of a sit-down with the Cobras and Blackstone Rangers, major violent gangs in Chicago. He ministered to the gang members in his gentle way, never wavering in his faith or in the gambits he used to implement it. Sitting on the floor in a dilapidated "slum" apartment, King offered a "seminar in nonviolence, trying to convince these kids that rioting was destructive and suicidal; and that the way to change a society was to approach it with love of yourself and of mankind, and dignity in your own heart. . . . He dealt with those kids with a reverence for their humanity, dignity, belief in their importance that he communicated to them, and with the patience of a saint."[29]

Things were more loony than ominous in Cleveland, where King came face to face with one of the city's black separatists, Ahmed Evans, who had predicted ghetto riots on the basis of astrological signs. His followers rejected King as an Uncle Tom and insisted that "Whitey" is "going to shoot you down" and "doesn't care about any black man."[30]

In a late-night talkfest with white confidant Stanley Levison, King marveled at Ahmed's exotic lingo: "They say everything in slang, like you are a 'mellow dude.'" When King preached about the encounter at Ebenezer, however, there was none of that startled distance. The wayward Ahmed loomed as "a brother" in need of redemption, as King humanized Ahmed, draining the demonic from the image of the wild-eyed nationalist. King told the congregation how he went to Cleveland and "they had a brother there who is the leader of the nationalists, the black nationalists of Cleveland, and he had announced the date for the riot to take place." A bemused King remarked, "First time that I'd ever seen the date set for a riot."[31]

After Ahmed pledged to run King out of town, King raced on over to "meet with Mr. Ahmed and his fellas and I was going to speak to 'em and talk to them as brothers . . . I didn't open my speech by criticizing or judging them, . . . [I didn't start out by saying] 'You are violent, you believe in riots, and you are killing the Negro race and hurting the cause of civil rights." Instead, after telling Ahmed that he understood his bitterness, King physically consecrated that bond. "I put my arms around

Brother Ahmed and pretty soon Brother Ahmed had his arms around me." Ahmed would proclaim King a "black brother."

In the face of challenges to cherished ideals from black skeptics, King was forced to take heed of the claims of those who mocked him. Yet in crossing over into rival black worlds, King showed the same principled resolve that he did when he crossed over into the world of philosophers like Martin Buber or the civic republican world of Thomas Jefferson before white audiences. His willingness to meet rival speakers both literally and symbolically on their own terrain applied mainly at the level of form, of showing respect and preserving face. But form was only the mechanism to create a stable occasion. Once established, the yielding gave way to King's determination to apply his Christian faith to the task of convincing his wayward brothers and sisters of "the better way."

Thus the vantage, and the advantage, ceded in entering the alien terrain were only apparent for a flickering instant; then King would turn the tables and begin reframing the definition of "standing up like a man." The tenets of his powerful Christian and democratic faith were never in competition with his equally powerful sense of black identity. The two were irretrievably tangled together, as they would be throughout much of King's talk. In the case of the gang members, the empathy King felt toward fellow blacks helped him gain an audience so he could convince them to adopt his faith in nonviolence and race-blind humanism. Here, then, was another aspect of King's "crossover" talk, and proof that he had to engage in the labors of translation and justification with certain black audiences no less than with white ones.

King was not even above sharing a laugh with Elijah Muhammad, the leader of the separatist Nation of Islam (NOI) and arch-symbol of black racism. The jocular moment came during King's only recorded meeting with Muhammad; presumably the encounter was the 1966 visit picked up by the FBI's listening devices that were hidden in Muhammad's Chicago mansion. The Nation's newspaper deemed the get-together a success. For once, the FBI and the NOI agreed: the Bureau's summary of the wiretaps dutifully reported a "very friendly" conversation. The meeting seems to have devolved into a fascinating, if oblique, ritual of black solidarity as the Messenger and King invoked their history as southerners. It's not clear if they realized another point of sharing: both Muhammad and King's fathers had been scarred as little boys by witnessing racist killings of black men in rural Georgia.

King asked the Messenger, "'Do you really believe that *all* white folks are devils? I know a lot of white people have a lot of devil in them, but are you going to say that *all* of them are devils?' Mr. Muhammad smiled. 'Dr. King,' he said, 'you and me both grew up in Georgia, and we know there are many different kinds of snakes. The rattlesnake was poisonous and the king snake was friendly. But they both snakes, Dr. King.' And the two of them, the Messenger of Allah and the apostle of Christian love, had a hearty laugh."[32]

It's easy to go astray when deciphering epithets like "devils" and "snakes," confusing the meaning of the community that does the judging with the one that does the insulting. As Dell Hymes warned, we "must first be sure of reading signs that are there, not signs imagined to be there." When Italian working-class toughs in Brooklyn told me in the 1980s that "the niggers all got that attitude . . . baaaaaaad," and then one minute later waved at their black friends, "niggers" may have signified not a racist epithet but something more idiosyncratic and local—a particular kind of black person. Malcolm X exploited similar ambiguities in his deployment of *devils*. For the acolytes, it was an esoteric term of art betokening the theological doctrine of genetically ordained white evil; for the secular street, it codified in one neat phrase a plausible verdict on white devilry.[33]

The distinction that King was trying to parse with Muhammad— "whites are devils" vs. "a lot of them have a lot of devil in them"—can be seen in part as a dispute over the rules that govern how carefully you generalize about other groups. As King formulated the line, despair produces bitterness, which "has not the capacity to make the distinction between some and *all*." There were, King once observed wryly, plenty of "black devils" too, a view surely supported by his belief in the omnipresence of sin. Meanwhile, the willingness to say nasty words like "nigger" or to collude with those who deploy such epithets reveals another feature of a community's "ways of speaking": the strength of taboos on coarse speech. Working-class speech often mocks the genteel equivocations of the middle class. In the Yiddishkeit world of Eastern European Jewry, in contrast to the *edel* (refined, in Yiddish) ideals of the more polished classes, "'to talk like a *proster*' means not only to talk inelegantly and ungrammatically but also that one is not above using 'ugly words.'"[34]

Jesse Jackson ran afoul of such *edel* fastidiousness when he used the words "Hymies" and "Hymietown" to refer to Jews and New York City in his talk with journalists. Although Jackson eventually "atoned," and though he surely "had issues" with Jews, it wasn't evident that "Hymie" was necessarily an anti-Semitic term. Actually, Jackson's jiving about "Mos" and "Mosela," his terms for a certain kind of stereotypical black person, sounds suspiciously like King's lampoons of befuddled rural Negroes. Even committed universalists are not above yielding to impolitic jokes or earthy riposte, as when cosmopolitan Jews, who might be squeamish about presenting themselves as "too Jewish" in mixed society, kibitz backstage about "the goyim." As the Reform Jewish leader Al Vorspan observed during the Hymietown episode, "I can recall . . . a thousand conversations . . . that I regard as parallel [with Hymie] . . . someone from the Jewish community . . . will say to me, not up on a platform, very off-the-record, just kind of schmoozing around, something about—'well, you know the schwartzes' [the Yiddish word for 'black,' often used pejoratively], or 'you know how the schwartzes are.'"[35] Seen from this vantage point, the rule Jackson broke was not the taboo on racism but the one on vulgar banter. This was the gist of Jackson's defense in his apology at the Democratic national convention in 1984—perhaps, he confessed, he was guilty of an error of "tone."

None of this contradicts the notion that the line between "all whites are devils" and "a lot of whites have a lot of devil in them" is a distinction with a difference. So too was former New York City mayor David Dinkins's insistence after a white mob in Brooklyn killed the black man Yusuf Hawkins that Bensonhurst did not kill Yusuf Hawkins; he was killed in Bensonhurst. Rev. Al Sharpton once insisted to me that he never referred to white people as "honkies." No, he insisted, he had referred to "crackers." "*Cracker* in our terms is like *redneck, racist;* it doesn't mean all whites. I never used it. *Honky* means all whites." Sharpton recalled going into a restaurant in upstate New York during the Tawana Brawley affair, and someone in his group would say, "'That looks like a real cracker.' It might be one [white] out of twenty."[36]

Yet from another angle, the difference between "all" and "a lot of" may strike some as quibbling. Much turns on what you mean by "a lot of." Occasionally, some of King's close colleagues sounded more like Muhammad than their iconic leader, as when executive staffer James Bevel excoriated "two million white savages in Alabama." At an SCLC meeting in 1965, Hosea Williams was carrying on about "Caucasians" to a mixed audience of civil rights workers: "I often use the term 'white folks.' I keep my foot on white folks' necks." Yet his concession to caution—"I don't mean all"—seemed modest, for he promptly went on to define "most" as "90%." "Your mommas and daddies messed up. White people got so much to repent for."[37] The inimitable Rev. C. T. Vivian, lacking Williams's street panache, and his vulgarity too, felt that King's faith in white redemptive capacity was a less than hard-headed empirical assessment; whites, he observed, had simply not shown the evidence to warrant that verdict.

Over time, King's caution about generalizing seemed to falter a bit. At times the difference between King's learned parsing and Williams's "your mommas and daddies" appeared more stylistic than substantive. "White brothers" transmuted into "sick white brothers," and then into still more jaundiced general assertions about white sickness. Upping the ante beyond "a lot of," King began to declare that "the vast majority of white Americans" were racist or lacked any commitment to racial equality. Portentously, "the white man" and "the black man" at times emerged as collective actors in their own right. Noting the "reversion to barbaric white conduct," King declared: "So let us say it forthrightly, that if the total slum violations of law by the white man over the years were calculated and compared with the law breaking of a few days of riots, the hardened criminal would be the white man." King said this in the context of the urban setting of Chicago, but he said something similar in the South. In Birmingham, at the tenth anniversary dinner of the Alabama Christian Movement, King remarked, "White America never did intend to integrate housing, integrate schools, or be fair with Negroes about jobs."[38]

King's growing sense of the stubbornness of the racial divide was reflected in his view of the power of words themselves. When King worried that whites might misinterpret the phrase "Black Power," he was recognizing the unpredictability of the meaning of words and the ability of listeners to imbue them with all kinds of significance. "So Black Power is now a part of the nomenclature of the national community. To some it is abhorrent, to others dynamic; to some it is repugnant, to others exhilarating; to some it is destructive; to others it is useful. Since Black Power means different things to different people and indeed, being essentially an emotional concept, can mean different things to the same person on differing occasions, it is impossible to attribute its ultimate meaning to any single individual organization."[39]

In King's later reflections on the word "black," language had become master to the speaker, resistant to any efforts to toy with its import. "Our society has messed this whole thing up because our very words, the semantics of the situation tend to make anything black on a lower level of reality, morality and everything else than anything white. We have got to re-order the very priorities of our vocabulary. Do you know that a white lie is better than a black lie so people say they tell a white lie, it is better. And you watch right through the whole vocabulary anything white is considered pure; anything black is considered dirty and low and evil." In another address, King noted that 70 of the 120 synonyms for "black" in Roget's Thesaurus "represent something dirty and evil—smut, anything low and degrading." All in all, "language conspired to make the black man feel that he was nobody, that he didn't count."[40]

King was acutely aware of his own shifting in his use of the terms "white man" and "black man." True, he still tended to apply all the caveats about his use of terms like "the white man," as he did in 1967, only months before his assassination: "It is not meant to encompass all white people—and I think it is very important to say this—for there are millions who have morally risen above prevailing prejudices." But that qualification didn't carry the same punch as the criticism that preceded it: he portrayed the white man not as a brother, not even a sick brother who needs our help, but as an opponent: "In using the term 'White Man,' I am seeking to describe, in general terms, the Negro's adversary."[41]

FOUR

Backstage and Blackstage

"Lil' Nigger, just where you been?"

The sense of beloved black community that guided King's encounters with "rude" elements outside the SCLC was no less evident inside, where he spent most of his time with an overwhelmingly black executive and field staff. The official aim of the Southern Christian Leadership Conference, "To redeem the soul of America," echoed Berry Gordy's positioning of Motown Records in the crossover market as "the sound of young America." Yet a variety of tendencies—race man ideologies, black Christian nationalism, the field staff's mystique of manliness—hinted at the countercurrents lurking close to the surface of a "universalistic" movement. These tendencies could be seen in the ribald humor, rowdy back-and-forth, and racial banter that served as markers of black fellowship. To fully grasp the reality of King's daily life in the midst of these forces of race, ideology, and talk, we will extend our focus in this chapter and the next to include the larger cast of characters with whom King spent time.

A deep sense of black Christian identity united the SCLC leadership. It was rooted in a distinctive black version of Christianity that emphasized

God's primal commitment to deliverance and a view of Jesus as an accessible savior who blessed "all God's children," even the least of these. No matter how much King and his inner circle differed in learning, background, and style, the Revs. Ralph Abernathy, Joseph Lowery, Andrew Young, James Bevel, C. T. Vivian, Fred Shuttlesworth, Wyatt Tee Walker, Bernard Lee, Bernard Lafayette, and Walter Fauntroy had all imbibed this black-inflected faith in separate black institutions. Wyatt Tee Walker's view, widely shared by the King coterie, that white Christianity is a religion of creed rather than practice, of the mind rather than the heart, was distinctive mainly for its ideologically elaborate character.

More secular sentiments of racial pride reinforced this sense of blackness, heightening the priority of black deliverance over the ideal of integration. As a little boy, King watched his father storm out of a shoe store after being told to go to the back. "There's nothing wrong with these seats . . . We'll either buy shoes sitting right here or we won't buy any of your shoes at all." Years later, King recalled, "I can remember him muttering: 'I don't care how long I have to live with this system, I am never going to accept it. I'll oppose it until the day I die.'" Moreover, "always alert to discourtesy or condescension coming from white persons," Daddy King discouraged his children from working for whites and demanded respect from whites. Once when a policeman reproached him, "Boy, what d'ya mean running over that stop sign?" Daddy King motioned at his son and rejoined, "That's a *boy* there. I'm Reverend King."[1]

Almost every member of King's coterie had grown up with such models of racial dignity. Joseph Lowery recalls asking his grandmother, a domestic worker forced to enter the house she tended through the back door, "how she handled it, 'cause I knew she didn't take no mess." The answer was a lesson in the theatrics of defiance. She went to the closet, got her apron, and, even as her mannerly white employers inquired, "How you, Polly," she would not speak. Then she opened the front door, swept the porch, and came back in with some fanfare. "As far as I was concerned that's the first time I went in the house," she told her grandson, who translates, "You know, existentially, *I hadn't been in the house* and the white folks never understood that, why she never spoke. She wasn't there. That's the sort of thing she could come home and share with her friends and laugh at the white folks."[2]

His colleagues teased Andrew Young for not being black enough, out of mistrust of his Howard University degree, membership in the Congregational Church, and his cheerful assumption of the task of negotiating with whites. As Young told it, no one "coveted [the job]. . . . They thought it was a waste of time and perceived it as 'sucking up to the white folks.'" In truth, Young's comfort with this task reflected the same race man sentiments that drove the suspicion of it. "My father taught me that putting white people at ease was a survival skill that signaled my superior intellect rather than inferior social status." His grandmother supplemented the lesson of racial pride: "If you don't fight 'em when they call you 'Nigger,' I'm gonna whip you myself if I find out about it."[3]

When it came to forming a mass movement, King and his colleagues chose an all-black—and all-Christian—organization dominated by preachers. The story of the founding period has been well chronicled by historian Adam Fairclough. He quotes the words of that rarity, a white Alabama liberal, Virginia Durr: "The Negroes are so proud of the fact that this is an all-Negro movement, led, financed to a large degree and activated by Negroes." Comments Fairclough, "It was obvious to [King adviser Bayard] Rustin and his colleagues that mass action in the South could best be promoted by an indigenous, independent, church-based organization of Southern blacks." As Durr saw it, however, SCLC's failure to include whites was "racist." Kivie Kaplan, an icon of Jewish liberalism on the NAACP board, was not so happy either about that triumph of Christian identity politics. He even asked King to change his organization's name: "I certainly would be happy that you have some Jewish leadership as well as Christian and possibly change the name to SOUTHERN LEADERSHIP CONFERENCE because I know that we do have Jewish leaders who are fighting for justice along with the Christian leaders." Only in 1966, "when its all-black board threatened to become an embarrassment, did King appoint whites to SCLC's governing body."[4]

A zanier example of this gap between official universalism and race loyalty occurred when the SCLC distributed a tape of King's 1965 Christmas sermon on black radio stations. Moments after King had preached that in Christ there is no East or West, no freedman or slave, an ebullient marketer's voice wished his listeners a beautiful black Christmas. "As a people, black people, how many of our gifts are an expression of our selves? In Chicago, SCLC's Operation Bread Basket is reminding people to use love and thought in selecting their gifts and to make their gifts an expression of

themselves. To give black art, black music, black books, and black prod-
ucts as Christmas gifts. They are celebrating a black Christmas." In case
that still wasn't enough blackness, the voice announced that "at the Martin Luther King black Christmas parade the Emotions sang a new song by
Purvis Staples. We thank them for the song, 'Black Christmas.'"[5]

The power of this black Christian identity was evident in the animosities that occasionally erupted between King's coterie of black preachers
and the interracial network of northern intellectuals and advisers who
crystallized into King's Research Group. The former were tied together
by the connective tissues of race, religion, inflection, world view, region,
humor, food, and history. In contrast, the whites in the group, many of
them northern Jewish New York liberals or leftists, came from an alien
culture. Capturing a certain undertone in the kitchen cabinet, Rev. Walter
Fauntroy, the former head of the Washington, D.C., office of SCLC who
went on to become the district's nonvoting Representative, referred to
"Tarzan liberals" whose fantasies of rescuing blacks created resentment. As
Lowery described it, "A lot of white liberals were being paternalistic and
. . . they never knew it; and sometimes you didn't call attention to it 'cause
you didn't want to get bogged down in it. [Often it was] unintentional.
We were too big, [we had] moved too far in the struggle to let that kind of
barrier emerge."

It seems that Harry Wachtel in particular, a New York corporate lawyer
who became an adviser to King, provoked racial animosities among some
of King's black colleagues who resented Wachtel's "quite assertive and
take-charge attitude." King's black friend and adviser, Clarence Jones,
was concerned enough to broach the subject of racial tension between
Wachtel and one of King's black lawyers, Chauncey Eskridge, with King's
Jewish confidant, Stanley Levison, who replied that Eskridge had always
been "a very good friend of mine and there was never any question of
Negro-white differences." Wachtel once raised a question about an SCLC
program dear to Jesse Jackson, who decried such skepticism coming from
"a slave master."[6]

Race was only one element in the mix of these skirmishes, which also
arose from regional and other stylistic differences. Was it more important
that you were black or that you were Christian preachers? I asked Rev.
Wyatt Tee Walker, who was the executive director of SCLC in the early
1960s. Well, he said, you can't really separate those things. In fact, King's

northern black advisers, including Bayard Rustin, Clarence Jones, and Chauncey Eskridge, were closer to the culture of cosmopolitan secularism and trade unionism than to the Southern Baptist preachers. As a result, the tussle between prophecy and bureaucracy cut across black-white tensions. The interracial Research Group was formed because Rustin, Levison, and the other northerners considered King and the preachers seriously uninformed about politics and policy. Blacks from the business world or academia who briefly found themselves in management positions inside the SCLC were shocked by the laxity that resulted from prophetic spontaneity.

Walter Fauntroy characterized the SCLC as a "preacheristic" movement. An entire executive staff meeting was given over to James Bevel's righteous charge that they should confess their infidelities to their wives. "King first said he would rather die, that they did not even know a chaste colleague in the pulpit except perhaps James Lawson . . . and that disclosure would do nothing except rupture families."[7]

At critical times of decision, King would leave the room and even mass meetings to pray, then enter dramatically to announce the Lord's verdict. When William Rutherford, a former business executive who became the executive director of SCLC in 1967, tried to get him to focus on a set of achievable goals, King replied, "I don't know that Jesus had demands." After Rutherford disputed his insistence that violence was their prime enemy, King "went into one of these preaching things," as Rutherford put it. Such God talk could serve as a manipulative pretext for closing down an argument. In the heat of a scrap, King deployed that trick against Bayard Rustin, according to a Rustin colleague who heard King say, "I have to pray now. I have to consult with the Lord and see what he wants me to do." In David Garrow's words, "Rustin, long familiar with King's proclivity for invoking God's name to avoid disagreements he did not care to hear, was furious. Seeking refuge in prayer—'This business of King talking to God and God talking to King'—would not resolve strategic questions."[8]

These dynamics of race, culture, religion, and region were reflected in King's personal relationships. By and large, black people, and especially southern black men, remained his main source of trust and solace. As fond as they were of each other, King's friendship with Stanley Levison lacked the sexual and racial joshing of King's offstage behavior with close black colleagues. Levison observed a "shyness" in King that was "accented, I felt, with white people . . . There was a certain politeness, a certain arm's length approach, and you could feel the absence of relaxation. As the years went on this vanished. But it was as if Dr. King's Southern background, largely with the black community, had its effect on him as far as thinking comfortably and easily in the company of white people."[9]

"Of course race made a difference," Wyatt Tee Walker says. "It was the way we spoke, the things we would say." And didn't say. The unspoken understandings that tied King and his preacher friends together encouraged certain conversations even as they squelched others. When King strayed from his marital vows at the Willard Hotel in Washington, D.C., and elsewhere, he did so in the company of other blacks. The eleven reels of FBI tapes record, in Taylor Branch's summary of what various FBI agents told him, "fourteen hours of party babble, with jokes about scared Negro preachers and stiff white bosses . . . sounds of courtship and sex with distinctive verbal accompaniment," including King's. Hoping to drive King to commit suicide, the FBI sent a package of those recordings to King, and it was opened by King's wife, Coretta. King played the tapes for Ralph Abernathy, Andrew Young, Joseph Lowery, and Bernard Lee. He told Chauncey Eskridge, the black lawyer with whom he apparently shared a lover, about the tapes, but not Wachtel.[10]

Within his circle of black friends and colleagues, King indulged in vulgar, ungrammatical, racial, lewd, and street talk. He simply hid such uncouth strains of his repertoire behind a veil of privacy. King's transgressions of dignity intruded even on official executive staff meetings, as a "rather surprised and shocked" William Rutherford discovered when he became the director of SCLC and tried to subdue the unruliness of a faith organization with the techniques of modern management. "SCLC was a very rowdy place," he observed, ". . . and the movement altogether was a very raunchy exercise." King was unabashedly part of the diffuse "ribald" atmosphere that Rutherford encountered. Garrow uncovered the story of an "Atlanta group party that had featured both a hired prostitute as well as the unsuccessful ravishing of a seventeen-year-old SCLC secretary." When Rutherford sought to discuss the incident with executive staff, virtually everyone present, including King, "cracked up in laughter."[11]

Dropping the public mask took place in various kinds of speech settings. After a celebrity crowd had departed from Harry Belafonte's apartment and King and Abernathy were alone with their hosts, Julie Belafonte brought out the Harvey's Bristol Cream bottle they reserved for King, and King and Abernathy fell into the ritualized play of informal banter, replete with gibes at "white people." King teased Abernathy, with whom he had shared jail cells, "Let me be sure to get arrested with people who don't snore." When Abernathy took umbrage, King gleefully retorted, "You are *torture* . . . White folks ain't *invented* anything that can get to me like you do. *Anything* they want me to admit to, I will, if they'll just get you and your snoring out of my cell."[12]

King often indulged in a more down-home kind of talk with his preacher colleagues. Once, the thin partition of a telephone receiver could barely keep the rival idioms, and the speech rules they marked, separate. According to Rev. Fred Shuttlesworth, King was "lecturing young President Kennedy by phone on the necessity of nonviolent 'creative tension' and he paused in mid-sentence to say, 'Wait a minute, Mr. President. Ralph, bring me a couple pieces of chicken, please, and bring some more of that bread! Fred, ain't this some great bread?'" That talk was not confined to the SCLC milieu. Walter McCall, King's old Morehouse and Crozer friend who had accompanied him on many culinary as well as erotic exploits, related, "He used to always have everybody rolling because you used to tell that he never did learn the finer arts of eating as his mother taught him. He'd take the food with his hand—the food would be very good—so he'd dip in there and start eating. We'd just—oh, boy—we'd just laugh at King. He'd say, 'Man, this food is good, man! I can't wait on youall.'" Later, King and McCall were in "truly a heavenly place" in New York, and "instead of King kind of putting on the dog in terms of table manners, he brought his same old country habits of eating there; and we just rolled. We just couldn't help from rolling."[13]

Nor did King refrain from racially tinged, politically incorrect joking. Walter Fauntroy chuckled as he remembered King's poking fun at a rural black man, one of King's bits fondly recalled by many of his colleagues. At the finale of the joke, the befuddled black man dissolves into a muddle of inarticulateness, then recovers and says, "You can't get there from here." In the more elaborate version that Young remembers, King set up the joke: "I was in Willacoochee, Georgia, looking for the Greater Mount Carmel Rising Free For All Baptist Church." He closed the joke in full-blown rural black idiom, telling how King and his retinue spot the man bounding after their car, and they pull over, and the man tells him, "Dr. King, Dr. King, I ax my brother for the church an' he say . . . he say you can't get there from here, neither."[14]

The use of the term "nigger" was unabashed, even as its meaning varied with the context in that circle. In the midst of a meeting, directed at Andrew Young, and prefaced by "Little," "nigger" could serve as a means to diminish or assert control. For Hosea Williams, "niggers" was a constant in his vocabulary, a badge of the unashamed earthiness he embraced when he proclaimed himself a man who had been sweating and eating greens his whole life. Williams once instructed a mixed group of civil rights volunteers on the etiquette of interracial sex inside freedom houses in small southern towns: "White women and niggers . . . If you just have to have some, go somewhere else up the road and get yourself some." King once cited William Rutherford's business credentials and Sorbonne doctorate; Williams answered, "That nigger don't know nothin' about niggers!" When James Bevel used the term in the midst of a staff workshop—"Niggers want to be white people rather than men that are loving and working, civilizing and humanizing . . . I'm a human being!"— the utterance was tinged with his mystical humanism and rejection of "enslaved consciousness." Often, the word served simply as an inside term of affection. Only moments before the bullet from James Earl Ray's gun struck, King spotted Andrew Young and asked with mock impatience, "Lil' Nigger, just where you been?"[15]

The point you need to understand, says Lowery, is that "nigger," like the rest of their racial ribbing, was never self-denigrating. Falling into his preacher rhythm, Lowery dubs it "the coronation of diminution." "When blacks tell racial jokes, it's really sometimes demeaning white folks, I hate to admit it, because it shows how insensitive or how ignorant white people were on black folks." As for "nigger" in particular, "it was taking what was meant for evil and transforming it into good. It was laughing at the white folks' enmity and hostility . . . This is what made King make fun of white people. We could use the terms they used in derision, we used [them] as legitimate." The same dynamic was at work when the assembled reverends made fun of "chicken-eating preachers." Whether it was white folks or "some black folks too" who had that image of blacks, in joking about it "we were admitting that we ate chicken, and there was nothing wrong with it." In the end, none of these high jinks were demeaning because "we enjoyed our blackness too much."

"Martin did have a side to him that was comfortable with the streets," Andrew Young observed. "He liked to get down and talk like a street brother when he was relaxing, blowing off steam. He teased, he could crack on you, insult you until the whole room was laughing 'til they cried . . . He could only relax that way with people he trusted, his closest colleagues and personal friends."[16]

King's "cracking" could be merciless. His lampoon of a stuttering preacher was so precise that people recognized the man within seconds of meeting him. Nor was King's jab at Abernathy for his snoring the only one he hurled. Once he gave Abernathy a hard time "about his consuming desire to give the really big speech—saying Abernathy needed to first become president of something, then suggesting he form the National Association for the Advancement of Eating Chicken. King led guffawing preachers as they 'cracked on Ralph' with ridiculous ideas for his organization."[17] According to some, another suggestion was lewder; Abernathy might head the "National Association of Pussy Eaters."

Meanwhile, the preachers teased Young for wearing "white man's shoes." After King's death, a roast of Young featured him staring at the mirror, saying, "I'm as pretty as Harry Belafonte." Young was not above retaliating, gleefully teasing Lowery for being "one of those curly haired Negroes, he's got good hair, he thinks his hair's better than everyone else." Once in a while King would restrain Hosea Williams when he was beating up on Young with a firm "Now, Hosea," but King could also leap right into the fray, taunting, "Andy, there's not a white man you wouldn't Tom." On another occasion, King promised, "Andy, when the Klan finally gets you, here's what I'll preach: 'Lord, white folks made a big mistake, today. They have sent home to glory your faithful servant, Andrew Young. Lord, have mercy on the white folks who did this terrible deed. They killed the wrong Negro. In Andrew Young, white folk had a friend so faithful, so enduring they should never have harmed a hair on his head. Of all my associates, no one loved white folks as much as Andy.'"[18]

Some of the edgier racial dynamics surfaced in the SCLC staff's response to Tom Houck, the white driver King enlisted late in his life. A teenager who came out of the Irish and German working-class world of

Somerville, Massachusetts, before moving South, Houck led demonstrations in his southern high school, quit to join the movement full time, and eventually became King's driver in 1967. Daddy King, who never entirely got over his deep suspicion of whites, used to marvel, "Look at Martin, he's got a white boy for a driver." But the younger King defended Houck. Resentment surfaced when Houck left the field staff for "the big house," a key marker for those never invited to the King home, and the field staff retaliated with grumbling: "Tom's the white son Martin never had" and "Be careful, that's Coretta's boy, you don't want to mess with him" and "Martin's got himself a white boy."[19]

As Houck tells it, "when Hosea [Williams] was around there were more racial overtones. I was harassed by the brothers," he says, more bemused than bitter. Williams used to call Houck "white boy" or "cracker boy." Much of this sparring was good-natured, but sometimes it was not. At one SCLC staff retreat, James Bevel's lower impulses must have overcome his spiritual convictions. A great womanizer who sometimes described himself as a "political sexologist," he had his sights set on a white woman, and he suddenly got up in Houck's face and badgered him, "How's it make you feel to see a nigger fucking a white woman?" In Chicago, Houck recalls, he came in for some misplaced anti-Semitic animus from local staffers who assumed that a fervent white enlistee in the black struggle had to be Jewish: "I thought we got rid of these Jew boys."

"It was hard being white in the movement," Houck says today. But none of that has diminished his memories of Bevel. "I loved Bevel," he says, and his face breaks out in a big grin. Such rituals of domination were "just the price you paid."

As important as blackness was to King and his inner circle, we need to be careful not to overstate its importance. If we reduce such less than genteel talk to race, we miss too many of the other dynamics that energized it. The distinction between black talk and white talk was never hard and fast. King's use of "crackers," "Little Nigger," and "chicken eating preachers" also declared his belonging to a world of rowdy masculinity that was only incidentally black. In fact, King did not clown around like this with most black people he knew, or in church or mass meetings. As John Lewis told me, despite their close, long-standing relationship, King never indulged in such banter with him, but then again, Lewis points out, he wasn't part of the workaday crew. Nor were field staffers privy to much of the carrying on with King either. Indeed, they were careful to restrain their own antics when King was around.

One could even say there was a certain race-blind universalism at work in the teasing of Houck as a "white boy." King did not insult people he didn't like to their face. That was true of the rest of the SCLC coterie as well. Says Lowery, "You could insult somebody [and] no one would get angry. You know, like when kids would play the dozens. You could play the dozens with friends. But you couldn't play otherwise, you'd get into a fight. It meant we accepted each other."[20] As Houck intuited, there was a world of difference between Bevel's taunt, "how's it feel to see a black man fucking a white girl," which had a nastier, racial edge, and the affectionate rituals of "giving the white man shit." The latter was a way of marking insider status.

How then to fathom the fact that, as one of the preacher colleagues stresses, they never said to Stanley Levison things like "Oh you Jewish rascal"? As a practical matter, the occasions on which King met with whites and the way these sessions were organized—scheduled meetings with an agenda and limits on time—tended to focus participants on the task at hand. Moreover, at times King did seek to tempt Levison into a more personal exchange. The obstacle then was not King's reluctance but Levison's seriousness. Stanley, his son Andrew explains, "had his own ability to get loose, he loved the Marx Brothers, but he was unable to cross culture and share the 'black thing.' He always wore a tie; he was a serious man. He could never swear around Martin, never say 'motherfucker.' He couldn't share in cracking jokes about the women they slept with." In contrast, even though Houck was a teenager at the time and way down in the hierarchy, logging hours together in the car provided time for King and Houck to kick back a bit. Houck recalls that King would sometimes use him as an explicator of the white experience. One time, King asked Houck if he knew what white people called the way black people smoked, wetting the end of the cigarette. He was referring to the colloquialism "nigger lipping."

As these layers of complexity indicate, there's a greater puzzle at work here: how big a deal was the absence of vulgar repartee in King's talk with Levison? Was that the only or the true measure of King's sense of intimacy? At first glance, it makes sense to think of earthy talk as genuine and spontaneous, but banter can be just as stylized as front stage talk. Even if the backstage allows frank talk on certain topics, it too is subject to its own taboos.[21] So before we romanticize the carrying on behind closed doors, it's only fair to point out what was so obvious to King: the immense egoism rampant among some of the same staffers with whom he kidded around. King distinguished between people who were relatively selfless—a transracial group that included Stanley Levison, Bernard Lee, Andrew Young, Joseph Lowery, C. T. Vivian, and Walter Fauntroy—and egomaniacs who were constantly plying their own agendas, such as James Bevel, Hosea Williams, and, later, Jesse Jackson. In one of the most fraught moments in SCLC history, King exploded at a staff meeting, "You don't like to work on anything that isn't your own idea. Bevel, I think you owe *me* one." As King went storming out of the room, Jesse Jackson yelled, "Doc, doc, don't worry! Everything's going to be all right." And King turned on him, "Jesse, everything's *not* going to be all right . . . If you're so interested in doing your own thing that you can't do what this organization's structured to do . . . go ahead. But for God's sake, don't bother me!"[22]

The encounters between King and Levison, on the other hand, reveal an intimacy that was rare for the time. They achieved a deep connection that both confronted race head on and transcended it. Always "Stan," Levison slept in the King home when he visited Atlanta. He was one of the first people Andrew Young called after King was shot in Memphis. Levison had no trouble serving a black man, selflessly as King judged it. Nor was he in thrall to some patronizing romantic ideal. Levison never hesitated to tell King things that he might not wish to hear, and King never hesitated to refuse his advice. The sharpness of Levison's disagreements with King and King's rejection of all kinds of advice from Levison underscore the mutuality at play.

Early in the relationship, King's New York-based literary agent was not happy that King had decided to work on the book *Stride toward Freedom* with black Alabama State professor Lawrence Reddick and not with a New York-based, presumably white professional. But Levison, as he wrote to King, saw the virtues of Reddick's "knowledge of the deeper meaning of the struggle . . . Such rapport necessarily rests upon the feeling that he is able to empathize fully because he is a committed person himself." King's agent and one of the white candidates, Levison continued, "did not fully grasp my feeling that a Negro more readily feels things that a white person comprehends with greater difficulty. This is the old story that too many white liberals consider themselves free of stereotypes, rarely recognizing that the roots of prejudice are deep and are tenaciously driven into the soil of their whole life." "Stanley," Andrew Levison observes pointedly, "had no desire to be a white Negro."[23]

King and Levison thus developed their own brand of closeness that reflected real people engaged in a common cause rather than some formulaic notion of intimacy. When King's longtime secretary, Dora MacDonald, worried over King's despondent state in 1967, she reached out to Levison to call him. As King's mood spiraled downward after a Memphis protest turned violent in early 1968, he called Levison and vented his intense feelings of despair. In Taylor Branch's words, King "relapsed into fears of ruin. He said influential black critics scented his weakness . . . and would reinforce the public damage." As King put it to Levison, "You know, their point is, 'Martin Luther King is dead, he's finished.'" These were not the only moments of vulnerability he shared with Levison, who recalled that being in solitary confinement was "the hardest thing" for King in jail. "When he was cut off from people, he really went into a depression. . . . He got his strength from people. When he was cut off from them he worried . . . he brooded, he felt bewildered. As a matter of fact, he told me one time that he broke down completely in solitary."[24]

As a "God-intoxicated" man, King found it hard to grasp Levison's secularism, and once they went at it on the religious front, surely as charged for King as race. "You believe in God, Stan," King insisted to Levison. "You just don't know it."[25] When they were forming SCLC and someone, focusing on the "Christian" in the title, pointed out, "Stanley's a Jew," according to Andrew Levison, "Martin said with a smile, 'We'll make Stanley an honorary Christian.'" Maybe not all Jews would have agreed, but it was the highest praise imaginable, and Levison cherished that moment. "The rest of his life Stanley told that story. He was so proud. He rarely bragged, but he'd always say, 'Martin made me an honorary Christian.'"

At one point on the FBI tapes of the Willard Hotel tryst, King is heard to cry out at the peak of sexual passion, "I'm fucking for God!" and "I'm not a Negro tonight."[26] In a moment of abandon, King could imagine escaping from blackness, at least for an evening. *Brother*hood was not so primal that he never wished to leave it. King was also not above admitting "whites" to the status of blackness too, if only in a moment of verbal horseplay. Daddy King had been fretting about his son's hiring Tom Houck to squire his grandchildren around Atlanta, but King would not be deterred. He insisted to his father, "Tom is more black than the blackest person who works here in SCLC. He ought to be over there with Stokely."

FIVE

Race Men and Real Men

"It is better to go through life with a scarred up body than a scarred up soul"

The Southern Christian Leadership Conference defined its backstage not only through the rites of race and ribaldry. Paradoxically for a nonviolent movement, a tough masculine culture flourished among the members of the SCLC field staff and the executive staffers who championed them. In certain respects King diverged from this model, despite his womanizing and raunchiness. King's empathy, epitomized by Jesus' example of tender masculinity, touted a "feminine" ethic of care and connection. Despite his guardedness, he was an expressive man who had no trouble revealing his emotions. In 1965 John Lewis, who was close to King even though he was then the head of the rival SNCC, watched King's tears welling up in Selma after Bloody Sunday as they listened to President Lyndon Johnson speak the words of the movement as his own, "We shall overcome."[1]

To fully understand King, we need to grasp the creative tension between his tender endeavor and the daily round of gritty practice that sustained it. Nothing better disclosed the realism at the core of King's movement, nothing more fully revealed the limits of the cartoon image of redemptive nonviolence as naïve and ethereal. This tension played out in Chicago in 1966 when the SCLC launched marches into white ethnic neighborhoods such as Gage Park. The upsurge of racist contempt across Chicago's bungalow communities had been revelatory, putting the spotlight on the racism of the northern white working class. Although Andrew Young placed a marcher in front of King as a protective buffer, when King joined the march into Gage Park, he was felled by a missile and dropped to the ground, bleeding from his head. That outpouring of hate rattled King, Andrew Young, and Ralph Abernathy as much as when they found themselves face to face with the killers of Michael Schwerner, James Chaney, and Andrew Goodman, three civil rights workers killed in Philadelphia, Mississippi, in 1964.

A tinge of bitterness seeped into King's comments during negotiations with Mayor Daley and the Chicago Board of Real Estate. "Our humble marches have revealed a cancer. We have not used rocks. We have not used bottles. And no one today, no one who has spoken has condemned those that have used violence. . . . Maybe we should begin condemning the robber and not the robbed." He then retrieved a crossover barb that he had used before when churning with anger at white hypocrisy: "No one here has talked about the beauty of our marches, the love of our marches, the hatred we're absorbing."[2]

An exhausted King did not hide his vulnerable state, something he usually confined to the safety of the black world. "If you are tired of demonstrations, I am tired of demonstrating. I am tired of the threat of death. I want to live. I don't want to be a martyr. And there are moments when I doubt if I am going to make it through. I am tired of getting hit, tired of being beaten, tired of going to jail."[3]

Bernard Lafayette, a former SNCC worker with close SCLC ties whom King would soon summon to the executive staff, had been training gang members to serve as marshals for the Chicago marches. When one of the Blackstone Rangers was getting out of hand and there was no arguing him out of his desire for reprisal, Lafayette explained the predicament to another gang member, who promptly decked his ornery colleague, slung him over his shoulder, and took him away. Was that Gandhian? I asked Lafayette. He laughed. "I guess I'm not a pacifist." As Lafayette put it slyly, "We had to go with the experienced. They had scars and could knock down bricks."[4]

In that punch-out, the classic dilemma of dirty hands entailed a literal laying on of hands. But Lafayette was not the only one in the orbit of prophecy who could get rough and tough in the service of a cheek-turning movement. The towering James Orange, the Parker High School football star who had joined the field staff as a youngster in Birmingham, discovered a new danger lurking in Chicago. Instead of disseminating Kingian language, he found himself a party to reverse translation. Orange tried to break up a rumble between gangs who were, in Fairclough's words, "disdainful of the church, antagonistic towards whites, and contemptuous of the word 'nonviolence.'" For his efforts, Orange suffered a busted nose and lip. As an undaunted Orange pressed on, instead of inducting the gangs into the Christian ethic, he was forced to use their language: "Listen you goddamn [expletive], I've whipped more white men and more niggers than any man in this room. Now you can kill me if you want to, but before you do I'm going to kill one from the Blackstone Rangers and one from the Cobras. Two of you at least are going to die before you kill me."[5]

Many on the field staff roster approached their task with a sensibility that was as much street as sublime. Lester Hankerson had been a pistol-packing gangster on the Savannah waterfront. Back in Albany, Georgia, J. T. Johnson and his buddies broke up a barbecue joint when they felt disrespected by whites. And Willie Bolden was certainly not at first an acolyte of nonviolence: "The idea of letting someone smack you was a foreign one. I wasn't nonviolent. I had spent four years in the Marines. I wasn't about to let people spit on me and slap me and not retaliate."[6]

What drew Bolden to the movement back in Savannah was not the ideal of beloved community but the "crazy," telling-the-man style of Hosea Williams, who would eventually help recruit him to SCLC. "Hosea," Bolden recalls, "climbed up on the statue of [the Indian chief] Tomochichi [in downtown Savannah]. He got the folk all riled up. I thought, 'That guy's got to be crazy!' He mesmerized me. In 1961, a black man stands up and talks about white folk like that just didn't fly. He was my kind of guy! I thought, 'I could do that.' This guy is tough."

"He got to be crazy" could also have been said about James Bevel, with his fierce faith, the yarmulke he wore as homage to the Old Testament prophets, and his wild disquisitions that lyrically mixed street talk, mystical Christianity, and an existential lingo of authenticity. Bernard Lafayette was privy to a Bevel caper. When they got out of their post–Freedom Ride jail stint, they stuck around Jackson, Mississippi, and began to organize some of the young toughs. Bevel disarmed them with this challenge: "You want to fight? We're going to fight the white folks downtown." And the toughs replied, "All right, I just got out of jail."

In the roughness swirling in the shadows of King, it's easy to see a vindication of necessity: delegating to proxies forbidden acts that morality denies but necessity obliges. When Wyatt Tee Walker dispatched James Orange to turn in false fire alarms to create havoc in Birmingham, he kept that bit of news from King. "Do what you gotta do," goes the moral rumination of the working class. The *gotta* reflects the pragmatic sociology of those who can't claim the privileges or immunity to act on their morality. In King's reference to Hosea Williams as "my wild man, my Castro," there was an acceptance not just of Williams but also of his kamikaze qualities as central to the King enterprise.

All of King's exalted language rested on a vast infrastructure that was very tough-minded. King may have preached at First African Methodist, but it was Willie Bolden and Big Lester who walked the aisles, recognized the thugs, and had the credibility to make them give up their weapons. King offered lofty musings on agape at the Birmingham mass meetings, but it was James Orange, Andrew Marrissett, and others—the network of young, street-wise volunteers organized by executive staffers like Andrew Young, Dorothy Cotton, and James Bevel—who mobilized the high school students who flooded Bull Connor's downtown, got doused by fire hoses, and won the day. In Chicago, Lafayette recalled, "We were able to reach [the gang members] because we were as tough, or tougher. We had been to jail, and we weren't afraid. They were taken aback." They explicitly appealed to the gang members' sense of manly shame, telling them it was one thing to stay in the safety of the ghetto "cussing out crackers," another thing altogether to march into these white ethnic neighborhoods that were full of "some serious white folks." Lafayette challenged them, "Are you tough enough to do this?"

The work of mobilization required talents other than toughness. A speech by King, only one moment in a stream of events, was preceded by meetings, requests, and exhortations. The work of getting frightened southern blacks in the spirit to receive King's word began well before King even arrived in town. Bolden became expert in sizing up a crowd and gauging their mood. What was the age of the crowd? Were they cowed and bedraggled or fired up? Did they need secular freedom songs or religious ones?

This was the same artistry of insurgency perfected by Andrew Marrissett, even if he lacked the ruffian swagger of some. His entrance into the movement came on impulse in 1963, when he leapt out of the school bus he was driving when he saw Birmingham cops beating a little girl in Kelly Ingram Park and carried her to safety. His SCLC missions, as he calls them, spanned a decade of organizing across the South. The children of Selma, who played their own heroic role in that resistance, named Marrissett, not King, as their hero; he was their good shepherd. "It was my Baptist upbringing, I was a missionary Baptist, which told us to love our fellow man and turn the other cheek. I never had hatred [for whites]—maybe dislike, and sometimes wonder—How can you do this, say this . . . lynch us?"[7]

As Marrissett describes the fieldworkers' role, if King was the gravy, they were the "potatoes." None of this intends disrespect for "Doctor King," he hastens to add. The movement needed the marquee speaker. Still, aside from an occasional glimpse of Moses, the field staff were often the links in the chain through which Kingian ideas trickled down to the masses. When Sheriff Jim Clark got sick—the Clark whose deputies had zapped the children of Selma with cattle prods—the children wanted to rejoice. But Marrissett told them, "No, no, go pray for him."

John Lewis recalled the frenzy of all this preparatory labor in Selma. Hosea Williams, Lewis's co-leader of the first of three attempted marches over Pettus Bridge on Bloody Sunday, "saw himself as one of Dr. King's field hands, getting out there on the scene, organizing the troops, preparing the way for Dr. King to follow. . . . That's essentially what everyone [in Selma] was doing during those first two weeks of January, preparing for King to come pull the trigger."[8] This mix of an iconic triggerman, executive staffers who loaded the gun, and a ground crew that lined up the targets reflected the logic of a division of labor.[9] Clearly, then, the sublime and the gritty were not just entangled; they were organically linked, the one dependent on the other, which is why King had no trouble acting as the unsentimental one. At one point, when pressed by a field staff disgruntled at being yanked from one town to the next just as they were putting down roots, King responded in a testy tone that would seem to violate his formulation of an I/thou relationship. James Orange recalled King "saying that we were shacking with the community . . . [and] we weren't gonna marry the community. Our job was to get stuff started and then move on and get stuff started in other areas."[10]

But there was still another dynamic at work in King's relationship to the field staff. The proprietary aspect of "my" in King's comment that Williams was "my wild man, my Castro" underscores that King did not merely accept the need for people like Hosea Williams but embraced them. Beyond the tacit coordination of lofty rhetoric and dirty hands, warm relations linked King and many of the ground crew. These were extraordinary people who had devoted their lives to the deliverance of black people. Some lived together, shared the peripatetic life together, even had Thanksgiving dinner together. In the process they shared key moments, some terrifying, with King. They were the ones who watched King's back. J. T. Johnson and Bolden were with King on the Meredith March when they spotted a pickup truck roaring up the road right at them, and they dove into a ditch. King, it seems, just stood there, refusing to flinch.

Eventually they made it to Philadelphia, Mississippi, where only one year earlier Chief Deputy Sheriff Cecil Ray Price and others had detained Schwerner, Chaney, and Goodman before releasing them to their death during Freedom Summer. When Price blocked King's way toward the lawn of the Neshoba County Courthouse, King asked quietly, "'You're the one who had Schwerner and those fellows in jail?' 'Yes, sir,' Price responded in a tone of sarcastic pride."[11]

Amidst heckling from a threatening crowd of whites, a shaken King memorialized the three martyrs: "In this county, Andrew Goodman, James Chaney, and Mickey Schwerner were brutally murdered . . . I believe in my heart that the murderers are somewhere around me at this moment." Shouts came back, "right behind you" and "you're damned right." "They ought to search their hearts," King told the crowd. "I want them to know that we are not afraid. If they kill three of us, they will have to kill all of us. I am not afraid of any man, whether he is in Michigan or Mississippi, whether he is in Birmingham or Boston." Suddenly, a crowd of white attackers crashed the line of marchers, hurling stones, bottles, and clubs.[12]

The camaraderie wasn't always somber. Many savored the times they played basketball with King or simply fooled around. Marrissett gently smiles as he remembers King's constant filching of his Kools cigarettes.

King, recalls J. T. Johnson, was "just a fun guy, he was just one of the boys. . . . He loved to play ball, he loved to play pool, he loved to *play*. He was just a guy who liked to laugh, just talk about things, stuff. You know, we'd talk a lot of trash." People just didn't get to see this private King, says Johnson. He "could get down to earth as much as anybody." Sometimes they would revisit scary moments, kicking back at the end of a day and re-hashing beatings like connoisseurs of suffering. King would "make a big joke" about it. "Our trash talking would be some of the experiences we had in the movement. You know, they whipped over so and so good and we'd talk about the beating we took, and we'd laugh about it."[13]

That frightful day back in Philadelphia, Mississippi, especially lingered in memory. "They almost got Ralph," King and his entourage chortled. After they dove into the ditch, Johnson continues, "We finally got on down to the courthouse, all of us, and we kneeled down, and Martin Luther King said, 'Pray, Ralph, pray.' So Ralph started praying and everybody's eyes was open . . . so we'd get back and we'd laugh, 'we didn't close our eyes, we were too scared to close them' . . . And that was the big joke. . . . We'd laugh about it 'cause nobody got killed and nobody got hurt." Andrew Young recalls one extra detail. "Martin—as he was fond of joking later—called on Ralph to pray, 'Since I sure wasn't about to close *my* eyes.' Martin, in telling this story, always added, 'Ralph prayed, but he prayed with a wary eye open.'"[14]

In the end, the bonds that linked King to the field staffers had a more spiritual aspect. Anointed or not, they all were working to deliver the captives. In terror and tears, they shared the sacrificial vocation. And they had accepted, some more perfectly than others, the good news of redemptive nonviolence. The field staff lived the boast, "we will win you with our suffering." In celebrating that doctrine, King sometimes merged his voice with that of Jesus, urging, "bless those who curse you." But in one fervent effort to explain that "way as old as Jesus saying / Turn the other cheek," King vaulted Jesus forward in time and switched places with him, making him speak King's words as if Jesus had been there in Yazoo City or Marion:

> And when He said that,
> He realized that
> turning the other cheek

might bring suffering sometimes.
He realized that it might
get your home bombed sometime.
He realized that it may
get you stabbed some time.
He realized that it may
get you scarred up sometime.
But he was saying in substance,
that it is better to go through life
with a scarred up body than a scarred up soul.
There is another way . . .
Ohhh, there is a power in that way.[15]

Certainly the field hands had been scarred up. At one retreat, King apologized that everyone had been so busy of late that "we on the executive staff often forget to express our gratitude to those of you who are working on a day-to-day basis in communities all over our country to make the American dream a reality; and I know how many of you have suffered, and I know how many of you have sacrificed. . . . Almost I found myself shedding a few tears this afternoon when I listened to Lester talk about what he had gone through in Mississippi and many of our staff members go through experiences not quite as bad as Lester that we often know nothing about. And I want to thank you because you have done this out of a loyalty to a cause . . . And you are to be praised for your willingness to suffer so creatively."[16]

Creative suffering had not come naturally. "We had to grow into it," J. T. Johnson says today, and they owed that all to King. The truth was that "we didn't know if we'd be violent or non-violent. [Accepting nonviolence] was pragmatic at first." In St. Augustine, Florida, Johnson and his colleagues would form a phalanx in front of the women and children. "We knew that if we retaliated everyone would be in danger, so we'd take the beating." Yet over time, something changed: "We talked about nonviolence and we preached it 'til we believed it. I practice it now." King had this aura about him, an uncanny power, and when he was present the fear and hesitation seemed to dissipate.

Willie Bolden too exemplified the vocation of suffering, although his nice straight teeth, long since capped, no longer bear the signs of the injuries he sustained in Marion, Alabama, the night of the shooting of Jimmie Lee Jackson, a young black man who had gone to the defense of his mother when lawmen assaulted her. Bolden, Big Lester, and several other fieldworkers who were "stationed in Selma" had gone over to Marion to mobilize the community for a King speech later that evening. When they returned to Selma to update King on the preparations, King explained he had been told, "Look, you need to rest your voice because you gotta do this thing in Selma tomorrow." He asked Bolden to stand in for him at the Marion rally.

As in Selma, the focus in Marion was on voter registration and the looming vote on the Voting Rights Act. The idea was to first awaken the people with rousing speeches, then a night march to the courthouse, with a few rounds of freedom singing. Bolden brought King's presence right into Zion Methodist Church. "I talked to them about Dr. King getting the Nobel Peace Prize and how he stopped off at Washington to garner support [for the bill and President Johnson asked] why are you doing that? You just came back from the mountain top [in Oslo]. And King replied, 'While it is true that I've had a mountaintop experience, I'm on my way back to the valley where my people are. President, we are going to get a voting rights act.'" Shifting back to Marion, Bolden raised the pressure on the audience. Even the great Moses could not do it alone; they had to do their part. "It is time that you stand up and be men and women, and stop scratching when you ain't itching and grinning when you ain't tickled."

The attack on the marchers began right after they left the church. The lights had gone out as if on cue; only the TV lights gave an eerie, lunar cast to the melee that exploded all around them. "This sheriff, and his folk and the Klan just jumped in and started beating us. The next thing I knew, some big sheriff had me jacked up in the back of my jeans, and the sheriff's going, 'What are you doing in my town, nigger, getting my niggers all upset? Where is that Martin Luther Coon.'" Bolden's devotion to his leader was too great to let such disrespect pass uncorrected. "And I said, 'You don't mean that. You mean *Dr.* Martin Luther King, Jr. He is not here, I'm here representing him.'" The sheriff replied, "Oh, you're one of those outside agitators," to which Bolden recalls answering, "Well, that's what you say."

The sheriff was furious. "That's when he stuck his pistol in my mouth, and cocked the hammer back, and got his hand on the trigger. And he looked at me and he said, 'Nigger, if you breathe, I'll blow your so-and-so head off.' I just looked him in the eye." The sheriff invited Bolden to "'breathe nigger.' When he snatched the gun out, that's when the teeth broke. He hit me upside the top of the head." Moments later, Bolden heard the sound of gunfire off in the distance; Jackson had just been shot over at Mack's cafe. As they dragged Bolden off, there was blood everywhere, even on the steps going up to the jail.

Throughout the years, the sacraments of blood would join King to his band of brothers, whether they were fighting for him or fighting to protect him. To this day, Bolden associates that madness in Marion with his beloved leader. "I can remember that little girl who wrote Dr. King a letter when he was stabbed in the chest. She had read where if King had sneezed he would have died, and she said to him, 'While it's not important, I want you to know that I'm a little white girl and thank God you didn't sneeze.'" Over the years, there were many days when Bolden had reflected, "Thank God I didn't breathe. I wouldn't be here telling you that story if I had."

Bolden's martial imagery—"We were prayer warriors"—comes close to capturing the blend of physical and moral courage displayed by the field-workers. That very image reflects the evangelical impact of King on so many of his colleagues. Bolden's induction into the movement came when Hosea Williams brought King to a Savannah poolroom. As Bolden recalls, an almost apologetic King began with a clear marker of racial camaraderie, "I won't take too much of your time, brother." As he did on similar occasions, sometimes in a somewhat strained fashion, he cited his exposure to Auburn Avenue, plus his expertise at pool, as a warm-up. In retrospect, Bolden can't believe how rude he was to King. He kept standing, and first hit the eight ball. But that poolroom palaver began what proved to be a life of Christian witness. Bolden today is Rev. (Willie) Bolden, pastor of a church in southwest Atlanta.

King cajoled Bolden to come hear him speak that night at St. Paul's AME, although Bolden did so furtively, walking two blocks out of his way to hide from "my boys" the fact that he was heading for church. But as he listened to King, Bolden wasn't so tough that he didn't feel undone by the man and what he said. He developed "chill bumps," and he was aware "that a man isn't supposed to make another man feel that way." After the address, Bolden went up to shake King's hand, and King recalled his name and said, "Willie, I'm glad you came." King's hands were soft, like a baby's, Bolden remembers.

To this day, Bolden can't quite define this quality in King's talk, but like J. T. Johnson he too glimpsed some special aura. When Bolden finally joined the SCLC, King gave him two books: the Bible and one by Gandhi. Bolden eventually got around to his Gandhi assignments and came to embrace them, and to practice them as well. He recalls the time in Greenwood, Mississippi, when a Klansman planted his foot in the crotch of a young boy and snapped his leg in three places. Every instinct urged Bolden to tear the racist thug apart, but instead he shoved him aside, scooped up the little boy, and carried him off. A little bit of King had been internalized, and there was a little bit of King in most of the others too—even Big Lester, who could backslide and get mean when he was drinking gin. But, Marrissett adds, "he loved Doctor King and would never do anything to hurt him." As King preached to a group of SCLC staffers at a retreat, Lester was amazing testimony to the power of "the better way" of Christian nonviolence to redeem the wayward. This was the soul force that King liked to trumpet, operating through a social movement that had the power to stir the soul not just of a nation but of a man like Big Lester.

Here then was another form of King's crossover talk—his ability to reach out to potential foot solders across the divide of vulgar and genteel, to tap something deep within some rough characters and enlist them in a sublime movement. Not only did the tender prophet move tough soldiers; in the process, the toughest soldiers succumbed to a certain tenderness.

SIX

The Prophetic Backstage

"Toughness and *a tender heart"*

"After a very hard and tough movement," Willie Bolden reminisced, "Martin would call for what we called a retreat—in the Army they call it R and R. . . . We would just play golf, basketball. Martin was an *excellent* athlete. Cat could really play basketball." A different King emerged at these retreats: "That's where he would not have to show the elegant part of himself with the tie. He wore open shirt, slacks, pair of trousers, maybe bedroom shoes if he felt like it, house coat." Bolden's grasp of the link between King's offstage demeanor and the material conditions of war—"in the Army they call it R and R"—reminds us that the vulgar banter that in part signaled shared blackness was embedded in a practical context of a liberation army on the move. As Bernard Lee, one of King's closest colleagues, told David Garrow, "Our joking, our playing, was about our *efforts*."[1]

Like any other army, King and his troops operated under conditions of intense stress. King's getting teary over the rough time Big Lester had in Mississippi was a tacit recognition that battered warriors needed time to recoup and repair. Some foot soldiers succumbed to post-traumatic stress that endured as frightening dreams for decades. The threat of racist violence was part of the texture of everyday life. "Our goal basically was to get through the day without anybody getting killed," says J. T. Johnson. He winces as he thinks of the Selma campaign when "we lost three or four."[2]

King suffered excruciating pressures, some unique and some just normal in any activist movement. He tended to succumb to the flu at the sharpest stress points of a campaign. He never chose the role of iconic leader; his life was beyond his control from the moment he was selected to lead the Montgomery boycott. The maniacal schedule, constant traveling, and shuttling from one speaking gig to the next devoured his private life. Such burdens were a factor in the melancholy to which King periodically succumbed.

One Sunday in 1959, as King prepared to join Daddy King in Atlanta as co-pastor of Ebenezer Baptist Church, word leaked out that he was going to resign from Dexter Avenue Baptist Church. Lerone Bennett could feel the thickening tension in the church. "King sat in the pulpit looking uncomfortable and preoccupied. Behind him in the choir, Coretta sat with the sopranos, giving no hint of anything amiss." Overcome with emotion, King announced he could not preach. Once the church was cleared of all but members, King, clutching the pulpit, told them, "For almost four years now, I . . . [have been] trying to do as one man what five or six people ought to be doing." As a result of the bus boycott, "I found myself in a position I could not get out of. This thrust unexpected responsibilities my way." He was their pastor, president of the Montgomery Improvement Association, head of the SCLC. There was the hopscotching across the nation to speak, the office chores, and "*the general strain of being known.*" He had been "giving, *giving*," and if things didn't change soon, "I will be a physical and psychological wreck . . . I have been too long in the crowd, too long in the forest." As he reached the end, King declared, "I can't stop now. History has thrust something upon me which I can't turn away. *I should free you now.*"

After he formally submitted his resignation, "King asked everyone to link hands and join him in the song. 'Blest Be the Tie That Binds.' As the melody rose and fell, Martin Luther King, Jr., broke down in tears in the pulpit that had carried him to fame."[3]

In the final year especially, the harsh response to his criticism of the Vietnam War, the vanishing allure of nonviolence, and the explosion of violence during an SCLC march in Memphis sent King into a tailspin. He worried about being consigned to irrelevance as militant rivals surpassed him. His closest colleagues observed a deepening despondency; they only divided on how much to chalk it up to physical, emotional, or spiritual exhaustion. "Late one night, King literally howled against the paralyzed debate [within SCLC]. 'I don't want to do this any more!' He shouted alone. 'I want to go back to my little church!' He banged around and yelled, which summoned anxious friends outside his room until Young and Abernathy gently removed his whiskey and talked him to bed." In the view of his close colleague Dorothy Cotton, King "was just really emotionally weary, as well as physically tired . . . That whole last year I felt his weariness, just weariness of the struggle, that he had done all that he could do."[4]

Meanwhile, the gap he felt between his inner self and his public image reinforced a profound sense of guilt which he vented to the Ebenezer congregation: "Martin Luther King too is a sinner." As the FBI cranked up its campaign against King by disseminating rumors of his promiscuity, King, according to David Garrow, "became so nervous and upset that he could not sleep, and was certain that the Bureau would do anything to ruin him. 'They are out to break me,' he told one close friend over a wiretapped phone line. 'They are out to get me, harass me, break my spirit.' The most intimate details of his personal life, King said, ought to be no business of the FBI's. 'What I do is only between me and my God.'"[5]

Above all, King lived with the ever-present threat of death from the very start of the Montgomery bus boycott, when his house was bombed. Toward the end, Levison and Rustin shared their fear that, as Rustin put it, "Martin was becoming a little too concerned about the possibility of death." Rustin voiced his misgiving to King, who "brushed [it] off. 'You think I'm paranoid, don't you.'"[6]

King's repertoire of death talk was eclectic. It took the form of disturbing unsettlement, as a rattled King rambled on at a Montgomery mass meeting—if "anyone should be killed, let it be me"—before collapsing at the pulpit.[7] It was combative when a younger activist would not relent in pressing King to join the Freedom Riders, and King lost patience with her: "I will choose the time of my own Golgotha." It was pedestrian, almost dismissive, with his battered field staff. "I may die in the movement, [but] I don't mind . . . I settled that [fear of death] long ago. . . . I don't think anybody can be free until you solve this problem."[8] It took the form of an out-of-body experience, when King was lying in a hospital after being stabbed in Harlem; according to Andrew Young, King was looking down on the scene and imagining a ring of black clergy eager for his death, and King was musing that he was not ready to go.

King could also quip about death, as he did after the pilot on a flight to Memphis apologized for a bomb threat that delayed takeoff: "Well, it looks like they won't kill me this flight, not after telling all that." Around the same time, on a tour across Black Belt towns, King's talk cycled from defiant rejection of bodyguards—"I can't live that kind of life. . . . I'd feel like a bird in a cage"—through resignation—"there's no way in the world you can keep somebody from killing you if they really want to kill you"—to a sardonic tone, after engine trouble made him late—"I would much rather be Martin Luther King late than the late Martin Luther King." It could soar with intensity: "I've been to the mountaintop . . . I'm not fearing any man. . . . Mine eyes have seen the glory of the coming of the Lord." And when he recalled how he would have died if he sneezed after a mad woman plunged a knife into him, it could exult in a praise song, "And I'm happy I didn't sneeze."[9]

These circumstances fueled King's need for retreat. Sometimes he sought an interlude of solace in the creature comforts of the steam room followed by a massage from the blind man at the Auburn Avenue YMCA, a remnant of a safe boyhood where he had spent hours playing basketball and ping-pong. Another pleasure of the flesh drove King to repair to various mistresses' apartments. A friend once raised "the subject of his compulsive sexual athleticism . . . after being prompted by a worried mutual acquaintance. 'I'm away from home twenty-five to twenty-seven days a month,' King answered. 'Fucking's a form of anxiety reduction.'"[10] The need for escape prompted King's jaunts to Jamaica, the Bahamas, and Mexico. There was only a "small circle of people King could get away with and not be bothered by the movement," Bernard Lee recalled. On one of those escapes, Adam Clayton Powell sent his boat over to pick up King and Lee and cooked up some greens for them, marveling, "Here, we've got soul food in the Bahamas!"[11]

Georgia Davis Powers, a Kentucky state senator who had an intimate relationship with King, captured his longing for normality in her auto-biography. They would share barbecue and watch the evening news to-gether. He teased her, gave her mischievous looks, and wanted to know what she thought of his new book. She called him M.L. and he called her Senator. When he returned to their temporary hideaway at a Chicago apartment, he told her about his day—helping Mahalia Jackson with some personal problems. She sensed his exhaustion and melancholy. "Suddenly M.L. said, 'I'm just as normal as any other man. I want to live a long life, but I know I won't get to.'" Before long, he was smiling, "looking into my eyes. Later he slept quietly and peacefully as I held him." He told her one night, "I just want to spend a quiet evening here with you without worrying about the problems that beset me." In April 1968, he called her and asked, "Please come to Memphis, I need you." In Memphis on the last night of his life, a few hours after he gave his "I've Been to the Mountaintop" speech, he slipped into her room at the Loraine Motel. "I've never been more physically and emotionally tired," he said, but the energy his final speech released in the crowd revitalized him. "'Senator, our time together is so short,' he said, opening his arms."[12]

King also found solace in more symbolic forms of retreat. King's death talk was not just a symptom of morbid obsession; his mock eulogies suggested an effort to defy their most dire implications through spoof and mockery, forcing such threats out of the macabre realm of the unspeakable. The compensatory joys of one instance of funereal joshing offered a counterpoint to one of King's late Ebenezer sermons in which he imagined his own death in a serious vein and also used the disciples' plea to Jesus, "I want to be on your left side and your right side," to reflect on the human desire for recognition.[13]

Quipping with his preacher colleagues, King gave a twist to the meaning of left side and right side, as Young recounted. "'Now y'all think they gon' get me. But all y'all gon' be out there jumping in front of the camera,' and he said, 'the bullet might be aimed for me but one of y'all going to get it. . . . But don't worry,' he said, 'I will preach the best funeral you ever had.' And then he'd start preaching your funeral: 'Andy Young . . . was a fine young man.'"[14]

Such whistling in the dark suggests the similar functions of gallows humor, the raucous party scenes, and joking around at retreats. They attested to the need to loosen the grip of seriousness, to lay down the burden of public commitment, and the public persona too, to escape a life utterly consumed by the movement and hemmed in by the Mosaic mantle. How better to escape somber excess than for the ambassador of agape to kid Andy Young for "sucking up to whites"? Such dynamics also help illuminate King's insistence on the Willard Hotel tape, "I'm not a Negro tonight." Though other meanings were doubtless at work in such cries, it is hard not to see them in part as a longing to lay down the burdens of race and movement and reclaim some essential humanity, to simply say "I'm a man."

It's clear, then, that less-than-sublime talk and conduct never operated solely as a sign of racial belonging for King and his colleagues; they served the needs of a social movement for solace and solidarity. Yet earthy backstage and sublime front stage were tightly coupled in a more direct manner. The late-night schmoozefests that encouraged raucous abandon, the staff retreats that featured jousting on the basketball court, also served as occasions of sacred reflection, sustaining an ongoing process of moral pedagogy.

King's role as prophetic teacher, a key part of his movement talk, had the same complexity as all his other forms of talk—something that gives pause to those who claim King's fancy sources were a way of gaining credibility with white audiences. At the SCLC retreats King used words like "ontological" and "existential" and reflected on big thinkers like Frantz Fanon and Erich Fromm. He even explored the tension between idealism and materialism in Marxism, with an aside on the more obscure Marxist Feuerbach before he transfigured Marx from secular intellectual into a more familiar figure: first a prophetic Jew, then a prophetic Christian. If you read Marx, he said, "You can see that this man had a great passion for social justice. You know Karl Marx was born a Jew, had a rabbinical background. And somewhere in those early days, I think Karl Marx probably turned to those statements and read Amos saying, 'let justice run down like waters, and righteousness like a mighty stream.' When he was six years old his parents were converted to Christianity, and so he had a little Christian background, too. And somewhere along the way he must have read where Jesus said, 'If you do it unto the least of these, you do it unto me.'"[15]

No matter how learned, King's reflections were never removed from the reality of life in the movement. King was responding to threats to the sacred teachings that gave his corner of the movement identity and endurance. A central function of the SCLC retreats was to fortify the organization's official values against nationalist and separatist challenges.[16] The defensive strain in King's addresses at the SCLC retreats of 1966 and 1967 was prefigured in the scuffling that erupted in a 1966 staff workshop, where Bayard Rustin's elegant musings could not blunt the force of rising questions about turning the other cheek. "White people are using nonviolence to exterminate black people," someone exclaimed. "I'm not saying we should resort to violence . . . [but] we're really carrying Negro people to their own death." Others cited the liability of the word "nonviolence" and wondered if it was time to junk it. There were angry invocations of "scars and beatings." Nonviolence, someone argued, "is a good weapon for [the flamboyant Georgia segregationist] Lester Maddox. . . . We're playing into their hands." Someone else said, "People are [getting] killed and we've done nothing about it."[17]

That quarreling reflected doubts about the King enterprise that were rampant in the black world at large. It raised the primal issues of "reverence for the movement and [King's] leadership," as Joseph Lowery remembers it, which is why it "would sting." King's dismay was ideological as much as personal. "It also might bring the thought to your mind, are we losing it? Are we losing control? Is the movement fading, you know? Are we really going to have to shift gears? And when you hear the constant cries about 'nonviolence doesn't work,' 'the hell with these crackers,' and 'I ain't turning the other cheek,' you begin to wonder, you know, about the efficacy of what you're doing. So that's hurting."[18]

King's address at the 1966 retreat aimed to shore up the primal faith. He told the gathering the biblical story of the three men who refused to heed King Nebuchadnezzar's command to bow down before the golden image, even at the risk of being thrown into the fiery furnace. "They stood before the king and said, 'We know that the god that we worship is able to deliver us, but if not, we will not bow.'" So too with King: his faith was not a "bargaining faith," was not conditioned on conditions. Surely the God of deliverance was no fair-weather friend; did he not pluck the three Hebrews from peril? Now King was ready to seal the deal. He pledged before the SCLC staff, "I, Martin Luther King, take thee, nonviolence, to be my wedded wife, for better or for worse . . . until death do us part."[19]

In threading his way from Frantz Fanon to the fiery furnace, King was reaffirming the Christian passion at the core of their movement. To call this slide from teacher to preacher imperceptible doesn't quite get it right, for it suggests the two roles could be disentangled. Never was the line between organization and prophecy murkier than when King preached to this preacher-laden community, in which even the unordained were sometimes called "Rev." Waiting around in airports, King and Abernathy rehearsed sermons with each other. Once, angry over President Johnson's stance on Vietnam, King began preaching to Bernard Lee and Andrew Young, and Lee had the idea of calling the White House. Much to their shock, Lyndon Johnson took the call, but King held back the homily.

What was more binding for the band of freedom fighters than this ritual of their shared faith? When King seemed about to wrap up in one such gathering, saying "finally," the audience responded with groans of disappointment. At times his audience seems in a light mood, and one hears in their laughter appreciation of a fellow practitioner's craft. At other times in staff retreats, board meetings, or settings with many SCLC preachers, it didn't take much for King's audience to recognize the signals of a more serious intention. A shift in cadence, the declaration "I'm gonna preach about it," or King's preface "I'm serious" alerted his audience that a prophetic, not an aesthetic, frame was in order. Sometimes, the signals were not clear. Rev. C. T. Vivian told me the story of the time King announced, "I'm gonna preach about it" and "We all thought he *had* been preaching!" At the start of a mass meeting in Alabama, King apologized, "I'm sorry I can't preach about 'em 'cause I don't have the voice, but I can at least talk about 'em and then I'll let Hosea and Bernard Lee and Albert Turner preach about it." Before long, King fell into a wild prophetic burst and was practically shouting, "I'm trying to save America!" As the audience erupted, King addressed them with what one can only imagine was an affectionate grin, "Y'all realize you gonna make me preach if you don't stop that!"[20]

At times one senses the audience moving beyond the chuckles of aficionados to a state of spiritual abandon. During a speech at an SCLC annual board meeting in a Washington church, King wandered into the biblical language of "But if you hath not love . . ." which seems to have nudged him out of his secular vein. "If you'll let me be a preacher just a little bit," he intoned, and the audience stirred. He recalled the night a man asked Jesus how he could be saved. But, King emphasized, Jesus did not tell the man to do this or that thing, but simply that he had to receive Christ. "Instead of getting bogged down on one thing"—now King's voice was quavering and the audience was crying out and applauding— Jesus said, "Your whole structure *(Yes)* must be changed." Without skipping a beat, King was ready to move out of biblical narrative back to the American present. Just as a man who lies will drink and steal and worse, King observed, "a nation that would keep people in slavery for 244 years will thingify them and make them things," and beyond that, will enslave its people economically and move with imperialistic swagger around the globe. "What I'm sayin' is that all these things tied together . . . We must say, 'America, you must be born again' [Applause]."[21]

King was hurtling toward the end, skipping from one favored snippet to another. This audience knew them all—"let us be dissatisfied," "do justly" and "love mercy" and "walk humbly with thy Lord," "justice will roll down like waters, and righteousness like a mighty stream," "the lion and the lamb shall lie down together," "every man will sit under his own vine and fig tree." King had now begun his approach to climax, and in a way related to the moment when he said "I'm fucking for God," he was leaping out of the Negro body in a less carnal sense, dissolving race into eternal grace before this audience of race men who were shouting as King cried out, "Then men will recognize that out of one blood, *(Yes)* God made all men to dwell upon the face of the earth *(Speak)* . . . until that day when nobody will shout 'White Power'; when nobody will shout 'Black Power' but everybody will shout 'God's power' and 'human power.'"

A less ebullient King preached to his SCLC comrades on November 28, 1967, during the buildup to the Poor People's Campaign in Washington. This was King's last staff retreat. King's troubled mood was heightened by the slow pace of recruiting three thousand volunteers to go to Washington as well as continual sniping by staff members against the project and fear of impending failure.[22]

Early on, King forewarned, "I'm serious about this, and I'm on fire about the thing." To critics of the Poor People's Campaign who had pointed to its lack of clear demands, King answered, "I don't know what Jesus had as his demands other than 'Repent for the Kingdom of God is at hand.' My demand in Washington is 'Repent America'"—here the audience broke into an aroused response. "And He just took that simple theme, and He fired up people." One man approached Jesus, saying, "'Master I fished all day and caught nothing.' He said 'Come on with me and I'll make you fishers of men.'" If King was Jesus, trying to fire them up, it was clear who they were and what their shared task had to be: to tap their own fire inside to arouse the fire in others, to fish for souls to go to Washington.

King told the story of one of those fishermen. "Old Peter vacillated and one day Jesus looked at him and said in substance, 'You are Simon now,' which makes you a sand but I'm expecting you to be like a rock. It was that pull of expectation that caused Peter on the Day of Pentecost to go off fired up with that something that he got to Jesus. And he preached until 3,000 souls were converted. Aren't we talking about 3,000? Now we can do that if we are fired up ourselves."

As always, the challenge to their task was in part inward: one had to be on fire to evoke the fire in others. Yet King's voice was suffused with a heaviness—not his usual slow-as-molasses preacher voice, but something more lugubrious. He had often seemed this way in the final year of his life, often would seem to be struggling with despair in the days ahead. By now the speech could not veil the sermon it had become, a rambling narrative of despondency in search of an antidote. Hope, he insisted, "has a medicinal quality." Was King trying to convince himself or his audience? King hoped only to move a sick nation back a bit in its "level" of sickness.

King confronted despair with a clutter of bits, swerving from social science—those who survived the concentration camps tended not to abandon hope; to baseball—the Dodgers pulled out a tight one in the last inning; to the laws of physics—"when two objects meet, the object with the greater power moves the other object"; to philosophy—"what existential philosophers would call 'the courage to be'"; to the Book of Revelation—"Make an end on what you have left, even if it's near nothing." Citing an unlucky Norwegian violinist whose A-string snapped and who "transposed the composition," King shaped his comrades into a crew of Norwegian violinists: "Our A-strings are broken in so many instances. . . . We in this moment have had our disappointments, we've had our failures, we've had our moments of agony." He admitted to mistakes the SCLC had made in so many places. He confessed, "I wish we had gone to Cicero," thinking of that tough racist town near Chicago and the strategic arguments that eventually prevailed against marching there in 1966.

Prophetic vanguard, apostolic circle—the "our" and the "we" in such moments referred not to the "our" of blackness or the "we" of humanity but to the warrior band of brothers, the "we" who should have gone to Cicero, the SCLC leaders who must remain "custodians of hope." The "we" is not racial or universal but organizational: the war-weary crew that, despite all differences and egocentric foibles and mistakes, would stay strong and engaged in the struggle.

The venue for this confession of "should have" is the safety of the retreat where King could unburden himself. In this most intimate lair, the most intimate act, it turned out, was neither ribald nor athletic nor madcap. It was prophetic. The backstage folded back upon itself, twisting into the public face of its officially stated purpose: to realize the Kingdom of the Lord on earth. All of King's talk of martyrdom, all the brooding on his death, burst forth in the identification of himself with Jesus, as he prepared to dispatch his disciples to Marks, Mississippi, and dozens of hamlets across the Black Belt and to the North to fish for souls.

None of this was really paradoxical. The tough and the tender, roughness and exaltation, "all God's chillun" and all God's children, backstage and frontstage, Christmas and black Christmas, Andrew Young and Hosea Williams, church and juke joint, executive staff and field staff, raunchy banter and fervent preaching: in the end, one can't separate these charged antinomies. They were all part of the King endeavor and the apparatus needed to produce it.

"None of us were saints," Andrew Young reflected. "Saints could not have survived the rigors of the movement. . . . We were flesh-and-blood human beings . . . We got our hands dirty with the labors of social change. We associated with racists and white supremacists. We negotiated and compromised with people who opposed everything we were trying to achieve. We were flawed and imperfect and we fell far short of the glory of God. But we changed America. And we did it without harming anyone, except ourselves."[23]

In the end, this pairing of opposites in the same man, the same organization, and the same movement was not mainly a testimony to King's divided nature or love of dialectic. It was testimony of a sociological sort: to the entwinement of church and insurgency, the mutual impact of each on the other, and the ingredients needed to fashion not just sublime performance, but even more important, an idealistic movement and the just society that was its intention. One could not create and sustain a prophetic army without dirty hands and warrior imagery. But a movement that lost its spiritual bearings was no longer a prophetic army. "I come with a sword," King quoted Jesus on another occasion. "Our movement," King insisted elsewhere, "was a special army, with no supplies but its sincerity, no uniform but its determination, no arsenal except its faith, no currency but its conscience. It was an army that would move but not maul . . . sing but not slay . . . flank but not falter . . . It was an army whose allegiance was to God."[24]

King acknowledged these very same sacred dualities to his disciples at the SCLC retreat a few minutes after he had preached the story of Simon. "I don't know if I'll see all of you before April," the master said. It turned out to be true—many of them would never see him again. The clock of King's life was running down. "But I still will feel as Jesus said to his disciples, as sheep amid wolves, be ye as strong and as tough as a serpent and as tender as a dove. And we will be able to do something that will give new meaning to our own lives and I hope to the life of the nation."[25]

Part II

SON OF A (BLACK) PREACHER MAN

"A fire locked up inside me"

He was "a preacher who could hoop Kierkegaard," says Rev. Joseph Lowery. He's thinking not of King but of King's favorite preacher, C. L. Franklin, one of the great figures of twentieth-century preaching, Aretha Franklin's Daddy and Daddy King's friend. Whenever in range of his radio ministry, the younger King never missed a chance to listen to that virtuoso known for his whooping and tuning. He even cut short SCLC strategy sessions to catch Franklin. "Martin couldn't hoop," says Lowery, who concedes he wasn't much of a hooper either. When they thought about Franklin's unique skills, the two men would crack up. "C.L. was the only guy we knew who could hoop Kierkegaard. We admired him so!"[1] Lowery's smile reflects his appreciation of the mixture: a technique associated with the wild style of the folk pulpit and the esoteric theories of a brooding Danish existentialist.

Actually, there's a bit of a question as to whether King could tune or whoop, both of which are generic forms of preaching. As for the looser practice of "hooping," a phrase that King and his colleagues used to mean intense, dramatic preaching, Lowery's SCLC colleague Rev. Wyatt Tee Walker told me of the time King, vigilantly scanning the room, asked him if the journalists had left "so he could hoop some." The main point here is not a technical one. It is that the Afro-Baptist feel of King's preaching was unmistakable.

Lowery ought to know. He was a formidable race-man preacher himself—he had been leading his own protests down in Mobile, and he came up to Montgomery with a sack of money for the boycott, thousands of dollars raised from offerings. Around that time, he and King had both preached at a ministers' convention where they sidled up to each other and engaged in the rites of "preacheristic exaggeration." "Man, you were wonderful! We got to preach to each other from time to time." Lowery was struck by the resonance of King's rich baritone, and its pathos too. "Martin had a beautiful voice for speaking but he couldn't sing a lick, I never knew why he couldn't sing 'cause he had such a melodious voice." While he "didn't develop the rhythmic tuning up that Baptist preachers had," Lowery recalls, "he developed his own rhythmic style, very moving. He had the ability to put into preacher tones the profundity of racism and racial oppression."

Then Lowery gets preacheristic himself. King, he says with his own lilt, "was blessed with the capability of adaptability." He was much more emphatic and enthusiastic with black audiences "because you responded to them as they responded to you. It was antiphonal. The white audience wouldn't bring out the emotion."

"When I'm before a black audience, I don't quote *The Courage To Be* and Tillich," observes Rev. Walter Fauntroy.[2] We're sitting in a room in the same church his father pastored in Washington, D.C. Like King, Fauntroy knew the transracial straddle. He had attended Virginia Union Seminary, known for the fervent preachers it produced, before heading north to Yale Divinity School. Returning to preach at his father's church, he didn't sing—that wasn't what trained ministers were supposed to do. That lasted about three weeks. There was a feeling among some in the congregation that with all his fancy education, maybe he felt he was too good to sing. But Fauntroy thought, "These people cooked chitlins and fried chicken so I could go to college."

Singing was only part of the learning curve involved. "When I came back from Yale to this congregation, Tillich meant nothing. What mattered was 'Can these dry bones live?' But if I'm out speaking at an Episcopalian church, then I'd go to Tillich." These things are elemental, he says, the basic tenets of any kind of public speaking: "You have to know your audience."

Lowery and Fauntroy, and Rev. Wyatt Tee Walker and Rev. C. T. Vivian too, all warn me not to confuse substance with the manner of performing it. What really mattered, the thread of King's constancy before white and black audiences alike, was Jesus Christ; the love God heaped on all his children, including the black ones; and God's resolve to deliver the captives.

These judgments place us in the right frame—the fraternity of craft—as we delve into the labor that constituted King's day job. The three chapters of Part II consider how the rival impulses of hooping and Hegel, rawness and refinement, played out in King's sermons. The learned preacher who held forth on agape never stopped being the prophetic preacher whose stylized passion signified the presence of a paladin God "who could make a way out of no way." At the same time, despite the racial communion King established with black congregations, King's spirituality was always devoted to the universal message of his faith. Formally, King's preaching was characterized by the same puzzles, hybrid qualities, and doubling of idioms that marked all his other talk. Substantively, the black stories he told never preempted the elemental force of his faith, his empathetic concern for ethnic strangers, and his role not just as the deliverer of his people but as a healer of all broken souls.

SEVEN

Flight from the Folk?

"Not a Negro gospel (No man)*; not a gospel merely to get people to shout and kick over benches"*

One could see the raw and the refined strains in King's preaching as phases of a career that recovered the passion expunged by Morehouse education and white learning. In such tellings, the moral and cultural force of the folk pulpit dissolved the refined gloss. This story line has some truth to it. Over time, the fervency of King's preaching quickened. Philosophical ruminations gave way to biblical parables. As the formal sermon structures loosened, King let loose with abandon, "blackening" his inflection and even mimicking the lingo of the street. The learned scholar went into quasi-remission; the great-grandson of a slave exhorter returned.

In part, this recovery reflected King's growing distance from graduate school. Southern black audiences played their part too, drawing him back to the wellsprings of ancient emotion and enveloping him in the sensuous immediacy of performance. His early preaching showed a preference for "reasoned argument and little emotion," according to Coretta Scott King. "Later, when he preached in the South to more emotional congregations, he became less inhibited. He responded to their expectations by rousing oratory; and as they were moved, he would react to their excitement, their rising emotions exalting his own. The first thunderous 'Amen' from the people would set him off in the old-fashioned preaching style. We called it 'whooping.' Sometimes, after we were married, I would tease him by saying, 'Martin, you were whooping today.'

"He would be a little embarrassed. But it was very exciting, Martin's whooping."[1]

It also makes sense that the adolescent posturing of the Morehouse ladies' man would be transformed by the sobering impact of the civil rights movement, the ascension to an iconic status that denied King a private life, and the constant death threats he got in return. The compulsive sexuality of his adult years has a driven quality that suggests more demonic sources than the sexual high jinks of the young playboy who fashioned an intricate system of rating female attractiveness. There were moments up in the pulpit when King laid bare not just the despondency of humanity or the race, but that of his own solitude. There's no reason to discount the influence of King's primal encounter with God during the Montgomery boycott. Spiraling downward into a dark, depressive funk, he had the equivalent of a born-again experience in which God spoke to him and he was pulled back to "the kind of religion my Daddy told me about."

While these undeniable changes over time in King's preaching certainly deserve mention, my emphasis is on the continuities that ran through King's various phases. At each stage, even as the precise ratio of raw and refined varied, the two were ever present, charging each other with creative energy. At each stage the substance of King's message varied less than the code, style, or voice in which it was articulated. And at each stage, different permutations of the same tension between race and humanity were evident. His more universalistic sermons never disguised the depth of his racial pride and love of black people. Some of King's most universal preaching was channeled through his "blacker," more prophetic style.

Refinement provides the starting point. When King returned to Montgomery in 1954, he was fresh from the Dialectical Society at Boston University and debates on Tillich. This was not so long after his courtship of Coretta—she noted his "intellectual jive" right off—during which he wrote, "My life without you is like a year without a spring time which comes to give illumination and heat to the atmosphere saturated by the dark cold breeze of winter. . . . O excuse me, my darling." Even a disingenuous catching of himself—"I didn't mean to go off on such a poetical and romantic flight"—could not slow the soaring language. "But how else can we express the deep emotions of life other than in poetry? Isn't love too ineffable to be grasped by the cold calculating hands of intellect?"[2]

The black minister who supervised King's preaching internship granted his "superior mental ability, clarity of expression," and "impressive personality" but voiced concern about "an attitude of aloofness, disdain & possible snobbishness which prevent his coming to close grips with the rank and file of ordinary people." There was about him "a smugness that refuses to adapt itself to the demands of ministering effectively to the average Negro congregation."[3]

There was also a tinge of embarrassment in King's distance from "Negro emotionality." "'David, I told you that I remember watching my daddy walk the benches when I was a little boy,'" King once told Ralph Abernathy. "Walking the benches referred to ministers who leaped from the pulpit in mid-sermon to preach ecstatically as they danced up and down the pews, literally stepping over the swooning bodies in the congregation. Abernathy knew that King considered it the most vaudevillian, primitive aspect of his heritage.

"'He walked the benches,' King repeated, in humiliation and wonder. 'He did it to feed and educate his family.'"[4]

Whatever the oedipal overtones, such distance continued when King returned to the South. In the writings he addressed to whites, King self-consciously strained to project the qualities of dignity and propriety. Early in his Montgomery ministry, King chastised a group of fellow black preachers. "Preachers? . . . We can't spend all our time trying to learn how to whoop and holler. . . . We've got to have ministers who can stand up and preach the gospel of Jesus Christ. *(Yes, All right)* Not a Negro gospel *(No man)*; not a gospel merely to get people to shout and kick over benches, but a gospel that will make people think and live right and face the challenges of the Christian religion *(All right, Yeah)*."[5]

Equating bench-kicking and the black gospel befits the Ph.D. who had read Buber. It was consonant with King's critique of a faith with "too much religion in its feet." Yet Coretta's recollection—at first "he leaned heavily on its theological aspect, for he was very self-conscious about anything that he considered too emotional"—is a bit too prissy. A better sense of that visceral distaste can be found in King's portrait of a young preacher "just jumping all over the pulpit and jumping out and spitting all over everything and screaming with his tune, and moaning and groaning."[6]

King's first pulpit upon his return to the South in 1953, Dexter Avenue Church in Montgomery, had a reputation for snootiness. Its members included many Alabama State professors and their families, which offered a good cultural fit for the high-flown, at times didactic King. The Dexter congregation was, in Ralph Abernathy's opinion, "habitually silent during the sermon. No matter how fervently they agreed with what was being said, you seldom heard an 'amen' or a 'hallelujah.'" The oft-told story of King's trial sermon, "The Dimensions of a Complete Life," features a triumphant wowing in which King examined John's vision of the New Jerusalem. The three dimensions—height, width, and length—gave King ample opportunity for lofty rumination. Like many of the early sermons that King delivered to black audiences and published in the white-targeted trade book, *Strength to Love,* "Dimensions" exhibited both the refined style that was always part of his black talk and his debt to white preachers. King took its very structure from "The Symmetry of Life," penned originally by the nineteenth-century New England minister Phillips Brooks. The borrowing from the sermons of more contemporary white liberal Protestant preachers was extensive.[7]

King's use of Exodus in his sermons might seem to be a counterbalance to these white sources. Ever since African slaves glimpsed in the Israelites' bondage a rippling reflection of themselves, what has been more identified with black preaching than the coming up out of bondage in Egypt? The "basis for our thinking together . . . is the story of the Exodus, the story of the flight of the Hebrew people from the bondage of Egypt," King announced in the first few sentences of "The Birth of a New Nation," his 1957 sermon recounting a trip to Africa for the installation of Kwame Nkrumah as president of the newly independent nation of Ghana.[8] Another of King's sermons, "The Death of Evil Upon the Seashore," echoed the title of C. L. Franklin's whooping prose poem, "Moses at the Red Sea," which broke into chanting at the close. King surely knew that version, which had circulated widely on vinyl on the Chess gospel label. Daddy King and his neighbor across Auburn Avenue, Rev. William

Borders of Wheat Street Baptist Church, had devoted an entire season to preaching Exodus.

Yet King's references to Exodus in his preaching were modest. Even more striking was the way he treated the theme when he did use it. In "Birth of a New Nation," King quickly removed himself from the folk tradition, improbably claiming he had come to see it "in all its beauty" after seeing the Cecil B. DeMille movie *The Ten Commandments* in New York City. Up front, he framed the story with a tepid slant that said as much about the human longing for freedom as it did about God's commitment to deliverance: "This is something of the story of every people struggling for freedom." The cursory Exodus references yielded to a temporal romp through the dissolution of imperialism framed by the schoolteacher's voice: "Prior to March the sixth, 1957, there existed a country known as the Gold Coast" in Africa. The chronicle of the demise of colonialism was followed by a biographical vignette of Nkrumah and a report from the installation itself.

Thus King's use of Exodus in this sermon, rather than inviting personal identification with a richly archetypal act, appeared as a series of intermittent time-outs from sociopolitical musing on the global march of freedom. And when it came time to evoke the hunger for freedom, King turned to Shakespeare's Othello: "Who steals my purse steals trash; 'tis something, nothing, 'twas mine, 'tis his, has been the slave of thousands; But he who filches from me my freedom robs me of that which not enriches him, but makes me poor indeed."

A related distance from the folk idiom characterized "The Death of Evil Upon the Seashore." King had again turned for inspiration to a Phillips Brooks sermon, "Egyptians Dead Upon the Seashore." King launched "Death of Evil" with a philosophical framing—"Is anything more obvious than the presence of evil in the universe?" He went on to evoke evil poetically through the biblical image of tares, a poisonous weed that appears in a parable of Jesus whose treatment King borrowed from George Buttrick, a distinguished Presbyterian minister and theologian who went on to serve as the head of Harvard's chapel. King moved from symbolist evocation to empirical validation with the example of "imperialistic nations crushing other people with the battering rams of social injustice." Jumping to a cosmopolitan vantage, he cited all manner of world religions that recognize the struggle between good and evil. He finished with a poetic mention favored by white liberal Protestant preachers: "Long ago biblical religion recognized what William Cullen Bryant affirmed, 'Truth crushed to earth will rise again.'"⁹

King mined not just the structure of sermons by popular white ministers but their quotes, references, and tropes. While imprisoned in Reidsville, Georgia, King wrote to Coretta to bring him a host of books that included not just his beloved *Increasing Your Word Power* but also Buttrick's *The Parables of Jesus*. According to Ralph Abernathy, King scoured the sermons of eighteenth- and early nineteenth-century clergy for "figures of speech and flights into rhetoric . . . [that were] . . . virtually unreadable to the average country preacher. As incredible as it may seem . . . much of what Martin said publicly had its origins in the works of clergymen long dead and in English as well as in American graves. He never traveled anywhere without a suitcase full of these musty volumes—leather-bound, with beautifully decorated end sheets and gold-tipped pages."¹⁰

For our purposes, the racial provenance of these borrowings is less illuminating than the self King crafted through them and the fact that he enacted it before black audiences no less than white ones. The King that we glimpse in these early sermons was learned, high-minded, didactic, worldly, and tolerant. He embodied qualities of mind as much as of feeling. The poetic sources he favored struck a majestic note of distance from the venal and gritty. The same King who cherished the sound of the opera *Lucia di Lammermoor* loved the sonorous sounds of Keats and Ovid.

King's language in these sermons also included a less poetic form of fanciness. His contrast of the realms of "is" and "ought" reflected the philosophical bent that King as theologian paraded throughout his preaching. King repudiated communism by observing that it strips human beings of both "conscience and reason. The trouble with Communism is that it has neither a theology nor a Christology; therefore it emerges with a mixed-up anthropology." In two adjacent paragraphs of "Antidotes for Fear," King cited Plato, Tillich, Aristotle, Aquinas, Epictetus, Thoreau, and Fromm. At times it seemed as if the language of high English, the vernacular, and even the Bible did not suffice to convey Christ's message. Luckily, the Greek language "comes to our aid beautifully," King instructed before parsing the distinctions between eros, philea, and agape. He even went so far as to use the word "ontological" in one homily, a word he favored so much that he pronounced it at a

Frogmore retreat with the SCLC staff. King got so carried away that he also used the term in a letter to a Dexter deacon and Boston friend, who replied that he "enjoyed reading it very much. Especially the part where you mentioned that the fellowship that you had with us was 'ontologically real' (smile)." The exchange provoked by King's soaring into the stratosphere anticipated the ritual joshing that Abernathy would direct at his friend in a mass meeting.[11]

As in "Birth of a New Nation," the learned teacher liked to play the global historian. He also called on secular authorities in the social sciences to buttress religious argument, as if the scriptures did not suffice by themselves. He offered cultural criticism that targeted the spiritual emptiness and materialism of a technological society. King's weakness for the therapeutic idiom underscored a worldly distance from fundamentalism. Noting "man's separation from himself," sometimes he preached an existential psychology that granted "the fear of death, nonbeing and nothingness." At other times, he cited Alfred Adler's notion of compensation for feelings of inferiority and Karen Horney's *The Neurotic Personality of Our Time*. In "Antidotes for Fear," he preached, "Many of our abnormal fears can be dealt with by the skills of psychiatry, a relatively new discipline pioneered by Sigmund Freud, which investigates the subconscious drives of men and seeks to discover how and why fundamental energies are diverted into neurotic channels."[12]

In "Loving Your Enemies," King taught that hate distorts the human personality. If you want to avoid becoming "a pathological case" full of "tragic, neurotic responses," then "the way to be integrated with yourself" is through "abounding love." King brought the implied authority of such clinical language into an explicit warrant that mimicked and supplanted the scriptural phrasing, "the Bible tells us." "Psychologists and psychiatrists are telling us today that the more we hate, the more we develop guilt feelings and we begin to subconsciously repress or consciously suppress certain emotions, and they all stack up in our subconscious selves."[13]

This cosmopolitan stance was accompanied by an apparent strategy of downplaying race. When King applied his sermonic themes to the black situation, he tended to blunt the force of black identity by placing it in a series of other examples that had nothing to do with race. In the 1957 sermon "Questions that Easter Answers," King succumbed to "despair every now and then" for his race. "*Why* is it that over so many centuries the forces of injustice have *triumphed* over the Negro and he has been forced to live under oppression and *slavery* and exploitation." But only a specific example of the larger theme of faith amidst futility, that ethnic worry claimed King's attention for just one of twenty-five paragraphs devoted to reminding the congregation that despite the "darkness and the agony and the disappointment that Jesus suffered," "Easter Sunday succeeds Good Friday." In one of the notable occasions when King broke into vernacular at Dexter, he parroted the "broken language" of the slaves he had just cited by reassuring "that it ain't gonna last always"—his answer to the perplexing question, "Why does God leave us like this? Seventeen million of his [black] children here in America." Typically, the racial suffering was dwarfed by more universal tensions, from being a cog in a vast industrial machine to guilt over adultery; by reflections on Jung, religion, and the art of sublimation; and especially by the solace only Christ can provide, "Come unto me, all ye that labor and are heavy laden, and I'll give you rest."[14]

That apparent skittishness toward particularism appeared in King's mentions of other religions. It was not that King was embarrassed by his Christian identity, but he worked hard to herald a tolerant faith that avoided triumphalism, that was curious about and conversant with other traditions. Befitting the boundary-straddler who had lived in multiple worlds, King was never so immersed in his own Afro-Baptist—or social gospel—traditions that he couldn't step outside and above them. As he noted early in "Death of Evil Upon the Seashore," "All of the great religions have recognized a tension at the very core of the universe. Hinduism, for instance, calls this tension a conflict between illusion and reality; Zoroastrianism, a conflict between the god of light and the god of darkness; and traditional Judaism and Christianity, a conflict between God and Satan."[15]

The learned content and borrowings from white ministers in King's Dexter sermons, like the seeming lack of prophetic fire in their written form, give a twist to the claim of theology professor James Cone that King quoted white theologians and philosophers before white audiences because "these were the persuasive authorities in the community" he was addressing. In downplaying King's august white sources to highlight the influence of the black pulpit, there was much in Cone's polemic that was insightful, and contrarian too. Most valuably, Cone grasped the dynamics of performance at work in King's white talk and the functions of citing fancy sources when trying to elicit financial and moral support from whites. But Cone came close to implying a false opposition between the opportunistic quality of King's white talk and the genuine quality of his black talk, as if both were not performances keenly tailored to the rhetorical occasions. In the process, Cone flirted with a romance of racial authenticity that seemed to say the real King was the black King, and the black King was the one who talked black, which in Cone's rendering meant the language of spirituals and the blues.[16]

The problem in Cone's analysis was not simply defining some alleged "real" King but identifying him with his race and the idiom and sources appropriate to it. As we will see more fully in Part IV, King was powerfully drawn to the social gospel, its white exponents, and their style. After all, he borrowed from Fosdick when he preached his trial sermon from the same Ebenezer pulpit that Daddy King ascended when he hooped and hollered. It is true that King's graduate school writings often sound forced, as if he was trying on an identity, regurgitating what his professors wanted to hear, or simply jumping through the hoops needed to earn that prized "Doctor" so he could get back to his cherished vocation of preaching. But if King recovered his true voice when he quit the fancy theology, he did so in part by adopting the words of white ministers such as Fosdick and Buttrick. Even more telling, as King's penchant for quoting Schopenhauer and Ovid while preaching at Dexter makes clear, he found in those "white" words a voice that was compelling before black audiences too, and would remain so even when he moved on to Ebenezer Baptist Church in Atlanta, where he hooped more fervently than he did at Dexter. Nor did King skimp on the fancy sources when he spoke at Morehouse, Spelman, Howard, Lincoln, and a host of other black colleges any more than he slighted these same references when he spoke at Cornell or Yale. All the while, he kept finding in black sources too, as well as in words and ideas that can't readily be jammed into the categories of race, a passionate voice before black and white congregations alike.[17]

To scramble the racial lines one more time, the romance of the folk that identifies the black component with the raspy and raw obscures the black sources of the high-flown style to which King was drawn. As James

Weldon Johnson observed in the 1920s, "The old-time Negro preachers, though they actually used dialect in their ordinary intercourse, stepped out from its narrow confines when they preached. They were all saturated with the sublime phraseology of the Hebrew prophets and steeped in the idioms of King James English."[18]

King's preaching style at Dexter also honored the black social gospel tradition he had learned at Morehouse from Benjamin Mays and George Kelsey. And his stylistic predilections were utterly in tune with the ideals of learning and refinement promoted by Mays, whose elegance spilled into all realms. King the B.U. graduate student who tooled around Boston in his own automobile had a closet full of splendid suits, but Mays, Russell Adams chronicles, "always dressed 'Gentlemen's Quarterly' style, usually some version of pin-stripe gray suit accentuating his height and lack of body fat. He was camera ready." Mays's favorite poem was "Invictus," penned by the nineteenth-century British poet William Henley. Like so many other Morehouse men of that period, Adams recalls the Phi Beta Kappa key Mays earned at Bates that always dangled from a silver chain linking his vest pockets. A half century later, Adams just as vividly recalls Mays's majestic aphorisms, more than a few of which migrated into King's standard repertoire: "As we stand in the vortex of injustice, have faith that God's mercy will assist us in our struggle to be free"; "the Arc of the Universe tends toward justice; the prayers of the abused and disfranchised will indeed be heard"; "Morehouse College is not expected to produce men simply glib of tongue and shallow of thought but rather men of moral depth, of trust and honor ever alert."

At some point during the early 1950s, Adams and a gang of fellow Morehouse men went over to Ebenezer to check King out when he was preaching while home from graduate school. They judged the performance "heavy," jargon of the day for knowledge and brilliance, and Adams recalls a reference to Maimonides. "When King spoke overly academic, we said he delivered a 'heavy' sermon for someone only a couple of years away from Morehouse." That was the word they approvingly applied to Mays's formal speeches, a style they imitated in their late-night arguments. "Like Martin Luther King after him, Mays said it better than we could, and for that we were grateful. Indeed we would have been disappointed had he descended to our level of style and diction. The elegance and eloquence of persons like Mays (and indeed of Marian Anderson and

Mary McLeod Bethune) reminded us of what was possible given sufficient opportunity."

As Adams indicates, elegance was hardly the enemy of race pride but its vehicle. Maybe Mays's fervor was controlled, but the fervor had more than a trace of folk passion. The "precisely selected words lovingly and rhythmically enunciated" paid homage to an African-American performance tradition whose love of sound was at once sensuous and theological. But Mays anticipated King in bridging one far more important set of oppositions. When he "reached the emotional part of his speeches," Adams says, "any line between Mays the elegant messenger and Mays the kinsman in struggle disappeared, *his* language ennobling our cause."

Nor did that kinship go over the head of the unlettered who "saw what a black man could *be* when they saw Mays, whose high falluting style contrasted with his forthrightness about his family background: he could talk about picking cotton—he was once a South Carolina cotton picking champ; he could talk about painting houses—he was an expert with the paintbrush and bucket; he would say things such as 'neither my mother nor my father could read; but I am here.' Virtually every year, Mays returned to his home town and gave a standing room only speech to audiences made of sharecroppers, maids and underpaid school teachers. One time, he introduced one of his semi-literate brothers to us in Sale Hall Auditorium, saying, 'My brother gave everything he could spare to help me stay in school.' I remember going back to my room, Graves Hall, Room 452, and crying without restraint at the sheer nobility of the gesture."[19]

Mays was only the most important of King's black models. Like Mays, no matter how much such men as Gardner Taylor and Vernon Johns, Mordecai Johnson and Howard Thurman differed from each other, they all were fashioning their own blend of polish and passion, the ethnic and the universal. For all his attunement to the folk, Sandy Ray, the minister of Brooklyn's Cornerstone Baptist Church in whose home King recovered after he was stabbed in Harlem, had a lovely poetic streak. In the sermon "Melodies in a Strange Land," he asked, "'How shall we sing?' We have symphonic souls. We have chirping, chanting spirits. We are on a rhythmic mission. Singing and praising God cheer us along the weary way." Confirming the poetic character of his own preaching, Gardner Taylor, Ray's Brooklyn neighbor over at Concord Baptist Church, soared himself in his eulogy at Ray's funeral: "At the height of his pulpit oratory it was hard to tell whether one heard music half spoken or speech half sung. And when the glad thunders of that voice reached his climactic theme, the heavens seemed to open and we could see the Lord God on his throne."[20]

The racial reading of King's preaching also fails to make sense of his relationship to spirituals and the blues that Cone identified with the black folk religion. King's musical influences were as eclectic as his spiritual ones. King loved black sacred music no less than opera, but his mentions of the blues often had a stilted quality. As his friend Walter McCall recalled, "King didn't come up in an environment where the Blues was heard too much . . . for the most part he didn't have an appreciation for the Blues as such."[21]

King and McCall took a course at Morehouse "where we analyzed various institutions and we analyzed many forms of the Blues . . . And the Blues, of course, where people truly understand them carry a kind of spiritual overtone. . . . It was from that point of view that King appreciated them." They dissected the philosophy of life implicit in lines like "I'd rather be a poor man with a penny than a rich man with a worried mind" and "a bad, bad whiskey made me lose my happy home." Clearly, King's cultural preferences didn't conform to neat racial categories any more than his literary and theological preferences did.[22]

There was one final irony in the romantic view of the "real King": his lofty sensibility appealed mightily to the folk. They didn't seem to care if King's quotes came from the black poet Paul Laurence Dunbar or from the white British poet William Cowper. "I never saw someone who could move unlearned black audiences with philosophy [as King did]," said Pius Barbour, who was capable of rather erudite speech himself. Did King lose his audience with his fanciness, I pressed Lowery, who broke into a smile, as if to say, of course not. "They loved it. They were thrilled that a black man was so learned. The knowledge made them trust him." In pointing to another dynamic, Rev. C. T. Vivian reached for the same word as Lowery: "Black people were thrilled to hear someone who was smarter than the white folks."[23]

John Fulgham, a deacon at Dexter, once confessed to King that as a football coach "our language is sometimes not so good, if you know what I mean." But that didn't interfere with his response to King's preaching: "You had to sit still and give an ear to Reverend King. One could not move when Reverend King was preaching. This preacher had something to say. He could deliver loud and forceful like the old Black preacher, yet Reverend King had a different style. Reverend King abandoned pulpit antics, acrobatics, and crooning. His was a refined yet spirit-filled type of preaching. It was a high type of preaching, yet the every day man or woman could grasp the content of every sermon."[24]

Likewise, the preacher cognoscenti who disbursed the honors for their professional brotherhood never doubted King's credentials as an Afro-Baptist member in good standing. In 1956, the young upstart dazzled thousands of members of the National Baptist Convention in Denver, "riding one of his ponies," as Lowery would put it, the tried and tested "Paul's Letter to American Christians," which owed much to the white minister Frederick Meek and his "Letter to American Christians." "Of course the center of attention was THE KING," Pius Barbour exulted. "Never in the history of the Baptist Denomination has a young Baptist preacher captured the hearts and minds of the people. . . . He just wrapped the convention up in a napkin and carried it away in his pocket."[25]

C. W. Kelly, pastor of Tuskegee's Greenwood Missionary Baptist Church, wrote to King, "It was indeed a masterpiece. . . . You will never be forgotten. The impression is everlasting. You spoke as a prophet and seer which you are. . . . How often have I stressed to my people their great error of 'making a living instead of a life.' I said just today, 'If the white man was as smart in his heart as he is in his head, how much better off our world would be.'" King preached so powerfully that Kelly, and others too, "wept like babies, and couldn't help ourselves, nor did we try. My, boy, God used you because you can be used by Him—and like Joseph, God is with you, because you are with God."[26]

In exhibiting his erudition, King was tacitly keeping faith with his audience, affirming its capacity to learn. In church, he was a teacher no less than a preacher. As Lowery says, to preach is merely to teach with emotion. "Maybe eros and agape and philea were strange and alien terms, but they became familiar. King was lifting them spiritually and intellectually." One of King's Dexter congregants marveled, "He uttered phrases that had never been heard. I have heard nothing like them since."[27]

In the end, the key thing was what King did to and with the various words he borrowed. Preaching "white" or preaching "black," King did not vest his sense of identity in language or any single aspect of it. He orchestrated a range of features of talk—code, idiom, voice, inflection, identity, ground, content, and others. One channel might serve as a conveyer of racial identity even as another channel evoked his Christian faith while still another paid homage to secular and civil forms of universalism. Often all these things were going on simultaneously in the very same sermon. Focusing too much on race and idiom obscures the hybrid quality of all of King's talk and his complex moves between the ethnic and the universal within his black talk and his white talk.

King was ever the mix-master, blending and layering different elements of talk. To get a sense of King's ability to imbue "white" sermon forms with a black feel, you only have to compare the written and the recorded oral version of "Love Your Enemies." In the published version, King added an Ovid quote and a reference to Nietzsche, while in the 1958 performed Dexter version, he included this observation: "Some people aren't going to like you because your skin is a little brighter than theirs; and others aren't going to like you because your skin is a little darker than theirs." More critically, the two versions didn't "sound" the same. At Dexter, King's tone has a quavering if quiet passion that roughens the polished surface. The phrase "Oriental hyperbole" sounds academic, but King subtly "swings" the pronunciation, giving it just a hint of a syncopated feel. He also embeds that phrase in a sequence that includes repetitions of two key words, "playing" and "serious," which he often used to project a gritty or "street" aura. So in "Loving Your Enemies," right after "Oriental hyperbole," he says again, "Because Jesus wasn't playing; because he was serious." One of various strategies for "taking the edge off," such tonal punctuation altered his didactic parsing of the Greek terms, as when a stuttering hesitation, "sort of," would diminish the fanciness of philea.

King even found a refined substitute for outright shouting. He didn't hoop at Dexter as he would at Ebenezer. But he did combine the rhythmic power of repetition and the emotive language of "crying out" with quotes from Ovid and Goethe, merging his voice with theirs and delegating the act of crying out to these paragons of high culture as he invited an undefined "we," plus the black man preaching, to share in that unison. "There is something within all of us that causes us to cry out with Ovid, the Latin poet, 'I see and approve the better things of life, but the evil things I do.' There is something within all of us that causes us to cry out with Plato that the human personality is like a charioteer with two headstrong horses, each wanting to go in different directions."[28] In a sense,

King transformed Ovid and Plato into surrogate prophets who cried out; simply saying the word "crying" was enough to stand for the deed.

King also blended different styles and techniques. Within the same sermon, King would lay down parallel versions of an argument, stating or evoking a theme in one idiom only to repeat or evoke it in the other. This could involve a brief nod to the vernacular. At other times, it involved a brief mention of the high code, followed by a restatement of his theme in the language of the black folk pulpit. This strategy of juxtaposition appeared in "Loving Your Enemies." Immediately after reflecting on "tragic, neurotic responses," King offered a spiritual warrant for the love "modern psychology is calling on us." "But long before modern psychology came into being, the world's greatest psychologist who walked around the hills of Galilee told us to love. He looked at men and said: 'love your enemies; don't hate anybody.'"[29]

The sermons King borrowed from Fosdick and Buttrick were hardly generic straitjackets. As Richard Lischer has noted, they were closer to loose outlines.[30] This made it easy for King to import all kinds of competing voices and themes, which is why there was no contradiction between white borrowing and black content. King could take the high-minded "Dimensions of Life" and dress it up or dress it down, preach it or pontificate it; he could also "blacken" or "whiten" it. In the late 1960s, King converted that exalted sermon he delivered at Yale and Cornell, as well as in London on his way to receive the Nobel Prize, into a paean to black pride. In short, the fact that King was not prepared to scuttle the universal vision of his brand of Christian faith did not mean he was cavalier about his blackness.

King's penchant for finding echoes in one idiom of a truth expressed in another was tied to the gift of translation that he displayed from the outset in his boundary-straddling roles. Both the echoing and the translating were emblematic of his playfulness with form. Early on, King discovered that he could use and meld forms. Instead of adopting them wholesale, he would infiltrate them only to mutate them into something different.

An understanding of King's gift for translation allows us to see aspects of "The Birth of a New Nation" that weren't evident at first glance. If secular observations trumped Exodus in sheer word count, it is also true that the sequence of Exodus interventions in the sermon tracked the movement of the Gold Coast from colonial bondage to black autonomy as

Ghana, providing a kind of ongoing translation. After he described the humiliation of colonial bondage, King noted, "There is something deep down within the very soul of man that reaches out for Canaan. Men cannot be satisfied with Egypt." Many paragraphs later, after a travelogue on the installation ceremony, he reminded the Dexter congregation, "This nation was now out of Egypt and had crossed the Red Sea. Now it will confront its wilderness."

As the end of "Birth of a New Nation" approached, the prophetic strain caught up to and overtook the secular. Prefiguring "I've Been to the Mountaintop," King reassured the people of Montgomery, "Moses might not get to see Canaan, but his children will see it. He even got to the mountain top enough to see it and that assured him that it was coming. But the beauty of the thing is that there's always a Joshua to take up his work and take the children on in. And it's there waiting with its milk and honey, and with all of the bountiful beauty that God has in store for His children." By this time King had come a good distance from DeMille's *Ten Commandments*. His chorus of interruptions provided a prophetic voice-over that created a parallel universe whose biblical reminders would culminate in the crescendo that delivered the final word.

Nor was the universal vision of the global march to freedom at odds with blackness. What was "blacker" than the Pan-African bonds that drew King to Ghana, or the emotive equivalence that King established between Africa's deliverance and the Negroes of Montgomery? Moreover, King injected a racial note into his depiction of Nkrumah's journey, which paralleled King's. After his various ventures in the great Western canon in London and the United States, Nkrumah, as King depicted it, declared, "I want to go home to . . . the land of my people." That very phrase recalls King's appeal to "my people" in the mass meetings.

As the sermon unfolded, King shifted into a more personal style of storytelling. Ensconced in Accra, Ghana's capital, he was jubilant to be among his own people. That telling sound figure, "Ohhh," alerted the Dexter congregation that something of moment was about to occur. "And ohhh, it was a beautiful experience to see some of the leading persons on the scene of civil rights in America on hand to say, 'Greetings to you,' as this new nation was born. Look over, to my right"—and here King named a number of important black politicians and a diplomat—"is Adam Powell, to my left is Charles Diggs, to my right again is Ralph

Bunche." At another point, he imagined those bonds more practically as the assistance that "American Negroes must lend" to the newly freed Africans.

After the ceremony King strolled the streets, observing the people's joy in freedom. He began to weep with joy too. He heard the sounds of little Ghanaian children and old people. "They couldn't say it in the sense that we'd say it, many of them don't speak English too well, but they had their accents and it could ring out 'free-doom!' And they were crying it in a sense that they had never heard it before." That chorus of crying freedom galvanized an arc of ancestral associations that would enter his "I Have a Dream" trope. Anchored in the continent of Africa and the streets of the city and its joyous people, King heard a crying out, but this time it wasn't Ovid. "And I could hear that old Negro spiritual once more crying out: 'Free at last, free at last, Great God Almighty, I'm free at last.'" In a typical exchange of identities, he conjoined the Africans' experience of actual freedom with the American slaves' vicarious anticipation of theirs: "They were experiencing that in their very souls." Again in an echo of "Dream," "we could hear it ringing out from the housetops." All this weeping and stirring, the commingling of slave and African voices, the anticipation of being "free at last," returned King to scripture. "This was the breaking aloose from Egypt."

In keeping with the rhythm of calm-to-storm, King prepared to bring it home, first geographically as he tightened the parallels between Egypt, Ghana, and the American Negro. Simultaneously he brought the Dexter congregation down to the concrete reality of their agony and lifted them up right into the Exodus narrative. For there were lessons in Ghana for the people of Montgomery, and things "we must never forget as we ourselves break loose from an evil Egypt." "Ghana reminds us that freedom never comes on a silver platter. It's never easy. Ghana reminds us that whenever you break out of Egypt, you better get ready for stiff backs. You better get ready for some homes to be bombed."

As King blurred Egypt, Ghana, and Montgomery, the line between Exodus and Resurrection blurred with it. "There is no crown without a cross. I wish we could get to Easter without going to Good Friday." But then, shifting, he prepared his audience: "before you get to Canaan, you've got a Red Sea to confront," and much more—"hardened heart of a pharaoh" and "prodigious hilltops of evil in the wilderness" and even "giants in the land." Still, there was no reason for despair, for the "beautiful thing about it is that there are a few people who've been over in the land. They have spied enough to say, 'Even though the giants are there we can possess the land.'"

Neither disguised nor denied, the prophetic voice and its celebration of deliverance were present throughout King's early preaching. King just didn't need to lean on the folk pulpit to broadcast it. Refinement did not vitiate the southern preacher's voice as much as translate it. And often King didn't even need to do that. These prophetic phrases, right out of the Afro-Baptist pulpit, were there in the sermons as delivered at Dexter and even in the written versions in *Strength to Love*. "Paul's Letter to American Christians" did not stint on the "white" voices that King would enlist in the crossover "Letter from Birmingham Jail." But the same un-attributed Buber slogan—segregation "substitutes an 'I-it' relationship for the 'I-thou' relationship"—could not silence the "crying out" of the prophet: "Yes America, there is still the need for an Amos to cry out to the nation: 'Let judgment roll down as waters, and righteousness as a mighty stream.'"[31]

There is no reason to regard King's cultured voice as any less black than the voice of the blues and spirituals. What James Weldon Johnson says of his own effort to capture the musicality of black preaching applies well to the learned endeavor that King and all his models were fashioning. (They included Mordecai Johnson, who shared a moment with King in Accra—standing on the sidelines, they smiled as Nkrumah squired the Duchess of Kent around the dance floor.) In *God's Trombones,* James Weldon Johnson found it necessary to go beyond the folk pulpit to honor it. "What the colored poet in the United States needs to do is something like what Synge did for the Irish; he needs to find a form that will express the racial spirit by symbols from within rather than by symbols from without—such as the mere mutilation of English spelling and pronunciation. He needs a form that is freer and larger than dialect, but which will still hold the racial flavor; a form expressing the imagery, the idioms, the peculiar turns of thought and the distinctive humor and pathos, too, of the Negro."[32]

Pulling to the close of the meandering "Birth of a New Nation," King was ready to bring the message home in a more spiritual sense. "Rise up," he told the Dexter congregation, "and know that as you struggle for justice, you do not struggle alone. But God struggles with you. And He is working every day." All the secular history dissolved in a more transcendent chronicle as King leapt from one millennial burst to another. No longer hemmed in by the particular vantage of Accra or Westminster Abbey, he found himself in that place of mysterious perception where he could see and hear and sense things that were not quite material. "Somehow I can look out, I can look out across the seas and across the universe, and cry out, 'Mine eyes have seen the glory of the coming of the Lord.'" He could see a great number "marching into the great eternity, because God is working in this world." Most powerfully, he could hear Isaiah: "that somehow 'every valley shall be exalted, and every hill shall be made low . . . and the glory of the Lord shall be revealed, and all flesh shall see it together.' That's the beauty of this thing: all flesh shall see it together: not some white and not some black, not some yellow and not some brown, but all flesh shall see it together."

EIGHT

Homilies of Black Liberation

"You are somebody"

"Birth of a New Nation" may not have been a typical King sermon. After all, the topical brew of Nkrumah, independence, and Africa naturally highlighted the theme of deliverance and its political resonance. Still, the implied dig at the film *Birth of a Nation* and the sympathy King felt toward the Ghanaians reflected black preoccupations that were even more pronounced in King's Ebenezer sermons.

Yet as we delve into that blacker content in this chapter and the even blacker style in the next, the same ambiguities of "blackness" that appeared in King's offstage palaver with friends surface here as well. Speaking to black congregations, King divulged things he tended not to flaunt in front of white audiences. But the tinge of black Christian nationalism never came close to a full-fledged "black theology."[1] Just as the cosmopolitan King who drew imagery, words, and form from white sources had ample means to express his blackness, King had no problem spreading the universal message of Christianity with the particular means bequeathed to him by the Afro-Baptist pulpit. In the end, even King's most intense preaching invariably returned to the primal ground of his universal faith.

This black perspective struck John Lewis the first time he heard King. Still a youngster tilling the soil in the fields around Troy, Alabama, in 1955 he happened upon a King radio sermon on WRMA out of Montgomery that "sat me bolt upright with amazement." The sermon was "Paul's Letter to American Christians." Lewis couldn't get over how King adapted Paul's rebuke of the church at Corinth for its "failures of brotherhood" to "what was happening here, right now, on the streets of Montgomery." Even as a boy, Lewis had bristled at all the preacher talk about "'over yonder,' where we'd put on the white robes and golden slippers and sit with the angels." But "this man spoke about how it wasn't enough for black people to be concerned only with getting to the Promised Land in the hereafter, about how it was not enough for people to be concerned with roads that are paved with gold, and gates to the Kingdom of God . . . [He] was talking about dealing with the problems people were facing in their right now, specifically black lives in the South. . . . I was on fire with the words I was hearing."[2]

If there was a contradiction between King's emphasis on black lives and his love of all God's children, it was institutional as much as personal or logical. Over and over when confronting black bitterness, King emphasized, "God is not interested just in the freedom of black people"— and he did so from a black pulpit. The racism that affronted Jesus' basic premise divided the church in two. As King preached in "A Knock at Midnight," "Millions of American Negroes, starving for the want of the bread of freedom, have knocked again and again on the door of so-called white churches, but they have usually been greeted by a cold indifference or a blatant hypocrisy." The very existence of a black church was hardly desirable. King's description of a "so-called Negro church" underlined its interim nature: "I say 'so-called' . . . because ideally there can be no Negro or white church. It is to their everlasting shame that white Christians developed a system of racial segregation within the church, and inflicted so many indignities upon its Negro worshipers that they had to organize their own churches."[3] Simply as a practical matter, black preaching was defined by the absent term, the schism that expelled blacks and tore humanity apart: the failure of white Christians to recognize black people as human beings.

King dwelled on "black lives" in his sermons in various ways. We've already seen hints of this in his comments on being married to a fine Negro woman, his empathetic response to black bitterness, and his experience in Ghana. In the protective space of Holt Street Church in Montgomery, Alabama, King gave voice to a black self-criticism intended for black ears alone, in which "we blacks" defined the focus of his attention. "This evening," he warned, he wasn't going to talk about the church, the federal government, or white liberals but "some things that we must do *(Yes, Amen)*, as Negroes . . ."

"Let us be honest with ourselves, and say that we, our standards have lagged behind at many points." Noting the high rate of illegitimacy and crime among Negroes, King asked the audience to step out of the black perspective: "What are the things that white people are saying about us?" Rejecting the white conviction that blacks wanted to marry white people, he did concede, "then on the other hand, they say some other things about us, and maybe there is some truth in them. Maybe we could be more sanitary; maybe we could be a little more clean . . .

"And another thing my friends, we kill each other too much. *(All right, Yes)* We cut up each other too much. *(Yes, Yes sir)*.

"We must walk the street every day, and let people know that as we walk the street we aren't thinking about sex every time we turn around. *(No, That's right)* We are not animals *(No)* to be degraded at every moment. *(Yeah)*."[4]

Typically, the blackness waxed and waned not just in the same sermon but in the same paragraph as King shifted in and out of an ethnic and a general "we." "The great problem of mankind today is that there is too much hatred around," King preached. Yet the forces that cleaved the church into black and white ghettos and produced the same need to split mankind and language itself into two camps intruded into the very act of preaching. "In America, the white man must love the black man, and the black man must love the white man, because we are all tied together in a single garment of destiny." That garment often seemed well-worn, if not threadbare, as King's voice quavered with urgency, "and we can't keep havin' riots every summer in our cities, we can't keep havin' all of these problems . . . Our white brothers must understand . . . the federal government has enough money to get rid of slums and poverty and get rid of these conditions that make for riots."

112

With the words tumbling out, King kept the run-on sentence running. "There's no point in continuin' to make up excuses, our white brothers have got to come to see one thing, we are in America, and we are here to stay and we got to learn how to live together, we ain't goin' nowhere." As King descended further into the vernacular, the congregation rustled, and King insisted, "There 22 million Negroes that we have counted up, the census figures give us that. Now they don't take under consideration the number of Negroes that <u>ran</u> when they saw the census man coming thinkin' it was somebody to collect a bill . . . There's at least 30 million Negroes in America," and then repeating emphatically, "and we are here to stay."[5]

The tone of "we are here to stay" was even more defiant in "Why Jesus Called a Man a Fool." Compounding the white failure to welcome was the failure of whites to recognize both black humanity and their own heartlessness. Even with King gamely clinging to the language of brotherhood—"Our white brothers must see this; they haven't seen it up to now"—the chasm between the races was widening. With the spoken emphasis on the words italicized here, an indignant King said, "It is *the black man* to a large extent who produced the wealth of this nation. *(All right)* And the nation doesn't have *sense* enough to share its wealth and its *power* with the very people who made it so. *(All right) And I know what I'm talking about* this morning. *(Yes, sir)* The *black man* made America wealthy. *(Yes, sir)*."[6]

Noting that "we've been here" and personalizing the refusal to leave ("I'm not going anywhere"), King rebuffed any talk of returning to Africa. "I love Africa, it's our ancestral home. But I don't know about you. My grandfather and my great-grandfather did too much to build this nation for me to be talking about getting away from it [Applause]." The last comment excited the audience into thunderous clapping and some yelling, and King shifted out of his indignation into a lyrical meter as he established a claim more primal than any official markers of history or civil religion:

> Before the Pilgrim fathers landed at Plymouth in 1620,
> We were here. *(Oh yeah)*
> Before Jefferson etched across the pages of history
> The majestic words of the Declaration of Independence,

We were here. *(All right)*
Before the beautiful words
of "The Star Spangled Banner" were written,
We were here. *(Yeah)* . . .

Black labor reinforced the belonging conferred by presence. "For more than two centuries, our forebears labored here without wages." They made cotton king; they fashioned the "sturdy docks, the stout factories, the impressive mansions of the South. *(My lord)*." This is why it was so galling that "this nation is telling us that we can't build." In a reprise of all who declared "no room at the inn," lily-white unions excluded blacks, denied them the ample salaries of the trades, "and they don't want Negroes to have it [Applause]."

Given King's long support for standard English, the lapses of *ain't* and the dropping of final *g*s (as in *comin'*) were significant. He had taught grammar classes to ministers. In the late 1950s, King complained, "But I have met more school teachers recently who can't even speak the English language. *(Yeah)* Wouldn't know a verb if it was big as that table . . . But for a college graduate to be standing up and talking about 'you is,' there is no excuse for it. *(Yes)*." That same scrupulousness was evident in King's citing of Sister Pollard's legendary words, "My feets is tired, but my soul is rested"—her answer to the bus driver's inquiry, aren't you tired? King often prefaced such affronts to diction with the careful distance of an adjective, labeling them as "ungrammatical profundity." So, as time went on, the lessening of King's compulsion to announce or comment on his swerves into ghetto-inflected street talk was revealing. In a 1967 appearance at New Covenant Baptist Church in Chicago, for example, he did not label Sister Pollard's insight "ungrammatical." King went further than simply dropping such preemptive apologies. "I just like to see that fellow Willie Mays," King attested in a conversation he retold for his Ebenezer congregation. "I said, 'He can really hit that ball.' And the person with whom I was talking said, 'He really can, but have you ever heard him talk?' Said, 'He can't talk too well.' I say, well, a brother that can hit a ball like that doesn't need to talk. [Laughter]."[7]

King's move into the vernacular reflected a larger aim of removing barriers to black solidarity. He warned the Ebenezer congregation that violence gave reactionaries "a good excuse . . . to destroy and kill many innocent Negroes in the process. A lot of folks want us to riot." In truth, no matter how much the desperation of "our brothers and sisters" was a response to their desperate conditions, such an approach was not just contrary to the teachings of Jesus but also self-defeating for the race as a whole. King once preached about a fellow theology student who was reluctant to invite his mother, who had struggled to put him through school, to visit: "The problem is I don't know if she would quite fit in this atmosphere. You know, her verbs aren't quite right; and she doesn't know how to dress too well." King told the congregation, "I wanted to say to him so bad that you aren't fit to finish this school. *(Yes)* If you cannot acknowledge your mother, if you cannot acknowledge your brothers and sisters, even if they have not risen to the heights of educational attainment, then you aren't fit *(Have mercy)* to go out and try to preach to men and women *(Amen)*." He castigated "our little class systems, and you know you got a lot of Negroes with classism in their veins. *(Sure)* You know that they don't want to be bothered with certain other Negroes and they try to separate themselves from them. *(Amen)* . . . [But] sometimes Aunt Jane on her knees can get more truth than the philosopher on his tiptoes *(Yes, Amen)*."[8]

King's 1967 sermon "Judging Others" implemented racial unity through a conventional parable, which King introduced with the line from Matthew, "Judge not that ye be not judged." If King's larger framework was always universalistic—self-righteousness "widens the gulf which Christian love should bridge"—the preponderance of examples involved bridging distance from other blacks. "I've looked at my black brothers and sisters so often caught up with dope in the ghetto and it's so easy to stand back and judge them. . . . But then somehow we must learn that that person who's a dope addict is a dope addict because so often circumstances have driven them there. We forget the system that made them that way." In King's mind, the hypocrisy contained in that inattention had a racial subtext. "And you know what makes me very angry about this thing? You know, I'm sick and tired of police forces in our nation merely arresting the Negro who's peddling dope, he's just out there selling a little dope . . . and they don't ever arrest the folk who really keep the policy going." Those folk, King emphasized, were in the highest echelons of society.[9]

King's preaching in "Levels of Love" epitomized the links between a racial "us" and the shared experience of racial victimization.[10] A stuttering hesitation of "uh, ah don't know" injected if not quite lewdness, then a certain folksiness into the discussion. "You just come to the point of sayin', uh, ah don't know, 'I just love her because she moooves me.'" Along with agape and philea completing the usual trinity, King added a new category. He equated "utilitarian love"—"one loves another because of the other's usefulness to him"—with what Jesus would consider the lowest kind of love. To get that idea across, King recounted a conversation he had with a white person during his travels in the larger white world, assuming the words—and thus the persona—of the white interlocutor.

Typically, he was on a plane when a white passenger told him, "'You know, I grew up with so much affection and love for, for nigras'"—King immediately interrupted himself to underscore: "he couldn't say 'Negro,' he said 'for nigras'—and he said that 'I always did nice things for nigras and I know that in my family we didn't grow up with any prejudice for nigras. We loved them. But over the last few years,'"—and now, as King narrated it, his interlocutor shifted into a personal "you"—"'since, ah, you nigras have been demonstratin', and, ah, you got others shoutin' 'Black Power' and, all of this, we just don't feel the same kind of love that we once had.'" (It seems that in the five years that had elapsed since King preached the same vignette at Ebenezer, either the white man had become more candid or King had become less squeamish about reporting racism in the raw. In 1962, King depicted the man as saying, "The thing that worries me so much about this movement here is that it's creating so much tension. . . . I used to love the Negro, but I don't have the kind of love for them that I used to.")[11]

But King turned the tables on the white man, assuming the superior role of teacher. Plaintively at first but with rising indignation, King continued, "And I said to him, 'Do you really think you *loved* us? Because if you really loved the Negro, ah, if you love a person, it isn't conditional whether that person stays in his place.' You see, this brother's problem was that he had affection for the Negro so long as the Negro patiently accepted his enslaved status. . . . But the minute the Negro decided that he was going to stand up and be a man, this man's love passed away. Well, it wasn't love at all. It was just a kind of utilitarian concern. Love is always unconditional."

If that brief definitional dip wasn't sufficient to lift the audience beyond the vignette, King ratcheted things up a notch: "Immanuel Kant, the great philosopher, said in one formulation of the categorical imperative that you must always treat persons as ends and never as mere means. And I know why Kant said that. Because the minute we treat a person as a means rather than an end you depersonalize that person and the person becomes a thing. This is exactly what happened to the Negro during the days of slavery. He was used for an economic end."

"Levels of Love" introduced one final category of love, humanitarian love, whose problem inhered in its abstract quality. What, King wanted to know, does it mean to love everybody in general? King pointed to the Southern Baptist Convention, which donated much aid to Africa out of its humanitarian concerns, but "if a black man went in the average southern Baptist church they'd kick him out. They love humanity in general but"—now King fled from the objective standpoint—"but they don't love *us* in particular [italics added]."

Sometimes in recounting his personal experiences, King presented distinctively "black" moments of insight and feeling as spontaneously occurring events. In his 1959 Easter sermon at Dexter, he described a thought that had come to him during his walk through Gethsemane on his recent trip to the Holy Land. He had just reached the Via Dolorosa, the Way of Sorrow through which Jesus passed on the way up to Golgotha. "The thing that I thought about at that moment was the fact that when Jesus fell and stumbled under that cross it was a black man that picked it up for him and said, 'I will help you,' and took it on up to Calvary. And I think we know today there is a struggle, a desperate struggle, going on in the world. Two-thirds of the people of the world are colored people. They have been dominated politically, exploited economically, trampled over, and humiliated. There is a struggle on the part of these people today to gain freedom and human dignity. And I think one day God will remember that it was a black man that helped His son in the darkest and most desolate moment of his life. It was a black man who picked up that cross for him and who took that cross on up to Calvary. God will remember this."[12]

On the primal ground of a faith defined by its universal message, King had an ethnic moment. He even remade God into a race-conscious deity for whom the color of the person who helped his son might matter. King didn't will these thoughts; he just couldn't help thinking them.[13] This resembled the kind of uncontrollable emotion experienced by those Jews of a certain generation who breathed a sigh of relief when they discovered that Son of Sam (David) Berkowitz, the serial murderer who terrorized Brooklyn and Queens in the summer of 1977, was only half Jewish. Some of those people were utterly embarrassed to admit to such a tribal way of being, which they experienced as unwilled and even unwelcome. It was a visceral twinge of Jewishness.

Such personal feelings at times served not just to give a black twist after an excursion into the universal but also as a way of connecting to something even more universal. Perhaps inspired by the Fourth of July holiday in 1965, King spoke in "The American Dream," a homiletic reprise of the final portion of the oration "I Have a Dream," on the "dignity and the worth of human personality" in a civil religious idiom unusual for his sermons. At first, his examples lay outside the black experience as he cautioned that the equality of all men "doesn't mean" every musician is equal to Verdi or Mozart, that "every literary figure in history is the equal of Aeschylus and Euripides, Shakespeare and Chaucer (Make it plain)," that all philosophers are on a par with Hegel or Aristotle. He continued in this high-flown fashion, citing "the words of a great Jewish philosopher that died a few days ago, Martin Buber. . . . '[Segregation is] wrong because it substitutes an 'I'-'it' relationship for the 'I'-'thou' relationship and relegates persons to the status of things.' That's it. (Yes sir)."[14]

With only the remark "I remember when Mrs. King and I were in India" to mark his shift from didactic to narrative mode, King recalled the words of the person who introduced him right before he spoke in the southern Indian state of Kerala to high school students from an untouchable caste: "Young people, I would like to present to you a fellow untouchable from the United States of America." That revelation incited a remarkable dance of identity: from resistance to an Indian pariah identity to an assertion of black identity to universalizing the condition of untouchability to a return to blackness enriched by the excursion.

To extend the untouchable status to blacks could be seen as a kind of sharing, the equivalent of when a black person tells a person who isn't black, "You're my nigger" or "You're my main nigger," or when King in effect said to Stanley Levison, "You're my main Christian." Yet King's initial response in India was less than thrilled. "I was a bit shocked and peeved," King admitted to the congregation, "that I would be referred to as an untouchable (Glory to God)."

King was being disingenuous, shaping the musings of "couldn't help thinking" into stylized form to better make use of them. G. Ramachandran, the secretary of the Gandhi National Memorial fund and a native of Kerala, had already made the link between American blacks and the caste system when he invited King to visit India. "We in India have watched with sympathy and admiration the non-violent movements of the Negroes in America." Ramachandran continued, "We expect you would be particularly interested to know how Gandhigi wrestled with the problem of untouchability in India."[15] Moreover, the entire episode sounds suspiciously like the one Benjamin Mays experienced when he traveled to India in 1936 and was introduced as "an untouchable who had achieved distinction." "At first I was horrified, puzzled, angry to be called an untouchable, but [then] . . . I realized, as never before, that I was truly an untouchable in my native land."[16]

King's miffed feelings at being called an untouchable quickly dissipated, giving way to one of those "started thinking" moments: "I started thinking about the fact that at that time no matter how much I needed to rest my tired body after a long night of travel, I couldn't stop in the average motel of the highways. . . . I started thinking about the fact that no matter how long an old Negro woman had been shopping downtown and got a little tired and needed to get a hamburger or a cup of coffee at a lunch counter, she couldn't get it there. *(Preach)* . . . I started thinking about the fact: twenty million of my brothers and sisters were still smothering in an airtight cage of poverty in an affluent society."

Only after the embrace of "my brothers and sisters" was King ready to pivot out of blackness and accept that foreign designation. "And I said to myself, 'Yes, I am an untouchable, and every Negro in the United States of America is an untouchable.'" King did not rest inside the untouchable identity. He reverted to the black position of "every Negro" and the familiar terms of "God's black children [who are] as significant as his white children *(Yes, sir).*"[17]

Convincing black children of their own worth was a struggle. King knew this firsthand as a father. Invoking his experience as an ordinary black man trying to shield his children from racism, King allowed the congregation of Mount Zion Baptist Church in Los Angeles to see through the outer veil of his private life. His daughter Yolanda had repeatedly voiced her longing to go to Funtown (a segregated amusement park), and the resolute leader of his people admitted the failure of nerve that led him to evade frank talk about racism. He perfectly captured the relentless insistence and singsong rhythm of a little girl who came bounding down the stairs and said, "Daddy, you know I been telling you, I want to go to Funtown, and they were just talking about Funtown on the television and I want you to take me to Funtown."

With his voice beginning to quaver, the distraught orator reflected, "And, ohhh, I stood there speechless. How could I explain to a little six-years-old girl that she couldn't go to Funtown because she was colored? I'd been speaking across the country talking about segregation and discrimination and I thought I could answer most of the questions that came up but I was speechless for the moment. I didn't know how to explain it. Then I said to myself, 'I've got to face this problem once and for all.'"

King heightened the verisimilitude of the moment with little details: "And I took my little daughter . . . and she jumped up in my lap and I looked at her and I said, 'Yolanda, we have a problem,' said, 'You know, some people don't do the right things . . . and so they have developed a system where white people go certain places and colored people go certain places.' And I said, 'They have Funtown like that so that they don't allow colored children to go to Funtown.'" King's wrestling, however, was not done. Afraid she might become bitter, he said, "all white people are not like that," but that was a prelude to the ancestral truth he was about to bestow on her, with the exact words his parents had used to induct him into a greater awareness of blackness.

"But then I looked down into her eyes and I said to her at that point, and I saw tears flowing from her eyes . . . I said, 'Yokie, don't allow anyone to make you feel you're less than them. Even though you can't go, I want you to know that you are as good as anyone who goes into Funtown.'" At this point the audience ratified King's words, moving beyond their previous rustling and breaking into forceful applause.[18]

The shift from "Yolanda" to "Yokie," her tears, and the eloquence with which King described his speechlessness all intensified the intimacy of the moment. Beyond the racial content, the fact that King tended to reserve self-disclosure for black audiences was a badge of racial belonging too. Much like his ethnic banter and raunchy joshing, King's Ebenezer preaching created a spiritual version of the black backstage. Such revelations were often tied to King's role as the head of an insurgency seeking to deliver black people, as when he offered a litany of movement disappointments: "I felt discouraged in Chicago. As I move through Mississippi and Georgia and Alabama, I feel discouraged. *(Yes, sir)* Living every day under the threat of death, I feel discouraged sometimes. Living every day under extensive criticisms, even from Negroes, I feel discouraged sometimes. [Applause] Yes, sometimes I feel discouraged and feel my work's in vain."[19]

Often when most in need of hope, King would invoke the Montgomery bus boycott, telling how "I was beginning to falter and to get weak within and to lose my courage *(All right)*." He had given a less than decisive speech at a mass meeting, and as he peered out at the audience, he could feel "the cool breeze of pessimism." Afterwards, Sister Pollard approached King, and said, "'Son, what's wrong with you.' Said, 'You didn't talk strong enough tonight.'

"And I said, 'Nothing is wrong, Sister Pollard, I'm all right.'

"She said, 'You can't fool me.' Said, 'Something wrong with you.' And then she went on to say these words: Said, 'Is the white folks doing something to you that you don't like?'"

After King's denial, Sister Pollard's command—"Now come close to me and let me tell you something one more time and I want you to hear it this time"—symbolized three aspects of closeness that were often tangled together: closeness between King and his congregation, between King and the extended racial family that Sister Pollard represented, between King and God. "'Now, I done told you we is with you. . . . Now, even if we ain't with you, the Lord is with you' *(Yes)*. And she concluded by saying, 'The Lord's going to take care of you.'"[20]

On that night of his "less than decisive speech" when he had such a difficult time at the podium, King had exhorted, "don't shoot, even though it may be difficult." He also said if "anyone should be killed, let it be me." By others' accounts, he apparently collapsed and had to be helped to a seat, but the *Montgomery Advertiser* carried his denial: "I shed no tears and nor was I overcome with emotion. To the contrary, I was calm and balanced throughout." He later admitted to being "in the grips of an emotion I could not control . . . for the first time, [I] broke down in public." His spare outline for the night's talk took note of recent bombings of "our churches . . . when men sink this low they have fallen to a level of tragic barbarity devoid of any moral sensitivity." Then King wondered, "Now why we have to suffer like this I do not know. But I am sure it has some purpose. It may be that we are called upon to be God's suffering through which [whom] he is working his redemptive plan."[21]

A comparison of two versions of King's account of his most extraordinary moment of vulnerability reveals the racial intricacy of King's confessional. The episode was his kitchen conversion during the Montgomery boycott when he suffered a failure of nerve in the midnight hour and then came to experience God in a new way. One version appeared in the white-targeted (and heavily white-edited and vetted) trade book *Stride toward Freedom;* the other rendition appeared in later sermons in black churches.

For King, midnight was always the time of need. In various versions of the sermon "Knock at Midnight," that "strange" time of unsettlement is the prompt for King to bind himself and his congregants in one mortal community of despondency. "Midnight is a confusing hour when it is difficult to be faithful." Midnight is a time of blurring, when the sharpness of colors gives way to the gray of eerie indistinction. It is a time of testing: will someone answer that knock? In a notable burst of emotion in a Selma mass meeting, it seems as if morning will never come. Even when dawn arrives outside, things are so bleak "it still was midnight."

Provoked by a racist telephone threat in the midst of the Montgomery bus boycott, King's prolonged midnight was not just a metaphor for the condition of man. It was linked to King's role in black deliverance; both his fear and his defiance embodied a collective fear and a collective longing to be free. Just as the line between King's sermons and his rally addresses was real despite its permeability, King's spiritual malaise was not entirely separable from the material reality he experienced as the leader of a social movement. The narrative structure turned on the three-part movement from the threatening phone call that triggered the incident, through an experience of flooding hopelessness, to resolution through God's intercession.

In *Stride,* King described the phone call in a straightforward fashion: "Listen nigger, we've taken all we want from you; before next week you'll be sorry you ever came to Montgomery." By contrast, the threat is more graphic and elaborate in a 1967 account inserted into a sermon, "Why Jesus Called a Man a Fool," which King delivered to a black congregation. "On the other end was an ugly voice. That voice said to me, in substance, 'Nigger, we are tired of you and your mess now. And if you aren't out of this town in three days, we're going to blow your brains out and blow up your house' *(Lord Jesus)*." In this and other tellings of the story to black audiences, King dramatically enacts the part of the racist speaker, accentuating the word "nigger" and infusing it with vicious contempt.[22]

The disparities in the two tellings intensify as a sleepless, rattled King descends to the kitchen. In *Stride*, King simply observed, "I got out of bed and began to walk the floor. Finally I went to the kitchen and heated a pot of coffee . . . With this state of exhaustion, when my courage had all but gone, I bowed over the kitchen table and prayed aloud." By contrast, in any of a number of versions of the kitchen experience enacted before black church audiences, the revelation was detailed, personal, and emotive, and King's voice trembled. "I sat there and thought about a beautiful little daughter who had just been born about a month earlier. . . . She was the darling of my life. I'd come in night after night and see that little gentle smile. And I sat at that table thinking about that little girl and thinking about the fact that she could be taken away from me any minute *(Go ahead)*." As King conveys his failure of nerve, one senses the congregation sympathizing, as their call and shout bucks him up, punctuates his words, and thereby shares in his classic expression of being prostrate before the Lord. "And I got to the point that I couldn't take it any longer; I was weak. *(Yes)* Oh Lord, I'm trying to be, I think I'm right . . . but I'm weak."

As in the Funtown chronicle, the expression of feelings of vulnerability was accompanied by a shift into the vernacular of "daddy" and "mama." "Something said to me, 'You can't call on Daddy now; he's up in Atlanta a hundred and seventy-five miles away. *(Yes)* You can't even call on Mama now. *(My Lord)* You've got to call on that something in that person that your daddy used to tell you about. *(Yes)* That power that can make a way out of no way.' *(Yes)* And I discovered then that religion had to become real to me and I had to know God for myself. *(Yes, sir)* And I bowed down over that cup of coffee—and I will never forget it. *(Yes, sir)* And oh, yes, I prayed a prayer and I prayed out loud that night. *(Yes)* 'But Lord, I must confess that I'm weak now; I'm faltering; . . . I'm losing my courage' *(Yes)*."

In this third phase of spiritual closure in *Stride*, King wrote of the encounter in a relatively clipped form. He simply felt the amorphous "presence of the divine," and the voice he heard was "an inner voice": "At that moment I experienced the presence of the divine as I had never experienced Him before. It seemed as though I could hear the quiet assurance of an inner voice saying: 'Stand up for righteousness, stand up for truth; and God will be at your side forever.' Almost at once my fears began to go. My uncertainty disappeared. I was ready to face anything."

Before black congregations, it was the black folk preacher who presented himself. God appeared as a fully formed actor in all his personality. The voice King heard was not always the vague "inner" one; sometimes it was God, or "the voice of Jesus saying still to fight on." That voice addressed him directly by name, "Martin Luther *(Yes)*." And King's finish was devastating in the intensity of his suffering. In one such version, he preached passionately, "The holy spirit filled me." In another, he began with the biblical "Lo . . ." As he often did, in "Why Jesus Called a Man a Fool" he merged his trembling, tortured voice right into the lyrics of "Never Alone," borrowing from its apocalyptic vision, and was near sobbing by the end.

> And I'll tell you,
> I've seen the lightning flash.
> I've heard the thunder roll.
> I felt sin-breakers dashing,
> trying to conquer my soul.
> But I heard the voice of Jesus
> saying still to fight on.

And then King fell into a chant, like a haunted man who couldn't stop repeating:

> He promised never to leave me,
> never to leave me alone.
> No, never alone.
> No, never alone.
> He promised never to leave me *(Never)*.
> Never to leave me alone.

In preaching to his Ebenezer family and other black churches, King made it clear he belonged to the black community. Some of these affirmations of blackness were confined to the oblique forms of implication and insinuation; others were more explicit. But these were all small signs of a larger vision of *brother*hood that went beyond the recognized strain of black exceptionalism. It emerged in ways that can hardly be treated alone because King's preaching tended to run them all together: the theme of somebodyness; the call for black self-love; the rituals of ancestor worship; the veneration of the songs of the slaves.

Some of these features were obvious. King's topical reflections on the civil rights movement and his constant return to the matter of racism gave an explicit black cast to his preaching. Defining the criteria for the "acceptable year of the Lord," King depicted God as carefully tracking the most minute details of southern racism and the civil rights movement. Even when presented as one instance of a more general feature of his theology or the human condition, subjects like the psychology of white racism or doubts about intermarriage declared his racial preoccupation. King's mentions of himself as the Mosaic leader engaged in the deliverance of his people further reinforced his totemic power as an exemplar of blackness.

As the diffusion of the 1960s slogan "black is beautiful" into his preaching indicates, King continued to range widely in praise of blackness with his usual hybrid versatility. Seemingly casual mentions of black pride—"There is a magnificent lady, with all of the beauty of blackness and black culture, by the name of Marian Anderson"—were compressions of an explicit racial perspective, and King had a cluster of heroes of the race he called upon recurrently. Preaching at Chicago's Mount Pisgah Missionary Baptist Church in 1967, he appropriated the loftiest of his white liberal sermon forms, "Three Dimensions," for a more ethnic end, turning the dimension of "length of life," the one that refers to inner powers of the self, into a meditation on racial pride. Instead of leaning on the British poet William Cowper, this time he enlisted the help of Rabbi Joshua Liebman's *Peace of Mind.* The relevant chapter was "Love Thyself Properly"—a typical postwar paean to self-realization. After establishing this general secular humanist—or perhaps Reform Jewish?—foundation, King enjoined, "And we must pray every day, asking God to help us to accept ourselves. *(Yeah)* That means everything *(Yeah)*." King proceeded to give the generic paean some ethnic edge with this leap: "Too many Negroes are ashamed of themselves, ashamed of being black *(Yes, sir).*"[23]

Having left the Jewish humanist sage behind, King swerved back to an old slave theme, invoking the idiom of somebodyness. King prescribed the act of saying as a therapeutic mandate: "A Negro got to rise up and say from the bottom of his soul, 'I am somebody. *(Yes)* I have a rich, noble, and proud heritage. However exploited and however painful my history has been, I'm black, but I'm black and beautiful.'"

"I am somebody" would seem about as universalistic as it gets, a Christian vision of democratic promise: equality of souls, equality of dignity. In one of those color-blind variants, King adopted Willie Mays's voice to draw out the larger lesson: "I may not be able to articulate my words, but I can be able to articulate a ball and a bat and I will rise up and be somebody in history. You can be somebody." Yet just as "all God's chillun" offered a blackened riff on the universality of "all God's children," somebodyness as preached to a "'buked and scorned" people was always freighted with overtones of racial healing. The same was true of "the least of these" and "all God's children." (As Eugene Genovese has pointed out, the slaves asked for recognition more than for forgiveness.) Even King's ostensibly Lockean examples—if you're a shoeshine boy or a janitor, be the best you can—were hard to separate from the racial history that imbued shoeshining and other service work with special black resonance. "And everybody that we call a maid is serving God in a significant way. *(Preach it)* And I love the maids, I love the people who have been ignored."[24]

The themes of somebodyness and racism were utterly entwined in King's preaching, and they often led right back to the primal kindred, the slaves. Noting that "today [we] find the tribal idea alive" in "white supremacy," King countered with the obvious, "God loves all of his children," and before long had deferred to the words of his predecessors. "You know the old slave preacher used to say this in beautiful terms . . . they had to live day in and day out, there wasn't nothing to look forward to morning after morning but the blistering heat, long rows of cotton, the rawhide whip of the overseer . . . women knew they had to sacrifice their bodies to satisfy the biological urges of the masters. As soon as their children were born, they were snatched from their hand like a dog snatches a bone from a human hand . . . They would pray over and over again that they did not count, that they did not belong, that they were nobody."[25]

Here King defined the role of the slave preacher as a surrogate of God who restored the humanity denied by the slaveowners with their perverted version of religion. That healing act began with a gaze full of pathos. "And that old slave preacher would look at his people, he would say to 'em,

'Now, all week long you been told that you are nobody, all week long you've been reminded of the fact you were a slave, all week long you've been called a nigger. But I wanna say to you,'"—and although the identity of the speaker here was not really murky, King's thickening of dialect created the impression that he had become part of the speech act too—"'You ain't no slave, you ain't no nigger, but you God's chillun.' And it was that affirmation that gave them hope. It was that affirmation that gave them something on the inside to stand up amid the difficulties of their days."

Moving back to the "we" of today, King soared: "Abused and scorned though we may be, God loves us. . . . There is a God who loves all of his children. Who loves his black children as well as his white children. And every man from the bass black to the treble white is significant on his eternal keyboard. We know that God so loved the world, and you know the thing I like about it, is that his mind is so big, that it can include everybody."

While heralding the "beautiful terms" of the old slave preacher, King was establishing a connection that was occupational as well as racial. That line was genealogical—his great-grandfather was a slave exhorter—as well as functional. Conferring somebodyness on all those "no d's" as well as the "Ph.D.'s," all the 'buked and scorned, he was carrying out the same role as a healer, and not just of forlorn souls but a forlorn people. King would even take that sacred endeavor of acknowledgment right into the churning energy of the mass meetings, blurring the line between insurgent rally and church service. And just as he would console, flatter, and lift up ordinary black people in the meetings, King gave praise in his preaching not just to Jesus but to the ancestors and all their descendants. They were not nobodies, and even more, in King's reckoning, they were a glorious people.

Preaching high or preaching low, from the early Dexter years through the late Ebenezer ones, King brought the voices of the slaves right into his preaching. Sometimes he defined them as victims of the rawhide whip. At other times, he credited their special insight. "The Negroes, many years ago, discovered something great and they were great psychologists." King's brief aside—"they didn't know the English language too well"—did not diminish the main point any more than qualifying Sister Pollard's profundity as "ungrammatical." "[But] they knew God, and they could say things that had a great deal of meaning, and with a profound psychological vision, they could say, 'I'm so glad that trouble don't last always.' *(That's right, All right)*."[26]

The core of the slaves' exceptionalism was a kind of endurance that was more than brute persistence. It was spiritual fortitude. This was the point of King's improvising on Howard Thurman's rumination on the slaves' relationship to Jeremiah's anxious question, "Is there a balm in Gilead?" "Centuries later our slave foreparents came along. *(Yes, sir)* And they too saw the injustices of life . . . But they did an amazing thing. They looked back across the centuries and they took Jeremiah's question mark and straightened it into an exclamation point. And they could sing, 'There is a balm in Gilead, to make the wounded whole. *(Yes)* There is a balm in Gilead to heal the sin-sick soul.'"[27]

It was in this appreciative spirit that King considered the slaves' capacity to create song, a symbol of the capacity to hope which itself defined faith in God. "The Interruptions of Life" drew out this link between hope and song. With "my" and "your foreparents" tightening the embrace of the racial family, King launched into a jubilant poem that bordered on song:

> And I'm glad this morning
> that my foreparents
> and your foreparents
> didn't jump.
> Stood back there
> during the dark days of slavery,
> in the anguish and the ache
> and the agony of slavery,
> but they didn't jump,
> they produced a song.
> And every now and then
> in the darkness of it,
> when they didn't have any shoes,
> they just say,
> "I got shoes, you got shoes,
> all of God's chillun' got shoes,
> When I get to heaven, gonna put on my shoes
> and I'm just gonna walk all over God's heaven

By and by, by and by,
I'm gonna lay down my heavy load.
I know my robes gonna fit me well,
'Cause I tried it on at the gates of hell."
Don't jump, just produce a song![28]

Once again, we don't need to square King's love of black spiritual music with his cultivated taste or the fact that he took Coretta to a highbrow concert on an early date. No more than his love of black people and of humanity in general were these things in competition. No more than Malcolm X's jail tutorial in the classic texts of white civilization did King's mastery of white texts, fluency in universalistic idioms, and ample supply of cultural capital extinguish his deep love of black culture. These things simply expanded the range of the genres he relished and the gambits he could use in moving audiences. In this case, the spirituals provided the means not only to venerate the ancestors but to declare his appreciation of black people now, of the culture and history they shared together, and his insistence on honoring it.

That history was the fount of so many of the things that were sacred to King. "Every now and then when it gets dark to you," King preached, "Go on somewhere and just start singing." As in that verse, singing, the ancestors, and morning were irretrievably joined together. "Our slave foreparents . . . were never unmindful of the fact of midnight, for always there was the . . . auction block where families were torn asunder to remind them of its reality. When they thought of the agonizing darkness of midnight, they sang:

"Oh, nobody knows de trouble I've seen,
Glory Hallelujah!
Sometimes I'm up, sometimes I'm down.
Oh yes, Lord,
Sometimes I'm almost to de groun',
Oh yes, Lord,
Oh, nobody knows de trouble I've seen,
Glory Hallelujah!"[29]

Neither was this imagery of midnight and morning separable from the capacity to dream, but with this qualification: before there was an American Dream, there was the ancestral dream of King's own people. "So many of our forebears used to sing about freedom. And they dreamed of the day that they would be able to get out of the bosom of slavery, the long night of injustice. *(Yes, sir)* And they used to sing little songs: 'Nobody knows de trouble I seen, nobody knows but Jesus.' *(Yes)* They thought about a better day as they dreamed their dream. And they would say, 'I'm so glad the trouble don't last always. *(Yeah)* By and by, by and by, I'm going to lay down my heavy load.' *(Yes, sir)*."[30]

NINE

Raw and Refined

"I'm gonna be a Negro tonight"

The richness of King's chronicle of black lives brings us some distance from his early cosmopolitanism. Yet even amidst the sessions of racial healing, there are ample hints that blackness for King was in certain respects incidental and interim, which prevents us from placing King's homilies under the rubric of "black theology." Just as he reproved those self-hating "Negroes" who distanced themselves from the sorrow songs of the ancestors, King never withheld his veneration of the slaves and their songs from white audiences either. King's reluctance to reveal himself before whites did not mean that he never admitted vulnerability to whites. If he told a less emotional version of his midnight crisis to the predominantly white trade book audience of *Stride toward Freedom,* it may be the written character of the enterprise more than the race of the audience that shaped King's telling. Just as revealing as the differences in the two versions is the fact that King did disclose to whites his vulnerability and Sister Pollard's nurturing of him. Later chapters of this book will explore a stylized form of self-disclosure that King employed in his crossover talk, even dropping it right into his speech at the March on Washington.

The line between blackness and whiteness remained as fluid as ever in other ways. Dwelling on black lives did not preempt King's empathetic leaps into the imaginative worlds of others. The ultimate meaning of such swerves during his Kerala visit was revealed when King overcame what he called his "peevish" feelings. At that point, he was ready to embrace the Indian version of the universal form of the pariah identity: "Yes, I too am an untouchable. And all Negroes are untouchable." Similarly, despite his own racial wounds, King never lost the ability to enter the white racist mind in order to transform vengeance into theoretical understanding.

In the sermon "Mastering Our Fears" King dissected "our white brothers'" irrational fear of "us" in a fashion befitting the former head of the sociology club at Morehouse. "Because the presupposition of *anyone* who has to make that an issue is that the Negro, the member of a so-called *outgroup,* has a kind of impurity, a kind of ah, of, ah, inferiority and a kind of ah, afflicted being that will contaminate the worthfulness and the purity of the in-group." For good measure, he threw in an existential expression: racism "thingifies" us, collapsing racial insult into a larger category of threats to being.[1]

In affirming black pride, King did not hesitate to draw from Rabbi Liebman and other white sources to justify it. Some fictive folk pulpit did not suddenly dispel all the authority of Immanuel Kant. Even as King occasionally flirted with the word "brother" as if it meant the racial family, he still applied that word to white people. As the music of Handel made clear, blacks held no monopoly over that special connection to song. Ultimately, then, King's most powerful moments of racial feeling disclosed the limits as well as the power of blackness in his life. If this was true of the black content of King's sermons, it was no less true of his preaching style.

Preaching to his home congregation, an indignant King told the Ebenezer audience that America needed to repent. The Vietnam War weighed on King mightily; lately he had been tortured by images of Vietnamese children whose flesh had been burned with napalm. Opening a magazine of the 1960s to "a picture of a Vietnamese mother holding her dead baby," King froze, recalled Bernard Lee. "Then Martin just pushed the plate of food away from him. I looked up and said, 'Doesn't it taste any good?,' and he answered, 'Nothing will ever taste any good for me until I do everything I can to end that war.'"[2]

Throughout the period of King's deepening resolve to speak out against the Vietnam War, both friends and opponents assaulted him with pragmatic considerations. Stanley Levison worried about the dilution of focus and monitored the impact of King's antiwar oratory on direct-mail contributions. Many SCLC preachers didn't think Vietnam deserved the same prominence as black liberation. In a sign of the racialism churning among the field staff, Hosea Williams and Ben Clark were "pretty adamant they didn't want white folks around," recalls one white staffer. Clark said, "Youall white folks move this peace symbol over to the white side of town."

As he often did, the cautious King took some time to weigh his course, but ultimately he rejected the cold ledger of cost and gain. "At times you do things to satisfy your conscience and they may be altogether unrealistic or wrong tactically, but you feel better," King told Levison. "I know . . . I will get a lot of criticism and I know it can hurt SCLC . . . [but] I can no longer be cautious about this matter. I feel so deep in my heart that we are wrong in this country and the time has come for a real prophecy."[3] As on so many occasions for King—before Birmingham, before the Poor People's Campaign—faith compelled a faith act, really a series of faith acts.

Up in the Ebenezer pulpit, King let loose in righteous anger, calling forth thunderbolts of judgment to rain down on the land. "God didn't call America to engage in a senseless, unjust war. . . . And we are criminals in that war. We've committed more war crimes almost than any nation in the world, and I'm going to continue to say it. And we won't stop it because of our pride and our arrogance as a nation." "But," King warned America, "God has a way of even putting nations in their place. *(Amen)* The God that I worship has a way of saying, 'Don't play with me.' *(Yes)* He has a way of saying, as the God of the Old Testament used to say to the Hebrews, 'Don't play with me, Israel. Don't play with me, Babylon. *(Yes)* Be still and know that I'm God. And if you don't stop your reckless course, I'll rise up and break the backbone of your power.'"[4]

Such admonitions hardly sounded like the cheek-turning saint of the King holiday. The savant who casually dropped Buber's name sounded more like some fire-and-brimstone shouter, issuing jeremiads. As with the black content of King's sermons, this interjection of a more fervent voice into King's talk was not entirely a late 1960s aberration of a despondent prophet adrift in the madness of the times. King's resort to the vernacular, "I'm not playin'," hints at a different kind of talk in King's early preaching repertoire. His prophetic voice, even when submerged during the Dexter years, managed to insinuate itself through subtle and not-so-subtle clues. The folksier style that King adopted in a Detroit church in 1954 around the same time he delivered "Three Dimensions" at Dexter also indicates we should not underestimate the power of the Dexter environment to shape King's style to its expectations.

Richard Jordan, a student at Alabama State College and an occasional driver for King, was amazed to discover this less restrained side of his minister. A deacon at Dexter where his family were longtime members, sometime in the late 1950s Jordan drove King up to preach at Sixteenth Street Baptist Church in Birmingham for the Women's Capital State Convention. The performance, Jordan observed, was "vintage King" and "moving as always." But he was "stunned when near the end of his sermon my pastor began to whoop." Jordan had never heard King whoop, had never seen him "bring it home" and get happy at Dexter. "After the service," Jordan continued, "I said: 'Reverend King, you whooped today.' I paused and added: 'I have never heard you whoop at Dexter.'

"'Well,' he began with a smile, 'the sisters at Dexter never talk to me when I am preaching like the old sisters did here today.'"[5]

One typically associates such fire with the Baptist firebrands who embarrassed the young King. But King too had fire—he could get fiery-glad, and occasionally fiery-mad, before the right kind of audience. The coexistence of fire and polish was no more contradictory than any of the other combinations of raw and refinement that King enacted in his oratory. The same mix of "high" and "low" could be seen in a paradoxical concession, dipping into the vernacular in the service of proper diction. Anticipating a time of integrated churches, King lapsed into "we going" and insisted, "Preachers? We going to get ready for integration, we can't spend all of our time trying to learn how to whoop and holler. *(Yes, Lord)* We've got to study some. [applause] *(All right, Yes).*" On that same occasion, right after he had criticized black ministers who preached a black gospel and dismissed it as a minstrel carnival—"Not a Negro gospel *(No man)*; not a gospel merely to get people to shout and kick over benches"—King immediately followed his seeming disdain with a shift in direction: "Now I'm going to holler a little tonight, because I want to get it over to you. *(Yes)* [laughter]. I'm going to be a Negro tonight [laughter]."[6]

"I'm going to be a Negro tonight" echoed the language from the FBI tapes, "I'm not a Negro tonight." Yet while both played with the idea of being a Negro as a state one could enter or quit, the jocular instance in the sermon lacked the ache of any real longing to flee blackness. Instead, it had the feeling of letting loose with one's own kind that typified King's banter with his SCLC colleagues. The inside joke functioned on many levels. Literally, it embraced a version of blackness conjured by white stereotype and snooty black prejudice. But it did so facetiously—no one really believed that King thought being a Negro could be reduced to hollering. At the same time, as with the kidding about "chicken eating preachers," it dared to speak the rude thought that maybe there was a bit of truth to it. This defiance of the need to step gingerly disarmed the sting of any cartoon rendering. Better yet, it created the opportunity for a good laugh at oneself and one's people.

In a whole host of ways, the more down-home voice implied in "I'm gonna be a Negro tonight, I'm gonna holler" could hardly be missed. The content of King's preaching motivated John Lewis to remain in the rhetorical moment, but it was its musical quality that first transfixed him, exuding a knowing familiarity that enticed Lewis to enter the occasion in the first place. "The voice held me right from the start," he said. Lewis recognized "[a] deep voice, clearly well trained and well schooled in the rhythmic, singsong, old-style tradition of black Baptist preaching we call whooping." All of its signature elements—the "cadence, with lots of crescendos and dramatic pauses and drawing out of word endings as if holding a note in a song"—made it sound "so much like singing. He really could make his words *sing*."[7]

Throughout his ministry, King's voice was as agile as a ballet dancer—twisting and turning, rising and falling in complex rhythms and moods. His emotive range increased less than its intensity. King's deliberate rhythm could congeal into a molasses-slow pace of near lugubriousness as he extended vowels for seconds. He could bend words and stretch them as if they were notes, shaping them into emphatic intervals. Quickening his rhythm, he might raise pitch and loudness, spiraling upwards toward a peak of near-shouting; then he might put on the brakes and swoop down to a whisper. His voice could tremble and quaver. King's use of repetition reinforced the power of his rhythmic waves. In front of the more responsive Ebenezer congregation, the density of sound was even greater. Here King came closer to full-throated versions of moans, shouts, and chant. The congregation propelled him forward on a tide of call and shout, ratifying his message and wrapping him in communal embrace.

All the while, King never abandoned that auditory mark he used as a substitute for whooping, the sound figure "ohhh." Sometimes it had a wincing quality. It could be filled with pathos, at times preceding King's tender "I know," as if he had leapt right inside the audience's mind to absorb their pain. A grave, admonitory quality could suffuse it. As a prelude to "it has a power," "ohhh" was a channel to divine mysteries when King sang praises to the better way of Jesus. These vocal accents explain why reading King's sermons, as opposed to hearing them, so often disappoints; shorn of lilt and resonance, pitch and inflection, they "sound" almost lifeless.

King's crescendos powerfully embodied the emotive quality of his preaching. King did not always end on a high; he could peak before the very end, then gradually come down to a more placid plane in a husky whisper, almost spent: "The interruptions are coming, / whoever you are / They are coming your way."[8] Such variation in timing intensified the power of his classic calm-to-storm runs. On occasion, King drew on the full array of millennial imagery, fusing the poetic and the prophetic as he brought the congregation to the heights of emotion with him. After combining the three dimensions of height, breadth, and depth into a complete life, King hurled himself right into the words of prophets as if no border could separate them, and as he did so, he came as close as he ever did to actually singing the climax:

> And when you get all three of these together,
> you can walk and never get weary.
> You can look up and see the morning stars singing together,
> and the sons of God shouting for joy.
> When you get all of these working together in your very life,
> judgment will roll down like waters,
> and righteousness like a mighty stream.
> When you get all the three of these together,

the lamb will lie down with the lion.
When you get all three of these together,
you look up and every valley will be exalted,
and every hill and mountain will be made low;
the rough places will be made plain,
and the crooked places straight;
and the glory of the Lord shall be revealed
and all flesh will see it together. . . .
When you get all three of these together,
You will recognize that out of one blood
God made all men to dwell upon the face of the earth . . .[9]

As the force of finishing blurred the borders among preaching, chanting, and singing, King at times glided from homily to song with no transition, going right into the words of the gospel hymn "Never Alone" ("I hear sin breakers") or the "Battle Hymn of the Republic" ("Mine eyes have seen the glory of the coming of the Lord"). These elements of song, moan, and chant were more than techniques. Just as the Afro-Baptist audience took "singing in the spirit" as a sign of God's presence, the intensity of King's cry, "Mine eyes have seen the coming of the Lord," offered a rapturous foretaste of eternity. Style was not adornment or accessory but a sign of the joyous message of love and redemption.

Even while hooping, King still drew on Shakespeare and Schopenhauer, still recited "sound and fury signifying nothing" and "life is endless pain with a painful end." The dignified King also got jokey, telling about the man who kept chickens in the basement of his house next to a river; after a flood drowned his prized birds, he complained to the landlord, who asked him, "Why you going to move? Why don't you try ducks?" As the congregation broke into laughter, King dissolved any trace of diminished gravitas, drawing out his moral prescription in a poetic chant: "Sometimes try ducks in your soul / Waters of disappointment can't drown you / Because you can ride about over the water, / just sail above it."[10] He became the wise older brother, telling about the time his foolish sibling gave in to all-too-human impetuosity and retaliated in kind when approaching night drivers failed to dim their high beams.

Prefigured by "the Bible tells us," King's increasingly stripped-down sermons vindicated their truth through extended biblical stories about

Silas in Crete, Lazarus and Dives, and Nicodemus. The most famous such sermon was "The Drum Major Instinct." Up front King announced, "And our text for [this] morning is taken from a very familiar passage in the tenth chapter as recorded by Saint Mark. Beginning with the thirty-fifth verse of that chapter, we read these words: And James and John, the sons of Zebedee, came unto him saying, 'Master, we would that thou shouldest do for us whatever we shall desire.'" When Jesus asks what he can do, they replied, "Grant unto us that we may sit, one on thy right hand, and the other on thy left hand, in thy glory." King took this premise of selfish desire and worked it not into a diatribe against puffery but a call to channel ambition into serving others and working for justice. Toward the end, King concretized this positive harnessing: don't remember me, he said, for the Nobel Prize and all the other accolades. "When I have to meet my day, I don't want a long funeral. And if you get somebody to deliver the eulogy, tell them not to talk too long *(Yes)*." Instead, they should say "Martin Luther King, Jr. tried to love somebody . . . did try to feed the hungry *(Yes)* . . . did try in my life to clothe those who were naked *(Yes)* . . . did try in my life to visit those who were in prison *(Lord)*." Then King squared the circle as he returned to the opening of the sermon. "Yes, Jesus, I want to be on your right or your left side, *(Yes)* not for any selfish reason. . . . I just want to be there in love and in justice and in truth and in commitment to others, so that we can make of this old world a new world."[11]

The finale of "Drum Major" might seem to reflect King's moroseness in the year before his assassination. Despite his own disavowal of any "morbid" state, his friends were struck by what they took to be his preoccupation with death. He seemed depressed, jittery, remote. Still, the admission that he wanted to be on Jesus' left side or right side, the meticulous dwelling on his own funeral, and the desire to control what people would say about him after his death reflected a general feature of his mature preaching: the willingness to let black congregations glimpse a more private inner man, not just the discouragement he felt as the deliverer of black people but a more universal anguish.

Unlike the professorial distance of King's early preaching, the quavering voice that often accompanied such revelations betrayed an intimacy that invited personal response. "I don't know this morning about you, but I can make a testimony. *(Yes, sir. That's my life)*," a fragile King confessed in

"Unfulfilled Dreams." Only weeks before his death, he described a civil war inside the soul: "And every time you set out to be good, there's something pulling on you, telling you to be evil. It's going on in your life *(Preach it)*." Maybe he was hinting at his own tortured soul when he admitted, "And there are times that all of us know somehow that there is a Mr. Hyde and a Dr. Jekyll in us. And we end up having to cry out with Ovid, the Latin poet, 'I see and approve the better things of life, but the evil things I do.' . . . Or sometimes we even have to end up crying out with Saint Augustine as he said in his *Confessions,* 'Lord, make me pure, but not yet.' *(Amen)* We end up crying out with the Apostle Paul, *(Preach it)* 'The good that I would I do not: And the evil that I would not, that I do.'"[12]

If there was any doubt that King was alluding to his own demons, he dispelled it moments later. "You don't need to go out this morning saying that Martin Luther King is a saint. Ohhh, no. *(Yes)* I want you to know this morning that I'm a sinner like all of God's children. But I want to be a good man. *(Yes. Preach it)* And I want to hear a voice saying to me one day, 'I take you in and I bless you, because you try.' *(Yes, Amen).*" Earlier King had come even closer to confession in the agonizing urgency of a 1965 version of "Is the Universe Friendly?": "St. Augustine, what have you figured? In your confessions, you talked how you used to live in adultery, you talked how one day you said Lord make me pure but not yet. You talked how you were destroying the fiber of your soul through lust and fornication and adultery. What happened to you Augustus?"[13]

But loneliness and suffering far outstripped sin as preoccupations in King's sermons. In these areas too, King showed doubt and despair, revealing a part of himself at odds with the qualities of control and poise that were key to his crossover rhetoric. There were times when King virtually sobbed the phrases, "never alone, never alone, never alone," with a naked quality that evoked his own longing. Friends and lovers glimpsed this deep solitude. His musings on philea, or friendship, in which he urgently invoked the friend to whom you can confess all your inner doubts, at times had an unsettling, personal edge.

Typically, though, King was not a supplicant in need of balm but its dispenser. Clayborne Carson rightly observes that King's Christology was more concerned with social teachings than with personal redemption.[14] But still another role, the therapeutic one of assuaging pain and restoring the spirit, came to the fore in some of King's most powerful preaching. In his "guidelines" for a church, King mentions right off "healing the broken-hearted" even before delivering the captives. In a churchly translation of his concern with "maternal" nurturing of black people, King was a consoler who never left his congregants in the dark places. "I love you, I'd rather die than hurt you," he told the Ebenezer congregation. He staved off their world-weariness with a joyous message of faith in God and the redemptive powers of Jesus Christ.

Captured by the poetics of darkness and light, the tension between hopelessness and hope was at the center of King's homilies, in its starkly personal as much as social or racial aspect. "Disappointment, sorrow, and despair are born at midnight," he told the Ebenezer congregants in "A Knock at Midnight," but, he reassured them, "morning follows. 'Weeping may endure for a night,' says the Psalmist, 'but joy cometh in the morning.'"[15] "Are you disillusioned this morning?" King asked the Dexter congregation. "Are you confused about life? Have you been disappointed? Have your highest dreams and hopes been buried? You about to give up in despair? I say to you, 'Don't give up, because God has another light, and it is the light that can shine amid the darkness of a thousand midnights. . . . They put the light out on Good Friday, but God brought it back on Easter morning.'"[16] In another sermon, after telling the story of the jilted lover who leapt to his death, King addressed his congregation directly with a personal "you" and "this morning" that anchored the story with an immediacy that flowed into the beat of the imperative, "Don't jump, Ebenezer":

> And I close this morning, Ebenezer,
> by urging you not to jump.
> When the interruptions of life come,
> reach down into the deepest bottoms of your soul
> and you will find something
> that you didn't realize was there.
> Don't jump this morning![17]

As with his backstage banter, King's religious images were shaped by the settings in which he deployed them. King also offered consolation in the mass meetings, but the theology of hope, lifted out of the church service, took on new meanings in the midst of mobilization. So it's important to state the obvious: the preacher King was a classical pastoral figure, counseling against despair, affirming the meaning of life in the midst of evil, spreading the good news of Jesus Christ and God's love.

Music for King was the incarnation of hope, even the capacity to hope; to make music was to make meaning. King drew out the more existential theology symbolized by "singing in the spirit," which he also translated into Tillich's language of "courage to be." Not long after describing the plunge of a jilted lover in "The Interruptions of Life," King launched into a remarkable prose-poem which gained power from the drumbeat that accentuated the close of each of four moments of musical creation— "Ohhh, when life's problems hit ya, / you don't jump! / But somehow think up a song, produce a song!" The first part began by repeating that sound figure:

> Ohhh, I would say to you,
> that Handel was down low.
> There was a day when Handel
> was all 'bout to break down physically,
> had no money,
> creditors were hounding him,
> ready to send him off to jail.
> And he had about given up.
> But he didn't jump,
> and I'm glad he didn't jump.
> Because at that last moment,
> he wrote "The Hallelujah Chorus"
> and "The Great Messiah."
> Don't jump, go produce a song!

King moved on to Schubert, who suffered a bad love affair. But instead of jumping, he created "Ave Maria" ("Don't jump, produce a song!"). King's kin—"my foreparents and your foreparents"—also knew the heartache of slavery. But they didn't jump either; they too produced songs ("Don't jump! Just produce a song!"). Finally, King turned to the people right in front of him with the direct address of "you":

> Every now and then
> when it gets dark to you,
> Go on somewhere

and just start singing,
Amazing Grace,
How sweet the sound.
That saved a wretch like me,
I once was lost
but now am found,
Was blind but now I see,
Produce a song![18]

Keeping faith lay at the heart of King's practical theology. Determination was essential to it, which for King was a special kind of moral stamina with "an in-spite-of" quality that the slaves had in abundance—"something on the inside." Things will fail you, the pleasures of the flesh will fail you, health will fail you. "But my ultimate faith is in the God of the universe, / The God who will make a way out of no way / The God who can transform dark yesterdays into bright tomorrows." This was the ultimate sense in which King's preaching voice was personal: in its faith in a personal God.

King began "Why Jesus Called a Man a Fool" by affirming that God—"And I'm going on in believing in him. *(Yes)* You'd better know him, and know his name, and know how to call his name. *(Yes)*"—with a seemingly gratuitous swerve into foreign "ways of saying" and a catalogue of his audience's verbal failings: "You may not know philosophy. You may not be able to say with Alfred North Whitehead that he's the Principle of Concretion. You may not be able to say with Hegel and Spinoza that he is the Absolute Whole. You may not be able to say with Plato that he's the Architectonic Good. You may not be able to say with Aristotle that he's the Unmoved Mover."[19]

These phantom abstractions were just a foil. At times, King's rebuttal took the subtle form of a gentle preface—"but sometimes you can get poetic about it if you know him"—that preceded King's heralding of a different way of knowing God, linked to his ancestors. "You begin to know that our brothers and sisters in distant days were right. Because they did know him as a rock in a weary land, as a shelter in the time of starving, as my water when I'm thirsty and then my bread in a starving land." On another occasion, King transmuted linguistic deficiency into moral sufficiency with more prescriptive force. "We don't need to know all of these high-sounding terms. *(Yes)* Maybe we have to know him and discover him another way. *(Oh yeah)* One day you ought to rise up and say"—and here the congregation came alive, greeting each of King's rhythmic phrases with a rising chorus of yelling that was especially marked on "my everything":

> I know him because he's a lily of the valley. *(Yes)*
> He's a bright and morning star. *(Yes)*
> He's a Rose of Sharon.
> He's a battle-ax in the time of Babylon. *(Yes)*
> And then somewhere
> you ought to just reach out and say,
> "He's my everything.
> He's my mother and my father.
> He's my sister and my brother.
> He's a friend to the friendless."
> This is the God of the universe.[20]

The juxtaposition of words like "architectonic" with sensuous images plucked from the folk pulpit and gospel music underscored the rival worlds King had known. Obviously, the equivalence of translation was only a guise. "All the words we don't need to know" were trumped by the need to "know him . . . another way." Such verbal acrobatics revived an old quarrel with King's graduate training and brought it right into the midst of Ebenezer Baptist Church. King's willingness to "get poetic about it" was a less Byzantine version of the repudiation that drove his dissertation. In his thesis, he had defended the theological approach of "personalism," which held that God was a distinctive personality, against the cold and abstract theology of Paul Tillich. Despite the abstruse refinements, the dissertation's argument repeated the same rejection of abstraction that was implied by "lilies of the field," "my mother and my father," and "bright shining star." There was a great irony here, which only underlined King's boundary-spanning role—crossing over into "high-sounding language" to repudiate high-sounding language.

King's sermons depicted a God who was both powerful and approachable. To those skeptics who went around pronouncing the death of God, King had a simple answer: if you can't prove God, you can't kill him either. As long as love was alive, God was alive; as long as truth was alive,

God was alive; as long as justice was alive, God is alive. "You can't kill God!" King practically shouted. "God can't die!" That God was as loving as He was immanent; he was the transcendent companion, the "friend to the friendless." King always reminded, "God so loved the world that he sacrificed his beloved son." This is what Titus, despairing in Crete, needed to understand. Maybe Crete was a hard place, full of evil beasts and idle gluttons. All of us, King reminded the congregation, know that place: We all struggle in our own Crete. "But whenever you struggle in Crete, don't think you're by yourself. He walks with you. He throws his long arms of protection around you. We're all God's children and He struggles with us!" And then King slipped into the words of the hymn, "You're never alone, you're never alone."[21]

To "never be alone!" is the promise in Hebrews, "For he hath said, 'I will never leave thee.'" As Matthew 28:20 puts it, "I am with you always, to the very end of the age." King constantly sampled from the hymn "Never Alone." In the sermon "Making the Best of a Bad Mess," the choir sang the song even before King began to preach. In his midnight show-down with despair, King heard "God promise he would never leave me."

In the safe embrace of the black church, King was not the purveyor of ethnic banter, ribald humor, and carousing companionship. Nor was he mainly a learned scholar or a movement leader or even a race man. Often a prophet, he was also the apostle spreading the good news of the Lord's redeeming grace. More than a deliverer, he was a healer of fractured souls, translating the ethic of love into tender practice with his own congregants. In these roles, Jesus was King's touchstone.

Abraham Joshua Heschel, the distinguished rabbi who was King's friend, may not have fully understood the intensity of King's relationship with his savior. Susannah Heschel, the rabbi's daughter, observed, "The preference King gave to the Exodus motif over the figure of Jesus certainly played a major role in linking the two men intellectually and religiously; for Heschel, the primacy of the Exodus in the civil rights movement was a major step in the history of Christian-Jewish relations." Rabbi Richard Rubenstein, who left a meeting of Conservative Judaism's Rabbinical Assembly in 1963 to support King in Birmingham, was struck by the primacy of "the basic religious metaphor, repeated by the Negroes over and over again . . . of Moses and the children of Israel. . . . There were almost no Christological references in either their preaching or their singing.

This was Mosaic religion. . . . No mention of the problem of the inner psychological man was made in the congregations we visited."[22]

That error grew out of the occasions on which Heschel and Rubenstein encountered King, as well as King's own rhetorical strategy in such circumstances. The logic of ecumenical black-Jewish encounters encouraged a focus on the shared iconography of Moses and the prophets, rather than a parading of King's love for Jesus. Moreover, the practical imperatives of mobilization in the big campaigns that drew rabbis naturally highlighted the theme of Exodus, the struggle with Pharaoh, and coming up out of bondage.

In ordinary sermons, however, the figure of Jesus overshadowed Moses.[23] Maybe the fact of a birthday partially explains the exultant homage to Jesus with which King closed his 1965 Christmas sermon. But the little boy who enraptured a church audience when he sang "I Want To Be More and More Like Jesus" grew into the man who never stopped offering praise songs to his savior. Toward the end of "Loving Your Enemies," King sang out, "And all around the world this morning, we can hear the glad echo of heaven ring," and then immediately moved into a hymn, "His kingdom spreads from shore to shore, / Till moon shall wane and wax no more." King heard another chorus singing, "All hail the power of Jesus' name!" and another one too: "Hallelujah, hallelujah! He's King of Kings and Lord of Lords. Hallelujah, hallelujah!"[24] Much like his own people, King would remind, Christ was rejected, scorned, and abused. Still, "he came in the fullness of time, and nothing could stop him. They tried it, didn't they?" As the tone of passionate, controlled urgency intensified, King fell into a hooping meter whose repetitions evoked the tidal power of "an idea whose time has come":

> Peter denied him,
> And that didn't stop him,
> Judas betrayed him,
> And that didn't stop him. . . .
> And then they took him to a cross,
> And that didn't stop him. . . .
> No grave could hold him.
> No nail was great enough
> to pierce his truth.

No hammer was large enough
to drive out his sense of compassion.
No cross was strong enough
to hold his justice.
No rock was powerful enough
to hold his sense of mercy.[25]

Wallowing in sin, Nicodemus did not grasp the simple remedy for what ailed him. King pointed out that Jesus "didn't say, 'Now Nicodemus, you stop gambling.' He didn't say, 'Now Nicodemus, if you, ahh, drink too much liquor, stop drinking liquor.' He didn't say, 'Nicodemus, if you are committing adultery, stop committing adultery.' He didn't say, 'Nicodemus, if you are stealing money, stop stealing.' . . . He looked at Nicodemus, and said, 'Nicodemus,'" and now King had reached the peak of his intensity, was practically shouting, "'You must be *born again.*'"[26]

You must be born again. A Lord that can make a way out of no way. The God my Daddy told me about. These declarations revealed the gap between King and secular liberals, as well as the non-churched part of the civil rights movement. The trappings of worldly learning never preempted King's bedrock faith in a personal God and his conviction that evil was ubiquitous in the world. When King preached against a religion with "too much soul in its feet," he did not do so in the name of a knowing rationalism so cultivated that it was "embarrassed to mention Jesus," as Abernathy described the Dexter ethos. He did so in the name of a "God that had to become real to me" in a way that God had not been at Crozer and Boston University, nor for that matter—and this is key—inside the walls of the Morehouse chapel or Ebenezer Baptist Church.

That fervent brand of religion did not contradict King's social gospel leanings. The one followed from the other. Prophetic chastisement was only the flip side of an intercessionary God with interests in this world that included race, social policy, and politics. "God," King would pronounce, "is not happy with the way his children are being treated." In "The Three Dimensions," descending from the topic of God's nature to the earthly realm of ungodly, racist, and "sick" southern governors, King was simply following out the logic of his conception of the almighty. "The God that I worship is a God that has a way of saying even to kings and even to governors, 'Be still, and know that I am God.' And God has not yet turned over this universe to [segregationist] Lester Maddox and Lurleen Wallace [wife of Alabama governor George Wallace]. Somewhere I read, 'The earth is the Lord's and the fulness [*sic*] thereof.'"[27]

King's answer to those blacks who wished he wouldn't preach so much about civil rights reflected his conviction that he had been called to the ministry. Maybe the congregation "called me to Ebenezer," King preached, "and you may turn me out of here, but you can't turn me out of the ministry, because I got my guidelines and my anointment from God Almighty. And anything I want to say, I'm going to say it, from this pulpit."[28]

The God who could make a way out of no way required a great deal of his flock: establishing His kingdom on earth. The teachings of Jesus merely fleshed out the nuances involved in applying God's boundless love to the full compass of humanity. Therefore, King did not offer a liberal rights model of justice. Over and over, he preached the biblical obligation of human beings to care, which entailed a refusal to stand on the sidelines like some hard-hearted bystander while the broken-hearted suffered. As King preached the parable of the Good Samaritan (with some help from George Buttrick), Jesus plucked the question "Who is my neighbor?" out of thin air and "placed it on a dangerous curve between Jerusalem and Jericho *(He did, he did)*." The priest and the Levite strode right past a man left half dead by robbers, but King generously credited them with fear; they asked the wrong question: "If I stop to help this man, what will happen to me? *(That's right)*." By contrast, the good Samaritan asked a different question, "What will happen to this man if I do not stop to help him?"

But who was that man? King stressed that it was "a member of another race, who stopped and helped him." In another version of King's description of the parable, he widened the racial distance to underscore the universality of his message. The Samaritan was "a half-breed from a people with whom the Jews had no dealings." As for the man in need, King depicted Jesus as "in essence" saying, "I do not know his name. . . . He is anyone who lies in need at life's roadside." The Samaritan's famous encounter ordained not so much a right to recognition as a duty to recognize that extended "beyond the eternal accidents of race, religion, and nationality." Such universal altruism applied to the farthest reaches of mankind. The words of the slave preacher, "you ain't no nigger," were only the particular form of the general norm.[29]

Could we say that the King who "had fire locked up inside," trumpeted his zeal for Jesus, and told Nicodemus he must be born again was the "blacker" King? Equally true is that the more King hooped it up some, the more he eliminated the clutter of learning and concentrated the purity of his message of universal love. And the more he hooped it up over his career, the more his compass spread beyond blacks to all sorts of half-breeds and strangers—Vietnamese children burned by napalm, the starving homeless on the streets of Calcutta, Soviet Jews threatened with "spiritual genocide," American Indians and poor whites and Mexicans and the others he devoted his movement to nourishing—even the white jailers he made "brothers."

In "Drum Major," King told how when he was in jail the warden and guards had come to his cell to chat him up and convince him that integration, intermarriage, and demonstrations were wrong. "So I would get to preaching, and we would get to talking," King said, and he told the congregation that he asked them what they earned. "And when those brothers told me what they were earning, I said, 'Now, you know what? You ought to be marching with us. [Laughter] You're just as poor as Negroes.'" King broke it down for them: "'You are put in the position of supporting your oppressor, because through prejudice and blindness, you fail to see that the same forces that oppress Negroes in American society oppress poor white people. (Yes) And all you are living on is the satisfaction of your skin being white, and the drum major instinct of thinking that you are somebody big because you are white.'"[30]

King's 1965 version of "Is the Universe Friendly?" underscored this sense in which his "black" homilies were only incidentally black. What could be friendlier than God's overspilling love for all men, the relentless way "He takes us in," as King liked to put it. "It was always thought in those early days that God was the god of a particular tribe," King reflected. The Babylonians had their god Mardu, the surrounding cultures had Yahweh or Elohim or Jehovah. But "Jesus Christ and the writers of the New Testament remind men that God is not the god of a particular race, God is not the god of a particular tribe, God is not the god of a particular group." In contrast to all the "particular gods" that appear throughout history, Jesus, King preached, was a new kind of king, and that newness was embodied in the intricate, race-blind verbal rules that Christ prescribed. "Notice that when it says the world or when it says 'man,' it isn't talking about any particular man, it isn't talking about any particular race." Rather, when "Jesus talks about Him . . . he says, 'We must say our father. Not my father, not your father, but our father.' Meaning he's everybody's father. And God so loved the world, the whole of mankind."[31]

In the end, what God required—not what man required—was key to the King endeavor, and blackness was always secondary in this larger scheme of things. Over the years, the formulation of that requirement varied, but not the fact of it or its substance. The larger world often failed to grasp the key influences on King, insists Rev. C. T. Vivian, eager to correct the record: the books of Matthew, Mark, Luke, and John. The mission of the "inconvenient hero," as Vincent Harding dubbed King, followed from the inconvenience of his faith. "King wasn't like a prophet," says Vivian. "He was an actual prophet."[32]

The calling was, as Rabbi Heschel grasped, an ambivalent one. "The prophet," he wrote, "is a man who feels fiercely. God has thrust a burden upon his soul, and he is bowed and stunned at man's fierce greed. Frightful is the agony of man; no human voice can convey its full terror. Prophecy is the voice that God has lent to the silent agony, a voice to the plundered poor, to the profaned riches of the world. It is a form of living, a crossing point of God and man. God is raging in the prophet's words."[33]

"And through his prophets," King preached to his Ebenezer flock in "Guidelines for a Constructive Church," "and above all through his son Jesus Christ, he said that 'there are some things that my church must do.'" King recalled the day when "our Lord and Master" had gone to the temple and declared, "The Spirit of the Lord is upon me, because he hath anointed me *(Yes, sir)* to preach the gospel to the poor, *(Yes, sir)* he hath sent me to heal the brokenhearted, to preach deliverance to the captives, and recovering of sight to the blind, *(Yes)* to set at liberty them that are bruised . . ."[34]

Part III

KING IN THE MASS MEETINGS

"The Lord will make a way out of no way"

"If we are wrong," Martin Luther King declared at the first meeting of the Montgomery Improvement Association that would take Rosa Parks's refusal to cede her seat to the next level of defiance, "Jesus of Nazareth was merely a utopian dreamer that never came down to earth *(Yes)* [Applause]."[1] Not quite a dare, the convoluted equation of the movement's mission with the ministry of Jesus was a daring display of King's boast that he had been anointed to preach the gospel of the Lord.

King was only one of many who perfected this hybrid talk that one could call a political sermon, even though the distinction in that term between politics and religion might have affronted the vanguard who were part of the army of the Lord. It's better to call it the prophetic tradition on the ground. The political culture fashioned by the churched part of the movement was a far cry from liberal perfectionism and sunny rationalism. At its core was the conviction of a twin presence: that evil was irrepressibly here in this world, but so was God and the possibility of realizing his Kingdom on earth.

This role was King's most decisive, the one that leveraged the others—hero of the race, racial ambassador, national icon. The glorification rested on a prosaic foundation of carpool pick-up points and the meetings needed to orchestrate them. Beginning with Montgomery and continuing to his death, King spoke at countless rallies convened to challenge racism, dismantle segregation, and achieve the vote. There were hallowed sanctums of legendary campaigns like Brown Chapel AME in Selma and 16th Street Baptist Church in Birmingham. There were vast mobilizations in Albany, Georgia and St. Augustine. There were rousing meetings in rural churches in Marion, Yazoo City, and Demopolis. In all these places passionate, often religion-soaked talk, a staple of claim and defiance in the southern movement, figured in King's addresses to black people. In all these places the rites of insurgency fashioned speech occasions with their own special feel, rules, and rituals.

It's fair to call them black occasions, as long as this is accompanied by the usual qualifications. Even in the early years, some whites were present, if only reporters or an occasional itinerant folk singer. After Bloody Sunday, the final leg of the jaunt from Selma to Montgomery included dozens of luminaries such as Marlon Brando and Rabbi Abraham Joshua Heschel. Police surveillance as well as FBI monitoring ensured some white presence, at least the furtive sort provided by wiretapping. When Wyatt Tee Walker noted elliptically at a Birmingham meeting, "I'm speaking in parables," King's colleague was not honoring the black preaching tradition but was alluding to the vulnerability of the meetings to penetration, as Bull Connor's conspicuous, stone-faced detectives attested.

The "blackness" of the occasions was relative in a more profound sense as well. King's efforts to mobilize southern blacks were enacted mainly in black churches.[2] The audiences were disproportionately female, often rural and unlettered, and intensely churched. But as with SCLC ideology and the ultimate concerns of King and his colleagues, the blackness was hard to separate from the Christian and southern character of the people and the places they gathered. The mix of qualities was embedded in the reassuring feel of church benches and preachers' cadences and the tropes of deliverance. "Sharecroppers, poor people, would come to the mass meetings because they were *in the church*," explained John Lewis. "People saw the mass meetings as an extension of the Sunday services."[3]

At the outset of the bus boycott, no one even thought to assemble anywhere but a church. That instinctive decision gave the mass meeting its basic expressive accessories—altar calls, fervent preaching, call and shout. At the start of the Montgomery bus boycott, after the tumultuous applause that greeted the entrance of King and Abernathy, the minister of music led the crowd in "What a Fellowship, What a Joy Divine," the first hymn of the Montgomery movement. "Unbeknownst to us," Abernathy reflected, "we were also creating the format for later meetings." Despite the rapture, then, the meetings were highly stylized, with their own conventions of performance. Accordingly, King's oratory was carried along by moans, shouts, rhythm, intensity, crescendo, and song. His repetition reinforced the poetry of insurgency, generating a pulse no matter what style of speaking he selected: "Today I want to tell the city of Selma *(Tell them, Doctor),* today I want to say to the state of Alabama *(Yes, sir),* today I want to say to the people of America and the nations of the world . . ." King brought church crescendos right into his meeting oratory. At the close of the Selma-to-Montgomery march, after all the buildup, he was hooping hope, transforming eschatology into political faith, and hurtling toward his peak, virtually singing, "Mine eyes have seen the glory of the coming of the Lord *(Yes, sir)."*[4]

There was thus a lively two-way traffic of common images, themes, and quotations between King's Sunday preaching and his mass meeting orations. The mystery of black song, the catechism of the spirituals, and the worship of slave ancestors made their appearance in both. The riff from Jeremiah ("Is there a balm?"), familiar lines from Longfellow, and the trinity of the forms of love migrated from church to movement. He also spoke the words of the prophets in the meetings, fusing Amos, the movement, and himself into a powerful "we" that lifted the prophet's words as if they were his own: "And we are determined here in Montgomery to work and fight until justice runs down like water *(Yes)* [Applause], and righteousness like a mighty stream *(Keep talking)* [Applause]."[5]

Over and over, King invoked Exodus, envisioning the promised land that awaited his people. Over and over, too, he invited his audiences to participate in the dramaturgy of resurrection, telling them in public what he wrote Coretta while he was in Reidsville State Prison: "This is the cross we must bear for the freedom of our people. . . . Our suffering is not in vain." As King entered Holt Street Baptist Church after he was convicted of violating the Alabama anti-boycott laws, a speaker hailed him as "he who [was] nailed to the cross for us" and "he's next to Jesus himself." Nowhere was the telling of the story of the cross as sustained, theatrical, and contrived as in Birmingham. "Ralph Abernathy and I have decided that we would like to feel we are suffering with Christ on the days that he suffered on the cross. And we are going to make our move [and go to jail] on Good Friday."[6]

King's meeting oratory was graced by the same blends and swerves that gave his sermons complexity. The specifics varied across settings, but the mix of passion and polish was a constant. He combined Longfellow with slave dialect. He could slide from poetry to prophecy to psychology. During that first Holt Street address, right after King flirted with the apostasy that maybe Christ never came down, the civil religious King pronounced, "If we are wrong, the Supreme Court of this nation is wrong *(Yes sir)*. [Applause] If we are wrong, the Constitution of the United States is wrong *(Yes)* [Applause]." The didactic King gave his theologian's parsing of the Niebuhr distinction, "I want to tell you this evening that it is not enough for us to talk about love . . . There is another side called justice. And justice is really love in calculation *(All right)*. Justice is love correcting that which revolts against love *(Well)*." In case that was too elliptical, he translated "correction" into its more vivid, vernacular double, handing over to "the God that stands before the nations" the task of saying, "Be still and know that I'm God *(Yeah)*, that if you don't obey me I will break the backbone of your power *(Yeah)*."[7]

King's grandiloquence was almost always at work, elevating the people and poeticizing their pain and struggle. The imagery of movement and stasis, midnight and morning, sun and darkness, warmth and cold provided physical depictions of the stride to freedom. He warned of a "season of suffering" and observed "majestic scorn" and shuddered at "alpine chill." Evil was not just incarnate in the world; it was "choking to death in the dusty roads and streets of this state." In little churches in Black Belt hamlets, he cited Carlyle and James Weldon Johnson.

King's place in a sequence, his frequent pairing with his sidekick Ralph Abernathy, only strengthened the impression of King's oratory as high-flying. Abernathy knew the precise moment to insert an "ah shucks now" or to berate his folk audience, "I knew the people of Selma were dumb and backwards but . . ." After insisting that "we don't want to be the white man's brother-in-law" but his brother, Abernathy looked around an Albany, Georgia, mass meeting and noted the variegated colors of the audience in a burst of poetry:

> And it appears to us
> As we look around this audience
> Tonight
> That it is *he*
> Who has tried to be our brother-in-law.
> [pandemonium, rich shouts, exclamations on the truth of the
>   poetry . . .][8]

155

The contrast between the two men could be seen vividly at one mass meeting in the aftermath of a flourish by King. Before he began to speak, the church was energized by the gut-wrenching version of a favorite song of the Birmingham movement, "99 and ½ Won't Do." As King explicated agape, philea, and eros, the call and shout faded. Soon after, the minister introduced Abernathy: "I wonder do you feel all right? I said, do you feel all right? All right, at this time, we're happy to present a man who knows his lesson," and Abernathy replied, "It's good to know your lesson, and it's good to know that you know your lesson, and it's good to know that somebody else knows that you know your lesson. I'm glad to be back home tonight."

Noting that he and King "travel all over the world" together, Abernathy wanted the audience to know that "there's one thing that we have that is different. He's a native of Georgia, and I am a native of Alabama. [laughter, clapping] And I been telling him all along that Alabama was alright, that the people of Alabama are all right . . . I been telling him that we know the meaning of that word he called eraas." Drawing the word out in an exaggerated, breathy fashion, Abernathy teasingly countered King with a more leering version of eros. "He says that eraas is that type of love that moooves you. And he went on to say what it might be." Here Abernathy began a syncopated rhythm that bordered on the profane—"It might be the way your lover walks. And it might be the way your lover talks"—and then shifted on a dime: "I was glad he didn't tell you what it *really* is. [laughter] But that's the way people talk from Georgia. In Alabama we'll take the 'it might be' out and let you know just plainly what it is."9

Was this the people's revenge on the pedant? Better to see it as a jocular version of the "dozens" that celebrated a united black community rich enough to span plain and fancy, high purpose and goofing. It also testified to the richness of the meetings themselves, where synergies of playful and somber, sacred and secular, inspired a buzzing creativity that further inspired King. If King's most celebrated eloquence was "more or less studied, polished," the extraordinary southern reporter Pat Watters could see up close from his perch in the meetings that "the eloquence he found in the little churches of the movement was something else—a weaving of appropriate themes from past speeches, sudden bursts of innovative, emotional talk out of the immediacy of events and the meeting, wonderous structuring of metaphor."10

The King who spoke at the meetings shared a great deal with the preacher King, but the parallels were never the whole story. The purposes were too different, the causal force of the occasion too great. King's rally talk often took place in the heat of battle under the watchful eyes of local lawmen, racist mobs, and Klansmen. After King had roused his troops to march out through the church doors, the occasion continued outdoors in a moving procession of singing, praying, and chanting. The end point, often institutions like the local registrar's office or the courthouse, and the litany of demands indicated the gritty purposes at work.

Accordingly, the King who performed here was not the ambassador of agape, even if he did preach the gospel of love. Nor was he an agent of theodicy, although he did speak to his listeners' perplexity at God's apparent passivity in the face of racist evil. If he dispensed balm to his black audience, those interludes yielded pride of place to his main business. The King of the meetings was an exhorter, leading his people up from bondage. Even as he communed with their faith and fervency, the mutual rapture they achieved inside the mass meetings always pointed beyond, to the larger environment of purpose and demand which convened those meetings in the first place.

The five chapters of Part III explore King's mobilization talk. Acknowledging the communion that King established with black people provides the starting point. Yet the "blackness" of even those moments was always qualified by other, universal concerns: the "blackness" pointed outward toward membership in the larger American order; it could never dislodge the inclusive tenets of King's Christian humanism; and it often was in the service of the universal needs of all social movements. Prefigured by the tensions in the SCLC between the tough and the tender, the decisive crossings in the meetings were as much between prophecy and pragmatism as between black and white.

TEN

Beloved Black Community

"There lived a race of people, black people, of fleecy locks . . .
who stood up for their rights"

It's a truism that the mass meetings inspired intense racial feelings. Less obvious is the intricacy of that communion as it spilled over from church to rally. As the choreography of King and Abernathy showed, a King speech was part of a field of black sound constituted by speakers' words, opening and closing prayers, congregational singing, gospel choirs, solo song leaders, amen corners, audience validations of "amen" and "well," moaning, chanting, groaning, sighing, yelling. The density of sound reflected the fluidity of boundaries between all the parties present, who often reached an emotive peak in freedom singing, in the interlinking of arms when singing "We Shall Overcome," and in countless small rites that affirmed a resonant black "we." This is why one can't really speak of King's rally talk as bounded bits of rhetoric. In a very tangible sense, King's black listeners were co-producers of those moments.

At the first meeting of the Montgomery boycott, the gentle applause that greeted King and Abernathy as they entered the church gradually intensified until it exploded into a full fifteen minutes of wild cheering. Just as "the sisters in Birmingham" catalyzed the whooping that in turn provoked their response, the same cascade of mutual provocation was at work on King even before he spoke his convulsive lines, "There comes a time . . ."

In Albany, Georgia, in 1962, the merging of black voices started before King ever got near the altar. Fifteen hundred residents had packed two nearby churches, Shiloh and Mount Zion, linked together by a jerry-rigged sound system. "The singing held everything together, even the two churches, which swayed in time to the same song, sending only a heartbeat of an echo back and forth across Whitney Avenue. King's progress through the nearby streets seemed to pass by conduction upstream through a river of sound." As King approached, the churches reverberated with the sound of "Aaa-men, Aaa-men, Aaaaaaaaa-men, A-men, A-men," which turned into "Everybody say freedom / Everybody say freedom . . ."[1]

"[A] great 'Yea' shout from the people" greeted King as he entered the church and headed toward the pulpit, "the shout grew louder, one sustained cry of joy and welcome," the people were on their feet, waving their arms, and King was waving back at them. At some point the shouting turned into singing, "a mighty resumption of 'FREE-DOM . . .,'" which turned into

> Martin King says freedom.
> FREE-DOM! FREE-DOM!
> Let the white man say Freedom
> Let the white man say Freedom
> Let the white man say Freedom
> Free-DOM
> Free-DOM.[2]

At that point, "Rutha Harris of the Freedom Singers . . . moved to the center of the platform and the din ceased abruptly, just in time for her overpowering contralto to switch songs:

> *I woke up this morning with my mind*

"And above the faint echo of Mount Zion, which could be heard making the transition in the background, the crowd finished her line:

SET ON FREEDOM
I woke up this morning with my mind
SET ON FREEDOM

"Three times she led them in this call and response, and then they all raised the one-word chorus:

HALLELU-HALLELU-HALLELUJAH!

"The verses kept rolling forth until without signal the sound collapsed all at once into silence. Pious souls would maintain long afterward that they thought the Lord Himself had arrived, so awed were they."[3]

Throughout King's addresses, the audience continued to energize him with their responsiveness. "Doctor King rose to speak, beginning slowly, almost falteringly, and moving soon into the singsong cadence of his delivery," telling them, "'Maybe you can't legislate morality, but you can regulate behavior *(yes. amen. AMEN),*' and reaching a fervor commensurate with the crowd's crying out: 'There must be repentance for the vitriolic, loud words of people of ill will, but also for the silence of good people! *(yes well amen).*" As he went through a long string of "How Long?" ("will we have to suffer injustice" and "will justice be crucified"), a man in the audience was his lone amen corner, "cry[ing] out basso punctuation to the questions: 'God Almighty . . .'"[4]

This merging of elements was epitomized by King's habit of "biting into" the applause, as the journalist Henry Fairlie described it, preaching over and into the rising response in a blur of sound. The impression of blending concealed an intricate pattern of control and release, hesitation and flow. Max Atkinson, a scholar of speech, described King's delivery like this: "King would bide his time" and resume right before the response had concluded. In "I've Been to the Mountaintop," he waited a full six seconds during the applause that followed the contrast of "I may not get there with you" and "But I want you to know tonight that we as a people will get to the promised land." "And six seconds, it will be remembered, is just the point at which the intensity of applause typically starts to fall away towards the eight-second norm. By waiting until then, Dr. King was able to continue totally fluently, without any fear of his next words being missed."[5]

This was not the least of the intricacies in "I've Been to the Mountaintop." Atkinson points to the moments of "marked increase in the intensity of the responses," such as the three-part list that concludes with "I may not get there with you" (four 'Holy's' and an 'Amen'), which "the audience regarded . . . as completion points requiring more decisive displays of approval." King telegraphed those points with a subtle shake of the head that came on the word "promised" in the phrase "Promised Land" and "as he was starting to say the word 'glory,' just before the final ovation got under way." The audience seemed to take that nod "as a signal that the end of an applaudable message was close at hand." Clearly, then, "when both the speaker and his audience repeatedly come in before the other has quite finished, a state of closely coordinated rapport exists between them, and the overriding impression is one of intense harmony, spontaneity and mutual understanding."[6]

Throughout King's oratory, the audience was exquisitely keyed to his rhythm, just as the lone man in the amen corner answered King's "How long?" with his own response. That same back-and-forth was replayed at the end of the Selma-to-Montgomery march, when some in the audience leapt into the fray, joining King, finding his cadence and eventually supplanting him in the rejoinder. Punctuation that occasionally broke into King's rhythm was revealing of the audience's state of mind. "I am in Selma," King said, and a voice intervened before he could finish, "You belong here."[7]

Such off-beat intercessions were evident during King's first rally speech in Montgomery. It had been agreed that the people would decide whether to continue the boycott. If there was any doubt, the people's feedback dispelled it. The people's eruption came in the midst of King's urgent repetition, the three sentences that each began, "There comes a time when people get tired." The crowd's roar ratified each of King's enumerations of their collective fatigue at "being trampled over by the iron feet of oppression," "being plunged across the abyss of humiliation," and "being pushed out of the glittering sunlight of life's July and left standing amid the piercing chill of an alpine November." King brought closure to their mutual ratification of resolve in one poetic finish, "There comes a time *(Yes sir, Teach)* [Applause continues]."[8]

King's sense of solidarity with his audience did not depend solely on the ineffable force of sound or style. He signaled his connection through explicit statements of affection for black people. After the long march from Selma to Montgomery in 1965, King dramatically intoned, "My people, my people, listen!" One of the rationales he offered at a mass meeting for being in Selma underscored that same ethnic feeling. Echoing the passage in "Letter from Birmingham Jail" in which he explained why he had come to that city, King cited more universalistic reasons as well. In Selma no less than Birmingham, it was the case that "injustice anywhere is a threat to justice everywhere." To defend his mission in both cities, he drew on the precedents of the eighth century B.C. prophets who took their "thus saith the lords" far from their hometowns. Yet in Selma he built up to one final reason: "So I'm in Selma because my people are here. I'm in Selma because my people are suffering." Backing away from the immediacy of "my people," King then merged his voice with the black voices who over centuries of oppression had sung that plaintive hymn now transfigured into a freedom song. "And I'm here to help you sing 'Come by Here'":

> Come by here my Lordy, come by here
> Somebody needs you Lord
> Somebody is suffering, Lord
> Somebody is being oppressed Lord
> Come by Here.
> And this is why I come to Selma.[9]

King's audience sometimes ratified that sense of connection in the same language. After a ten-minute warm-up of hand-slapping and rousing choruses of "Give me that old-time religion" that shifted into chants of "freedom now," one local minister cradled King in the embrace of community as the audience interjected "speak" and other sounds of assent throughout. "Ladies and gentlemen, . . . you are privileged to have one of the greatest men that God has ever breathed life into. And if there is a Negro in this audience who doesn't feel that way I'm ashamed of you . . . Dr. Martin Luther King is a great man within his own right. *(Speak)* He has suffered perhaps more than any living human being this day for us. You can remember when the knife was plunged into him and that would have been enough to stop almost anybody but he has gone on because he loves his people *(Well, God)*."[10]

With just a hint of vernacular humility, King responded with the story of the woman whose employer said to her, "Ann, I hear that you're getting ready to get married," to which she replied, "No, . . . but thank God for the rumor." Amidst the church's laughter King quickly added that all the nice things said about him couldn't possibly be true, "but thank God for the rumor." He further ratified the reciprocity of the regard by saying, "It's great to be back with you and to see you tonight in such large numbers and with such overflowing enthusiasm."[11]

He suffered *for us*. He loves *his people*. *My people* are suffering. This was the King that blacks of the Black Belt saw: a champion of all the abused and rebuked people, but especially them.

Nowhere was the role of assuaging the wounds of the race more evident than in King's rumination on somebodyness in Selma in which he had quoted "Come by Here My Lord." Just moments after he invoked two hundred and forty-four years of slavery that "so often [make us] feel we don't count," and just moments before he recited the lines that "fleecy locks and black complexion / Cannot forfeit nature's claim," King assured his audience, "I come to tell you tonight in Selma, 'You may not have a lot of money. You may not have degrees . . . You may not know all of the intricacies of the English language. You may not have your grammar right. But I want you to know that you are just as good as any Ph.D. in English. I come to Selma to say to you tonight that you are God's children and therefore you are somebody. I come to tell you that every man, from bass black to treble white, is significant on God's keyboard."[12]

Earlier in the speech, King recalled growing up in that safe world of Auburn Avenue where he was told the catechism of the race, "You are as good as any other child." He recounted how he used to get on segregated buses as a boy: "My body day after day took a seat on the back, morning after morning my mind would sit up on the front seat. And I said to myself, 'One day my body is going to be up there where my mind is.'"[13] Here the mind had to conjure what the body was denied; vicarious realization was what kept hope alive. Such compartmentalization was a way of refusing to concede the virtue of necessity.

This loving embrace of their possibilities as human beings was key to King's communion with his rally audiences. The younger, more radical, and secular activists in the Student Nonviolent Coordinating Committee may have bridled at what they saw as King's grandstanding and pomposity, but at least some of them were awed by the feelings he stirred in ordinary black people. As they moved deeper into the Delta during the

Meredith March, Cleveland Sellers described a scene that unfolded "several times each day. The blacks along the way would line the side of the road, waiting in the broiling sun to see him. As we moved closer, they would edge out onto the pavement, peering under the brims of their starched bonnets and tattered straw hats. As we drew abreast someone would say, 'There he is! Martin Luther King!' This would precipitate a rush of two, sometimes as many as three thousand people. We had to join arms and form a cordon in order to keep him from being crushed.

"I watched Dr. King closely on several such occasions. The expression on his face was always the same, a combination of bewilderment, surprise and gratitude. He would smile a little, nod his head in a thank-you gesture and touch as many of the reaching hands as possible. Sometimes we would halt the line of marchers while he delivered a speech, promising that things were going to get better and urging them to register and vote.

"It's difficult to explain exactly what he meant to them. He was a symbol of all their hopes for a better life. By being there and showing that he really cared, he was helping to destroy barriers of fear and insecurity that had been hundreds of years in the making. They trusted him. Most important, he made it possible for them to believe that they *could* overcome."[14]

This mix of trust, faith, and care helps explain why his folk audience remained ever receptive to even King's most soaring rhetoric. "I heard [Rev.] Woods use some big words today, and Woods is a great user of big words," said Rev. Fred Shuttlesworth in Birmingham. But his next observation applied even more powerfully to King. "And he has big meaning with his big words. Any time a man goes to jail, he qualifies himself to use big words or any other kind of words he wants to use."[15]

King's qualifications were unimpeachable. As shown by the constant appendage of "Doctor," speakers' introductions of King at the mass meetings attest to their pride in a black man who was so learned, eloquent, and important that he could raise their struggle to world-historical importance. "This the first time perhaps in the history of this country, and in fact there is no perhaps about it, this is the first time beyond a shadow of a doubt that we have been privileged to have a Nobel Peace Prize winner to come and spend days and weeks with us." Sustained applause would break out at the mention of "a Ph.D. from Boston University," as it did when

Abernathy declared, "The Nobel Peace Prize didn't honor King; he honored the Nobel Peace Prize."[16]

In the process, King honored the race. Concerned about the substance of their suffering, few who heard King doubted the sincerity of his faith in them, the spirit that was upon him, his resolve to free them. Quibbles about style or idiom could not obscure any of it. As in his preaching, telling the people of Albany and Selma they were God's children offered more than personal consolation. King's loftiness spread the sublime onto a "'buked and scorned" people. The narrative lifting constituted a lifting of the race as well. Rather than creating distance between speaker and audience, King's elevation reached down to his audience and lifted them up, placing everyone on the same level.

This was ethnic fellow-feeling in its happiest, most noble guise, full of grace and humor. But the communion sometimes acquired more ominous tones. The racial import of "us" was especially stark when the forces of racism revealed their murderous intentions. In such moments, even King's ability to sublimate raw emotion could falter. "The day was a dark day in Birmingham. The policemen were mean to us," a subdued King said in a voice you don't often hear in King's oratory on the ground—not just plaintive, perhaps stunned, surely sobered, as if the nakedness of white depravity had depleted even King's ability to poeticize.[17]

King pronounced the almost childlike simplicity of *they were mean to us* only hours after Bull Connor had unleashed the infamous rampage across the city. "They got their violence and resolve and turned them loose on nonviolent people. Unarmed people. But not only that, they got their water system working, and here and there we saw the water hose with water pouring on young boys and girls, old men and women, with great and staggering force." Still struggling to absorb what had happened, King repeated, "Birmingham was a mean city today."

One can detect more than a glimmer of the anger roiling right beneath the surface of the control King usually projected in the meetings as he said defiantly, "Let's let them get their dogs and let them get their hoses, and we'll leave them covered with their own barbarity. We will leave them standing before their God and the world splattered with the blood and reeking with the stench of our Negro brothers."

The opposition between *their* and *our* has rarely been greater; do these whites even share the same God with King and King's people? Later in that same mass meeting, King told the story of spotting a tank, and asking what it was, and someone told him, "Well, that's Bull Connor's tank," and King told the audience, "and you know it's a white tank," which provoked laughter. King's riposte followed: "Now I want to say tonight that they can bring their dogs out, they can get their water, and even Bull Connor can get his white tank, and our black faces will stand up before the white tank [Cheering]."

As the antagonistic synergy of white tanks and black faces suggests, there was an interplay between the acute sense of racial consciousness and the external force of racism that sharpened it. Such small contexts were never separate from the larger environment. As the 1960s unfolded, those contexts were increasingly hostile to jovial preachments. It's not so much that King's idealism gave way to cynicism; his realism, at once theological and sociological, was too ingrained from the start. But if his spiritual faith in white redemptive capacity did not plummet, his appraisal of the depth of white racism and the degree of correction needed surely mounted. This was the context in which King's lofty assertions of blackness in the meetings began to be laced with strains of racial resentment and victimization.

This narrative of the black nation in exile reached caustic expression in the rallies King addressed in February and March of 1968 as he swept across the Black Belt to mobilize for the Poor People's Campaign. "There is trouble in the land," King announced portentously at a Greenwood, Mississippi, meeting in a voice of anguished urgency. He was fresh from Marks, Mississippi, where hours before he had heard from the impoverished mothers who lived in a feudal world of shacks and sharecropping. "There is something wrong with America," he orated. "There is still something wrong with Mississippi. And we are going all out this time to start getting America straightened out." His voice quavered as he thought about people living in rat-infested, roach-filled slums, about the Marks children with their bellies distended from hunger, barefoot children who shivered through the night because their families could afford neither shoes nor blankets. "And I said to myself, God doesn't like this, and we are going to say in no uncertain terms that we aren't going to accept it any longer."[18]

King's effort to ease the audience into the new task—"This time we're dealing with poverty"—could not suppress the relentlessness of race. Almost immediately King added, "And the poorest of the poor are the black people of this country." Weaving in and out of appeals to poor and black identities, he kept returning to the latter, promising a festival of blackness in the nation's capital. To compensate for the sense of homelessness America had bequeathed to Negroes, King said they would create a new town imbued with blackness. "In our shanty town we're gonna teach black culture. We haven't been told enough about ourselves." Punctuated by a black "we," the preacherly refrain "we want the world to know, we want our children to know," and the pointed language of "come by here," King's words celebrated black insight and talent:

> We want our children to know
> that Einstein is not the only scientist
> that came into being.
> We want them to know that
> George Washington Carver came by here.
> We want the world to know,
> and our children to know,
> That Shakespeare, Euripides, and Aristophanes
> were not the only poets
> that came in the world
> but Countee Cullen and Langston Hughes
> and Paul Laurence Dunbar came by here.

The substitutions of Hughes, Cullen, and Carver for the Lord in "Come by Here" were positive ones. Just as the Lord, and King in Selma, had come by here (but Einstein and Euripides only "came in the world"), King was enlisting heroes of the race to tell the people of the Black Belt that they were not "nobodies." But King's segue out of poverty talk into a familiar chant—"This is *our* country. . . . Before Jefferson wrote the beautiful words of the Declaration of Independence, we were here. *(All right)*"—did not just trump civil religious imagery with a more primordial one of race. Nor did that construction culminate in a testimony to the slaves' fortitude, as it did in Albany, six years previously. Rather, the retrieval of collective memory was surrounded by grievance—"this is our country, we built it"—and a crystallized sense of a malevolent "they." "They said" simply piled an additional layer of white insincerity on top of the original crime of enslavement, hinting at the relentlessness of white sinfulness: "They kept us in slavery 244 years in this country, and then they said they freed us from slavery, but they didn't give us any land. Frederick Douglass said we should have forty acres and a mule."

This refusal to welcome was no remnant of archaic history. "And they haven't given us *anything!* After making our foreparents work and labor for 244 years—for nothing! Didn't pay 'em a cent." That same jeering edge was implicit in King's observation, "Our young black boys and our young white boys are forced to fight together and kill together in brutal solidarity in Vietnam and when they come back home they can't even live on the same block."

In Montgomery a few weeks earlier, King had seemed to honor the claims of civil religion. "We hold these truths to be self-evident," he told the crowd, "that all men are endowed by their creator with certain inalienable rights, that among these are life, liberty, and the pursuit of happiness." "That's a beautiful creed," King granted. "It didn't say some men, it said all men. It didn't say all white men, it said all men, which includes black men. Each individual has certain basic rights . . . [that are] God-given." But this nod to Jefferson mainly served to highlight the sinful mendacity of those who spouted it. If the tone of King's original statement was perhaps ambiguous, the tone of his repetition, "now that's beautiful," confirmed the sarcasm of his words. Lest there be any ambiguity, King went on to say, "America has never lived up to it. And the ultimate contradiction is that the men who wrote it owned slaves at the same time."[19]

King then launched into a devastating chronicle of the captive black nation; his contrast of whites' honeyed words with their evil deeds paralleled Malcolm X's analysis of white "tricknology." King's recourse to the collective "white man" only underscored his main point that "racism is very deep in this country." "Do you know that in America the white man sought to annihilate the Indian, literally to wipe him out, and he made a national policy that said in substance, the only good Indian is a dead Indian? Now a nation that got started like that has a lot of repentin' to do."

A twist on American exceptionalism intensified the impression of American barbarity. The nation's effort "to destroy absolutely the indigenous people" was unprecedented for a conquering nation "coming in." At least no other nation in the New World ever attempted such a thing. "We got to tell America the truth," King insisted. "And where the black man is concerned, let me tell you something. It's a serious thing that America did to the black man." Even after the Emancipation Proclamation said "we were free," America "didn't even give us any land to make that freedom meaningful. It was like putting a man in jail, and keeping him there for many years and discovering that he's not guilty of the crime for which he was convicted."

That wasn't the end of the torment blacks had to undergo. "And then you just go up to him and say, 'You are free,' but you don't give him any bus fare to get to town. You don't give him any money to buy some clothes to put on his back or to get on his feet in life again. Every code of jurisprudence would rise up against that. But this is exactly what America did to the black man." The nation could have provided a program or reparations instead of leaving him penniless and illiterate after 244 years of slavery. Calculating that twenty dollars a week for the four million slaves would have added up to eight hundred billion dollars, King noted acerbically, "They owe us a lot of money."

There was still one more sadistic turn to come that revealed the depth of racism in this nation. At the time of this hard-hearted refusal, America was showering its "white peasants from Europe" with largesse, and here King ticked off the gifts in excruciating detail: land in the West, land grant colleges to disseminate expertise, county agents to implement that learning, low-interest loans to mechanize, and, up to the very present, millions of dollars in subsidies to farmers not to grow crops. The vagueness of the likely agents of that evil signaled the power of the righteous indignation coursing through King: "And these are the very people telling the black man that he ought to lift himself by his own bootstraps. It's a nice thing to say to a man, 'Lift yourself by your own bootstraps,' but it's a cruel jest to say to a bootless man that he ought to lift himself by his own bootstraps."

At one point, imagining the right-wing repression that was in the offing, King dropped his voice down to a near-whisper. "And you know what? A nation that put as many Japanese in a concentration camp as they did in the forties—you remember that?—could put black people in concentration camps. And I'm not interested in being in any concentration camp. I been on a reservation too long now."

These particulars gave rise to a damning inference about the nation. "We read on the Statue of Liberty that America is the mother of exiles," but, King observed in a resonant phrase, whites "never evinced the same maternal care and concern for its black exiles who were brought to this nation in chains." (In an SCLC retreat around the same time, King heightened the contrast: "But pretty soon we realize that America has been the Mother of Exile for its white exiles. It has been a dungeon of oppression and deprivation for its Black exiles.")[20] Blacks themselves had absorbed that fact into the most intimate regions of their psyche and song: "And isn't it the ultimate irony . . . that the Negro could sing in one of his sorrow songs, 'Sometimes I feel like a motherless child.'" As the audience erupted in applause, King demanded, with his voice rising in intensity, "What sense of estrangement, what sense of rejection, what sense of hurt could cause a people to use such a metaphor?"

There remained a difference, however, between "maternal chill" and "white devils." Nor did King ever resort to the face-slapping staccato of Malcolm X's curses of blue-eyed, foul-smelling apes. At the same time, even if King's recital of the evil that whites had committed against Indians, Japanese Americans, and his own people was not quite "telling the white man about himself," as Malcolm X described his life mission, King was certainly telling black people something about the white man (and we shall see, he would tell white people something about themselves too). If we leave aside the matter of audience and venue, King's maternal chill mimicked Malcolm X's charge to the white man: "It has never been out of any internal sense of morality or legality or humanism that we [blacks] were allowed to advance. *You have been as cold as an icicle whenever it came to the rights of the black man in this country.*"[21]

Still, in the end, the "blackness" of the mass meetings could never crowd out the key elements of King's mission. As a formal matter, the mix of rhetorics, the invocation of white sources before black audiences, the willingness to step into the white racist's imagination, the empathy disclosed in that venturing, the call to transcend vengeance, the shifts between Afro-Baptist and civil religious idioms, the emissary role King played when he brought news from presidents and attorneys general right into the local scene—all these things defined the cosmopolitan character of King's endeavor. In the mass meetings as in church, King constantly enlarged the imagination of his audience, citing parallels with Gandhi's mission to free India or the effort of "our brothers and sisters" in Africa and Asia to "throw off the shackles" of oppression.

In the midst of a long academic explanation of Jim Crow replete with references to "class structure," King inserted the phrase, "I want you to follow me through here." Segregation was not just an emanation of the emotion of hatred, King explained. "As the noted historian, C. Vann Woodward, in his book, *The Strange Career of Jim Crow,* clearly points out, the segregation of the races was really a political stratagem employed by the emerging Bourbon interests in the South to keep the southern masses divided."[22]

That reach for theoretical distance was simply one of the ways in which King sought to control volatile feelings through empathy, forgiveness, and understanding. Here the contrast between King and his sidekick Abernathy couldn't have been greater. When Sheriff Jim Clark shoved Mrs. Annie Lee Cooper, one of the Selma protesters, with enough force to knock her down, Abernathy decried Clark's "devilish" ways, warned that "they're gonna get rougher than they got today and you may as well brace yourself," and said, "They're against us because we're black." He soon got tangled up in a contradiction between his certainty that Mrs. Cooper "did not do any such thing [as hit Clark]" and the advice that parents often dispensed to children on the first day of school: "Don't you bother anybody. But if they hit you . . ." Having primed the audience by hesitating, he didn't even need to complete the thought.[23]

All the while, Abernathy vividly depicted the white abuse of black womanhood and the black men's longing for vengeance. "I saw it the other day," Abernathy said gravely. "They threw to the ground a Negro woman. A fine Negro woman! Wonderful Negro woman! . . . They took their billy clubs and punched them in her stomach. Took their feet and placed them on her wrist . . . I saw them as they held her in the most inhuman fashion. I saw the Negro men in that line that were ready to go and get them [laughter, applause, assent]." Only then did he dampen down emotion. "But I heard the voice of Martin Luther King saying, 'Be calm . . . just take it in a nonviolent manner.' . . . Thank God for Martin Luther King. If not some blood would have been shed."

In contrast to Abernathy, King kept the raw facts of the episode at bay, approaching it circuitously through a sociological generality ("when the opposition gets pushed up against the wall, whether it's legally or morally, they react in strange ways") and a bit of what he deemed "psychological theory" that required a voyage into the white man's mind. The heart of

171

the problem was the role of guilt, "haunting, agonizing guilt," in white backlash. On the one hand, King explained, guilt may inspire the guilty to "repent" and mend their "evil and unjust ways." But like the drunk who recoils from counseling only to drink more, "some of our white brothers drown their guilt about how they've treated the Negro by engaging in more of the guilt-evoking act." Dropping for a moment into the vernacular—oppressors will "beat on you"—he warned that whites aimed to provoke violence with their "brutal language and through brutal methods and through outright physical violence inflicted upon us."[24]

King's voyage into the psyches of white racists had a political motive. It reflected his understanding that achieving social justice for black people required not just symbolic swagger but also a disciplined movement whose eye was forever on the ultimate prize. At the same time, these ventures were inseparable from the spiritual core that drove them: King's faith in redemptive love, which remained impervious to all the other incidental pressures. King never abandoned his evangelical mission, bringing the good news of "the better way" of Jesus Christ to suffering black people. As a result, King's musings on the totems of the race who "came by here" could not diminish the urgency of his need to minister to a rainbow of all the afflicted.

In the Poor People's Campaign, King explained at various rallies, "We going to have Mexican Americans joining with us, we're going to have American Indians, they're poor too, we're gonna have Puerto Ricans joining with us, and we gonna have Appalachian whites, who will join with us, because some of them are getting enough sense to know that the same forces that oppress the Negroes oppress poor white people." That invitation sharpened tension within the SCLC between race man sentiments and its leader's vision of beloved community. Many of King's executive staff colleagues, the SCLC board members, and fieldworkers were less than thrilled about King's effort to move the focus beyond blacks. In the backstage huddles before the polyglot gatherings, some of King's black colleagues made insulting and patronizing comments about Puerto Ricans and poor whites. In David Garrow's account, an aide told a staff meeting, "I do not think I am at the point where a Mexican can sit in and call strategy on a Steering Committee." Another aide said that the Hispanic leader Reies Lopez Tijerina "didn't understand that we were the parents and he was the child."[25]

For King, racial matters could never be so simple—not even his own deepening anguish over racism. As barbed as the imagery of black exile and maternal chill may have been, it didn't trump the universal terms of his anointment. The Master's words, "I was hungry, and ye fed me not," rang in King's ears. All of God's children, not just the hungry black ones, deserved succor. The point of the Good Samaritan story was to nurture half-breeds and strangers, not just one's own kind.

So in a perfect union of material task and narrative form, King's rising concern for the poor was matched by the rising prominence of the parable of the rich man Dives and the beggar Lazarus who came to his gate. Throughout the final years, King cited the story before black audiences and white ones, in ramshackle churches and the National Cathedral in Washington, D.C. It leapt from church homily right into rally talk. At a wild meeting in Montgomery to drum up support for the Poor People's Campaign, King warned that "Jesus reminds us that once a man went to hell because he forgot the poor. There was a man by the name of Dives. Then and there he passed the poor man by the name of Lazarus. You remember the story."

But, King underscored, "There is nothing in that parable that Jesus told us that Dives went to hell because he was rich." On the contrary, "Jesus never made a universal indictment against all wealth." King conjured up that parable's "long distance call between heaven and hell with Abraham in heaven talking with Dives in hell. Abraham was a real rich man. It wasn't a millionaire in hell talking with a poor man in heaven, it was a little millionaire in hell talking with a multimillionaire in heaven." King explained Dives' unhappy ending this way: Dives did not even acknowledge the presence of the gimpy beggar who every day, with sores all over his body and hardly able to walk, managed to get himself to Dives' gate. All Lazarus needed was a few crumbs from his table, somebody to care. "Dives went to hell because he passed by Lazarus every day but he never really saw him. Dives went to hell because he allowed Lazarus to become invisible."[26]

Even when King didn't mention Dives and Lazarus by name, the drama of invisibility and acknowledgment played out in many of King's final mass meetings. So did the obligation to translate the theology of recognition into physical acts of seeing and listening. King had affirmed that duty at least as far back as *Strength to Love*. The difference a decade later was equally physical. No longer abstractions, the poor had acquired an immediacy that derived from King's encounter with them. King's sensitivity to the pain of the least of these was hard to miss back in Marks, where he was deeply unsettled by the poverty he saw. Watching underweight children whose lunch was one quarter of an apple and a few crackers, Abernathy looked over at King. "I saw that his eyes were full of tears, which he wiped away with the back of his hand." King was "strangely silent" for the rest of the day, and back on the motel bed that night, he just "stared at the ceiling for a long time, then spoke to me. Ralph, he said. I can't get those children out of my mind. . . . We've got to do something for them. . . . I don't think people really know that little schoolchildren are slowly starving in the United States of America. I didn't know."[27]

Having come to see and hear the poor more clearly, King told the audience in Greenwood, Mississippi, that he was determined to "force America to see and hear the poor." They would need to go to Washington in great numbers "so the entire nation will have to hear and see the poor." For King, the equations were clear: America was Dives, striding right past Lazarus, the children of Marks. There was no room for the poor at the American inn.[28]

In demanding that Dives-America look at the poor, King was never more like his beloved Jesus. Yet in the throes of the Greenwood rally, Jesus never sounded more down-home, and southern too. With the audience responding to each of his phrases with squeals of delight, King conjured up the carnival of recognition that Lazarus was about to stage for Dives in Washington. "Oh, we going to have a time," King shouted out over and over in his most countrified voice. "And we gonna have 'em comin' from everywhere. We going to have 'em coming by horse and buggy, moving on down the highway, moving toward Washington." He promised them not just that festival of blackness, but music and plenty to eat. But more than anything else, the great American refusal to see required florid visual drama to coerce that seeing. Politics was about to become performance art.

As the audience gave off shouts, King merged himself with the poor of the Black Belt in a determined "we," telling them how they would ride into Washington on their mule train "and we gonna take some of these shacks that we have to live in, and we're gonna put 'em on a truck, and we gonna take them right up to Washington and present them as a gift." If their segregationist senators "won't see ya down here in Mississippi," in Washington, "we goin' by to see brother Stennis and brother Eastland." King concluded with a threat: "And I tell you this. They better see us. Because, if they refuse to see us, they won't do no business in their office. We'll just go in the office . . . and we'll just take our blankets and have somebody bring us our coffee and our chicken, right on up there, and we'll just stay in and sleep in and eat right in those offices." The audience roared.

Chicken-eating Lazarus was no longer waiting at the gate; he was about to walk right into Dives' home. "We're going to make America see the poor people," King said. "We're all poor, and we're all deprived of that which we should have." As King said earlier, "We not playin' about this thing!" And then, distending the word *time:* "We goin' to have a *tiiime* in Washington!"

From his first oration in Montgomery to the latter-day mobilizations for the poor, King never stopped reprising the role of the old slave preacher who "came by here" to tell his people, "you ain't no nigger." But for all the familiar accents, it's important not to lose sight of an essential point: the carnival of the poor brought out the brash emphasis on action that distinguished King's rally oratory from his preaching and infused his signature themes with new accents. Thus the campaigns for rights in Albany, Birmingham, and Selma changed the character of the need and the suffering in "Somebody needs you, Lord" and its lamentation, "Somebody is suffering." The suffering was neither the ancient suffering of the race nor that of "my [black] people" in general, nor the cosmic "trials and tribulations" that dominated King's homilies of hope in church. In the meetings, King placed suffering and need alike in a tangible context: the people in need were the Negro people of Selma who were standing up and fighting for rights and respect. Their suffering was spatially and organizationally embedded—the suffering that had come to them because they stood up and joined the liberation battle.

Accordingly, the solidarity King touted was not the emotional unity of victims who shared the tragic history of the race, but the political cohesion of fighters who had been aroused to reverse that history. On the last night of his life, speaking before a vast room full of black sanitation men on strike, King warned of the danger of internal bickering. "We've got to stay together and maintain unity" if "we are determined to be people," if "we are God's children," if "we don't have to live like we are forced to live." He reminded the strikers of Pharaoh's devious strategy for maintaining power: "He kept the slaves fighting among themselves. [Applause] But whenever the slaves get together, something happens in Pharaoh's court, and he cannot hold the slaves in slavery."[29]

King's efforts to fashion community typically appealed to elevated moral purpose and shared sacrifice. In the 1963 Birmingham campaign, King stressed the need to "live a sacrificial life during this Easter season and even after the Easter season." The Mosaic leader known for his love of elegant suits and silk sheets explained to his church audience, "Now you see that we have on blue jeans and gray work shirts. We're wearing these things not merely to engage in some theatrical gesture . . . [but] to symbolize our determination to sacrifice during this period . . . We are not going to buy suits or shirts or shoes or socks or anything in the downtown of Birmingham, Alabama until the walls of segregation crumble."

The urgency of maintaining the boycott wore down even King's reserves of high-mindedness. His appeal to "every freedom-loving Negro of self-respect . . . to refuse to shop in the stores downtown" contained only a hint of scorn for those blacks who remained aloof from their people's struggle. But then King spoke what had been only insinuated: "Now we're asking you, my friends, not only to stop buying yourself but tell your neighbors and when you see any Negro shopping downtown, realize that that Negro doesn't have any self-respect. And he isn't fit to be free." King granted that a few people might not have heard of the boycott yet. "But I think the vast majority of Negroes have heard about this movement. And that means that anybody who goes downtown to shop is going down in defiance of this movement. And they are traitors to the Negro race."[30]

The alterations in King's signature riffs as he shifted from preacher to exhorter were visible in his very first speech at the start of the bus boycott in Montgomery, where he linked the celebration of black people to straightening backs rather than straightening Jeremiah's question, "Is there a balm in Gilead?" King's subtle slap at all racist stereotypes was a key part of this first speech as a civil rights leader. He told a church full of maligned people that he appreciated them. It was not just that they were noble, but that the act of defying segregation was noble. It was not just that Rosa Parks was a fine person—"Nobody can doubt the boundless outreach of her integrity (*Sure enough*). Nobody can doubt the height of her character *(Yes)*, nobody can doubt the depth of her Christian commitment and devotion to the teaching of Jesus *(All right)*." Her act of protest was fine too. By next moving immediately to applaud the black audience's new refusal to be "trampled over by the iron feet of oppression," King was associating their pride with more than their reserves of hope, as in "there is a balm in Gilead," but with a different kind of moral courage linked directly to marvelous militancy.[31]

King's intuiting of that buried desire was reflected in the imagery of fatigue. He told a packed and pulsing crowd at Memphis's Mason Temple, "We are tired . . . We are tired of being at the bottom. *(Yes!)*" Over and over, he channeled the wisdom of Sister Pollard, "our feets is tired." In a rally in Greenwood, Mississippi, punctuated by fervent applause, he declared, "We're going to Washington to say we're tired. We're tired to have to live in shacks. Rat-infested, roach-filled slums. We're tired. We are tired of not being able to get adequate jobs, we are tired of doing full time work for part time income. We are tired of our children getting inferior education. And we are tired of making so little money that we can't even get the basic necessities of life."[32]

The fatigue of the burdened protagonist of so many gospel songs was a weariness with the world. By contrast, the "tired" state of the people of Montgomery was not the weariness that ached to escape from this world. Sister Pollard's soul wasn't tired. She was tired of being mistreated, and thus was ready to act, not rest. King understood this: "We, the disinherited of this land, we who have been oppressed so long, are tired of going through the long night of captivity. And now we are reaching out for the daybreak of freedom and justice and equality [Applause]." Reaching out and waking up. The captive black nation had had it with captivity.[33]

This was the key aspect of the "New Negro" that King heralded constantly from the mid-1950s on. No longer downtrodden, black people were full of robust energy to struggle with the world, to transform it. That is why the most electrifying moment in the Holt Street speech was the roar that ratified King's insistence, "There comes a time when people get tired."

In his own Afro-Christian way, King was mimicking Marcus Garvey's exhortation, "Up you mighty race." The exuberance of King's performance of black majesty reinforced the message implicit in his novel deployment of the "fleecy locks" trope from his preaching. The critical move was not the familiar one of King reveling in blackness through the Englishman's idiom, but the political extension involved in linking it to collective protest.

King closed his first Montgomery speech by imagining the judgment of history that would validate their majesty: "Somebody will have to say, 'There lived a race of people *(Well),* a *black* people, *(Yes, sir)*'"—and then he seamlessly slipped in Cowper's line "'of fleecy locks and black complexion' *(Yes).*" But rather than following through with the usual completing couplets from Cowper, King inserted this twist of collective identity—"a people who had the moral courage to stand up for their rights. [Applause] And thereby they injected a new meaning into the veins of history and of civilization."

ELEVEN

The Physics of Deliverance

"The acceptable year of the Lord is this year"

The defiant strain that entered King's oratory at the mass meetings raises a question about the balance of fresh and familiar in freedom preaching and singing. Did the presence of chant, moan, and crescendo mark the retrieval of an established black culture that was simply occurring in a novel political context? King himself argued that freedom songs were "adaptations of the songs the slaves sang—the sorrow songs, the shouts for joy, the battle hymns, and the anthems of our movement . . . We sing the freedom songs today *for the same reason* the slaves sang them, because we too are in bondage and the songs add hope to our determination that 'We shall overcome, black and white together, We shall overcome someday.'"[1]

And yet the new accents in King's mass meeting oratory should make us skeptical of his emphasis on the continuity with the ancestors. Did the slaves really hope that blacks and whites together would overcome? Or did they just want to be free? In truth, King was taking liberties, blurring the difference between hoping to be delivered "someday" and struggling to free oneself on "this day," even if one sang "someday" in the process. The "it" in "I'm gonna let it shine, let it shine" may have been the familiar "light of mine" that was equivalent to the "me" in "Jesus loves me," or even the light of the race more generally. But people were also declaring their unembarrassed love of black song, sermon, and spirit, which they were letting shine too, and letting it shine before white people while demanding entrée to the larger order. This was the novelty of the "fleecy locks" passage as King performed it in the meetings—not just the word "black" nor the reveling in collective defiance but yoking the two together in such a public manner. That is why we can't really think of the mass meetings only as a black sanctuary for "my people."

Making black culture, humanity, and resolve visible was a key part of King's meeting oratory. There was an opportunistic aspect to this: ever aware of the sympathy and indignation created by racist attacks on noble black protesters, SCLC crafted its spectacles of suffering with its eye always on the media, the White House, Congress, and public opinion. But the more local displays were all the more poignant for their innocence. The singing and praying that began in Brown Chapel became a continuous stream that flowed outside as the people walked out into the world. In Albany, Georgia, a great shout went up, "'Now! Now!' People begin clapping in the same, complex, increasingly fast way they had that other night, clapping and stamping their feet in the same rhythms, shouting again in unison: 'FREEDOM FREEDOM FREEDOM FREEDOM . . .' Then, after being told to observe the traffic lights, a teenage girl said, 'Yes, Lord, I'm ready to go,' and they stepped out of the church, all the while singing 'Ain't go' let nobody turn me round' as they headed down the block toward the police."[2] Such acts did not stop once the protesters were out in the public space where whites could see them. In Selma, King led the protesters over the crest at the top of the Pettus Bridge, then continued down the slope of Route 80 toward Lowndes County, knelt, and began praying in front of George Wallace's state police.

Clashes between the police and protesters persisted through threats and attacks by vigilante gangs and racist officials. When a sheriff invaded a black church in small-town Georgia and swaggered about, saying, "We don't wanta hear no talk 'bout registerin' to vote in this county," the congregants began to hum, "We'll Never Turn Back." As the singing became louder, "Some sister began to moan till you could hardly hear the sheriff over the singing and moaning. The sheriff didn't know what to do. He seemed to be afraid to tell the people to shut up. . . . Those beautiful people sang that sheriff right out of their church! That was some powerful music."[3]

Andrew Marrissett, the SCLC fieldworker, still shakes his head in wonder at the "miracle" he was part of when Bull Connor's troops parted and he and hundreds of his colleagues marched on through singing "I want Jesus to walk with me." When Connor ordered them to disperse, they knelt in prayer. But Rev. Charles Billups leapt up and yelled, "The Lord is with this movement! Off your knees. We're going to jail!" The police stood transfixed and silent. Bull Connor cried, "stop 'em, stop 'em!" The growling police dogs calmed. The firemen too seemed frozen as Connor yelled, *Turn on the hoses, turn on the hoses.* "I saw one fireman," Andrew Young remembered, "tears in his eyes, just let the hose drop at his feet. Our people marched right between the red fire trucks." As Connor stood there cursing, one woman called out, "Great God Almighty done parted the Red Sea one mo' time!"[4]

The insurgents converted small-town jails and prison work farms into venues for sacred black performance. In Savannah, Andrew Young calmed down a paddy wagon full of unnerved youngsters who couldn't breathe as the police closed the windows to intensify the heat. "Look, they are trying to get you to crack up. They want you to scream and holler and plead. That would demonstrate that you are niggers who got out of your place. . . . You've got to use mind over matter." As they sweltered and dripped with sweat, he had them imagining they were approaching cool water and then said, "We're going to wade in the water"; having led them into the pool, he shifted to a whisper-soft singing of the Exodus spiritual, "Wade in the water, wade in the water."[5]

Perhaps the most touching of these encounters involved the children of Selma, hundreds of them between the ages of six and eighteen. During the rout of the innocents in the mid-1960s, a posse of Jim Clarke's police with cattle prods force-marched more than two hundred barefoot young protesters through the countryside. Once, while the protesters were testing to see if the local movie theater was obeying the 1964 Civil Rights Act, Clark's deputies hit one of the youngsters with a blackjack and burned others with a cattle prod, and Clark "threw his billy at someone. One of us picked it up and said, 'Here it is, Sheriff' and handed it to him." Another teenager recalled, "We were marching and singing 'I Love

181

Everybody,' and one of them stuck me with the cattle prod and said, 'You don't love everybody,' and I said, 'Yes, I do.'"[6]

Malcolm X made fun of the idea of a movement that sang and prayed. But it was one thing to bait whites from Harlem street corners; it was quite another for black people in St. Augustine to come out of their houses to face down the Klan marching through their streets and to address them with a defiant form of crossover talk, "You can't make me doubt Him, You can't make me doubt Him." In that move from black sanctuary to the larger white world, the tension heightened right before the church doors burst open and the marchers moved out into the world. For many, the singing and praying steadied their nerves as they glided across the threshold. It was as if the rhythmic resolve of "I'm on my way to Freedom Land" flowed right into the heart. In "Terrible Terrell" (County), "forty beleaguered believers in democracy, among them little children, sang, 'We are climbing / Jacob's ladder' and then, standing in a circle, hands joined, building their courage, sang 'We Shall Overcome,' verse after verse, before finally going out to face what might be waiting in the southern summer night from the whites."[7]

That link between vulnerability and song, speech, and sermon underscores the functional dynamic at work in King's mass meeting oratory. The rallies did not just reflect the growing audacity of black people; their purpose was to generate and sustain it. As part of that mission, King tried to change black people's sense of time as much as of space. These shifts mirrored the edge King was injecting into Christianity, an edge that blurred the lines not just between ethnic church and public square but also between sacred time and profane time, the time of this world and that of the next.

Grasping the meaning of King's shift from preaching to exhorting requires a small detour to examine the complex relationship between black religion and the political culture that the churched part of the movement was fashioning. To do this, it is necessary to draw out a theme only hinted at in the last chapter. When he spoke in the mass meetings King dipped into his sermons, yet he fiddled with them too, and both the dipping and fiddling were shaped by the practical imperatives of mobilization. While religious rhetoric proved "useful" in this endeavor, its usefulness was not self-evident—thus the fiddling. King and the others had to engage in a good deal of labor to make the most productive use of the religious language. The remaining chapters of Part III consider how King "used" religious and other narratives to "solve" various dilemmas of insurgency.[8]

Michael Walzer puts the point with typically elegant economy: "Most of the reinventions [of Exodus] have been the work of religious men and women who found in the text not only a record of God's action in the world but also a guide for His people—which is to say, themselves . . . Within the sacred history of the Exodus, they discovered a vivid and realistic secular history that helped them to understand their own political activity." As Walzer says, our subject "is not what God has done but what men and women have done, first with the biblical text itself and then in the world, with the text in their hands."[9]

A look at what King did with biblical and other texts in his hands exposes a paradox that won't be fully explained until the final chapter of Part III. King's passionate, at times millennial rhetoric obeyed a rational logic. This was true in the obvious sense that his oratory in the meetings was a means to ends that were quite different from those at play in church contemplation or backstage talk with friends. It was also true in the more exact sense that one of the major tasks King set for himself was to provide rational justifications for participating in dangerous protests. At the same time, to prefigure the end point, King's larger Christian faith subverted the clever logic it was forced to honor, giving a spiritual cast to the very meaning of what was rational.

Deciphering this paradox requires understanding King's words in the light of the meetings' aims. To use King's own words, there was not just a "transphysics" of deliverance but a "physics" too,[10] which hinged on the brute fact of insufficient numbers. Despite King's imagery of "a people who stood up for their rights," there weren't enough defiant individuals to populate the networks of defiance. Each audience had to be transformed into warriors for this more seditious purpose. That required inspiring, persuading, prodding—at times even shaming and chastising.

This need to produce a flow of bodies willing to defy segregation and then to retain them in the struggle conditioned all of King's meeting talk. "The only thing we had was our bodies," one activist recalled. "They were welcome to our bodies, and they could use our bodies the best way they saw fit. And so this was the thing. We put our bodies on the line." When the first wave of freedom riders were battered and bloodied by the vigilantes who firebombed their bus and tried to burn them alive, a new wave of martyrs, this time from Nashville, stepped forward to replace them with new bodies. Rebuffed by the city commission in Albany, Georgia, King said, "Well, there are two ways that you can communicate. One is with your words, and if they don't get over, you have to communicate with your action. *(yes, yes)* The students of the student sit-in movement were able to communicate something by keeping their mouths shut and their bodies active that I could have never communicated in words."[11]

In Montgomery in 1955, the leadership needed to keep the bodies off the buses, to inspire them to walk, and to maintain their resolve over the long haul. The Montgomery Improvement Association closed its meeting with a rousing hymn, and the huge church trembled from the vibrations. "The only question left to answer, both for them and for us, was: How long could we keep it up?"[12] Years after the ecstasy of the Albany movement had given way to demoralization and cynicism, one activist got the churning dynamic just right: "We were naive enough to think we could fill up the jails. [Sheriff] Pritchett was hep to the fact we couldn't. We ran out of people before he ran out of jails."[13] State action involving terror and vigilantes amplified all the inherent obstacles to insurgency, as did the strategic design of creating bloody spectacles for northern media consumption. "I want to make a point that I think everyone here should consider very carefully if he wants to be with this campaign," King warned the SCLC staff before Birmingham. "I have to tell you that in my judgment, some of the people sitting here today will not come back alive from this campaign."[14]

In Birmingham, the sheer scale of action, which expanded to include a mass boycott of downtown stores, sit-ins at lunch counters, and filling the jails, ratcheted up the demographic need. "We are just getting started," King told a group of ministers. "We are going to continue demonstrations everyday until the white people of Birmingham realize that we are going to get what we want. . . . We are going to fill all the jails in Birmingham. We are going to turn Birmingham up side down and right side up."[15]

Despite Rev. Fred Shuttleworth's formidable organization and King's theatrical jailing, on one occasion after hours of preaching King and Abernathy still had only a dozen bodies to show for their effort. As Glenn Eskew summarizes the situation, "Apparently, the SCLC had expected the very presence of Martin Luther King to draw hundreds of protesters into the movement. That had not occurred. Only a small percentage of Birmingham's black population had supported the campaign, and an even smaller proportion had volunteered for direct action protests . . . the black community appeared too alienated and disinterested [*sic*] to get involved."[16]

Symbolic maneuvers—celebrations of "jailbirds"—and organizational innovation—using the format of altar calls to come to the podium and witness for the movement—were deployed to entice and induce. Serendipity saved them temporarily, as the mingling of decidedly less than nonviolent bystanders swelled the ranks of insurgency and created chaos. Eventually, such accidental participants did not suffice. This was the context in which children came to figure mightily in the physics of collective action: having run out of adult bodies, the movement compensated with younger ones. The same adaptive logic gave birth to a full-blown field staff who became adepts at mobilization.

No matter how much the brand of "fire no water could put out" defied the laws of physics, the very transphysics that King invoked paid homage to the "physics" it had to overcome. No matter how much King quoted the adage "my feets is tired but my soul is rested," an effective movement had to obey the logic of feets too. Deliverance required attaining a threshold of bodies, no matter how spiritualized, to do some very bodily things.

Between the big causes and the felt grievances, there was an intimate zone of indeterminacy that governed each person's often split-second decision to walk out of the church, march to the courthouse, brave the dogs and hoses. If leaders could waver, ordinary people often required nudging over the threshold of reluctance.[17] In Andrew Young's reckoning, "powerful folk oratory was necessary to preach people out of their fears." As Willie Bolden recalls, "Sometimes, they were just so high from freedom singing, they didn't need any preaching, they were ready to go, and we just marched them right out the church." In Danville, Virginia, Reverend Lawrence Campbell preached, "God did not tell [the children of Israel] to turn around but God told them to go forward"; by the end he was praising God's miraculous powers in a near trance, pounding the lectern and chanting, "How I got over, How I got over, How I got over," hoping the God-ordained movement of the Israelites out of Egypt and God's wonders to perform might propel black Virginians out of bondage.[18]

Over and over King chanted, "Keep this movement moving"—an imperative that could veil neither its pleading nor the wishing it sought to transform into reality. "Now let me say this. The thing we are challenged to do is to keep this movement moving . . . As long as we keep moving like we're moving, the power structure of Birmingham will have to give in."[19] Velocity and friction, vacancy and replacement: these were all part of the deliverance equation too.

For all the rapture and religion, the movement was still a movement. Maybe King could turn mass meetings into sessions of racial psychodrama, but the dilemmas he confronted were universal, common to all mobilizations: shaky commitment, the pull of family life, the power of state repression, fear of being fired. King's audience could claim no immunity from transaction costs, rational expectations, and disappointment with public involvement. And because talk is cheap, verbal art remained a powerful weapon for the movement leaders in managing these vulnerabilities.

These vulnerabilities crystallized into four dilemmas confronted by King in his rally talk. The dilemma of rationality provoked the query, is it reasonable—or, as much evidence suggested, futile, masochistic, or even suicidal—to mobilize against segregation? The dilemma of despondency—really a subset of the first problem—led to the query, how do I vanquish pessimism? The dilemma of agency provoked the query, do I have the power to affect my own future, and if so do I have the gumption not to await the Lord but to act on such powers? Finally, the dilemma of solidarity generated the query, am I alone in this effort or do I have powerful allies to lean on? To its often anxious audience, the new activist political culture shouted back, with freedom lyrics to boot: defiance is rational ("We shall overcome"); there are good reasons not to yield to hopelessness ("Paul and Silas were bound in jail but . . ."); even the least of us can boast pride and power ("Ain't gonna let nobody turn me round"); and no matter how oppressed, black people are not alone ("God is on our side").[20]

If religion was to help in this effort, first King had to validate its place in the struggle. Legitimacy and immediacy were tangled together in what was essentially an argument about time: that the time for action was now, that God was in this world now, that it was proper to deploy religion on behalf of such earthly matters. That God had blessed the enterprise was obvious to King, but not to every potential recruit to the movement. To impart righteous urgency to the quest for freedom, black religion had to be worked over and even argued against. Prophetic political culture had to be fashioned as much as reclaimed.[21]

The earthly import of the deliverance theme of the spirituals had long given way to the flight from the world represented by gospel music's ethos, "good news in bad times." In retrospect, one can glimpse oblique hints of resistance, and more explicit ones too, in certain strains of the folk tradition, but as Benjamin Mays observed in *The Negro's Church* and knew firsthand from his own childhood pastor, most black churches preached an otherworldly gospel.[22] King himself described the Reconstruction-era implicit bargain under which blacks got Jesus and whites got the world. King had always decried an ethereal Christianity that heralded Christ only after the cross.

Clerical reluctance was more than diffidence. The cantankerous James Bevel was initially convinced that the proper purview of Christian faith was crown-wearing. As a student at Alabama Baptist Theological Seminary, he initially remained aloof as fellow seminarians John Lewis and Bernard Lafayette threw themselves into the network of Nashville nonviolence energized by Revs. James Lawson, Kelly Smith, and C. T. Vivian. One night in the midst of a dorm bull session, Bevel asked John Lewis, "Why you always preaching this *social* gospel and not the *Gospel* gospel," John Lewis recalls. "'Well,' I said, parroting the words I'd heard Dr. King speak in Montgomery, 'I think we need to be less concerned with getting people up to those streets paved with gold and more concerned about what people are dealing with right here on the streets of Nashville.'

"'John,' one of the others said, shaking his head, 'you gotta stop preaching the gospel according to Martin Luther *King* and start preaching the Gospel of Jesus *Christ*.'"[23]

In a sense, Bevel at this time was anticipating Rev. Jerry Falwell's 1965 "Ministers and Marches" sermon, in which he decried King's Christian activism and the flooding of rabbis and ministers into Selma after Bloody Sunday. "The Christian's citizenship is in heaven. Our only purpose on this earth . . . is to know Christ and to make Him known . . . Preachers are not called to be politicians but to be soul winners."[24]

Yet even if one narrows the focus to those strains of black religion with a more worldly emphasis, the belief that freeing the captives is God's constitutive act did not by itself generate participation. Prophetic preachers

have invoked the theme of deliverance for various ends, including counseling patience because God will eventually deliver. In his dazzling "Moses
at the Red Sea," C. L. Franklin preached, "But you know God always has
his Moses on hand," though Franklin allowed that his name might be
George Washington Carver as much as Frederick Douglass. Franklin's
concern was the realm of personal trials no less than bondage, and the
message included an appeal to patience: "Oh, wait a little while, / . . . Just
wait on him. Just wait on him / He'll lead you across the Red Seas. / He'll
make you overcome your enemies."[25]

King did not seek to affirm the value of deliverance or a yearning to
be free, but actually to deliver his people. You could say he was engaged
in applied theology: to transfer the optimism of his people's faith that
God would deliver them to their efforts to deliver themselves, to their
hunch that their efforts would achieve success, and to their search for the
guts and gumption to stride out of the church and face snarling dogs
and growling Klansmen. To unleash the convulsive power of his faith,
King had to draw out its worldly import, and where this was lacking, to
invent it.[26]

All this explains why in launching the siege of Birmingham King had
to open up a war on two fronts, not just against Bull Connor but also
against the black ministers who remained aloof or opposed to the Birmingham campaign. Before an audience of two hundred ministers, he offered a genteel yet testy rejoinder. "Only a 'dry as dust' religion prompts a
minister to extol the glories of Heaven while ignoring the social conditions that cause men an earthly hell." But then King attacked his clerical
audience in more personal terms: "I'm tired of preachers riding around in
big cars, living in fine homes, but not willing to take their part in the
fight. . . . If you can't stand up with your own people, you are not fit to be
a leader!"[27]

Later that night, the less varnished Abernathy, reporting on that same
meeting to a large church audience, lit into those "Uncle Toms" who were
thwarting the insurgency. "We had a roomful of the elite, the Bourgeoisie,
the class of Birmingham who are now living on the hill, learning to
talk proper," declared the best buddy of the paragon of proper talking.
"They've got their hair tinted various colors, trying to fool somebody. Year
before last they lived like us, across the railroad tracks, took baths in a tin
tub, and went to an outhouse. Now they are strutting around proper.

How did they get rich? We made them rich." Abernathy was just getting warmed up. "You ought to threaten to cut the preachers' salaries if they don't stand up with you for freedom. They say this is the wrong time and yet they have had 350 years. I want to know when the devil gives the right time."[28]

On the surface, King's rejection of "dry as dust religion" tracked his fancier repudiations drawn from Buber and Tillich in "Letter from Birmingham Jail," ostensibly addressed to the Birmingham white ministers and one rabbi who had criticized his actions. In both cases, King advanced a social gospel and all of its temporal corollaries: the danger of patience and the urgency of action. And in both cases, too, his anger at those who counseled waiting was palpable. Yet in contrast to the whites he addressed in "Letter" as third-party outsiders to the movement, King sought to enlist his fellow black ministers in the freedom struggle. His attack on his colleagues took as its vantage point not the universality of profession in "Letter" ("My dear fellow clergymen"), but love of one's race. Just as King proclaimed in Selma, "I am here because my people are suffering," he castigated the black ministers of Birmingham for insufficient racial loyalty—"If you can't stand up with your own people, you're not fit to be a leader."

King's excoriation and Abernathy's lampoon of clerical procrastination were small signs of the civil war erupting within Afro-Christian life. Disputes over "the right time" were at the heart of it. Unfortunately, the Birmingham ministers' indifference to "earthly hell" was no aberration. King was painfully aware that many black churches were making no effort to deliver the captives. "You know, there are some Negro preachers that have never opened their mouths about the freedom movement . . . And every now and then you get a few members [who say]: *(Make it plain)* 'They talk too much about civil rights in that church' *(That's right).*"[29]

King's reply flowed from his belief that a minister "must be concerned about the whole man. Not merely his soul but his body. It's all right to talk about heaven. I talk about it because I believe firmly in immortality. But you've got to talk about the earth. It's all right to talk about long white robes over yonder, but I want a suit and some shoes to wear down here. It's all right to talk about the streets flowing with milk and honey in heaven, but I want some food to eat down here."[30]

Beyond infusing an otherworldly religion with social relevance, King also drew on religion to underscore the urgency of putting one's body on the line. As always, he invoked secular rationales too. The practical aim of the rhetorical adjustments we examined in the last chapter, such as linking "fleecy locks and dark complexion" to "standing up," was to entice the audience into direct action. Most of the themes in King's secular musings on time—the danger of patience, the evil of "normality," the folly of procrastination—were designed to alter perceptions of the temporal horizon of deliverance. His speech "Three Words" was an obvious invitation to testimonies of urgency. King's questions—"What do we want?" "Where do we want it?" and "When do we want it?"—drew resounding replies of "all (our freedom)," "here," and "now." Calling on "every Negro citizen," and every white one too, to join the movement, King said, "I ask you to decide now, not tomorrow, not later on tonight, but I urge you to start to decide at this minute, remembering a tiny little minute, just sixty seconds in it, I didn't choose it, I can't refuse it, it's up to me to use it. A tiny little minute, just sixty seconds in it, but eternity is in it! God let us use the minute [cheering]."[31]

None of these rationales exceeded the passion of King's explicitly sacred exhortations to join the fight. As King told it, a minister acquaintance had run up against grumbling about his activist preaching from his own congregation, but King told him to pay it no mind because they didn't "anoint you to preach. (Yeah)." It was God who "anointed. . . . Some people are suffering. (Make it plain) Some people are hungry this morning. (Yes) [clap] Some people are still living with segregation and discrimination this morning. (Yes, sir) I'm going to preach about it. (Preach it. I'm with you) I'm going to fight for them. I'll die for them if necessary, because I got my guidelines clear."[32]

Even when King emphasized that "I am here [in Selma] because my people are suffering," he also cast participation as a righteous obligation in the same terms he used in the context of an address to whites in "Letter from Birmingham Jail." Had not the eighth-century prophets "carried their 'thus saith the Lord' far beyond the boundaries of their hometowns," had not Paul left Tarsus to preach the gospel in hamlets and cities across the Greco-Roman world? "Like Paul, I must constantly respond to the Macedonian call for aid."[33] The equivalences that King was making had a near-algebraic clarity: the prophets and disciples were doing God's work, the movement was doing God's work, King was doing God's work. The implication was clear: you should do God's work too.[34]

God's single command to King during his midnight crisis was the order to participate: "And he said to me, 'Martin Luther, stand up for justice.'" If the Lord told him to stand up for justice, King in turn told others to stand up with him. This trumpeting of a collective obligation to fight was evident in the "we" that runs through the series of "If . . . then" constructions in King's first address at a Montgomery mass meeting. Translating the cosmic storm into historical form, King brought Jesus into the very heart of the movement, onto the streets of Montgomery, into church. That was the implication of the statement that we have seen, "If we are wrong, God Almighty is wrong. And Jesus . . . never came down to earth *(Yes)* [Applause]." You can almost hear the crackling of electricity in the church as the audacity of those words sinks in. Who in that audience was prepared to entertain this apostasy: Jesus never came down, we are wrong?[35]

The Jesus who "came down" was not simply the tender lover who preached agape but a manly figure who was not afraid to fight (nonviolently). "Do you know Him? / Jesus Christ / Our son," went the freedom song. "He is my lawyer / . . . The first man on the battlefield / And the last to leave." At an SCLC retreat, King made Jesus a virtuoso of mobilization, the fisher of fishermen. King's efforts to justify putting children on the front lines in Birmingham drew power from this vision of a young Jesus as a radical insurgent who walked the earth.

The searing images of children bounced across the pavement by high-pressure hoses had provoked national condemnation of the movement's turn to the young to replenish the battered army. Mass jailing and the threat of school expulsions had heightened parental anxiety, which Rev. Wyatt Tee Walker tried to counter. "Your mommas and pappas and preachers ought to tell them, 'Don't you dare go to jail,' and wink your eye at them." We need one thousand young people in jail, Bevel told the audience at East 16th Street Baptist Church. Once, he might have exempted not just children but mothers and black men with jobs. "But it's not a civil rights struggle, it's a struggle for the Kingdom of God to come . . . the struggle of righteousness against evil. Christ himself could not exempt you from the struggle. Can you imagine . . . yourself going up to the gates of heaven, lining up behind John, who's walking with his head in his hands, he's lost it fighting for the Kingdom . . . And every person that knows anything about God ought to be involved in the struggle for the Kingdom."[36]

At last, King weighed in. "And don't worry about your children," King reassured the crowd. "They are going to be all right. Don't hold them back if they want to go to jail. For they are doing a job for not only themselves but for all of America and for all mankind." Suddenly, King swerved into scripture—"Somewhere we read, a little child shall lead them"—which provoked the audience into responsiveness. "And remember there was another little child just twelve years old and he got involved in a discussion back in Jerusalem as his parents moved down the dusty road leading them back to their little village of Nazareth."

In his mid-1950s sermon "Rediscovering Lost Values," King had used this same story of the Passover journey when Mary and Joseph lost Jesus as an allegory about remembering sacred values. ("They didn't mean to forget him . . .") But in the mass meeting venue, rocked by the sound of "I'm on my way to Freedom Land," King seized on the story as a parable of engagement. "And when they got back and bothered him and touched him and wanted him to move on, at that moment he said, 'I must be about my father's business.' *(All right)*." As if no further transition were required, he substituted the Birmingham kids for Jesus as the subject of Jesus' sentence: "These young people are about their Father's business. *(Yes)* And they are carving a tunnel of hope through the great mountain of despair and they will bring to this nation a newness and a genuine quality and idealism that it so desperately needs."[37]

The indirection of King's roundabout construction, "if we are not right, then Jesus never came down to earth," is hard to miss. That is also true of the parallel drawn by "there was another child," which spread the aura of godly purpose from Jesus to black protesters. These were less direct versions of Bevel's statement that "we read these Bible stories and we say, 'Oh, that used to happen.' God does everything that he did then, he does it now. . . . The leader of the movement is God himself."[38]

The intricacy of such moves underscores the final way in which King relied on religion to impart urgency to participation. In a fashion more oblique than invoking explicit duty or God's command, King tried to prompt action through evocative rhetoric and metaphoric parallels. This often poetic transfer of qualities between the sacred and the secular, like the exchanges between sermon and speech, was two-way. Even as King's strategy of elevation lifted ordinary black people into biblical narratives, the very context of direct action entailed a "bringing down" of the sacred into the present. This was the significance of King's resorting to the continuous biblical present in such claims as "We are marching through the Red Sea." Septima Clark, a legendary movement figure active in the citizenship schools, experienced the hypnotic power of King's biblical analogies: "As he talked about Moses, and leading the people out, and getting the people into the place where the Red Sea would cover them, he would just make you see them. You believed it."[39]

John Lewis was also struck by King's ability to draw the listener into his dramaturgy. That power was only fortified by the deep resonance of the stories themselves among his prime southern audience. Once again, speaker and listener together played a role in endowing movement events not just with biblical meaning but with God's approval.

"We were God's children, wading in the water," Lewis reflected on his third, and finally successful, attempt to cross Pettus Bridge. At the very start, King had invoked the Israelites' time in the wilderness as they headed off to Montgomery. A few weeks after Lewis reenacted the pain of the first and foiled Bloody Sunday march on its fortieth anniversary in 2005, he fell into a hushed state of reverie as we sat in his office on Capitol Hill. Back in 1965, as the marchers made their way across Lowndes County, Lewis was feeling not quite that "God is on our side but we were on his side. As we walked and marched during those five days, I felt like I was marching and walking with the holy spirit. We were caught up in something, allowing ourselves to be used by God Almighty. . . . One day, the heavens opened up, it rained and it rained. I felt like the Lord our God was speaking to us."

As Lewis recalled, "Our struggle was the modern day struggle of the children of Israel, and we were on our way out of Egypt land to a better land, to a Promised Land. [Like] the children of Israel, we were in a strange land, and from time to time we had to sing a strange song. And so we sang our songs of deliverance"—now Lewis shifted to a rhythmic song-chant—"we would sing 'Go down Moses, go way down in Egypt land, and tell old pharaoh, to let my people go, go down in Alabama, go down in Selma, tell Sheriff Clark, tell George Wallace, to let my people go.'" Lewis was not alone in feeling that Martin Luther King had been ordained, almost like a modern-day Moses. "Montgomery was not necessarily the Promised Land, but it was a different place, it was a different land because people had told us we would never make it across that bridge." That's why so much emotion was released early in the march when they crossed over the Alabama River: "We were crossing our own Red Sea, our own river of Jordan."[40]

King's evocative immediacy was evident in his speech after the marchers finally arrived in Montgomery. Like his equation of black audience, slave forebears, and Israelites, King's shift into slave dialect when he sampled the lyrics of "When Joshua Fit the Battle of Jericho" was standard fare. But the decisive move came when King merged Joshua's army with the Selma protesters and made their connection tangible: "The pattern of their feet as they walked through Jim Crow barriers in the great stride toward freedom is the thunder of the marching men of Joshua *(Yes sir)* and the world rocks beneath their tread *(Yes sir)*." *Is*. Not *is like*.[41]

The Kingian refrains, taken out of the church sanctuary and placed in the civic spaces of courthouse alleys and insurgent marches along Route 80, were changed in the process. The equivalences became more exact. The deliverance King celebrated was not the hypothetical or archetypal one that keeps hope alive, which might unfold in some vague hereafter or abstract "there." The link between the marching armies of Joshua and those of Selma was graphically literal, the actual "thunder of marching feet" *here,* up and over Pettus Bridge. Once again, King was not affirming the value of deliverance or faith in its eventual arrival but the process of actually achieving it, and not just acts of deliverance by God but by ordinary black people. King was tying his audience's sense of black exceptionalism to the character they showed in tumbling down walls, not to their capacity for faith or hope as he often did while preaching. Jeremiah gave way to Joshua.

In Birmingham just before he and King were arrested on Good Friday, Abernathy's almost casual blurring of realms attested to the obviousness of their linkage: "I been with him [King] in the fiery furnace, and I'm not going to let him down now; I been with him in the lion's den, I'm not going to let him down now. I been with him on Patmos Island, I'm not going to let him down now."[42] Such transfers of energy from the sacred to the worldly imbued the movement with the legitimacy of God's sacred purpose.

This legitimation by intimation was evident in the sermon-like climaxes with which King sometimes closed his mobilization talk. The mixing of earthly and biblical time, pulling the temporal horizon into the present, evoking God's presence in the movement and his approval too, the heightened sense of immediacy of deliverance, the claim to prophetic vision ("I can see")—these were all present in King's transition from calm to storm in countless towns across the Black Belt. They were present at the end of the Selma to Montgomery march, when he declared, "Our God is marching on. / Glory, hallelujah! Glory, hallelujah! / Glory, hallelujah, Glory, hallelujah! / His truth is marching on." It was evident up on the mountaintop in Memphis, when he was near shouting, "Glory hallelujah, mine eyes have seen the glory of the coming of the Lord!" It was evident in Selma when he reprised "I Have a Dream," declaring, "Free at last, free at last, thank God almighty, I'm free at last," as if the movement had completed its godly work.

There would seem to be an irony here in using otherworldly ecstasy to mobilize ordinary black people to take practical action. In the black performed sermon, the intensity of the climax offers a foretaste of the Kingdom to come. "As the sermon progresses," Richard Wright observed, "the preacher's voice increases in emotional intensity, and we, in tune and sympathy with his sweeping story, sway in our seats until we have lost all notion of time and have begun to float on a tide of passion. The preacher begins to punctuate his words with sharp rhythms, and we are lifted far beyond the boundaries of our daily lives, and upward and outward, until drunk with our enchanted vision, our senses lifted to the burning skies, we do not know who we are, what we are, or where we are."[43]

In truth, any irony was only apparent. King's crescendos may have kept the notion and emotion of foretaste, but they changed what was being tasted and the location of the Kingdom. The transport provoked by King aimed not to take the listener out of history but to bring God into it. The very meaning of freedom in various "Dream" performances—"Free at last, free at last"—altered in the enacting of it, merging the "freedom to go home to my Lord" with the freedom to vote, the rapture of God's coming with the rapture of freedom's coming.

Mine eyes. Have *seen*. Such sensuous acts of seeing God offered the same blurring of the immediacy of perception and the abstraction of God that appeared in the old spiritual recommissioned as a freedom song, "Over My Head I See Freedom." For King to say he had seen the coming of the Lord moments after beholding the promised land of freedom, and to have glimpsed both in the context of struggle, was to commingle the two—to make the same elision that marked Fanny Lou Hamer's melding of deliverance and redemption in her hybrid lyrics, "Go Tell it on the Mountain" (a song of welcoming the savior), to which she added the Exodus twist, "to let my people go." It was the same transition effected by all of King's praise songs that mixed the glory of the movement with the glory of the Lord, thereby summoning God's authority on the movement's behalf. It was not just that "God is on our side," as the freedom song put it. Mobilizing for freedom was the enactment of God's will.

Over and over, King orated, "God is moving *here*." The "here" in "Come by here, Lord" defined the physical place to which God must come, and King too, since he lyrically substituted himself for God as the one who had "come by here." The "here" was vividly concrete—in the alley where those petitioning for the right to vote had been herded day in and day out; on the courthouse steps where Jim Clark punched out C. T. Vivian and knocked down Mrs. Cooper, and Andrew Marrissett cried out, "Why are you beating us?" Just as the "we" had acquired meanings more precise than "someone is suffering," the targets of the struggle acquired the same specificity: not the struggle against pharaohs in general but the political struggle against their own hometown pharaoh, Jim Clark.

King's mixing thus repeated the more general stance of freedom songs, which replaced an otherworldly end ("I woke up with my mind on Jesus") with a historical one ("I woke up with my mind on freedom"). "Keep Your Eye on the Prize," culled from the hymn "Keep Your Hand on the Gospel Plow," had already concretized God's place in the civil rights movement. The people engaged in the Albany, Georgia, insurgency concretized the song further, thereby muddying the meaning of "the other side"; to the biblical verse—"Jordan River is deep and wide / We'll find freedom on the other side"—they added a more tangible one: "Albenny, Georgia lives in race / We're goin' to fight it from place to place / Keep your eyes / On the prize / Hold—On."[44]

It was in Albany that Ralph Abernathy told the audience, "Now nobody can enjoin God. I don't care what kind of injunction the city attorney seeks to get, he cannot enjoin God. This is God's movement *(yeah, Amen)*." After listing all the powers and principalities to whom Albany did not belong, he closed with "*All-benny* belongs to God," and then fell into a prayer which restored God's proprietary interest in their struggle with lines that King favored as well—"For the prophet said: / 'The earth is the Lord's / And the fullness thereof / The world and they that dwell therein'"—before closing, "And this is God's world / This is God's *All-benny!*"[45]

Sacred and secular; church and movement; sermon and speech; prophecy and pragmatism, biblical time and now. Was there a danger that all this mixing would confuse the realms? That it might secularize and thus trivialize the spiritual? It's just as true that King and the others were sacralizing the secular. They did not find it hard to tell the two realms apart; they refused to.

It took the interpretive efforts of King and the rest of the movement to make the bridge from moral culture to political culture. They had to apply the cosmic optimism implicit in the slaves' assertion, "there is a balm in Gilead," to the tangible realm of the freedom struggle. They had to shift the time line so that God's commitment to liberation would be realized not in some vague jubilee but here on earth, now. And they had to adapt the principle of hope embodied in God's primeval act of deliverance to their own efforts to deliver. In doing so, they were doing more than expressing some underlying tradition of prophecy deliverance or the social gospel; they were working it, applying it, and thus making it new.[46]

The obligation to preach "the acceptable year of the Lord" was crucial to the enterprise. But when is that? "Some people reading this passage," King conceded in a sermon at Ebenezer, "feel that it's talking about some period beyond history." But no, King insisted: it is "the year that is acceptable to God because it fulfills the demands of his kingdom." And that year is not simply inside history, it is now and not later. "The acceptable year of the Lord can be *this* year . . . The acceptable year of the Lord is any year *(Amen)* when men decide to do right."[47]

At this point King let loose a machine-gun volley of repetition—eighteen sentences all beginning "The acceptable year of the Lord is . . ." that defined the eclectic nature of doing right: it includes not living riotously, and loving one's neighbor—even women "not using the telephone . . . to spread malicious gossip." It is also "when"—and here King tinkered some, expanding the human role over God's by inserting "men will allow"— "justice to roll down like waters, and righteousness like a mighty stream *(Yes)*." An acceptable year is also "that year when people in Alabama *(Make it plain)* will stop killing civil rights workers and people are simply engaged in the process of seeking their constitutional rights."

This is the social gospel mandate, spinning in a wild, widening gyre, beyond seminary and sermon too. "It seems that I can hear the God of the universe smiling and speaking to this church, saying, 'You are a great church *(Glory to God)* because I was hungry and ye fed me . . . I was naked and ye clothed me . . . I was sick and ye visited me . . . I was in prison and ye gave me consolation by visiting me. And this is the church that's going to save the world.'"

TWELVE

The Rationality of Defiance

"There is a Balm in Gilead"

Could one really see freedom "over my head"? In any case, that misplaced concreteness had a corollary. If freedom was that near, it had to be close at hand. The clincher was the line that followed it: "There must be a God." If freedom validated God's presence, then freedom must have been part of God's design, and surely a person could reasonably imagine its imminent arrival. Both of these bestowals—imminence on freedom, legitimacy on the movement—were thus bound up with perceptions of the possible. If this was truly "God's Albany" and not police chief Laurie Pritchett's, perhaps a victory really was gloriously in the making.

Convincing southern blacks that the attack on segregation was not irrational or suicidal was daunting. King had to make the case that deliverance was a rational goal in the face of good evidence to the contrary. The movement argued that deliverance was possible, likely, even inevitable. To mobilize bodies and prevent defections, King sought to shape his audience's appraisals of the rationality of protest. First, he harped on the ordained victory and glorious future that would redeem the privations and danger of present action. Second, through maneuvers that ranged from the imperative to the rhythm of repetition, he evoked the feeling of movement forward, of acceleration to an end point. Finally, he answered pessimism with an applied theology of hope that compensated for disappointments.

King's rhetoric of assertion brimmed with exultant positivity, as he held out the "glittering future" that awaited black people. Before memorializing a string of civil rights martyrs, he intoned, "In the glow of the lamplight on my desk a few nights ago, I gazed again upon the wondrous sign of our times, full of hope and promise of the future *(Uh huh).*"[1] The triumphalism of his constant climaxes, "Mine eyes have seen the glory of the coming of the Lord," offered a millennial version of the civil religious equivalent, "the day of man as man."

As we have seen, the story of Exodus offered special resonance, a mirror in which the movement caught a glimpse of itself and provoked itself to action. The lyrics of freedom songs amplified familiar plot points; "Wade in the Water" combined the emphatic imperative to act with the back-stiffening certainty that "God's gonna trouble the waters." "Oh Mary Don't You Weep, Don't You Moan" carried the heartening reminder, "Pharaoh's army got drownded." More generally, Exodus fused the logic of inductive possibility—the escape from bondage—and deductive inevitability—deliverance was God's prime act, unfolding over and over again through history. In either case, the denouement of Exodus held out the hope of a wondrous payoff.

At a meeting in 1965, SCLC and SNCC were talking about sending two spies into Lowndes County to assess the environment for registering blacks to vote. King "abruptly started reciting by heart the passage from Hebrew scriptures about Moses sending twelve scouts into Canaan to scope out the Promised Land. When they came back after forty days, two of the scouts encouraged the Israelites to fight for the Promised Land of milk and honey; the other ten terrified them with reports of giants who would slaughter them." King detailed the defiance of the command of God and Moses to go forward, after which God sentenced the Israelites to forty years in the wilderness. Only the two courageous spies, Joshua and Caleb, were ever permitted to enter the Promised Land. "After reciting his Torah portion, King was followed without pause by other preachers in the circle: Abernathy, then C. T. Vivian, then Hosea Williams, all speaking from memory. The land of milk and honey, one said, would be a land flowing with black people exercising the vote."[2]

More typically, King tended to avoid sustained biblical narratives in favor of compressed clips and momentary mentions. Encouraging blacks during the Montgomery bus boycott to walk and not to get weary, King envisioned "a great camp meeting" of "freedom and justice." "God is leading us out of a bewildering Egypt," he pronounced, "through a bleak and desolate wilderness, toward a bright and glittering promised land."[3]

It would make sense that Resurrection would operate differently from Exodus. Yet that was not entirely the case. If the slaves commingled Moses and Jesus,[4] a different similarity, rooted in the functional needs of mobilization, governed King's use of the two stories. In both cases, he exploited a common temporal structure—suffering yielding to an ordained end point—to convince participants why reasonable men and women should accept the risks of defiance. As he told the people of Montgomery, "We have lived under the agony and darkness of Good Friday with the conviction that one day the heightened glow of Easter would emerge on the horizon. We have seen truth crucified and goodness buried, but we have kept going with the conviction that truth crushed to earth will rise again." Elsewhere, he insisted: "The cross we bear precedes the crown we wear. To be a Christian one must take up his cross, with all its difficulties and agonizing and tension-packed content and carry it until that very cross leaves its marks upon us and redeems us to that more excellent way which comes only through suffering."[5]

Oppressed blacks, Keith Miller observes, "could easily take prophetic and eschatological assurances that their movement formed a sequel to God's narrative of Exodus and Resurrection."[6] But King didn't limit himself to these grand stories to coax people into the struggle. He exploited all sorts of pledges that future rewards would far exceed present costs—from naturalistic ones (the season of suffering would give way to a different season) to civil religious and global equivalents (freedom's global march). Even King's most biblically resonant language spoke to the hard-boiled gamble involved in the decision to participate: the rewards at stake discounted by the probability of attaining them. The unique contribution of Exodus and Resurrection was to convert a gamble into a guarantee.

King drew the attention of his audience to the fruits that would accrue to their investment of effort. That emphasis on the end point—glittering mountaintop, valleys exalted and mountains made low, Resurrection, the beautiful symphony of brotherhood, tumbling walls, gleam of light, promised land—transformed random, discrete happenings into a sequence charged with unfolding purpose. But King also reflected on the process of getting there. Exodus especially resonated with this theme of the journey to freedom—the vexing phase of marching as an interlude between bondage and liberation: the flight from Egypt, crossing the Red Sea, and wandering in the wilderness that didn't feel so different from the trek across Lowndes County.

King exalted the idea of forward motion as much as the destination. He loved to herald the "stride toward freedom"—the title of his first book. Like an accent mark, he constantly interjected the phrases "Walk together, children" and "Get on your walking shoes." Linking journey and destination, movement and reward, only accentuated the likelihood of success. King did so poetically, with and without echoes of Exodus. "We've come a long way since that travesty of justice," he observed after the trek from Selma, then slipped right into a quote from James Weldon Johnson: "We have come over a way / that with tears hath been watered. *(Yes, sir)* / We have come treading our paths / Through the blood of the slaughtered. *(Yes, sir)* / Out of the gloomy past, *(Yes, sir)* / Till now we stand at last / Where the white gleam / Of our bright star is cast *(Speak, sir).*"[7]

Gandhi's march cast the same connection between effort and reward, the march and liberation, in a useful historical form. Gandhi, King emphasized, "started with just a few people. He said to 'em, 'Now we're just gonna march. If you're hit, don't hit back. They may curse you. Don't curse back. They may beat you and push you around, but just keep goin'.'

"'They may even try to kill you, but just develop the quiet courage to die if necessary without killing—and just keep on marchin'.' *(yea-eeah)*.

"Just a few men started out, but when they got down to that sea more than a million people had joined in that march . . . and" [voice excited] "Gandhi and those people reached down in the sea and got a little salt in their hands and broke that law, and the minute that happened *(all right)* it seemed I could hear the boys at Number Ten Downing Street in London, England, say: 'It's all over now.' [pandemonium].

"There is nothing in this world more powerful than the power of the human soul . . ."[8]

King also rendered the link between journey and destination in a more organizational vein, in the form of the protest march. At Holt Street Baptist Church, King's "until" was a pledge of victory and the payoff that would vindicate the sacrifice that went into achieving it. "Let us march on ballot boxes until the salient misdeeds of bloodthirsty mobs *(Yes sir)* will be transformed into the calculated good deeds of orderly citizens. *(Speak, Doctor)* Let us march on ballot boxes *(Let us march)* until the Wallaces of our nation tremble away in silence." And then, adding a more preacherly element to the mix, King instructed the audience, "Let us march until . . . we elect men who will not fear to do justly, love mercy, and walk humbly with thy God."[9]

As the insistence of the refrain "Let us march" indicates, King also evoked the impression of inexorable movement, accelerating rush, and imminent arrival that reflected the entwining of immediacy and rationality. Imperatives, the drumbeat of repetition, the continuous present, the rhetoric of proclamation, and crescendo all created auditory and kinetic equivalents to ordained arrival at the destination.

The imagery of one of King's favorite lines from Amos, justice rushing down like water, suggested the unstoppable realization of freedom—a biblical equivalent of gravitational force. Rhythm and repetition built up a similar feeling of momentum, sometimes intensifying a sense of agency along with rationality. After declaring his fierce resolve—"We are not about to turn around. *(Yes, sir)*"—followed by his insistence—"We are on the move now. *(Yes, sir)*"—King began a chant, "Yes, we are on the move and no wave of racism can stop us. *(Yes, sir)* We are on the move now. The burning of our churches will not deter us. *(Yes, sir)* The bombing of our homes will not dissuade us. *(Did you hear him, Yes sir)* We are on the move now. *(Yes, sir)* The beating and killing of our clergymen and young people will not divert us. We are on the move now *(Yes, sir)*."[10]

The commanding power of King's imperatives, along with the lilting rhythm that rocked them along, reinforced the impression of propulsive motion. "Keep this movement going! Keep this movement rolling! In spite of the difficulties! And we are going to have a few more difficulties! Keep climbing! Keep moving! If you can't fly, run!" As the crowd now joined him, revving up the intensity and amplifying the force of their locomotion, King kept chanting, almost breaking into a shout: "If you can't run, walk! If you can't walk, crawl! But by all means keep moving!"[11] As

King finished, the sound of the freedom song lines, "Oh Lord I'm running, I'm running for freedom," rang out through the church.

King's use of a biblical present did not just heighten the sense of God's presence in the movement; it also heightened the expectation of success. The phrase "We are moving through the Red Sea of injustice" borrowed the inevitable denouement to assuage any doubts about what lay in store. King's insistence that "the marching feet of Joshua's army are the marching feet of the Selma marchers" applied the known victory of tumbling walls to the struggle whose outcome was not yet self-evident.

King used another version of the continuous present to cast a hoped-for-future as an achieved fact, as if the rhetoric of proclamation were sufficient to induce the wished-for result. We might call it the prophetic present. Sweeping across the Black Belt in the run-up to the Poor People's March, resolved to mobilize thousands of soldiers for his liberation army, King began his pronouncement of steely resolve in the future tense. "Now we are going to Washington. I'll tell you, we got to keep attention on the problems of the poor." Envisioning mule trains of poor people "coming up" out of the Southland, he pledged to keep the power center of the nation "locked up in the sense we're going to be on them." At a certain point King seemed to pick up on the feel of "coming up out of," and his voice quickened portentously. With the audience rumbling and applauding, King offered his vision, still in the future tense: ". . . and the Mississippi people will join the Alabama people and the Alabama people will join the Georgia people and the South Carolina people and they're just moving on up . . . As we get toward Washington, somebody around the administration in the departments of government will come to the window."[12]

At this juncture, with what sounds like a biblical "Lo, will look out, somebody will say," King now moved fully into preaching mode, just moments from crossing into that prophetic present with the trembling emphasis placed on the very first word, "Where are they coming from?" His language echoed Paul's exchange in Corinthians, "I asked the angel: Who are these? And he answered and said to me: These are they who are sent forth in the day of the resurrection to bring the souls of the righteous, who intrepidly walk according to God":

> I can hear somebody say,
> "They're coming up out of Mississippi

And Alabama and South Carolina.
Who are these people?
These are they!
They are coming up
out of their trials and tribulations.
These are they!
They are coming up out of their agonies, poverty.
These are they!
They're coming up
out of years of hurt and deprivation."

With barely a transition, King shifted biblical verses while maintaining that position of clairvoyance from which he was able to hear and see the unseen and the unheard:

And I can hear somebody else sayin'
"I see 'em coming, how many?"
And I can see somebody trying to tell 'em,
And pretty soon I hear a voice,
"I looked, and I watched and it seems to me
It's a number that no man can number."

Exhortation, incantation, and proclamation were all elements of the rhetoric of assertion that sought to turn wish into reality. They developed in language the momentum that King sought to inspire in action.[13] Through the flow and beat of his verbal performance, King created the same kind of pulse as the freedom singing that primed the audience for a King appearance. All the elements in the field of sound amplified one another, creating an auditory rush that was the sound equivalent of the sensuous image of "freedom rushing down like water." The rousing rhythm of "I'm on my way to Freedom Land" evoked the arrival of a future that was yet to be realized, adding a collective exclamation mark to King's propulsive oratory.

Fittingly, anticipation and proclamation both came to a peak in King's crescendos. King was jumping the gun a bit when he crossed over into a rapturous present tense at the conclusion of speeches in Selma and Detroit: "Free at last, free at last, thank God almighty I'm free at last." But the taste of freedom embodied in that anticipatory present wasn't really a lie either. Merging history and eternity, the rapture of God's coming and that of freedom's coming, permitted the vicarious experience in the present of a not-yet-attained state. Similarly, in declaring "mine eyes have seen," King was heightening an impression of the imminence of freedom itself no less than of God.[14]

Yet proclaiming hope was no guarantee. To achieve freedom in language was one thing; achieving it in life was another. The movement faced brutal oppression, setbacks, and demoralization. Sometimes, no amount of oratorical power could move people out of their lethargy. There were times when a sullen or fearful audience provoked King's colleagues, and one could hear in their rising shrillness an angry disappointment in the people. "Is anybody gong to jail—to join Dr. King?" a staff member asked in St. Augustine. "Who would like to be a witness for our leader?" It would be "the *worst* thing that ever happened to the Negro in America," another staffer pleaded, "if you don't follow him to jail. If you don't see the significance of this man's suffering and share it, then it's empty and meaningless and worthless." He warned if they didn't act, they would be parties to "crushing the greatest leader that the Negroes in America have ever known." Another jeered, "You can't reason with some people. The excuses they come up with! Some of you Negroes ain't ever going to be free."[15]

Confronting despondency was simply the flip side of King's more optimistic efforts to affirm the rationality of protest. King's reassurances sought to mitigate cost, risk, and despair. As a religion of the oppressed, Afro-Christianity had long dealt with the problem of evil and suffering. It fashioned a vision of endurance implicit in "holding on," a spiritual version of the secular fortitude in the injunction to "keep on keeping on." Beyond the vision of the suffering servant, the indomitable spirit of slave religion managed to produce a spirit of joyous affirmation. As always, the context of struggle in the movement added its own twists to despondency and the imagery King used to alleviate it.

King was at his best as a counselor against despair. Not only did his predilection for dialectic mesh with the stark poetics of biblical contrast, but the imagery of darkness and lightness offered metaphoric means to lift the spirit. In the low moments of the valley, King affirmed the "glittering mountaintops" that awaited the people. He imagined the problem of hope laterally as well as vertically, telling his audience not to worry about the young children in Birmingham: "And they are carving a tunnel of hope through the great mountain of despair." To move forward was to endure in time, and King's poignant warning—"we're in for a season of suffering"—implied a season of redemption to follow.

These metaphors affirmed the same temporal vision as Resurrection and Exodus—faith that the cosmos was a moral one, underwritten by God's redemptive love and commitment to justice. Like a cheerleader, King offered counter-depressive aphorisms to rouse the spirit: Love will not go unredeemed; God will make a way out of no way; my God is a good God; my God is marching on. Such phrases echoed the theology of hope King preached to his congregation, to whom he offered balm that would "make the wounded whole." In the mass meetings, however, King dispensed a different kind of balm for a different kind of wound. He gave solace not to sin-sick souls but to those who suffered from the sin-sick racism of others, and he offered it to them not as victims but as fighters. Mobilization narrowed the principle of hope to the tangible needs of the movement: to keep disappointment at bay and assure ultimate triumph.

King's appeals to faith had a deductive quality similar to his proclamations of victory. Both proceeded as if insistence alone would bring freedom into being. Faith was the ultimate warrant, trumping all tangible evidence of failure: "But I submit to you this evening that if we will only keep faith in the future we will be able to go on, and we will be able to gain an inner consolation and an inner stability that will make us powerful and . . . give us strength to carry the struggle on. . . . As I try to talk with you on the eve of a great action movement, don't despair. It may look dark now. (yeah) Maybe we don't know what tomorrow and the next day will bring. But if you will move on out of the taxi lane of your own despair, move out of the taxi lane of your worries and your fears, and get out in the take-off lane and move out on the wings of faith (yeah), we will be able to move up through the clouds of disappointment. (yeah) . . . and we will see the sunlight of freedom shining with all of its radiant beauty."[16]

Once again, the line between deduction and induction was at times muddy. In the throes of struggle, King and the others often focused on vivid precedents of rescue and persistence that suggested eventual triumph even in the midst of troubles. The first verse of "Hold On," like its subtitle of "Keep Your Eyes on the Prize," did not just shift attention from the "gospel plow" of the original version to Freedom's sweet name. It also moved time from a millennial future to an earthly one that would redeem all pain and indignity. Maybe the movement suffered defeats, but if you kept the faith, suffering would yield to future reward. After all, "Paul & Silas began to shout / The jail doors opened and they walked out / Keep your eyes on the prize, Hold on."

The press of mobilization worked the same specialization of meaning on the query "How long?" That was the cry of the prophet Habacca to God: *How long, oh Lord, will you make me look upon injustice?* In a time of turmoil in the kingdom of Israel, Habacca kept calling the people to righteousness, but they did not listen. King posed his version of that query in Montgomery after the march to Montgomery. He had also raised it in a Selma rally meeting, during the Albany campaign three years earlier, and in a Durham, North Carolina, mass meeting. Every generation has been provoked by that same perplexity. In 1992 in a sermon preached to his Brooklyn congregation, Rev. Johnny Youngblood also wanted to know, "How long, oh Lord, must I call for help, but You do not listen. . . . Why do You make me look at injustice? Why do You tolerate wrong?"

On the surface, Youngblood's lamentation seems to echo King's. Youngblood spoke that refrain of incomprehension to his riled congregation on the first Sunday after the Los Angeles riots, provoked by an all-white jury's acquittal of the police whose gratuitous beating of Rodney King was captured on video. Youngblood quickly established the psychic condition of preacher and congregants alike: "Brothers and Sisters, we are Christian realists here. We have come to praise God without a doubt. But all of us are affected by the Los Angeles situation. And we need the Lord to speak to us. Don't we need him to speak to us!"

Youngblood seemed to be struggling with the same emotions as his congregation. "We come before you as black men. . . . Rodney King could have been any one of us." In a dangerous moment, he almost seemed to inflame the sense of racial wound. "I do not necessarily condone the violence," but "the only worse thing that could have happened is nothing at all." Having made Rodney King every black man, he later made them all Samson—"you just don't kick a man when he's down." Was he justifying their thirst for vengeance? For a moment, he seemed to teeter on the edge of yielding to the desire to bring the whole place toppling over. "Satan, we going to tear your kingdom down."

Having ventilated that feeling, Youngblood was ready to sublimate it. At the outset, he had invoked Judges' praise for God: "I trust in God wherever I may be. No, I'm never, I'm never all alone, I know that God, He watches, He watches me." To all these wounds, in all this perplexity, he held out the hope of just deserts. "Don't you remember the Lord saying their blood shall be required at the hands of those who take their lives. That a sinner may go a thousand years but will not go unpunished." Maybe they kicked Rodney when he was down but "we must not despair and allow humiliation to have the last word because, y'all, listen, we are humiliated." Jesus was also down, whipped and buried, but "God got off his throne and said, 'Evil, you've had your way.'"[17]

King and Youngblood both deployed the same query, spoke as black men and Christians, and offered reassurance to their anxious audiences. Still, the two uses of that query could not have differed more. Youngblood sought to buttress faith in God in the face of the perplexity of enduring evil. By contrast, King invoked Habacca not against nihilistic skepticism but to shore up faith that the pain incurred in protest would be vindicated by eventual success.

This linkage of "How long?" with the calculus of likely success was obvious in Albany, Georgia, when King said, "Now I know that it gets dark sometimes and we begin to wonder: How long will we have to face this? How long will we have to protest for our rights?" Three years later King asked the same question in Montgomery after the march from Selma, and his stance was equally combative rather than spectatorial or meditative. *How long?* referred to the encounter with pain in the course of movement struggle, not with pain as a general feature of human existence. "I must admit to you that there are still some difficult days ahead," King told them. "We are still in for a season of suffering." He was so close to his people that he could almost leap right into their minds. "I know you are asking today, 'How long will it take?' *(Speak sir)* . . ." and he condensed all these doubts into a string of questions that included, "When will wounded justice, lying prostrate on the streets of Selma and Birmingham . . . be lifted from this dust of shame to reign supreme among the children of men," and "When will the radiant star of hope be plunged against the nocturnal bosom of this lonely night *(Speak, Speak, Speak)*, plucked from weary souls with chains of fear and the manacles of death?" and "How long will justice be crucified *(Speak, Speak)*, and truth bear it? *(Yes sir)*."[18]

A rough journey haunted King's posing of those questions. The distance to travel from the wounds of Selma to crashing down Jericho's walls was great. Here is a partial tally of the steep price paid by people in King's personal orbit just to walk to Montgomery, let alone to achieve voting rights: Rev. Bernard Lafayette, in the early days of Selma, bashed on the head; Rev. C. T. Vivian, who called Sheriff Jim Clark a Nazi right to his face, smashed and bleeding; Hosea Williams and John Lewis, trampled and reeling from Bloody Sunday; James Orange, beaten and then taken to the jail in nearby Marion; Willie Bolden, dispatched by King to Marion, his mouth bloodied; all the kids assaulted with billy clubs and cattle prods. Beyond King's personal coterie, there was Viola Liuzzo, felled by a Klan hit team following King's speech in Montgomery; J. T. Johnson and Hosea Williams had implored her not to make the dangerous night run back to Selma. The same night when Willie Bolden had his teeth shattered, Jimmie Lee Jackson was shot in Marion, where Coretta King was born and the parents of Andrew Young's wife still lived. Jackson had gone to the defense of his mother, who was attacked by rampaging lawmen.

Preaching at Zion's Chapel Methodist Church in Marion, Alabama, a few days after Jackson died, James Bevel played his part in the task of reassurance. According to Charles Fager, the white volunteer who shared a Selma jail cell with King and Abernathy in Selma, Bevel began by preaching on the murder of another James, as chronicled in Acts 12: "[King] Herod killed James, the brother of John, with a sword; and when he saw that it pleased the Jews, he proceeded to arrest Peter also." But Bevel's point was not to dwell on Jimmie Jackson, or thoughts of revenge. "'I'm not worried about James anymore,' Bevel shouted; 'I'm concerned about Peter, who is still with us. James has found release from the indignities of being a Negro in Alabama . . . James knows the peace this world cannot give and lives eternally the life we all hope someday to share.

"'I'm not worried about James. I'm concerned with Peter, who must continue to be cowed and coerced and beaten and even murdered.'"

A host of voting rights initiatives in surrounding counties depended on Bevel's ability to rescue Peter. Bevel found guidance in Esther 4:8, the passage where Mordecai gave a copy of the decree to kill the Jews to show to Esther, "and to declare it unto her, and to charge her that *she should go unto the king, to make supplication unto him, and to make request before him for her people.*" As Fager continues his chronicle, "There was a decree of destruction against black people in Alabama, Bevel went on, but they could not stand by any longer to see it implemented. 'I must go see the king!' he cried, again and again, and the answering shouts from the people grew to a full-throated chorus of approval. His intuition about their readiness was correct: *'We must go to Montgomery and see the king!'*[19] Thus was born the idea of the Selma to Montgomery March and all that would follow from it: Bloody Sunday, the march to Montgomery, President Johnson's address to the nation, and eventually the Voting Rights bill of 1965.

A few days later at Jackson's funeral in Marion (there was another ceremony as well at Brown Chapel in Selma), anticipating that Jackson might not be the last of the martyrs, Abernathy said simply, "We are gathered around the bier of the first casualty of the Black Belt demonstrations. Who knows but what before it's over you and I may take our rightful places beside him." Jackson's mother, still bearing the marks of the injuries she suffered moments before her now dead son came to her rescue in Mack's Cafe, was weeping as King rose to speak. He seemed to be struggling with his own despondency; according to one observer, "A tear glistened from the corner of his eye."[20]

King did not have to look far for a model for his remarks that day: the notes he made for the funeral were handwritten over a typed copy of his funeral oration for the four little girls blown up in Birmingham. As he did in that previous effort at exaltation, he recited his usual aphorisms of hope—"God still has a way of wringing good out of evil" and "unmerited suffering is redemptive." He conjured Jimmie Jackson, "speaking to us from the casket, and he is saying to us that we must substitute courage for caution." Did the "still" in "God still has a way" betray a tinge of doubt in King, or simply his recognition of the alpine chill unleashed by the killing of Jackson? Despite the sublime language, King did not submerge all of his bitter anger. "Who killed him?" King wanted to know, and his answer implicated many: the brutality of lawless sheriffs, and every politician who "fed his constituents the stale bread of hatred and the spoiled meat of racism," and a "Federal Government that is willing to spend millions of dollars a day to defend freedom in Vietnam but cannot protect the rights of its citizens at home."[21]

These were precisely the circumstances in which King felt pressure to maintain an appearance of strength in front of his people lest they waver too. But a private remark after the funeral provides a clue to what the inner man was feeling. King had been preoccupied with death for days now, not just Jackson's. Malcolm X had only recently been assassinated. Marching with the procession to the grave, King said to Joseph Lowery, "Come on, walk with me, Joe, this may be my last walk."[22] This had a more urgent tone to it than King's typical joshing. The Justice Department had made King privy to the details of the Klan plot to kill him in Marion on February 16, but the assassins could not get a clear shot. On the final leg of the trek to Montgomery, others on the front line would adorn themselves in suits in order to confuse any potential assassins.

Bloody Sunday only added its own menacing accent to King's posing the question "How long?" by the time the marchers reached Montgomery. Despite all the pain that King refused to rationalize and the string of black martyrs he was about to memorialize, King could still foretell a glorious future, not of the black man and the white man "but the day of man as man." He would soon assure his people that "our God is moving on." Presumably, so would the movement.

Yielding to the seductive force of the folk antiphonal, King fashioned Habacca's ancient question, the audience's same anxious query, and his answer, "Not long," into a rite of tender communion. He consoled them with a medley of hope culled from a litany of his favorite aphorisms, all with the force of certitude.

"I come to say to you this afternoon, however difficult the moment *(Yes sir)*, however frustrating the hour, it will not be long *(No sir)*, because truth pressed to earth will rise again *(Yes sir)*.

"How Long? Not long *(Yes sir)*, because no lie can live forever *(Yes sir)*.

"How Long? Not long *(All right, How long)*, because you shall reap what you sow. *(Yes sir)* . . .

"How Long? Not long, because the arc of the moral universe is long, but it bends toward justice *(Yes sir)*."

If that still was not enough assurance, he soon trumped all the others:

"How Long? *(How long)* Not long, *(Not long)* because: 'Mine eyes have seen the glory of the coming of the Lord.' *(Yes sir)*."[23]

In the tenderness of "my people, my people," in the empathetic anticipation of his people's pain, "Our God Is Marching On" overflowed with pathos. But King didn't have to reach too far to experience pain. Bowing down over his kitchen table at midnight, he too had wondered "How long?" The answer provided by his theology of hope simply poeticized the hard-boiled issues at stake: the pain and effort and discouragement would be redeemed by a not-so-distant triumph.

Never was this poeticizing force as powerful as in one burst of outright preaching in Selma in 1965 that hearkened back to a key moment in the battle between midnight and morning. Detailing the anxious moments and blasted hopes of the Montgomery bus boycott as day moved into night and back to morning, King kept the beat with the punctuation, "it was still midnight," as the audience interjected throughout, "Well" and "Yes sir" and "Speak." Recounting his own vulnerability back in Montgomery, he explained, "But I had to stand up before them and tell them the truth. I didn't quite know how to talk that night, I didn't have the same kind of fervor and the desire to get it over. But I got up and tried to say something. And I said something like this: 'I must be honest with you my friends, tomorrow, we're going to court . . . and I must be honest enough to say . . . they're going to rule against us. At this point, I can't tell you what will happen after that but I urge you to go on in the faith that has carried over all of these months.' And I concluded by saying that the same God that has carried us through experiences in the past, the same God who can make a way out of no way, will give us a way out of this dilemma." It is not clear whether King's despondency deepened the audience's own doubts. In any case, he admitted, "Even after I finished speaking, I still saw that cool breezes of pessimism were flowing all round that congregation."[24]

The interplay between King's own anxiety and the force of "the same God who can make a way out of no way" seems to have nudged King into the cadence of preaching. He began to pick up intensity, steadily building to a more joyous finale, with the audience calling out its shouts at the end of each line.

> It was midnight,
> darker than a thousand midnights.
> I went to bed and I couldn't sleep too well that night.
> It was dark,

the darkest hour of our struggle in Montgomery,
it was midnight in all of its dimensions.

King and Abernathy and a host of other leaders went down to the court,

> The sun had come up
> but it was still midnight for us.

King could see that despite the brilliant arguments of their lawyers, the judge was not listening,

> And I sat at that head table
> as chief defendant with the lawyer
> and I watched.
> And it was moving on toward noon
> but it was still midnight,
> still darker than a thousand midnights.

King peered across the room and saw people buzzing and leaving, he could tell something had happened, but

> Deep down within,
> it was still midnight.

At that point, an AP reporter informed King that the Supreme Court had held Montgomery's system of segregated buses unconstitutional. King began building to the finale,

> Morning had come,
> It was midnight
> but morning had come,
> And I got up from the table,
> and started running around the courtroom,
> telling the news,
> and I got back to
> one of the fine sisters in our movement,
> and she jumped up and she said,
> "Good Lord almighty,
> God done spoke from Washington." [pandemonium]

As the Selma audience broke into applause, King was ready to make the parallel exact, and he interjected the word "here" to ground them back in their struggle, only moments before allowing Howard Thurman's voice to carry them,

>And I'm telling you here,
>And so I'm here to tell you tonight,
>don't despair.
>I must admit
>there are some difficult days ahead,
>It's still midnight in Selma,
>but the psalmist is right,
>"weeping may tarry for a night
>but joy cometh in the morning."
>Centuries ago,
>a great prophet by the name of Jeremiah
>raised a great agonizing question.
>He looked out and he noticed,
>the evil people often prospering,
>And the good and righteous people often suffering,
>and he wondered about the injustices of life,
>and he, he raised the question,
>"Is there no balm in Gilead?
>Is there no physician there?"
>Centuries later,
>our slave foreparents came along,
>they had nothing to look forward to,
>morning after morning,
>but the sizzling heat,
>the rawhide whip of the overseer,
>and long rows of cotton.
>They too knew about the injustices of life,
>but they did an amazing thing!
>They looked back across the centuries,
>And took Jeremiah's question mark
>and straightened it into an exclamation point,
>and in one of their great spirituals,
>they could sing,
>"There is a balm in Gilead,
>to make the wounded whole,

there is a balm in Gilead,
to heal the sin-sick soul."[25]

After King told of his own need for balm, the local preacher under-scored the impact of King's preaching: "After listening to this dynamic message coming from the very soul of our leader, I'm sure you can join in that old hymn, I feel like going on. I feel like going on. Yes, our nights are dark but we feel like going on."

King's speech in Memphis the night before he was murdered gave the usual tension between hope and despondency an uncanny aura. Coming at a low point in King's spirits, "I've Been to the Mountaintop" paraded King's own capacity for hope, and by extension his audience's. In the weeks before, King had been a haunted, at times disconsolate man. When a worried Abernathy broached the subject, King had reassured him, "Don't worry Ralph, I'll be okay." Only hours before the speech, a demoralized King had begged off, telling Abernathy he didn't feel up to it. But as the hall filled, Abernathy called to tell King he had to come by. King finally entered the hall. Bolts of lightning lit up the auditorium.

King rehearsed the gritty details of the sanitation men and the boycott of various bakeries. But as he approached the end, King made himself Moses, climbed the mountain, and glimpsed the promised land of freedom. "I just want to do God's will. *(Yeah)* And He's allowed me to go up to the mountain. *(Go ahead)* And I've looked over *(Yes sir)* and I've seen the Promised Land *(Go ahead)*."

It might seem insensitive to emphasize the exchange dynamics at work in millennial preaching. But it is not a stretch to discern motives of a kind of utility at work amidst the ecstasy. The opposite is more nearly the case. To ignore the balancing of cost and reward would require us to deny what was spilling over the surface of King's talk, to ignore his own take on the meaning of his life and of the movement he embodied.

It's not that King didn't momentarily think about himself up on the Memphis mountaintop. "Like anybody," he conceded, "I would like to live a long life—longevity has its place"; but then he quickly cautioned, "But I'm not concerned about that now. I just want to do God's will *(Yeah)*." With eerie premonition, he told the crowd, "I may not get there with you. *(Go ahead)* But I want you to know tonight *(Yes)* that we, as a people, will get to the Promised Land." Soon he went flying past some ineffable barrier, moving beyond Exodus in one convulsive final push. "And so I'm happy tonight; I'm not worried about anything; I'm not fearing any man. Mine eyes have seen the glory of the coming of the Lord. [Applause]."[26] Immediately afterwards, King fell back, his face glistening. By every account, there was a sense in the room that something extraordinary had transpired.

In reassuring the crowd, King was refiguring success and failure, and thus the incentives for acting, through two extensions. First, he was inviting his audience to think about victory in collective terms. The point was that even if "I don't get there with you, it doesn't matter to me." What matters is what happens to "we as a people." That move implied a second one. King fleshed out the incentives which the garbage workers—and black people more generally—had for acting even if he died, not by abandoning the calculus of pain so much as extending the horizon beyond the narrow one of now. The "we" that constitutes a people, and here it carries the ethnic drift of "my people, my people," eventually will get there—if not the generation of Moses, then the one of Joshua.

In all the appeals to hold on, in all the antiphonal replies of "Not long," in all the reminders that "mine eyes have seen the glory," civil rights preachers and singers appealed to deep strains of Christian stoicism and African-American optimism. In the midst of that borrowing, King and the movement altered the very meaning of those concepts just as they did so many other ones. The retrievals mobilized themes of hope normally associated with passivity and surrender to God in the pursuit of action. As a result, stoicism came to signify not enduring the injuries of the world until one could "go home to my Lord," but having the resolve and stamina to fight those slights and remain in the struggle and create a world without them. Where evidence in favor of optimism was lacking, the deductive certainty provided by faith offered a consoling substitution.

The Christian political culture that was enacted in civil rights preaching, exhorting, and singing was able to exploit the most millennial strains in the folk religion for this-worldly ends. The otherworldly contributed something critical which did not confine itself to the great beyond: a temporal structure with a clear end point; the faith that ultimate ends would achieve realization; anticipation of the Kingdom to come; the belief that the universe had moral purpose. Black performance in the movement took liberties with these yearnings, commingling them and the emotions they catalyzed: salvation, Canaan, freedom, crossing over, the Jordan River, resurrection. In the immediacy of the moment of speaking, boundedly rational expectations were converted into boundless anticipation.

THIRTEEN

The Courage to Be

"This Little Light of Mine"

In firing up faith in victory, King sought to change his audience's sense of the ratio of risk to reward. Such figuring resembles the process Doug McAdam dubbed "cognitive liberation."[1] Yet as canny as his analysis is, the phrase doesn't capture the wild spirit that was part of the rallies. In lifting ancient restraints on black anger, freedom singing was playing with dangerous emotions—the humiliation of silence, the longing for payback. When black protesters facing white segregationists broke into the lyrics, "I've got the light of freedom, I'm gonna let it shine," they were exorcising demons of debilitating inferiority, ingrained passivity, and paralyzing fear. The meetings were psychic cauldrons that unleashed the powers of the self.[2]

To begin to rethink reward and punishment in the way King suggested required the imagination to view oneself as a powerful person able to control one's own fate. Just as "estimations of the likelihood of success" were hard to disentangle from faith, acquiring a sense of "agency" may have entailed something as simple as plain old guts. Cultural selection tended to call forth leaders who were not inhibited by fear. When Wyatt Tee Walker stated that the movement needed a dozen people ready to give their lives for the race, he wasn't playing, as King might have put it. But if King was part of this community of the brave, there simply weren't enough fearless souls to generate the manpower needed for liberation.

King expressed this gradient of feistiness in various classifications of Negroes, ranging from slavishness to defiance. At the Jimmie Jackson funeral in Marion, King went so far as to accuse blacks of some complicity. Jackson, he said, "was murdered by the cowardice of every Negro who passively accepts the evils of segregation and stands on the sidelines in the struggle for justice." "You know," he had reflected some years earlier, "one of the great tragedies of this hour is that you have some Negroes who don't want to be free. *(Yes, Amen)* Did you know that? *(Yes).*" Exodus psychology provided one way to make sense of people's failure of nerve, the problem that "in every movement toward freedom some of the oppressed prefer to remain oppressed." "Almost 2800 years ago Moses set out to lead the children of Israel from the slavery of Egypt to the freedom of the promised land. He soon discovered that slaves do not always welcome their deliverers. They become accustomed to being slaves. . . . They prefer the 'fleshpots of Egypt' to the ordeals of emancipation."[3]

King did not, however, descend to the shock therapy that James Bevel deployed in the meetings to heighten black courage. "Negroes are sick," Bevel declared baldly on the Good Friday when Martin Luther King went to jail. Echoing Christ, Bevel wanted to know, *Do you want to be healed? Do you want to get well?* Slavery, segregation, and racism "have made a lot of people sick. . . . So sick they haven't realized yet they are children of God. . . . There are a lot of sick black people right here, right here in Birmingham." Relentless, he told them, "It has nothing to do with Bull Connor. . . . [It] comes back to the Negro people in Birmingham, do *you* want to be free?" For a moment, he took the edge off. "I was tricked for years. I thought white folks was keeping me from being free. . . . [But] white folks can't keep us from being free. Oh no! . . . White folks don't control freedom. . . . You decide." He briefly struck a tender note: "I wish I could write a prescription and give every Negro his . . . courage. I can't do that . . . I can simply ask the question like Christ asked, 'Negroes in Birmingham, do you want to be free?'" But then Bevel felt the Holy

Ghost moving, recalled how a dead man once got up. "When the Holy Ghost get in a man, he's bound to resurrect. And in Alabama and Georgia, I see Negroes coming to life, dead men. The question is, really do you want to be free? . . . Just get up and start walking."[4]

Nor did King follow the tack of Abernathy, whose speeches often provoked through burlesque. "Do you want to be free?" he too would call, waiting for the ricochet back, before taunting his audience, "I can't hear you. I don't want to have to say the Negroes of Selma don't want to be free." He described the ancient masks of servility that blacks wore around whites as scratching when they weren't itching, laughing when they weren't tickled. Ever alert to the humiliation of emasculation, he told the story of a plantation darky's transgression as if he could laugh them into action. The once servile man went up to the plantation to milk the cows when he came upon the boss man, Mr. Charlie, and said, "Good morning, Charlie." And the white man said, "John, now tell me, are you sick? . . . You know you have no business calling me Charlie. Do you want me to take you to the hospital?" So the Negro replied, "No, . . . I just want to know how is Ann doing?" And the white man said, "Now I know something is wrong with you!"[5]

At this point, John ratcheted things up an ideological notch. "Listen here, Charlie. You know the freedom riders came through here the other day and they told us . . . about our freedom and I want you to know from now on, you ain't going to be no Mr. Charlie. You just Charlie." As for Miss Ann, "it's just gonna be Ann. From now on, it ain't gonna be Miss Nothing, it's not going to be even Mississippi, it's just gonna be plain ole Ssippi."

King too sought to fortify the powers of the self. Rather than hector or shame, he tried to coax, inspire, cajole, argue, and even proclaim his listeners into feistiness. "Let no force, let no power, let no individuals, let no social system cause you to feel that you are inferior," he commanded. He could offer general affirmations of responsibility and "the courage to be." In Albany, Georgia, King placed the burden for black freedom squarely on the shoulders of Negroes themselves, yet without Bevel's baiting: "'It has already been said here tonight, and I want to say it again: the salvation of the Negro in Albany, Georgia, is not in Washington. . . . The salvation of the Negro in Albany, Georgia, is not forthcoming from the governor's chair in the state of Georgia.' Slowly, solemnly. 'The salvation of the Negro in Albany, Georgia, is within the hands and the soul of the Negro himself.'"[6]

Typically, King fortified his basic point through echoes and parallels. In the same speech where he wandered from black history to Gandhi's March to the Sea, he burrowed deep down into the source of black people's transcendent power. "For centuries we worked here without wages. We made cotton king. We built our homes and homes for our masters, enduring injustice and humiliation at every point. And yet, out of a bottomless vitality, we continued to live and grow. If the inexpressible cruelties of slavery could not stop us, certainly the opposition that we now face cannot stop us [pandemonium]."[7]

At first glance, the celebration of the slave ancestors resonates with familiar preachments on somebodyness. The purpose King invoked in Selma ("I come back to Selma to tell you are God's children") echoed his mission of racial healing in his sermons ("They call you a nigger, but I'm here to tell you . . ."). It is hardly surprising that the same language of healing black souls marked Jesse Jackson's signature refrain in the 1970s, "I am somebody," given that Jackson had scrutinized King's moves and lifted them all. Jackson fashioned a street-wise persona, replete with gold chains, leather jacket, and an Afro aimed at younger northern ghetto blacks. He "blackened" the prophetic Christianity, adding the chorus "Black Power, Black Power" and the phrase "Nation Time," with its Nation of Islam resonance. The key difference was that Jackson aimed to rouse the spirits not of a southern audience burdened by vicious racism, vigilante terror, and state violence, but a demoralized urban underclass suffering from anomic despair, broken families, crime, drug addiction, and unemployment. He thus anticipated the therapeutic idiom that runs through urban black Christianity today, with its mix of themes of fractured selves, the crisis of masculinity, and the idiom of recovery.[8]

By contrast, somebodyness, as King deployed it in Selma, did not aim to console but to provoke. The point of King's recollection of getting on a bus as a boy and imagining sitting up front was not to reiterate that one day his body would be up there with his mind. It was to spur the practical acts that were bringing the body up front with the mind. King's poetic fusion of "fleecy locks" and "the measure of the mind" followed his central emphasis on "things that we must do" to prepare for "freedom Monday," when the movement would test public accommodations and register to vote. Desegregating "our minds" was only a prelude to the "plan for Selma. We are not here to merely engage in high-sounding words. We are not here merely to talk about freedom. We are here to do something about freedom." Segregation, King stressed, was "a system of adultery perpetuated by an illicit intercourse between injustice and immorality"; it was "a new form of slavery covered up with certain niceties"; it was "a cancer on the body politic that must be removed." "Must be removed" was the critical point: the people of Selma were showing they now had the resolve to remove it. "And on Monday we are going to say to Selma in no uncertain terms: 'We are through with segregation, now, henceforth, and forever more.'"[9]

In the meetings, racial elevation aimed not to lift the spirits of the race as an end in itself, but to stoke the gumption needed in the struggle. By the same token, King did not cease his flattery but simply changed its terms to focus on qualities other than faith and hope. The insurgents' militancy was "marvelous," their crusade for freedom was "holy," their resolve was "majestic." King praised his Selma audience, saying, "I am absolutely convinced that the Negro people of Selma, Alabama have been captured by this idea [of freedom] whose time has come." Shifting to a more vivid, personal present, King then addressed not the "Negro people" but "you," citing the unmistakable signs of freedom: "I can tell by the way you sing. I can see it on your face. I can see it in all of your expressions. I can hear it in the magnificent outpourings of your ward leaders. The word on your lips tonight is freedom and I know that the people of Selma, Alabama are determined to be free."[10]

King was not exaggerating so much as encouraging the heroism of the often unlettered folks who were making a revolution: "I don't know how many historians we have in Birmingham tonight, I don't know how many of you would be able to write a history book, but you are certainly making history and you are experiencing history and you will make it possible for the historians of the future to write a marvelous chapter. Never in the history of this nation have so many people been arrested for the cause of freedom and human dignity *(Well)*."[11]

The apotheosis of agency in King's meeting talk played out in appeals to manhood. As King made a point of mentioning in his book *Stride toward Freedom,* the one white man active in the Montgomery boycott,

Reverend Robert Graetz, drew his biggest applause line when he told a mass meeting audience of thousands, "When I was a child, I spake as a child. . . . But when I became a man, I put away childish things."[12]

The rising up of the children provoked volatile feelings of pride and humiliation, which at times got tangled up with generational tensions and a subtext of failed fathers. William "Meatball" Dothard, one of the young activists in Birmingham, stood up at Sixteenth Street Baptist Church and criticized the cowardly elders. "Tomorrow, students are gonna show you old folks what you should have done forty years ago. They're gonna make you ashamed to see that they have to go through what you should have gone through earlier for them, to make their life better. [They] don't want their parents to work five days a week making 15 dollars a week cooking for somebody else, still be called 'girl.' . . . They want their mom called 'Mrs.' . . . Parents, let the children go [to jail] . . . They sing a song every night, 'If you don't go, don't hinder me.'" A few moments later, he merged the voice of an eight-year-old boy who had gone to jail with a line from a favorite freedom song: "Do you know why [he decided to go to jail]? He said he 'woke up that Saturday morning with freedom on my mind.' . . . Let them go get what you supposed to have gotten a long time ago." As the church erupted, there was a call for jailbirds to come down to the front of the church.[13]

An eight-year-old jailbird was an emblem of the rising courage among black people that King and other speakers sought to spread and fortify. A powerful assent rose up from the Selma audience when Ralph Abernathy commanded, "Now you put it in the record that the Negro is not afraid of the white man. Used to be afraid of him, but we're not afraid any longer. No, No. Negroes are standing up everywhere today, all over the nation." This was the true meaning of the unleashed power of Annie Lee Cooper that drew the sympathy of nonviolent blacks and the astonishment of some of the white officials present at the melee. Throughout his reflections on the white psyche, even King seemed reluctant to chastise Mrs. Cooper for abandoning nonviolence. Abernathy put it with typical directness: "She just couldn't take it any more." Charles Fager captured the frenzy of Cooper's resistance. "It was one push too many: with a curse under her breath, she turned around and slugged Clark near the left eye with her fist. She was a tall, powerfully built woman, and Clark staggered to his knees under the blow; as he did, she hit him again." She stomped on the foot of one of the two deputies who rushed over to help and elbowed him in the belly. Even as a third deputy joined the fray and they wrestled with her, "the sheriff got up, lifted his billy club, and struck at her head. But she grabbed the club and hung on, knocking Clark's white helmet off. . . . Finally he wrenched it free, his hands trembling visibly, and cracked her on the head."[14]

To inspire manly action, King associated black forebears and ancient songs with acts of spectacular defiance, even of death. In St. Augustine, where the Klan marauded through the streets, King acknowledged the presence of death in his daily round while pushing agape to the limit. "I got word way out in California that a plan was under way to take my life in St. Augustine, Florida. Well, if physical death is the price that I must pay to free my white brothers and all of my brothers and sisters from a permanent death of the spirit, then nothing can be more redemptive."

Far from the "effeminate" weakness that some blacks saw in such unfathomable altruism, King's attitude declared a fearless immunity to intimidation. "You know they threaten us occasionally with more than beatings here and there. They threaten us with actual physical death. They think that this will stop the movement." This was the context in which King sampled the more martial strains in the sacred tradition. "We have long since learned to sing anew with our foreparents of old that"—and then he let them speak for him:

> Before I'll be a slave (yes. all right. well?)
> I'll be buried in my grave
> (amen. amen.)
> And go home to my Father (amen.)
> And be saved . . .[15]

None of this may have had the aura of masculine bravado displayed by more "Custeristic" black nationalist figures who vowed they would not be taken alive. But after its own fashion King's statement of resolve—"Before I'll be a slave"—did promise a fight to the end. Despite the line "And go home to my Father," King was defying death, not courting it. His statement in Selma was even more direct: "Nothing will stop us, not the threat of death itself. The only way we can get our freedom is to have no fear of death. We must show them that if they beat one Negro, they are going to have to beat a hundred, and if they beat a hundred, they are going to have to beat a thousand. We will not be turned around."[16]

To the degree that King was stating his own defiant credo—no calculus of cost, no flicker of fear, could cow him—he was enacting his own sublime version of the archetypal badass who, as sociologist Jack Katz describes it, transcends rationality by forcing *others* to calculate the consequences of the irrational things the badass might do. What could be "badder" in this sense than Rev. C. T. Vivian's laughter when Klansmen held his head under the water as he desegregated the St. Augustine beaches? Even today, Vivian cackles as he recounts that incident to me. That's how *bad* he still is.[17]

As the years went by, King's defensive language, in which he preempted objections by stressing that nonviolence was not something weak, sentimental, or frightened, gave way to more emphatic assertions of "Olympian black manhood." "We are tired of our men being emasculated so that our wives and our daughters have to go out and work in the white lady's kitchen," King said to a packed and pulsing crowd at Mason Tabernacle during the Memphis sanitation men's strike. "When the Negro confronted tear gas and screaming mobs and snarling dogs," King told an annual SCLC meeting in 1967, he "moved with strength and dignity toward them and decisively defeated them. And the courage with which he confronted enraged mobs dissolved the stereotype of the grinning, submissive Uncle Tom."[18]

Manhood found expression in the movement's version of a martial identity. When Andrew Young remarked to a Birmingham mass meeting, "We are warriors," and hastened to add, "but nonviolent," the accent fell on the first note, not the second. The same ideal was present when Young virtually taunted men standing on the sidelines in St. Augustine, inviting them to join the predominantly female band of protesters. In the midst of the mass meetings in Birmingham, Ralph Abernathy praised Fred Shuttlesworth as a man who had "been in battlefield a long time," and he and King both celebrated black "freedom fighters."

The emergence of the captive black nation into a nation of black warriors achieved lyrical expression in King's sampling of the spiritual "Joshua Fit the Battle of Jericho" in "Our God is Marching On." His martial cry in dialect provided the right counterpoint to the tender antiphonal of "how long?/not long." It also allowed the current insurgency to be sanctified by the forebears. And depoeticizing the connection between biblical deliverance and the civil rights movement transformed ordinary black people into heroic biblical actors capable of rocking the world. These things were effected through a parallel set of "tellings." "The Bible tells us that the mighty men of Joshua merely walked around the walled city of Jericho *(Yes)* and the barriers to freedom came tumbling down *(Yes sir)*." King then shifted the subject of "tells us," allowing the slaves to tell the biblical story: "That old Negro spiritual *(Yes sir)* 'Joshua Fit the Battle of Jericho' . . . tells us that . . . 'And the walls come tumblin' down.' *(Yes sir, Tell it)* / Up to the walls of Jericho they marched, spear in hand. *(Yes sir)* / 'Go blow them ramhorns,' Joshua cried / 'Cause the battle am in my hand.' *(Yes sir)*."[19]

In ceding authority not just to God but to the ancestors, King presented himself here as a mere vessel, the channel through which the words flowed and which consecrated a race of warriors. "These words I have given you just as they were given us by the unknown, long-dead, dark-skinned originator. Some now long-gone black bard bequeathed to posterity these words in ungrammatical form, yet with emphatic pertinence for all of us today."

King never stopped rejecting "that strange illusion which says that the Negro doesn't really want to be free. It's that strange illusion that only the agitators are making a lot of noise and arousing the people, but at bottom they don't want to be free. They said this in Africa. They said it for years in Algeria. And so this goes through all our struggle . . . But . . . there is deep down within the soul of the Negro a new determination to be free . . . *(yes)*.

". . . We are making it clear that we are going on to the end in order to achieve justice . . . we've gone too far now to turn back [great shout].

". . . So we will have to demonstrate to them by our very lives and our willingness to suffer . . . [Drowned out by shouts and applause.] So, my friends, we call on you now to get ready. *(get ready, get ready)* Get ready for a significant witness."

Not long after King finished, with a rousing "Get on yo' walkin' shoes. Walk together, children. Dontcha get weary," Ralph Abernathy followed up with exquisite choreography, telling them, "And fellow soldiers in the army, I just had to come back. I could not let anything stand in my way.

Because I told you the other night-that-I'm-not-goin'-to let"—and then, along with the crowd, breaking into sound—"Chief Pritchett / turn me 'round / Turn me 'round, Turn me 'round / . . . Keep on a-walkin'-Yeah! / Keep on a-talkin'-Yeah! / Marching down the / Freedom highway."[20]

Evident in King's cry to "get ready for a significant witness" and Abernathy's orchestration of "I'm-not-goin'-to-let" to elicit participation, civil rights preaching and singing repudiated diffidence through its expressive means as much as its argument. The larger field of sound amplified the chorus of resolve, imbuing the audience with kinetic energy. All of King's verbal acts were wrapped in this auditory embrace, usually preceded by exhortations from the field staff as well as hours of freedom singing, including stalwart selections like "Ain't gonna let nobody turn me around." In Birmingham, the audience was primed by Carlton Reece's freedom choir and chorus after chorus of "I'm on my way to Freedom Land," including such celebrations of indomitable will as "If my mother won't go, I'll go anyhow" and "If you don't go, don't you hinder me" which migrated back into the oratory. The chorus's immediate repetition of the singer's line reinforced the sense of emphatic collectivity. The singing was more free-form in Albany, almost a dub sound stripped down to beat and rasp, but it emphasized the same psychic underside of deliverance, the way insurgency both required transformed identities and transformed them too.

Freedom singing had a thrust beyond language. For a people who had repeatedly been told they were nobody, the simple act of lifting one's voice could be a subversive notion, declaring one's presence. The amplification of voice, the power of rhythm, the complex interplay of singer and chorus, the grasping of hands, the thunderous stamping of feet—all these practices created emotive rites of community, dissolving the multitude of individual I's into a communal wave.

King too merged his voice with the freedom hymnal, flowing right into the words of the song, "Before I'll be a slave, I'll be buried in my grave." More often he built up his own rhythmic message of refusal that was meant to imbue his audience with a sense of power. After declaring his fierce resolve—"We are not about to turn around. *(Yes, sir)*"—followed by his insistence, "We are on the move now. *(Yes, sir),*" King began a virtual chant that signaled the unstoppable rush of freedom:

Yes, we are on the move
and no wave of racism can stop us. *(Yes, sir)*
We are on the move now.
The burning of our churches will not deter us. *(Yes, sir)*
The bombing of our homes will not dissuade us. *(Yes, sir)*
We are on the move now. *(Yes, sir)*
The beating and killing of our clergymen and young people
    will not divert us.
We are on the move now. *(Yes, sir)*[21]

Such back talk, at least as King spoke it, might seem gentle, even gen-teel in its at times stentorian formality, but all matters of style aside, it re-mained a form of "telling the man." The spiritual "Go Down Moses" de-picts a distinctive form of the act of speaking truth before power. "Tell old pharaoh, to let my people go" involves a brute confrontation, the making of a claim to the face of power. In the early days of the movement, the metaphoric aspect of many spirituals provided protective cover for direct assault. But over time the rhetoric of telling underwent revealing alter-ations: in the character of the language—from oblique to literal to pro-vocative (from tell old pharaoh to tell Bull Connor to calling him a "steer")—and the setting of the telling—from the black talk of backstage to direct public address.

In advance of King's entrance into a rally, ordinary black people had of-ten rehearsed this defiant voice, refusing to flinch as they named the most fearsome names and dressed them down: Bull Connor, George Wallace, Jim Clark. In preparing crowds for a King appearance, field staffer Willie Bolden liked to use dramatic gestures, pointing a finger at the self to ex-pand it when they sang, "I ain't gonna let," and then back out at the phan-tom adversary, "nobody turn me around." Speaking out the name of ad-versaries was practice for the real thing.

"For example, if we were in Alabama, we would say"—and here Bolden begins a kind of whispery, speedy, mumbling song-chant, skipping over the words—"'We ain't gon' let nobody tear apart, turn around, we ain't let nobody, you're going keep on walkin', keep on talking, nothing is going to keep us, . . . ain't let it go by.' Just being able to say it [was critical]. It was important to them to be able to call their names because they knew that these people like George Wallace and Bull Connor were racists. [But] though they may have talked about them in their little group, there were never any public announcements, if you will. But here you are now, you've got 300 folks down in front of the county jail, singing 'ain't gonna let nobody,' and then you call it out, Bull Connor's name, and you see him standing there and he can't do anything about it . . . 'I can actually call Bull Connor a racist to his face, you ain't gonna let nobody turn me around,' to his face. And that helps give them the courage so they can express themselves openly and singing songs like 'Oh freedom, oh freedom.'"[22]

Abernathy was a master at eliciting the glee of back talk. Once in a Birmingham rally, he was giving a lesson in black history that celebrated the black martyrs who died for America. Ranging widely from the black fathers and sons who "gave their red blood" on the beaches of Normandy to Crispus Attucks, "a black man [who] was the first to give his red blood" in the Revolution, he suddenly turned to the white reporters, affectionately taunting them, "I don't see you writing it down . . . Write it down, you all don't know it." He drove the audience wild with his outrageousness, declaring that since he had been dragged to America he was not going back to Africa "until the Englishman goes back to England, until the Italian goes back to Italy, until the German goes back to Germany . . ."—he kept naming potential returnees—"and until the white man gives this country back to the Indians," at which point the audience erupted in wild assent. Turning the podium "doohickey" (the recording bug planted by the police) into an intimate prop, Abernathy invented a humorous version of crossover talk intended to cut the white man down to size. "Doockhickey, can you hear me," he said, and went on to commune with Bull Connor, then mused out loud that he had heard that "Bull Connor teaches Sunday School," so he knows his Bible. "Bull's gonna look up and see a number, he's gonna say, 'This is the number no man can see.'"[23]

King's back talk offered a different kind of joy, the pleasure of resolute dignity. "Beatings," he said, "will not deter us." At other times, the address was to a vague collective—"I'm gonna say to Selma" or "Birmingham was a mean city today." As in Bolden's experience, often the biggest charge came with the dead-on address of individuals. "We are not," King declared, "going to allow Sheriff Clark to intimidate us. Sheriff Clark violated the injunction [clapping]. We must have the vote. We're going to march down, we have the will to say, 'If something isn't done, we will fill up the jails of Dallas County.'"²⁴ Telling pharaoh rather than Bull Connor was an indirect mention that left some maneuvering room, but that disappeared when King dared Governor Wallace by name. Whether "telling the man" or refusing to be turned around, King was once again enacting his own Christian version of manhood, sifting out the violent retaliation but nevertheless "not fearing any man."

Still, enduring feelings of weakness remained a threat to resolve. Black preaching and gospel music had long shown a confessional side in which participants revealed helplessness. In "Precious Lord, Take My Hand"— King's request to saxophonist Ben Branch minutes before he was assassinated ("Ben, play it real nice")—the singer virtually sighs, "I am tired, I am weak, I am worn." These disclosures were often accompanied by requests for help that flowed through traditional channels of imploring. Just as call-and-shout was easily transferred from church to rally, the movement was able to apply the forms of confession and supplication to the distinctive kind of weakness of spirit that arose in the course of mobilization.²⁵

In a small black church encircled by the Mississippi state police, as a group of young people prepared to walk to the courthouse and sit down, the pastor intoned to his frightened congregation, "Oh Lordy, oh Lord, we need you right now, Jesus. Can't get along without your help, my father. Oh Lord, oh Lord. Don't leave us right now. You know what we're goin' up against, Jesus, you don't come, Lord, we can't stand the storm. Come on, my Father. Help us on every weak and leaning side. Build us up where we're torn down. Give us more power, my Father."²⁶

If such prayers recall timeless themes of weakness, to treat them as signals of surrender neglects the milieu in which they were uttered. As always, context changed meaning, transforming flight from the world into its opposite. Intoned, preached, sung, and wailed in movement settings, confessions of vulnerability no longer signified debilitating passivity. Nor did the immensity of God's power swallow the self and underscore human powerlessness. Dependence and agency, surrender and freedom, were not opposed terms in civil rights argument. Bearing witness to the former enhanced the latter. Even if the form was common to both, to cry "I'm so weak" in the endeavor of flight from the world was not the same as asking the Lord to steady one's nerves so one could remain in the freedom struggle and transform the very world that was making one weary. Prostrating oneself before the Lord was only one moment in a stream of activities which the participants experienced as "standing up like men"; it brought God psychically into the struggle in this world so that one could remain standing even in the face of brutal policemen and Klan viciousness.

The anthem of the movement, "We Shall Overcome," perfectly distilled this tension between agency and resignation. The overcoming in the original version of "I Shall Overcome" does not change the world, nor does it seek to. Overcoming takes place not in this world but in the next. The self is overcome with weary resignation. The freedom it envisions is the freedom to go home to my Lord. But in the hands of the movement, the hymn was transformed into the thunderous resolve of "We Shall Overcome," with the accent often placed on the "shall."[27]

It mattered that the resolve was communal. "They always stood up to sing 'We Shall Overcome,'" Pat Watters observed, "with arms crossed in front, hands clasping the hand of the person on either side, the hand clasps forming a chain of all those gathered together, in the churches, on the streets and sidewalks of the demonstration confrontations, in the jails, wherever the movement manifested itself, swaying from side to side, forming in their unity and communion something larger, greater than the sum of their number, ordinary people finding in each other and within themselves things, qualities they never knew they possessed."[28]

King did not often show his weakness in the meetings, saving such exposure for sermons and the more intimate setting of SCLC retreats. The Mosaic mantle laid on his shoulders weighed heavily. In one sermon, he did bare his soul as he reflected back on the threatening phone calls he had received early in the Montgomery campaign. "I was beginning to falter and to get weak within and to lose my courage. *(All right)* And I never will forget that I went to the mass meeting that Monday night very discouraged and a little afraid, and wondering whether we were going to win the struggle." In another sermon, King owned up again to "faltering; I'm losing my courage. *(Yes)* And I can't let the people see me like this because if they see me weak and losing my courage, they will begin to get weak. *(Yes)*." All of King's efforts in the meetings were to buck *them* up, rouse *their* spirits.[29]

Still, the interplay among vulnerability, supplication, and defiance was crucial to King's own ability to stay in the struggle. As we have seen, in one Selma mass meeting King did refer to his moment of despondency back in Montgomery. That reference followed the bout of preaching in which the morning of hope struggled against the despair of midnight. It is unclear what set him off—perhaps the word "midnight" with all its personal resonance, perhaps the celebration of "the amazing thing" of "our slave foreparents." But as he pulled up out of that ancestral reverie, he added an improvised verse to "There is a Balm in Gilead" that celebrated the continuity with the ancestors by attributing the topical lyrics to them:

> They had another verse
> sometimes I must confess
> that I have to sing it,
> "Sometimes I feel discouraged in Alabama,
> sometimes I feel discouraged in Mississippi,
> sometimes I feel discouraged in this struggle,
> sometimes I feel my work's in vain.
> But then the holy spirit
> revives my soul again
> There is a balm in Gilead,
> to make the wounded whole."[30]

This fleeting nod to discouragement reminds us that King's confessions of weakness in church were inseparable from his faith in his own insurgent powers and thus his mobilization talk more generally. "The midnight hour," Ray Charles sang around the same time as King's encounter with God, "has left me lonely"; but King's midnight was not personal solitude or a broken heart. Enmeshed in his efforts as the leader of a social movement, King's despair was brought about by the brute dangers of protest, the death threats that were intended to scare him into silence, and his failure of nerve as a leader of the Montgomery boycott. "Nigger," the voice on the phone had said, "we're tired of you and your mess." This was the moment when the "God my daddy told me about" commanded him to "stand up for justice," and to help him do so salved his wounds with balm. "He promised never to leave me." Fortified by the primal companion who would always be with him, a replenished King returned to the fray.

As the imploring tone of "Oh Lordy, oh Lord, we need you right now, Jesus. Can't get along without your help, my father" makes clear, the effort to impart a sense of bold self often merged with the need for allies. The pledge of God that restored King's spirit—"He told me, you'll never be alone, never"—was also a declaration of solidarity. The support that flowed from this cosmic alliance was no more separable from the assertion of the self than estimations of possibility were from faith in one's own power and feelings of group support.

Of course, support was not always spiritual. "And I want you to know that you are not alone," King told the people of Birmingham. He said the same thing in Selma. He was bucking them up with news that powers and principalities—the Justice Department, the Attorney General, "and if Bobby [Kennedy] doesn't call, then we'll go right to the President"—were also on their side. Still, God was the movement's secret weapon: a force multiplier and cosmic compensator. The movement often followed the testimony of resolve, "we shall overcome," with the lyrics "we are not alone, we are not alone," hinting at the presence of God made more explicit in the verse, "God is on our side, God is on our side." That's precisely what one huddle of protesters stranded on Pettus Bridge sang out in the midst of the Bloody Sunday rampage, as Alabama state troopers on horseback flailed them with whips and hit them with truncheons.

How could the God who made a way out of no way not fail to trim segregationists down to size? The movement constantly invoked the immensity of God's powers to even the playing field. "Thou who Overruled the Pharaohs / Overruled the Babylonians / Overruled the Greeks and Romans / You alone is God / Always have been God / God in man / God in love / May our suffering help us." "Who is Mayor Stimson?" Reverend Campbell asked in a righteous, almost belittling tone, and before long he was whooping God's terrifying strength.

Thus did the power of God magnify the power of the protesters by dwarfing their enemies. When Abernathy intoned poetically, "This is God's Albany," he was serving notice not just to chief Laurie Pritchett but also to the Negroes of Albany. King's sermonic jab—"God didn't anoint George Wallace"—had the same twin meaning: inflating black people, deflating racists.

Conjuring this angrier God of correction like a fearsome ally ready to go up against a bully, King hurled the prophetic threat of the great equalizer at the very first meeting of the Montgomery Improvement Association. "The Almighty God himself is not the only, not the God just standing out saying through Hosea, 'I love you, Israel.'" He is also the God of retribution provoked by evil in the world who "stands up before the nations" and warns if they don't do right, "'[I] will slap you out of the orbits of your national and international relationships.' *(That's right)* Standing beside love is justice *(Yeah)*."[31]

Fear, as we have seen, was most intense at the stress points: before striding out of the church, in the midst of the approach to racist sheriffs and the fire hoses, in the eye of a racist mob. In these moments of transition, song, prayer, and chanting could steel the will. Facing down a cordon of Alabama state police on the other side of the Selma River, King began the march by invoking the Israelites' time in the wilderness: "Almighty God, Thou hast called us to walk for freedom, even as Thou did the children of Israel. We pray, dear God, as we go through a wilderness of state troopers that Thou wilt hold our hand."[32]

In the virulent atmosphere of St. Augustine in 1964, the marchers really needed everlasting arms to lean on. Andrew Young, King's surrogate in the city, wondered whether the "cadre of determined, nonviolent warriors," mostly women and teenagers, would be up to the task. "After I prayed," Young remembered, "one of the good ol' sisters sang out in a loud, clear voice: 'Be not dismayed, whate'er betide, God will take care of you. Beneath his wings of love abide, God will take care of you.' Then everyone joined on the chorus: 'God will take care of you, through every day . . . all the way; He will take care of you, God will take care of you.'"

With spirits fortified, the group marched on down the street toward the gathering, still singing softly, "God will take care of you." Yet this was, in Young's retrospective words, "an affirmation of faith," still to be tested. "And I thought to myself, *It's one thing to sing this in church where it's easy to believe it, but the song says through every day, and this is nighttime in St. Augustine.*" As they approached the mob, Young heard chains rattling and bottles shattering. "I began to understand what it meant to 'walk through the valley of the shadow of death . . . [and] fear no evil' . . . I was not afraid for some reason."

Suddenly out of nowhere, Young was grabbed, punched, and stomped. At the time, Young did not know what was happening, but luckily Willie Bolden had his back, literally. The mob, certain that the punishment meted out to Young would deter the marchers, faded away, but Young got up and insisted, "We can't stop now, let's go." The straggling band of non-violent marchers moved forward.

"I don't know what motivated us to march on, but it certainly wasn't cheekiness. It was closer to faith and determined belief that 'the Lord will make a way out of no way.'"[33]

FOURTEEN

Free Riders and Freedom Riders

"They can put you in a dungeon and transform you to glory"

The fact that King's incandescent rhetoric was helpful in dealing with some of the basic problems of mobilizing closes some of the distance between righteousness and rationality. That is not the same thing, however, as reducing his righteous passion to utilitarian motives. To view King's tactics only as shrewd ways of framing an argument misses the core of what he was up to and radically compresses the vision of rationality he operated with. The opportunistic possibilities of his moral argument depended on a moral community of fervent faith, and that was the least of the complexities engaged by King's "usage." To illuminate these rich ambiguities in the relationship between morality and rationality in King's mobilization talk, it is useful to briefly consider the distinction between freedom riders and free riders.

Seeking to explain why reasonable people might refrain from collective action that could benefit them, scholars came up with the concept of the "free rider," an individual who wonders why he should fight for prized goods like clean air or voting rights if even the indolent will enjoy the fruits of his initiative. Free riders thus hold back, letting others pay the cost of acting. Meanwhile, they bide their time, until what goes around comes around—to them.[1]

Free riders ride free in another sense. They are liberated not just from the risk of being a chump but also from the encumbrances of the social relationships that sustain participation. Whether or not the free rider realizes it, the liberty attained is paradoxically bittersweet. Avoiding cost simply means the accession of a different order of costs, like emptiness and solitude. As the economist Albert Hirschman observed, the experience of underinvolvement can disappoint.[2] Sitting on the sidelines can be a lonely business. Staying above the fray deprives the free rider of the rewards of fellowship and sisterhood. And it can expose you to other costs, including guilt and regret. There is also the risk of charges of treachery. "Which side are you on?" sang the civil rights movement, a question that could devolve into a taunt in the very next verse: "Are you going to be an Uncle Tom or stand up like a man?" Later, as more militant sentiments took hold, the sting of noninvolvement was amplified by more cutting charges. Seen in the context of the mounting cost of disengagement—the cost of intimidation, of failed self-esteem, of exclusion from blackness—participation, no less than nonparticipation, could seem to offer more payoffs of a certain sort.

Yet if we turn away from such high theory, it becomes less clear that this sort of hypothesizing gets it right, at least when applied to the freedom riders or to the larger universe of those who walked, marched, swam, preached, sang, chanted, or sat down for freedom. Such people came forward to deny a cramped view of reward and punishment. John Lewis and the entire band of freedom riders turned a deaf ear to all those colleagues who told them, *You cannot go. You are asking to be killed. You are committing suicide.*

It's not that King and his colleagues were saintly masochists. As supremely indifferent to pain as many freedom riders may have seemed, the point is not to sentimentalize them. In truth, the differences between them and free riders were murkier than the sharp contrast between sacrifice and selfishness allows. As the previous two chapters have made abundantly clear, the leaders, and followers too, did not always shrink from shrewd assessment before they leapt into the fray. In seeking to alter his audiences' perceptions of success, depreciate the sense of costs, intensify rewards, and highlight long-term gains over short-term setbacks, King was honoring those very calculations.

At times, this yielded a certain division of occasions and a corresponding division of talk. On countless nights, King would move in sequence through the same gamut of moods, from rapture to savviness to carousing, as he left the fervor of the meetings for the leadership huddle back at the Gaston Hotel in Birmingham to weigh tactics and then, as the night gave way to early morning, to eat ribs and tell preacher jokes.

"We were asking these people to go into the streets," Ralph Abernathy reflected, "and to accept whatever punishment the white community had to offer, whether jail or beating or death; and we were asking them to take this risk *without ever assigning a hand in their own defense*." "We're only flesh," said John Lewis, whose body bore the stigmata of countless beatings. "I could understand people not wanting to get beaten anymore. The body gets tired. You put out so much energy and you saw such little gain."[3]

Moral action, then, did not inhabit a zone of absolute purity. It too was subject to hard-boiled assessments of effect and instrumentality. King knew that the ethos of redemptive suffering had specific conditions. Without some practical payoff, its legitimacy as well as its market would erode. Why else did he plead to white moderates, give me some victories to compete with the black nationalists? Hardheaded pragmatist that he was, King fully understood the limits of moral exhortation. As David Chappell has stressed so powerfully, mimicking King's own words, there was nothing soft or naïve about either King's politics or his anthropology. Over the course of the 1960s, as black capacity to believe the white man "would really open his heart" to black moral appeals rapidly diminished, King had no trouble grasping the exchange logic of that black nationalist rebuke we encountered earlier, "Nothing hurts a nigger like too much love." More than a wry lampoon, it was a sophisticated gambit that sought to reverse the sublimation of pain into pleasure by the movement claim that "suffering is redemptive."[4]

Nor was King above shrewdly choreographing moral spectacles whose payoff lay in the righteous indignation they aroused among the national television audience. The *New York Times,* and just about everybody else, roundly criticized King for moral callousness during the Children's Crusade in Birmingham, when he calculated the gains to be had from deploying thousands of school children and put them up against Bull Connor's dogs and hoses. Even if James Bevel pushed him into it, the long-resistant King finally yielded because the movement had run out of bodies. In the end, demographic necessity gave birth to theological flexibility.

As some sheriffs belatedly discovered, against the brute calculus of state coercion and vigilante terror the movement often struck back with simply a more sophisticated accounting system as it fashioned games of tacit co-ordination in which only one party truly understood the *real* rules. As Glenn Eskew chronicles, after one of Bull Connor's dogs lunged toward a bystander that the national media mistakenly identified as a protester, "a jubilant [Wyatt Tee] Walker [was] jumping up and down with Dorothy Cotton and other SCLC workers saying: 'We've got a movement! We've got a movement. We had some police brutality. They brought out the dogs. They brought out the dogs. We've got a movement!' A disgusted [James] Forman, the director of SNCC, found the response 'very cold, cruel and calculating to be happy about police brutality coming down on innocent people, bystanders, no matter what purpose it served.'"[5]

The street smartness of various guardians of the local state varied a good deal on this point. Early on, police chief Laurie Pritchett in Albany, Georgia, understood that the pain the demonstrators absorbed was a rational investment—except for the blacks. He had seen the payoff that came in the media spectacles and aroused public opinion, and thus Pritchett was able to orchestrate King's defeat through his restraint. He redefined the terms of the game. By contrast, after initially hewing to a stance of restraint in Selma, Jim Clark and George Wallace's head of the State Police, Al Lingo, finally lost it and began cracking heads. As Abernathy had warned at Kiowa Baptist church, "It's gonna get rough. . . . We knew Jim Clark's niceness just couldn't last." Unlike in Albany, movement savvy trumped cracker emotion, and the upward cascade began, this time for King and his people, who were able to mobilize third parties: the national television networks that broke into the screening of *Judgment at Nuremberg* with pictures of Bloody Sunday; the clergy and congressmen and others who came flooding from across the nation into the Selma backwoods. Before long, Lyndon Johnson had taken to the airwaves to declare "We Shall Overcome," and the momentum for the Voting Rights Act accelerated.

With his at times brooding, almost haunted nature, King recurrently yielded to demoralization, and then would ask the investment question: "Is it worth it?" Over time, encounters with the local southern state, the seeming betrayals of the Kennedy administration, and the ferocity of white backlash produced skepticism about what David Garrow called "the oratorical illusion," the belief that one could appeal to the moral conscience of whites. Nonviolence was based on an empirical guess—an estimate of latent white decency—and when that guess was falsified by the evidence, as it was after four little black girls were blown up in a Birmingham church, as it was in Gage Park, Chicago, its attractiveness would shrink. The rare thing about King was that he was impervious to such estimations, even if his mood was fragile. But the people he depended on surely were not.

Yet as useful as it may be to identify the calculation involved in movement protest, it is important not to overstate the case, at least for the kind of people who devoted their lives to the movement. At a certain point, if you stretch the concept of cost and benefit to include all sorts of psychic and spiritual rewards and punishment, the concepts distend beyond recognition into the shapeless realm of tautology. Just as surely, we begin to overlook the special spirit that moved the movement and the moments at which it was decisive. The freedom riders of the early civil rights movement would have struck the too-clever-by-half free riders as perversely eager to pay dearly for the privilege of riding. When they clambered aboard the buses, they were envisioning the punishment that awaited them. Their preparation for action readied them not for the denial of pain, but for its almost sensuous anticipation. It really did not seem to matter to them. They rode not *for* free but *to be* free. There was a difference.

So there were many who found King's exceptional boast—"We will win you with our capacity to suffer"—unfathomable. Where's the boast in the absorption of pain? Does not the reasonable man, the shrewd man, look for ways to reduce costs? They preferred a rival notion of exchange: tit for tat, negative reciprocity, vengeance. What kind of people flaunt their cowardice, Malcolm X fumed. Many southern blacks, especially among the unchurched, who never ceded their right to retaliate or to pack weapons, viewed the calls for turning cheeks and loving enemies as a slavishness which, as Walter Kaufmann restated Nietzsche, "would like nothing better than revenge." Slave morality means "being kindly when one is merely too weak and timid to act otherwise."[6]

The verdict of timidity seems hard to sustain if applied to King and his coterie. Unlike free riders, men like Vivian, Shuttlesworth, and Bolden were not afraid to limit their boldness lest others profit from it. Rather than dipping their toe in the water nervously, "freedom riders" leapt right in. Before he plunged into a segregated swimming pool, J. T. Johnson did not stop to consider that the motel owner was about to throw acid into the water and burn him. Rather than mulling over every risk, these movement leaders were the initiators of cascades of actions that shaped *other* people's calculations of cost and pain. Like the badasses that Jack Katz described, blasé about "rationality" unless they were defying it, they forced other people to reckon the consequences of what they, the badasses, might do.

But this was not the least of it. The freedom riders could often seem not just stubborn or righteous but crazy or masochistic. At times, the spilling of blood seemed to spur them on. Diane Nash was not deterred when she was told that it would be suicide for her band of Nashville freedom riders to join in after the first wave was decimated. "'We fully realize that,' she said, with a touch of irritation in her voice, 'but we can't let them stop us with violence. If we do, the movement is dead.'" When a young C. T. Vivian was called "boy" while being booked in the Jackson, Mississippi, jail, he replied, "My church generally ordains *men,* not boys." The officer rose and raised his billy club, saying, "I'll knock yo' fuckin' black nappy head through the goddamn wall if you don't shut yo' goddamn mouth, nigger." As James Farmer recounted, Vivian "smiled even more broadly, looking the officer coolly in the eye." And later, when the freedom riders were transferred to Hinds County Prison Farm and Vivian refused to finish his answer with the phrase "Sir," "almost instantly, came the sound of weapons against flesh. The thud of a slight body falling to the floor. . . . When C.T. was led back down the corridor, there were bandages over his right eye and his T-shirt was covered with blood. The huge guards, half carrying him, appeared frightened. There was a smile on C.T.'s face."[7]

Or take Fred Shuttlesworth. He called the melee that left freedom riders dazed and bloody "glorious . . . here, Negroes and whites are being beaten together, are riding and suffering together, are praying and working together."[8] Maybe that mulish man was crazy or maybe he was just a man with "with fire locked up inside," as the title of his biography suggests, when he proclaimed that "not enough Negroes are ready to die in Birmingham." Farmer marveled at Shuttlesworth's courage in leading him through a white mob: "Never before in my life had I seen such physical courage.

"He walked right into the mob, elbowing the hysterical white men aside, saying, 'Out of the way. Let me through. Step aside.'

"Incredibly, the members of the mob obeyed. I walked behind Fred, trying to hide in his shadow. Looking back on it now, I can only guess that this was an example of the 'crazy nigger' syndrome—'man, that nigger is crazy; leave him alone; don't mess with him.'"[9] The sociologist Aldon Morris quotes from Glenn Smiley's recounting: "Once [Shuttlesworth] told me, after he had been chain whipped by going into a white group that chased him and whipped him with a chain, that 'it doesn't make any difference. I'm afraid of neither man nor devil.' . . . Now Martin [King] and these other guys just wouldn't allow their fears to govern their actions. Now this is courage. This is bravery. Not Shuttlesworth. I think Shuttlesworth, his bravery is in defiance of possible consequences. But that's the way he is."[10]

It's important to understand these instances as more than reflections of "character." Whatever features of temperament helped calm the nerves, in all these cases courage reflected larger cultural preachments. The leaders did not simply act out their inner resolve but their sacred principles too, and they created moral teachings and institutional mechanisms to disseminate that courage to others. That, after all, was the entire adaptive logic that gave birth to and sustained the mass meetings.

That mantra of the movement originally said by Sister Pollard, the elderly "freedom walker" in Montgomery—"my feets is tired but my soul is rested"—proclaimed a spiritualization of suffering that was central to the identity of the churched side of the movement. Her elegant repudiation of materialism defined the rival definition of rationality that was central to its logic. It helps explain why Bevel and John Lewis didn't panic when they integrated a White Tower burger joint during the first Nashville sit-ins launched by Kelly Smith, and a cloud of poisonous insecticide filled the room. "Then I heard Bevel's voice . . . It was his preaching voice, raised even louder than the machine churning out that poison. Bevel had begun to whoop, reciting the words from the Book of Daniel, where an angel appears before the kingdom of Nebuchadnezzar and warns the people to bend before God or be thrown into the fire and smoke of hell.

"*And whoever falleth not down and worshipeth,*' Bevel chanted, his eyes squeezed shut, *'shall the same hour be cast into the midst of a burning fiery furnace.*'

"Then he started singing. Then he chanted some more, about the three Hebrew children—Shadrach, Meshach and Abednego—who were saved from that furnace."[11]

In the end, this alchemy was as radical as any other aspect of King's movement oratory: He and the others were engaged in a larger effort to transform the very meaning of what was rational. They were seeking to shift not this or that preference but the entire way of approaching the question of worth, value, and meaning.[12] Here, ultimately, was the paradoxical revenge, the payback, if you will, on an overly shrewd conception of what King and his colleagues were up to. The whole calculus of pain and gain was put in question if King and the others could play with, play havoc with, their meaning, taking the empty rationality of the most cramped sort and standing it on its head, adding a whole new dimension of spiritual costs and rewards like justice, dignity, fairness, redemption, godliness, and going home to my Lord to the equation.

King achieved this inversion through a series of his beloved contrasts. A reward as much as a punishment, suffering was redemptive. Jail became a badge of holiness, the embodiment of the body's transcendence. They can put you in a dungeon, he orated in Albany, Georgia, "and transform you to glory." He would proclaim in the meetings, "I'd rather live with a scarred up body than a scarred up soul." Getting doused with high-pressure fire hoses was a "baptism." Rested souls trumped tired feet; soul force could vanquish physical force. King swore that the "spiritual anvils" of the movement would "wear out many physical hammers." Their "breastplates of righteousness" would protect them from all material harm.

The subversion of meaning reached its ultimate form in King's contrast of physical and spiritual death. It's worth returning here to his comments in St. Augustine: "You know they threaten us occasionally with more than beatings here and there. They threaten us with actual physical death. They think that this will stop the movement. I got word way out in California that a plan was under way to take my life in St. Augustine, Florida.

Well, if physical death is the price that I must pay to free my white brother and all of my brothers and sisters from a permanent death of the spirit, then nothing can be more redemptive."[13]

In urging people to pay the same price he was willing to pay, King had to force them out of "the valley of fear" where life was governed by a budget of mundane risk—the cost of getting shot, a lost job, a bombed house. But there was a higher plane to live on, as the previous analysis of "I've Been to the Mountaintop" has prefigured. In Selma, King said, "I've never known anybody to achieve freedom until somehow they were willing to say within that death is not the ultimate evil. The ultimate evil is not to have something for which you will die if necessary. That's the most evil thing in the world. If we are going to be free, we have to be willing to suffer and sacrifice for that freedom if necessary."

Repeating his earlier declaration of purpose, "I come to tell you tonight," King celebrated a number of those sacrificial acts, each introduced by the refrain, "The South is better today": "because Medgar Evers lived in Mississippi and died in Mississippi"; "because three young civil rights workers . . . died on the soils of Mississippi"; because "back in 1965, Rosa Parks lived in Montgomery, Alabama, [and] like Martin Luther of old who said, 'Here I stand, I can do none other, so help me God,' she said in substance, 'Here I sit and I can do none other, so help me God.'" If black people now had the freedom to go places they once could not go, "Don't forget that somebody suffered that you may go there."[14]

For his intensely churched audiences, King did not need to say the obvious: Those who died so that others could live were godly. The protesters were also engaged in a kind of transubstantiation involving water and fire. In Birmingham, King scoffed at the city's fire hoses with a sectarian inside joke, told in the voice of the oppressors. "We tried to use water on them and we soon discovered that they were used to water, for they were Methodists or Episcopalians or other denominations, and they had been sprinkled. [Cheering] And even those who hadn't been sprinkled happen to have been Baptists. And not only did they stand up in the water, they went under the water." But it was the special fire of the protesters, the fire locked up inside them, that neutralized the power of the water. After Bull Connor had left the movement stunned and bleeding, King told a gathering that unarmed truth had the power to disarm enemies. "They just don't know what to do. They get the dogs and they soon discover that dogs can't stop us. They get the fire hose. They fail to realize that water can only put out physical fire. But water can never drown the fire of freedom."[15]

Some of King's most intense oratory came when he sacralized these moments of standing up like Christian warriors in the battle of spirit and state. He did so in a low moment in Selma. He did so in Memphis on the last night of his life. And he did it in a mass meeting in Montgomery in early 1968. He was warning against the futility of violence and the right-wing repression that rioting invited, telling his audience that "they" surely could handle violence. "I seen 'em try to handle it, but they didn't know. I remember when we were in Birmingham, Bull Connor was always happy when somebody behind the lines would throw a rock or throw a bottle. . . . They knew how to deal with it because they were experts in violence."[16]

Evoking the spiritual force of nonviolence at work on the streets, King began to build intensity, and the crowd was with him all the way.

> And then we would just pour out
> of the 16th Street Baptist Church,
> by the thousands,
> and Old Bull would say,
> "sic the dogs on 'em."
> And they did sic the dogs on us,
> And we just kept on walkin',
> Singing "ain't gonna let
> nobody turn me around."
> And then Old Bull would say
> as we kept moving,
> "Turn on the fire hoses,"
> And they did turn 'em on.
> But what they didn't know was
> that we had a fire that no water could put out.
> And we went on singing
> in the midst of the water hoses,
> "over my head I see freedom in the air."
> And then Bull would say,
> "pour 'em in the paddy wagon,"

And they threw us in,
And we were sometimes stacked up in there,
like sardines in cans,
but as the paddy wagon pulled away,
we were singing, "We shall overcome,
deep in my heart, I do believe!"

Part IV

CROSSING OVER INTO
BELOVED COMMUNITY

"The day of man as man"

Whether exhorting southern blacks, rousing his congregants, or joking with colleagues, Martin Luther King did not shy away from speaking as a black man to other black people. As we have seen in the first three parts of this book, he hooped it up, invoked fleecy locks, and told black people they were somebody. The King who spoke in black spaces beyond white scrutiny was often a more ethnic figure than the orator familiar to the public imagination, the crossover artist who reached out to the nation and, while arousing its collective conscience, emerged as its totem. Mythical moments of his oratory have been absorbed into the weave of the culture as emblems of principled idealism. Who can tell today if "I Have a Dream" belongs more to civil religious hagiography or to pop culture iconography? But no matter how it is used or abused today, King's clarion call to "Let freedom ring" still stands as a symbol of the nation's principled, if often latent and corrupted, idealism.

Part IV of this book considers the vibrant power of King's crossover ventures. Their surprising twists made hash of polarities like black and white, integration and nationalism. The first of these five chapters examines the tension between artifice and authenticity that sometimes diminished the power of the written and spoken words that King addressed to whites. As the following chapter reveals, King's rhetoric of mankind spilled over into life as intimate cultural encounters with white liberal Protestants and Jews that collapsed the barrier of race. The third chapter in this section confronts the mix of deference and edge that energized King's "legitimacy talk," and his use of shared sources to persuade white audiences to support the movement's goals and methods. The next chapter chronicles the "rudeness" that lurked beneath the surface of the exquisite manners that accompanied King's efforts to justify his cause. In the final chapter I look at the postethnic achievement of King's public ministry, the way he mixed displays of blackness into his affirmations of mankind before white audiences, concluding with a detailed examination of "Letter from Birmingham Jail" and "I Have a Dream."

Those most famous appeals represent only a fraction of the speeches and writings that King directed at whites. From virtually the start of the Montgomery bus boycott, he moved in widening circles, beyond the ethnic world out into the larger white universe. His forte was the ability both to console and provoke black audiences and to convince and inspire white ones. With blacks, he was a therapist, cheerleader, and goad. With whites, he was a far-ranging minister without a portfolio: emissary, gadfly, tour guide, fundraiser, ambassador, teacher, translator, conscience, go-between, a bridge between black community and white nation.

Inevitably, a life predicated on such straddling generated its own vexations. As the work of spies, ethnographers, and undercover cops attests, shifting in and out of audiences and identities can be stressful. The quandaries of authority and authenticity are always dicey. King was vulnerable to all the dilemmas that emerge in jobs that span boundaries: gaining entrée to new worlds, markets, and genres; keeping potentially incongruous performances separate from each other; maintaining fluency in multiple codes; and countering resistance and mistrust from the home community.

These dilemmas varied with the volatility of the milieus in which King practiced his crossover craft. In the early years, King was able to harmonize his black and white practices. The two sustained each other. King garnered acclaim from the white world: he was *Time* Magazine's Man of the Year; he won the Nobel Peace Prize; he huddled with presidents. All the while, most black people saw him as a heroic deliverer.

As the years went by, King found the balancing act ever more precarious. In the turbulence of the 1960s, the imperatives of mobilizing blacks and persuading whites continued to pull against each other. It was also harder for King to connect to either white or black audiences. As the old Democratic coalition fractured in the wake of white backlash and the Vietnam War, whites were less enthralled by King and the inconvenience of his prophetic stance, or they became distracted by other concerns. To black people disenchanted with the pieties of integration and turning the other cheek, moral exhortation to whites looked like obsequiousness, betrayal, and self-hatred—or just plain pointless. Toward the end of King's life, the Harlem congressman Adam Clayton Powell assailed him for "catering to whites."

Some time before that, Powell's constituents had accosted King with cries of "Uncle Tom," as if a world of mixing was tantamount to perfidy. Such charges wounded King deeply. He succumbed to snappishness, as David Levering Lewis captured King's mood in his comments to the writer Robert Penn Warren: "I guess you go through those moments when you think about what you're going through, and the sacrifices and sufferings you face, that your own people don't have an understanding— not even an appreciation, and seeking to destroy your image at every point." But King managed to pull himself out of that flash of frustration. "You know, they've heard these things about my being soft, my talking about love, and they transfer their bitterness toward the white man to me." He was convinced that "all this talk about my being a polished Uncle Tom" would fade.[1]

We saw how Andrew Young's flair for diplomacy with whites made him the brunt of black barbs within the SCLC. Young tells of the time he was getting ready to meet with the Birmingham Board of Trade. "When I came out in my suit, James Orange . . . and Fred Shuttlesworth would tease, 'Andy's going to "Tom."' And everybody would laugh. I'd respond, 'Any of you all are welcome to go with me, come on.' But going to negotiate with white folks was not their idea of a good time."[2]

Their reproach applied better to King, but Young was a safer target. As much as anyone, Young understood the betwixt and between zone that King inhabited. There were others in the movement who could energize a crowd of blacks to action, sometimes with more effect and virtuosity. But they could not secure the attention of the larger white world or the specialized white publics that King addressed. King's uniqueness, as Young understood, involved this capacity to translate the black experience for those outside it.

"There has to be a synthesis," King said of this juggling act. "I have to be militant enough to satisfy the militant yet I have to keep enough discipline in the movement to satisfy white supporters and moderate Negroes." Was this possible in the late 1960s? King himself was not so sure.

"You just can't communicate with the ghetto dweller and at the same time not frighten many whites to death," he admitted to one questioner. "I don't know what the answer to that is. My role perhaps is to interpret to the white world. There must be somebody to communicate to two worlds."[3]

FIFTEEN

Artifice and Authenticity

"I have other sheep that are not of my fold"

The charged question of the genuineness of King's oratorical outreach to whites has been a persistent one. Thoughtful commentators have sensed a forced quality in some of King's talk to whites, as if the fancy vocabulary was either a contrivance, excessive zeal for white approval, or opportunism. Decades ago, theology professor James Cone noted the cunning in King's mentions of white theologians and philosophers, as if he quoted them only because whites found them convincing: such references "were primarily for the benefit of the white public." Similarly, Keith Miller described King's graduate school writings on "erudite metaphysical topics" as characterized by "a peculiarly crabbed, stilted, self-conscious prose that does not sound remotely like the King his friends knew or the later King."[1]

King's seminary classmate Marcus Garvey Wood, the pastor of Baltimore's Providence Baptist Church, may have been thinking of the Crozer years as an artificial interlude when he wrote King to congratulate him after the Montgomery bus boycott: "I know you are preaching like mad now. You have thrown Crozer aside and you have found the real God and you can tell the world that he is a God who moves in a mysterious way. That he will be your battle ax in the time of war."[2]

A look at this issue of sham and wiles as it emerged in a few specific instances underscores the considerable caution needed in fathoming King's white talk. His plagiarism on his doctoral dissertation provides the most blatant case of writing in a voice that was not his own. King swiped whole paragraphs from others without attribution, and he did not admit the swiping or get permission for it. In this instance, inauthenticity devolved into duplicity. The efforts to account for this painful lapse differ a good deal, but they tend to emphasize King's disengagement from his scholarly words.

Some have sought to exonerate King, claiming that this was his way of resisting the white world's definition of intellectual property. In this rendition, King was in sway to the oral tradition of the black folk preacher convinced that only God could own the Word. How many black preachers cited precedent when they preached "Can These Dry Bones Live"? The revealing thing about Rev. Wyatt Tee Walker's comment that he liked to preach the sermons of Vernon Johns was the apparently offhand way in which he offered this tribute to the preacher he "worshipped." When he sampled Isaiah, Jesus didn't stop to offer a footnote either.[3]

Reflecting the skepticism shared by a number of King scholars, David Levering Lewis offered a judicious retort to this casting of King as a champion of some populist notion of intellectual property: "It is compellingly evident that Dr. King, of his own volition and intellect, formally endorsed and claimed to subscribe to the elementary rules of the academy of learning." But Lewis too perceived a dynamic of resistance beneath the surface of King's polish. It simply took a less earnest form. Given the "demeaningly modest" expectations of King's professors, who must have colluded with King in his flimflam, Lewis speculates, "almost certainly, an alert striver like Martin Luther King, Jr., would have sensed instantly the racial double standard for his professors." He concludes, "Finding himself highly rewarded rather than penalized for his transparent legerdemain, he may well have decided to repay their condescension or contempt in like coin."[4]

Both of these explanations are compatible with a more straightforward emphasis on King's devotion to the vocation of minister and the waning of his enthusiasm as he moved from the preaching emphasis of seminary to the academic concerns of a doctoral program in theology. As one of King's B.U. classmates, Cornish Rogers, recounted to David Garrow, King "told me, fairly early, that he was not a scholar, and that he wasn't interested, really, in the academic world." Maybe, Garrow considered, the posture of the worldly philosopher was a pose; maybe King was "a young dandy" before all else. King "was by no means fully at home with the dense and often abstruse theological texts that he was assigned to master. King wanted a Ph.D. in order to credential himself as someone far more learned than the average Baptist preacher. . . . It is no exaggeration to say that in his course work at Boston University, Martin Luther King, Jr., was to a considerable extent going through the motions."[5]

King's typical addresses and writings to a white audience offer a better test of the charge of contrivance. Especially in the words he wrote rather than spoke, King's tendency to play the scholar could project an affected and pompous persona. It has often been noted that in *Stride toward Freedom,* his account of the Montgomery boycott, this philosopher-King put himself forward as a self-styled big thinker who systematically worked through Hegel's dialectic, parsed Nygren's reading of agape, counterposed Niebuhr's realism to Rauschenbusch's idealism, and parried Tillich's existentialism with the foil of Brightman's personalism.

King could get so carried away with his fancy language that his trade book editors had to tone it down some. Melvin Arnold, the Harper editor of *Stride toward Freedom,* worried that King might appear too friendly to socialism. "This [passage] suggests that you place Marxism and traditional capitalism on the level of absolute equality," he said. But Arnold also cautioned, "You are vastly more at home with theoretical concepts and theoretical terms than 99% of your readers. (That is why, I think, you want to hold on—earlier in the book—to the word 'zeitgeist'! Some readers will think that 'zeitgeist' refers to an Ogpu [the spy agency that preceded the KGB], FBI, etc; others will think that you want to show that you know more than they do.)"[6]

The crowded production process that shaped King's crossover ventures also magnified the risks of sounding artificial. Compared to his black performances, much more of King's white talk—trade books designed to shape informed opinion such as *Stride toward Freedom, Why We Can't Wait,* and *Where Do We Go From Here?,* or speeches to Jewish audiences—

was heavily edited or initially drafted by others. Substantial portions of the literary handiwork of Stanley Levison, Bayard Rustin, Clarence Jones, Ed Clayton, and others appeared under King's name. The editors who worked on *Strength to Love* did more than sift out sentences that might have smacked of sympathy for socialism; they removed passages that they feared would provoke readers, as well as some of King's preacherly repetition. "King's assessment of segregation as one of the 'ugly practices of our nation,' his call that capitalism must be transformed by 'a deep seated change,' and his depiction of colonialism as 'evil because it is based on contempt for life' were stricken from the text."[7] For all these reasons, irrespective of the race of the audience, it is not surprising that the books fall into stretches of lifeless prose, leaden policy reflection, and vapid cultural criticism.

"Letter from Birmingham Jail" engages the issue of artifice in a different fashion. King presented "Letter" as an anguished outpouring, a direct response to the eight white clergymen who had criticized his protests in Birmingham. At best, the earnestness was something of a pretense. King never bothered to reply personally to his critics, a failure they found wounding and even exploitive. For all the Kantian injunctions to treat people as ends, King treated them as means to his larger political goal. He had been flirting with the idea of a jailhouse epistle for some time. When the Birmingham newspaper ran the clergymen's critical letter while King was in jail, timing and place combined to give King his perfect opportunity.

The symbolism of a letter composed inside jail was certainly not lost on King. The effort of King and his coterie to reshape the "spontaneous" and "private" epistle through countless drafts after he was released and to shop the letter for prominent placement was calculated. Hermine I. Popper, King's Harper editor for *Why We Can't Wait,* his story of the Birmingham protests which incorporated a version of "Letter," caught several references in the early drafts to events that couldn't possibly have happened while King was still in jail. She wrote King that "to sustain the biblical aura of the letter, it remained essential to maintain the appearance that King had written the entire composition while incarcerated."[8] And so "Letter" was moved along through the machinery of an organized public relations effort.

All of King's addresses to white audiences were shaped, in varying degrees, by the same forces that shaped the scripting of "Letter." Compared with his private repartee, preaching in black churches, and rally exhortation, the crossover King was pressed through the filter of a wary and often hurried production process. These forces came together in concocting the initial image of the Gandhian King.

Stride toward Freedom casts King's insurgent role as the natural culmination of a deliberate philosophical process. Only when he came to Crozer, he said, "did I begin a serious intellectual quest for a method to eliminate social evil." Nor had the seminary student studied Gandhi "seriously" until he attended a talk on Gandhi by Howard University president Mordecai Johnson. The impact was "electrifying." The studious King ran out and bought a trove of books on the Mahatma, which further "fascinated" him. "The whole concept of 'Satyagraha' . . . [which King translates as "truth force" or "love force"] . . . was profoundly significant to me. As I delved deeper into the philosophy of Gandhi my skepticism concerning the [social] power of love gradually diminished." Before long King was singing praises to Gandhi as "the first person in history to lift the love ethic of Jesus above mere interaction between individuals" into "a potent instrument for social and collective transformation." Here was the "method for social reform that I had been seeking for so many months."[9]

This vision of a dramatic odyssey hardly squares with the King who was dragooned into leading the Montgomery boycott. Moreover, the black and white proponents of Gandhi who descended on Montgomery during the boycott tried to bring King under the spell of a doctrine whose strange lingo declared its distance from the traditions of ordinary Montgomery Negroes—including King. Surely King's love of ribs and chitterlings was out of sync with the vegetarianism of "the little brown man," as King sometimes referred to Gandhi. Francis Stewart, one of King's white friends at Crozer, recalled that King got into "a pretty heated argument" with the pacifist A. J. Muste at Crozer in 1949. "King sure as hell wasn't any pacifist then."[10] Probably what drew him to Mordecai Johnson's Gandhi talk, which was billed as a sermon, was Johnson himself and his spellbinding oratory. King's embrace of nonviolence was rooted in Jesus' disavowal of the ethic of revenge. He made sparing use of Gandhi in mass meetings, giving him a cameo appearance in Albany, Georgia, where the March to the Sea offered an example of what a social movement based on Christian principles might accomplish. King's lone mention of Gandhi in his 1965 Gandhi Lecture at Howard University came in the title of the event.

The gap between homegrown belief and foreign doctrine created tension, at times with a partially religious or racial subtext. King had sent a draft of a chapter from *Stride toward Freedom*, "Pilgrimage to Nonviolence," to his Morehouse theology professor, George Kelsey, a notable black proponent of the social gospel. Perhaps sensing an overly generous crediting of Gandhi, Kelsey called for a "sharpening of the fact that the movement which you so nobly led was Christian in motivation and substance. Christian love remained on the 'ground floor.' Gandhi furnished the techniques, including the 'operational principles.'" Kelsey went on to emphasize, "I reserve such words as 'substance' and 'philosophy' for [the] Christian Faith." Less gently, some Ebenezer members bristled over the fact that King didn't learn anything from Gandhi that he hadn't learned in his Ebenezer Sunday school class.[11]

When Glenn Smiley, a white organizer for the Fellowship of Reconciliation (FOR), the Gandhi-influenced interracial pacifist group that included Bayard Rustin, was credited at an FOR meeting with preparing the way for the Montgomery bus boycott, King's secretary responded huffily. In her letter to King reporting on the meeting, she wrote, "I explained that white people just do not go into Montgomery and teach the Negroes anything."[12]

Smiley himself couldn't deny the superficiality of King's knowledge of the Gandhian philosophy or his commitment to it. King, he could see, "had Gandhi in mind when this thing started . . . but is too young and some of his close help is violent. King accepts . . . a body guard, and asked for a permit for them to carry guns. . . . The place is an arsenal. King sees the inconsistency, but not enough. He believes and yet he doesn't believe." Bayard Rustin had to warn a pacifist colleague who accompanied him to the King residence, "'Bill, wait, wait. Couple of guns in that chair. You don't want to shoot yourself.'"[13]

One evening not long into the boycott, Rustin pressed King on the issue that Gandhian principles "called for unconditional rejection of retaliation." Gandhi, he explained, recognized that most of his followers accepted nonviolence only pragmatically, which was why it was essential that movement leaders not betray the values of nonviolence by tolerating guns and guards. The movement, King countered, "*is* nonviolent," without yielding the right to self-defense. "We're not going to harm anybody unless they harm us." King even told an interviewer in 1956, "When a chicken's head is cut off, it struggles most when it's about to die. . . . A whale puts up its biggest fight after it has been harpooned. It's the same thing with the Southern white man. Maybe it's good to shed a little blood. What needs to be done is for a couple of those white men to lose some blood, then the Federal Government will step in."[14]

King did mention Gandhi, along with Thoreau, in his preaching from time to time, and not just upon his return from India in 1959. In his 1966 appearance in a Los Angeles black church, King even attained a degree of passion: "No, we need not hate / We need not use violence / There is another way / The way as old as the insights of Jesus of Nazareth / As modern as the techniques of Mohandas K. Gandhi. / There is another way." Yet the parallel mention of Gandhi and Jesus is deceptive. Typically, the Mahatma mention played a mainly rhetorical role, doing its part to create a contrast between "as old as" and "as modern as"; and King rhythmically accentuated the drawn-out phrase, "Mohandas K. Gandhi," for its dramatic effect. As the pulse of "there is another way" and the auditory punctuation of "ohh" indicate, the Gandhi references were subordinate to the expressive code of black preaching that carried them. The passion of the passage derives from "the better way" of Jesus Christ.

Still, the false notes in King's crossover talk should not be exaggerated. King's output to whites was diverse in form, style, purpose, context, audience, medium, passion, intimacy, anonymity—and affectation. Nor was there a single white audience any more than there was a single black one. King's angry reply to white critics in "Letter from Birmingham Jail" obviously differed from the mutual warmth of an appearance at the Rabbinical Assembly of Conservative Judaism with his friend Rabbi Abraham Joshua Heschel, yet the indignation in one and the pleasure in the other were both genuine. Clearly, none of the strategic considerations in "Letter" deprived King's voice of its deeply felt passion. If the parts of "Letter" were something of a jumble, the mosaic that King composed from them was based on his own signature phrases, quotes, and techniques. He relied on that same process of collage production for his rally speeches and sermons.[15]

Similarly, King remained an active participant in collaborations with ghostwriters. The King who emerges from the transcripts of his FBI-monitored chats with Levison hardly seems pliable. Instead he sounds like a president brainstorming with his staff for an inaugural speech: he mulls, objects, weighs, suggests, vetoes, and chides. That process was especially intense in the preparation of the speech King envisioned for the March on Washington in 1963. King's vigilance was increased by the high stakes and tricky political currents swirling about the event. Clarence Jones and Stanley Levison had worked up an early version. A stream of advisers weighed in, and King went through additional drafts. The night before the march, Jones played with language about executive orders while others lobbied for a call for full employment. Eventually, as Drew Hansen, author of *The Dream,* relates, King "put an end to the barrage. 'My brothers, I understand,' he said. 'I appreciate all the suggestions. Now let me go and counsel with the Lord.'"[16]

King was not happy with the initial draft that Levison and Jones provided for what would prove to be his most controversial speech, "Beyond Vietnam: A Time to Break Silence," which King delivered at Riverside Church on April 4, 1967. The speechwriters' caution reflected the real dangers in such a public rebuke of the war. The last thing the civil rights establishment wanted was to get into a smack-down with President Lyndon Baines Johnson. When King read the draft, he told Jones, "You've gotten conservative on me. You're supposed to be my 'take no prisoners' guy! This [speech] is too wishy-washy. I can't equivocate when we're bombing innocent women and children. And it's destroying the moral fabric of our country. Clarence, I love you like a brother. But you should know I'm a minister of God before I'm a civil rights leader. This is about morality, not politics!"[17]

So King accepted "the vocation of agony." He told the Riverside Church audience about the cascade of accusations that were leveled at him because of his speaking out on Vietnam: "Why are you joining the voice of dissent?" "Peace and civil rights don't mix." "Aren't you hurting the cause of your people?" From the outset, King reminded them, he and the SCLC had refused "to limit our vision to certain rights for black people." He recited that Langston Hughes plaint, "O, yes, I say it plain, / America never was America to me, / And yet I swear this oath—/ America will be!" Despite the assuaging note of "will be," the "never was" hinted at the seditious stance with which King was flirting—a stance above loyalties not just of race but of nation. "The true meaning . . . of compassion and nonviolence . . . helps us to see the enemy's point of view, to hear his question."[18]

Here was the radical force of the Word that was upon King. At stake was nothing less than what King described in the speech as the "meaning of my commitment to the ministry of Jesus Christ," which superseded his commitment to blacks and their deliverance. Did his critics not know "that the Good News was meant for all men—for communist and capitalist . . . for revolutionary and conservative? Have they forgotten that my ministry is in obedience to the one who loved his enemies so fully that he died for them? What then can I say to the Vietcong or to Castro or to Mao as a faithful minister of this one?"

Was this an empathetic entry into an alien viewpoint or, as some Americans took it, giving aid and comfort to aliens, not just the Vietcong but the alleged communist enemies supporting them? But King disavowed the petty sentiments of tribe. "Somehow this madness must stop. We must stop now. I speak as a child of God and brother to the suffering poor of Vietnam. I speak for those whose land is being laid waste, whose homes are being destroyed, whose culture is being subverted. . . . I speak as a citizen of the world."[19]

The establishment struck back hard. The *New York Times,* liberal senators, and the NAACP board all condemned King. "A Time to Break Silence," a *Washington Post* editorial charged, was full of "bitter and damaging allegations that . . . [King] . . . did not and could not document . . . sheer inventions of unsupported fantasy." The *Post* even cast King's prophetic stance as a betrayal of blacks: "The Government [of President Johnson] which has labored the hardest to right [historic] wrongs, is the object of the most savage denunciation. . . . King has diminished his usefulness to his cause, to his country, and to his people."[20]

King did not come late to his principled obstinacy. An early stylistic spat between King and Bayard Rustin underscores King's confidence in his own instincts. When King was about to deliver the speech "Give Us the Ballot" at the 1957 Prayer Pilgrimage for Freedom at the Lincoln Memorial in Washington, Rustin had objected to King's use of the word "give" in the title, a pleading request that he thought northern blacks might find demeaning. He wanted King to declare forthrightly, "We demand the ballot." "No, King said, that wouldn't convey the rhythm and music of his natural delivery. When Rustin insisted on his point, the young preacher, then only twenty-eight, issued this gentle reminder: he needed no advice from Rustin in the art of engaging and inspiring an audience."[21]

By contrast, Stanley Levison—white, secular, a New York Jew, King's "honorary Christian"—not only entered the mind of the black preacher but found his prophetic pulse where Rustin had missed it. In 1967 Levison wrote a *New York Times* op-ed piece, to run under King's name, which he read to King in a telephone call that was monitored and transcribed ungrammatically by the FBI. "Let us save our national honor, stop the bombing. Let us save American lives and Vietnamese lives, stop the bombing. Let us take a simple instantaneous step to the peace table, stop the bombing. . . . Let our voice ring out across the land to say the American people are not vainglorious conquerors, stop the bombing." King replied, "Well I don't think you need to change that a bit that is excellent. It really gets everything I need to say and it opens up just right. . . . That last part is beautiful for a speech."[22]

Talking by phone three months after King's death, Levison and Rustin hearkened back to that early period when they sat around madly dashing off phrases and ideas and, as Rustin put it, "created the direction" for King. Levison qualified that a bit: "No, I don't want to take too much on it because the man was very independent always. But I do think we helped direct the mode in which he was going. Remember when we used to sit up in your place late at night writing those things?" "We were analyzing Martin," Rustin chimed in, "and saying 'how did he view these kinds of problems.' . . . It was not we directing him so much as we working with him and giving expression to ideals we knew he had or would quickly accept." As Rustin elaborated, "I don't like to write something for somebody where I know he is acting like a puppet. I want to be a real ghost and write what the person wants to say."[23]

A similar seriousness characterized King's growing engagement with Gandhi's legacy. King simply absorbed its lessons not as a solemn theologian or spiritual seeker but as the leader of a movement refining his repertoire of protest. Even before that process took hold, King had grasped the predicate of Niebuhr's view that groups were more immoral than individuals: moral suasion required the bite of pressure to implement it. King had also noted that Gandhi lived the themes of suffering and sacrifice that so entranced King in his own faith. Beyond these generalities, however, he knew nothing about insurgency. In Montgomery King was mainly winging it. But if Gandhi's "technique," as Kelsey had phrased it, had offered a nice rhetorical foil to the "spirit" of Jesus, it was the substantive intricacies of techniques of loving coercion that would now resonate with King. Ranganath Diwakar, a disciple of Gandhi who met with King in Montgomery in August 1959, "convinced Martin that he, too, must set an example of physical suffering." It was no accident that two weeks later King opted to go to jail and surrendered himself to the Montgomery authorities. During all his subsequent jail stays, King adopted Gandhi's habit of fasting.[24]

With his usual gift for flattery, King declared upon arriving in India in 1959, "To other countries I may go as a tourist, but to India, I come as a pilgrim." As Lerone Bennett observed, King was as much "impressed by Gandhi's living monument, [Prime Minister] Jawaharlal Nehru," as by anything else in India. Over dinner, Nehru told King about his own campaign on behalf of the untouchables. "To King's surprise, Nehru even endorsed the idea of national atonement, of special and intensive efforts to root out the effects of thousands of years of soul-destroying oppression." Retracing the steps of the great Salt March made vivid the power of a national movement that gave its adherents both the ethic of "soul force" and, to use David Levering Lewis's term, "a tactical breviary" that included boycotts and mass meetings, strikes and nonpayment of taxes, and the pageantry of moral dramaturgy. King left India with a heightened sense of the place of Montgomery in a much broader global struggle for justice. He also returned, as Bennett put it, "convinced more than ever of the necessity of massive government intervention and of the efficacy of love."[25]

King's encounter with India epitomized the vitality of his engagement with all kinds of "foreign" influences and the openness and empathy he brought to all his dealings with the world.[26] These constancies outstripped the variations of source or style. Always, there was the driving force of his prophetic faith. Always, there was his effort to enlarge the imagination of his audience. And always, there was his immense capacity to observe parallels and translate the foreign into his audience's experience. All the while, however, King sifted out the accoutrements that he found unappealing. No matter how attractive Gandhi's asceticism with respect to possessions may have been, the sexual self-denial went by the wayside, as did the alien religious sensibility of Hinduism.

There was no better symbol of the authenticity of King's crossing over than the words of Jesus he invoked in his very first sermon at Dexter upon his return from India: "I have other sheep that are not of this fold." As King told it, Jesus grasped that there were others who embraced the spirit of his teachings, even if they were not in his immediate camp. Preaching at Dexter on Palm Sunday, King granted that it might make sense to "think about this wondrous cross," but he begged the congregation "to indulge me this morning to talk about the life of a man who lived in India." Ever the border-crosser, he was now prepared to return to India with Dexter in tow, so they could experience together what he had found in that faraway land. The homily was studded with strange names—Dandi, Ahmadabad, Porbander.[27]

Just as he converted Stanley Levison into an honorary Christian, King made Gandhi into a Negro and a Christian of sorts. He recounted how, when Gandhi lived in South Africa, the ticket takers on the train he was riding noticed "that he had a brown face, and they told him to move on to the third-class accommodation." Gandhi looked "at his people as they lived in ghettoes . . . [and] were humiliated and embarrassed and segregated in their own land." King told how the untouchables suffered from their own version of a Jim Crow life. But if they suffered from an Indian version of invisibility, Gandhi overcame the gulf: he made them visible, even within his own household. As King told it, Gandhi's upper-caste wife thought "he was going crazy" when he made up his mind to adopt an untouchable girl. "'We are not supposed to touch these people.' And he said, I am going to have this young lady as my daughter."

Throughout his sermon, King preached the irrelevance of labels or source, language or fold. Praising God toward the end, King noted, "We call you different names," and he ticked off Allah, Elohim, Jehovah, Brahma, and even the architectonic good. The important thing was not something as mundane as religious affiliation but Gandhi's exemplary acts, which indicated a gracious, forgiving spirit. Just as King ventured beyond his Afro-Baptist world to engage all sorts of people, Gandhi, King explained, devoured the words of Tolstoy, the Sermon on the Mount, and Thoreau. What did it matter if he was, in Jesus' terms, "not of my fold"?

He refused to hate, he turned the other cheek, and he walked in the way of love. "It is one of the strange ironies of the modern world that the greatest Christian of the twentieth century was not a member of the Christian church."

As King compressed the distance between folds, the Indian holy man even began to sound like the Montgomery preacher; at least as King rendered him, Gandhi seemed to be parroting King's lines, and he had acquired a bit of Afro-Baptist cadence and the cry of the mass meetings. "And Gandhi said to his people, 'if you are hit, don't hit back; even if they shoot at you, don't shoot back; if they curse you, don't curse back *(Yes, Yes)*, but just keep moving. Some of us might have to die before we get there; some of us might be thrown in jail before we get there, but let us just keep moving.'"

Ultimately, the weight of evidence closes the debate on the real King by revealing the genuine quality of his outreach. The artifice lies in any simple division between King's talk to blacks and his talk to whites. It was not, it turns out, the whiteness of King's sources that corrupted his voice on his dissertation; it was the particular white sources he was recycling, and the state of mind of the cyclist. Before both whites and blacks, King displayed the same penchant for exalted phrases, elevated his audiences into cosmic narratives, and exhibited the same blending that gave all his talk a universal quality. Nor did any of his high-minded moments diminish his sense of blackness, whether he paraded it exultantly before whites or only hinted at it with a barely marked word. As King practiced it, crossing over signified the expansion of tradition, not its diminution. His mixology was a bold and comfortable claim to multiple codes, identities, and traditions. Brotherhood endured right alongside *brother*hood. Or, to put it more formally, King's ties with whites proliferated in tandem with his "blackening" voice before black audiences—and white ones too.

SIXTEEN

Practicing What You Preach

"And yet our legs uttered songs"

 King's oratory could seem untethered from the practical work of mobilization, but it did not float in rhetorical space. Like King's black talk, his addresses to whites were embedded in personal and organizational relationships. Before we delve into the words themselves in the next three chapters, it is useful to examine some aspects of the context that shaped King's outreach to whites: the rearrangement of relations between the races in the nation; the connections the movement itself was forging between blacks and whites; and especially the networks that channeled King's oratory and created a shared culture between King and his Jewish and liberal Protestant allies.

At the grandest level, King's talk to whites reflected the multiplicity of opportunities that were being generated by the breakdown of racial partitions in post–World War II America. The obvious signs included a whole range of challenges to the racial status quo—ideological attacks on racism; government action resulting from Supreme Court decisions, executive orders, and such local experiments as the desegregation of police forces; and the force of nascent black insurgency. Also during the years when King was working out his remarkable synthesis, a similar blurring of racial boundaries was occurring in the realm of popular music. Its most visible symbol was the "Sound of Young America" that Berry Gordy was creating at Motown Records, which adapted rhythm and blues to appeal to both whites and blacks.

This line of musical development was anticipated by the Drifters, whose various phases spanned the entire range of raw and refined, race music and American music. In their mid-1950s incarnation headed by Clyde McPhatter, the mournful sound of Bubba Thrasher on "I Should Have Done Right" affirmed the link to gospel as much as R&B. The 1950s and early 1960s saw the emergence of a large number of soulful singers, whose auditory maneuvers offered a secular equivalent to whooping: James Brown's sobbing bleats, the gospel funk of Solomon Burke, Ray Charles's wail, the raspy country pleading of Otis Redding, Wilson Pickett's screaming of notes rather than noise,[1] the breathless intoning of Gene Chandler, and Garnet Mimms's keening on "Cry Baby." But in 1959 the Drifters, with Ben E. King as lead singer, produced the "cleaner," orchestral sound of "There Goes My Baby," violins and all, that prefigured the fusion Berry Gordy would refine at Motown.

Working out that soul hybrid carried dangers for civil rights leaders as well as artists. The practical question was how to maintain expressive intensity without making it too "foreign," too black, for the white market. This concern prompted Stanley Levison to object when King and a consultant were exploring the idea of airing recordings of King's sermons on the radio. According to the consultant, after Levison "heard some of the tapes that I was going to use, which was Martin preaching in a black church, for instance, he didn't want that to go on for all the public to hear, so I said, 'why?' And he said, 'That's the black idiom.'" As David Garrow explains, Levison feared that black voice "would not play well with potential northern contributors."[2]

The balance could tip in the other direction as well. Too much polish or pop imitation—the obligatory "The Four Tops on Broadway"—and the music would brighten, and whiten, too much. Symbolized by the draconian regimen of correct diction and grooming that Motown imposed on its less varnished artists, too much effort to cater to a white audience could risk turning the translation of a black musical tradition into its corruption.

White consumption of black culture was not a guaranteed sign of racial tolerance. Fleeting dips into blackness may have been little more than musical curiosity for the white teenagers of Albany, Georgia, who overheard the freedom songs of the mass meetings in 1962 and later that summer "sat under the trees one night at the resort, Radium Springs, and sang together: 'Kum-bi-yah.'" Such mutual surveillance and cultural exchange have had a long lineage in the South. Black preachers were never entirely cut off from white preachers, who in turn eavesdropped on their black counterparts. From minstrelsy up through contemporary "wiggers," the white aficionados of hip-hop, such encounters have been replete with voyeuristic zeal and racist contempt as well as appreciation. In the early 1950s, James Brown performed at Deep South universities that never would have countenanced black people in a dorm or classroom. There was even a black band who called themselves "The Five Screaming Niggers," who did cover versions of "Shout" at drunken Colgate College bashes in the late 1950s and 1960s.[3]

Yet the meaning of such cultural exchange is never independent of the terms of exchange and the larger milieu that shapes them. Borrowing in a world of Jim Crow, *Birth of a Nation,* and Dorothy Dandridge is not the same as in a world of civil rights ferment and its aftermath, of Putney Swope and the Black Pack—or, for that matter, a world of Philip Roth, *The Feminine Mystique,* and Stonewall. And it's especially not the same as in today's more mixed-up world of Oprah, *Chappelle's Show,* and "Chef" on *South Park.* Like King's endeavor, soul music too offered a chance to transcend aesthetic "neighborhood" with musical "brotherhood," a cultural adventure that anticipated the slipping over of the hip-hop nation into "Hip Hop America," to borrow Nelson George's title. Like the civil rights movement, soul music brought black cultural forms proudly out into the larger civic arena. Sundering the link between art and tribe, it was accompanied by white appreciation too.

King's imaginative ventures into Jewish, liberal Protestant, German, untouchable, worker, black nationalist, and even racist white identities were matched by the empathetic voyage of a bevy of incipient "white Negroes," from businessmen to A&R personnel to house band members, who appreciated black culture. Etta James captured one of those experiments: "I dug how [the Greek-American soul man] Johnny Otis reinvented himself as a black man. . . . His soul was blacker than the blackest black in Compton." It was a white southern member of the horn section in the Stax house band, not Isaac Hayes, whose praise of the rougher rasp of southern soul was a transracial dig at the Motown sound. Meanwhile, James Brown drew the inspiration, and chords too, for the rhythm and blues classic "Lost Someone" from country singer turned reluctant rockabilly artist, Conway Twitty. In all this mixing it up, one can see glimmers of a new racial order of permeable borders as opportunities to try on identities and appreciate cultures other than one's own—in the process not just making them one's own but casting doubt on the very meaning of "own."[4]

The second aspect of the context of King's crossover ventures was a special case of the first. The civil rights movement itself became a place in which new crossings between the races were anticipated, rehearsed, and fashioned. King's moral witness to whites was only one form of crossover culture linking the races in new forms of exchange. As the chapters in Part III made clear, black people's mobilization talk was never self-contained. It pointed outward in exultant, at times jousting, encounters with the state and civil society. The children of Selma who called out "we love you" to the sheriff burning them with cattle prods were only an idiosyncratic manifestation of such engagement.

Detectives on Bull Connor's surveillance detail, a staple of the mass meetings, got the chance to experience a conspicuous version of racial tourism. Seated night after night in the rapturous churches, some of the monitors seemed transfixed by the loss of control of black women "screaming" and "falling out." Apparently riled by criticism of Bull Connor, one detail opined that such criticism was a tool "to get a spontaneous reaction from the audience." They went on to speculate, "Apparently the only thing that held them under control was the absence of vines suspended from the ceiling." The detectives also took note of whites in the audience, such as "a beatnik type character, shabbily dressed, with long hair, ankle length boots, and long white socks."[5]

Yet at least one policeman appeared to change over time into a connoisseur who occasionally hazarded critical appraisals of black performance, enlivening the voice of deadpan observation and racist voyeurism with the judgment that one speech by Rev. Charles Billups was "unimpressive." Some members of the unit even began to refer to their detail as "going to church," according to James Baggett, director of the Birmingham Public Library archives, who is working on a biography of Connor. The men's own evangelical and Pentecostal style of worship, he points out, made some of them comfortable with the fervor of the meetings.

There were also more sympathetic encounters whose exuberance on occasion tipped toward the humorous. In St. Augustine, the mother of Massachusetts governor Endicott Peabody and a bunch of Reform rabbis descended on the scene. Al Vorspan, the former director of the Social Action Committee of Reform Judaism, described the meeting, in which one of them got so caught up in the fervor that he leapt into a Jewish form of whooping. Two years before, Rabbi Israel Dresner had found himself next to King at a black church in Albany, Georgia, as they both sang, "John the Baptist was a Baptist." Now in St. Augustine, Dresner "astonished his colleagues with call-and-response preaching that evoked a tumultuous response. Carried away, he retained his customary long-windedness beyond the endurance of several rabbis who, wilting from fatigue in the Florida heat, discreetly chanted *genug*—Yiddish for 'enough already.'"[6]

Such acts of trading places allowed moments of trying on the identity of the other. The crossings flowed in all directions. In the workshops in Montgomery, Nashville, and Birmingham, sometimes blacks played the role of demonic white racists in exercises designed to teach the victims of such insults the discipline not to respond in kind. John Lewis writes, "It was strange—unsettling but effective, and very eye-opening as well—to see a black student pushing a white off a chair, screaming in his or her face, 'Coon!' and 'Ape!' and 'Nigger!,' or to see a white student shoving a black, yanking his or her hair, yelling, 'White trash!' and 'Nigger lover!'"[7] The anthem of the movement, "We Shall Overcome," provided a perfect emblem of these dynamics. White unionists and a white folk singer played a role in turning the personal flight from the world of the original hymn, "I Shall Overcome," into the collective resistance of "We Shall Overcome."

The third aspect of the context of King's outreach to whites involved the web of connections through which his crossover oratory flowed from movement to nation. King forged a host of personal relationships which snaked through the larger field of expanding possibilities.[8] In the beginning, King was the beneficiary of luck—the serendipity of the outsiders who descended on him, including Stanley Levison and Bayard Rustin, who emerged as gatekeepers to donors, editors, and influentials of all sorts. A stream of ideas, strategy, and resources flowed back in the reverse direction to King and his prophetic coterie. An ongoing feature of Levison's role was to serve as King's eyes and ears in the white world.

Over time, King cultivated a presence in the world of liberal white Protestantism. He also circulated through the world of synagogues and Jewish ethnic defense organizations. The Jewish segment of King's networks overlapped with the broader liberal alliance of the time, and King forged close relationships with a number of important unions and segments of the Democratic Party. Anticipating the emerging post–New Deal liberal order, King developed ties to movie stars and other entertainers, major national magazines and important newspapers, television shows such as "Meet the Press," the foundations, and Ivy League and other universities. As part of his fund-raising efforts, he dined with wealthy liberals in Manhattan and Hollywood. Eventually, King's ties to the Vietnam peace movement deepened, and he was a star attraction at antiwar rallies.

These networks were vital channels in the crossover enterprise. They linked King to worlds beyond the black community. They provided venues for King's performances before special white audiences. They created the opportunity for encounters with whites that blossomed into shared culture and warm feeling. This was most obviously true with white Protestants from liberal denominations. The streaming of his words into this religious distribution network gave King access to an audience of thousands. In addition to face-to-face appearances, King reached them through articles in *Christian Century*, for which he served as an editor-at-large, and *Pulpit*. Every one of his trade books was published by Harper, whose religion list had featured the stalwarts of liberal Protestantism.[9]

King had long studied the paragons of liberal homily, but now he joined these previously remote figures on the circuit that stretched from Detroit's Lenten Series to the Chicago Sunday Evening Club to Riverside Church. Harry Emerson Fosdick, Robert McCracken (Fosdick's successor at Riverside Church), J. Wallace Hamilton, George Buttrick, and E. Stanley Jones had preached in these venues, as had the theologians Paul Tillich and Reinhold Niebuhr. Even if they were not King's literal ancestors, they were his adopted kin, and he honored them, incorporating their words, ideas, and metaphors into his oratory. "The Man Who Was a Fool," which King preached at the Noon Lenten Series in Detroit and at the Sunday Evening Club in Chicago, owed more than its title to George Buttrick's explication of the parable of the rich fool. King wove into his sermon Buttrick's language that "Jesus made no sweeping indictment of material wealth" and his distinction between "the 'within' and the 'without' of our lives." The version of "Loving Your Enemies" that King delivered in 1961 at the Noon Lenten Services of the Detroit Council of Churches drew much from Fosdick's sermon "On Being Fit to Live With," including his discussion of agape, eros, and philea.[10]

Could such borrowings seem more chutzpah than homage? After all, if McCracken had read King's sermon on communism in *Strength to Love,* he might have felt he was in a strange kind of echo chamber, with his own words flying right back at him. A certain degree of pique would have been natural. Yet it seems that McCracken and countless others did not fuss about such appropriations.[11]

In borrowing from such figures, Keith Miller argues, "King took pains to ensure that his sermon reflected a broad homiletic consensus." Yet the idea that King "took pains" to secure approval may not fully capture the nuances of King's hybrid efforts. Even if not entirely guileless, King's renditions were from a repertoire of "ponies he liked to ride." Better yet, the ponies were race-blind. As we have seen, King preached "Three Dimensions," "The Man Jesus Called a Fool," and many other sermons to black congregations as well as white ones. It made sense that King was echoing a sermon by the Presbyterian minister Frederick Meek when King preached to the United Presbyterians. After all, King's "Paul's Letter to American Christians" owed its basic conceit to Meek's sermon, "A Letter to American Christians." But recall that King electrified ten thousand black Baptists with the same rebuke of a soulless white Christianity. Far from "taking pains" in a white setting, King was citing language that he deployed before all kinds of audiences.

King's personal copies of the books of these ministers indicate his heartfelt grappling with this liberal Protestant material. The underlining and the scribbling of inspired sermon ideas suggest the primal acts of incorporation through which he took them in and chewed them over. King anticipated his own sermon "Paul's Letter" with the note he wrote to himself on his copy of Meek's "A Letter to American Christians": "The division in the churches appalls me (i.e. Negro and White)." Inspired by Niebuhr's *Moral Man and Immoral Society,* King jotted down on its opening pages this idea for his sermon "What Is Man?": "the individual sin becomes a social sin." In his copy of J. Wallace Hamilton's *Horns and Halos in Human Nature,* Hamilton's musing, "So, when I get the blues about human nature and when I am tempted to lose faith in people or in the future, I turn to Christ," prompted King to scrawl his own points such as "man's persistent tendency to overlook this duality—either we overstate the evil or we overstate the good."[12]

King's addresses to white Protestant churches thus differed from his other crossover appearances. Negotiating the tricky currents of the Holocaust and Israel, King needed guidance when he spoke to Jewish groups. But on the Protestant circuit, he was preaching to the converted. In his own mind, and the mind of the audience, King was not just a civil rights leader but a preacher too, not just a Christian but a Protestant with allegiance to a social gospel. King had been studying the work of these Protestant thinkers since he was a teenager, and they reciprocated with praise and affection. As Miller describes it, "Warmly welcoming him to Riverside Church, McCracken repeatedly negotiated a spot on King's jammed schedule and always expressed exuberant pleasure at King's appearance."[13]

The parallel with Elvis Presley, stealing away from his family's Pentecostal church to head to the black church one mile away, is not too long a stretch. The same savoring was at work. Presley, and a broader group of the white, country-oriented Sun Records coterie, soaked in the powerful preaching and gospel music of Rev. Brewster. Presley returned at night to hear the radio broadcast of Brewster's Camp Meeting of the Air. The Reverend, writes Presley biographer Peter Guralnick, "constantly preached on the theme that a better day was coming, one in which all men could walk as brothers."

Across Memphis Sam Phillips, the founder of Sun Records, "listened on his radio every Sunday without fail, and future Sun producer Jack Clement often attended with his father, a Baptist deacon and choir director, 'because it was a happening place, it was heartfelt, and that's what was happening in Memphis.'" A similar appreciation, at once human and cultural, prompted Phillips's love of rhythm and blues no less than rockabilly and led him to guide Presley toward a more blues-oriented sound, like his cover of Arthur "Big Boy" Crudup's "That's All Right (Mama)" in the legendary Sun recording sessions. As a child, Phillips had wondered, "Suppose that I would have been born *black*. . . . I think I felt from the beginning the total inequity of man's inhumanity to his brother. And it didn't take its place with me of getting up in the pulpit and preaching. It took on the aspect with me that *someday I would act on my feelings, I would show them on an individual, one-to-one basis.*"[14]

If King "took pains" to align himself with some "consensus," it was one he had deeply internalized. In that sense, King was borrowing from himself as much as from outside sources. But he was also borrowing from the band of black mentors who had helped enlarge that "white" consensus, inducted King into it, and pioneered the crossover path. Benjamin Mays spoke at the Sunday Evening Club. William Stuart Nelson, dean of the Howard University School of Divinity, published in *Christianity Today*.

These men did not enter white settings just to mingle and make nice. In his 1953 address to the American Baptist Convention, "There is Power in That Cross," Gardner Taylor lamented, "What an insuperable burden we put upon the Christian evangel by our reservations and by our bigotries." The Protestant voice, he said, muted by expedient silence in the face of racism and anti-Semitism, "has become . . . a faint and powerless echo" that mocks the grandeur of Christ and "our gospel [which] says to us that every creature, every human soul, is of infinite and endless worth to the heart of God." Repeating arguments he had made to the World Baptist Convention in the 1940s, Mays insisted in a 1952 address at Yale Divinity School: "Segregation on the basis of color or race is a wicked thing because it penalizes a person for being what God has made him. . . . And to do this is tantamount to saying to God you made a mistake in making a man like this. Of all the sins, this is the greatest."[15]

When his turn came to reach out to white Christians, King employed not just the words and ideas of Buttrick, Fosdick, and McCracken but those of Mays—the notion that racism implied that God made a mistake; the appeal to the "interrelatedness" of all humans (that phrase itself, and the John Donne line—no man is an island—that validated it); the scientific support which anthropologists Ruth Benedict and Margaret Mead gave to the idea that the races differed precious little; the mantra, "We are tied together with an inescapable destiny," which was what Mays told the seniors at the 1945 Howard University commencement. King's observation in both *Stride toward Freedom* and *Strength to Love* that segregation "distorts the personality" and hurts the one who hates was vintage Mays: "The chief sin of segregation is the distortion of human personality. It damages the soul of both the segregator and the segregated."[16]

Mays, Thurman, and Johnson found something more beguiling than a platform in the white world. Mays knew firsthand that the pastor of Shilo Baptist Church, the church he had attended as a boy in backwoods South Carolina, could make "broken down" Negroes shout as he offered them detailed visions of damnation in hell and heaven's joy. But at Bates College in Maine, Mays discovered a thrilling message of liberation in the writings of Walter Rauschenbusch and the evangelical strain of social gospel liberalism. This was the same doctrine that Gardner Taylor and Vernon Johns imbibed at Oberlin.[17]

King may have thrilled to read Rauschenbusch's call for an "earthquake" of social action to respond to earthly injustice, and he saw it as appealing to his optimistic faith that "the universe was friendly." But decades earlier, the idea that the teachings of Jesus had social application was for Mays "like food to a starving man!" writes historian Randall Jelks. Even after he became president of Morehouse College, "Mays would demonstrate his gratitude" to Rauschenbusch by editing the first collection of his writings, which appeared decades after the great evangelist of the social gospel had died. For Mays no less than King, there was no unbridgeable chasm between so-called "white" culture and so-called "black" culture. The meanings they found in the white world offered a universal idiom that helped make sense of the black—and the human—plight.[18]

King's black models also found something less metaphysical in the white liberal pulpit: moral support for their effort to condemn racism as un-Christian. Through repeat invitations and their own racial witness, those white allies embraced the emphatic message of their black colleagues. More than a "universal human ailment," according to Niebuhr, racism was "the most recalcitrant aspect of the evil in man." Fosdick pronounced racism "as thorough a denial of the Christian God as atheism and . . . a much more common form of apostasy." In this nook of spiritual learning, whites and blacks were forging a spiritual counterculture. The standing applause that greeted King as he entered the Sunday Evening Club in 1958, even before he preached a word, indicated clear approval for his activist endeavor.[19]

The crossover King was only one figure in a collective endeavor. His outreach to liberal Protestants moved along the tracks others had laid down. Just as Willie Bolden and J. T. Johnson, the heritage of the folk pulpit, and the rapture of the meetings prepared Black Belt audiences for a King performance, the entire roster of black and white liberal Protestant preachers prepared the way for King in these more rarefied settings.

One might suppose this milieu exacted a steep cultural price of admission: an implicit pledge to give "no offense" by parading ethnic identity.[20] These were the years before "the decline of the Wasp," before multiculturalism and identity politics. But if King did not flaunt his mentions of race, neither were they trifling. The oppositional Christian culture being forged here allowed more than a dollop of blackness in the social gospel mix.

Howard Thurman's shifts between black and universal perspective in two books he wrote in the 1940s anticipated the promise of King's hybrid strategy. *Deep River* is a rumination on the richly spiritual character of the slaves that enters the imaginative universe of the spirituals and translates them for outsiders. This was where King found the rendering of balm in Gilead—and its affirmation, "They did an amazing thing!" Still, *Deep River* has the gossamer feel of reverie, the wispy distance of a trance. Thurman's *Jesus and the Disinherited,* a book that King carried around with him, has an earthier quality in keeping with its concern with social oppression. Despite the vibrancy of its humanistic vision, the racial awareness is always present.

Thurman mentioned the flak Jesus took from those who thought love for "those beyond the household of Israel" was a perversion. He also recalled the response of Jesus to a "Syrophoenician" woman who had pleaded with Jesus to help her children. "What right has this woman of another race to make a claim upon me?" Jesus wanted to know. "What mockery is there here. Am I not humiliated enough in being misunderstood by my own kind?" The story ends with a rejection of the tribal ethic.[21]

At one point, Thurman disclosed a personal story that exposed an intimate secret of the race. Drilled into him by his grandmother, it was "given to her by a certain slave minister who . . . held secret religious meetings with his fellow slaves. How everything in me quivered with the pulsing tremor of raw energy when, in her recital, she would come to the triumphant climax of the minister: 'You—you are not niggers. You—you are not slaves. You are God's children.'" This is the passage that King dramatically tweaked into the dialect of "you ain't" and imported into sermons at Dexter and Ebenezer for the purpose of racial healing rather than transracial understanding.[22]

Like Thurman, King felt no need to veil his black identity at the pulpits of high Protestantism or in the books that targeted the same audience. Even the written transcript of "The Christian Doctrine of Man" that King preached at the Noon Lenten appearance exudes Afro-Baptist passion. Shifting from exposition to the language of "crying out," King infused emotion with the drawn-out "ohh," and voiced his ethnic concern for his black brothers: "But in the midst of your creed, America, you strayed away to the far country of segregation and discrimination. *(Say it, Amen)* You've taken sixteen million of your brothers, trampled over them, mistreated them, inflicted them with tragic injustices and indignities."[23]

King attributed those words to God in a manner that recalls "Paul's Letter to American Christians." This God, who cares so much, directly addresses America as "you," and insinuates himself into the midst of the nation's racial struggles, is a warm, inviting personality. Echoing all of his preaching before black congregations about God—*He takes you in*—King reassured his audience in Detroit: "The God of the universe stands there in all of His love and forgiving power, saying, 'Come home. *(Yeah, Amen, Amen)* . . . But America, I'm not going to give you up. If you will rise up out of the far country of segregation and discrimination *(Amen)*, I will take you in, America. *(Amen, Amen)* And I will bring you back to your true home.' *(Amen)*.

"And when a nation decides to do that, when an individual decides to do that, somehow the morning stars will sing together. *(Amen, Yeah)*, and the sons of God will shout for joy *(Yeah, Amen)*."[24]

It wasn't the energy of a live audience that prompted King's expression of black concerns and Afro-Baptist accents in front of whites. King did not disguise his sense of blackness in the white-vetted trade book *Strength to Love*. In one of the sermons in that book, "Shattered Dreams," after listing Darwin, Helen Keller, and Handel as among those who "exchanged their thorns for crowns," King moved to a black vantage point. "We Negroes have long dreamed of freedom, but still are confined in an oppressive prison of segregation and discrimination." The veneration of the ancestors appeared as more than just a faint insinuation: "Our slave foreparents" survived "in spite of inexpressible cruelties," King almost boasted. He commemorated their suffering—"the slaves . . . were taken from Africa, they were cut off from their family ties and chained to ships like beasts. . . . When women were forced to satisfy the biological urges of white masters, slave husbands were powerless to intervene." King had no qualms about parading the slaves' language for the white liberal Protestant readers of the Harper religion list: "By and by I'm gwin to lay down this heavy load."[25]

King's commingling with Jews had different accents and antecedents. Shared regard for the Hebrew prophets compensated for the absence of a shared Christology. The secular indignities experienced by pariah peoples gave the mutual identification special resonance. Paul Robeson, who was able to sing in Hebrew Kol Nidre, the opening prayer of the Jewish Day of Atonement, caught the blues sensibility of two peoples: "The Jewish sigh and tear is close to me." The *Yiddishe Taggeblatt* gave rave reviews to Mendel, the Black Cantor. As for Reb Tuviah, a black artist who performed in Yiddish and Hebrew before throngs of Lower East Side immigrants, he was incomparably versatile. He starred in the bawdy "Yenta Talebenta," while his version of "Eli, Eli" "conveyed more deeply . . . Jewish sorrow, the Jewish martyrdom, the Jewish cry and plea to God, than . . . could have ever been imagined." Image and metaphor did not flow in one direction. The *Daily Forward,* the Yiddish newspaper, depicted lynching as "pogroms."[26]

A consecration of this mutual sympathy came one month before King's death at a gathering of the Rabbinical Assembly at the Concord Hotel in the Catskill Mountains of New York. Right before King ascended the podium, he was greeted by the sound of one thousand rabbis, linked arm in arm, singing "We Shall Overcome"—in Hebrew. In stretching that capacious "we," they were bearing witness to the same elasticity of community that King did when he invited burly union men to sing the same song, although that time decidedly in English.

King's personal relationships reinforced the bonds of shared sensibility. Bayard Rustin was a philo-Semite for whom the liberal-labor-black-Jewish coalition endured as an article of faith. As for Stanley Levison, it is true that he was hardly a "Jewish Jew." About as Jewish as it got, recalls Andrew Levison, Levison's son, was a Passover in which the Egyptians were the capitalists and the Jews the proletarians. This made sense in that left-wing culture in which Rustin once took Andrew to see a cowboy movie and cheered on the Indians, all the while yelling out in his British accent, "Get those Europeans!" But Stanley Levison grasped the importance of cultivating the ideological support of Jewish liberals and the dollars of Jewish donors. From the start of their relationship, he encouraged King to speak to secular ethnic defense groups such as the American Jewish Congress. Over time, King developed friendships with a number of key rabbis in various denominations, including the whooping rabbi Israel Dresner, Maurice Eisendrath, and many others.

In Atlanta, following Rabbi Jacob Rothschild's outspoken calls for racial justice, a hate group bombed The Temple, as the Reform Jewish synagogue was known. As early as the late 1940s, he had invoked these lines of Isaiah for their racial import: "Your hands are stained with crime— / wash yourselves clean. . . . Devote yourselves to Justice / Aid the oppressed." Rothschild did not shrink from discomfiting his comfortable congregation. "We have committed no overt sin in our dealings with Negroes. I feel certain that we have treated them fairly. . . . No, our sin has been the deeper one, the evil of what we didn't do." As Melissa Fay Greene chronicled, Rothschild recited all the evils inflicted on the Negro: "Deep voiced, angry, looking back and forth from scripture to the black slums of his adopted city, Rothschild was in the grip of divine vision, of righteous anger." "There is only one real issue," he told his congregation. "Civil rights." Constantly, he named as his favorite verse of the Bible, "Then I heard the voice of my Lord saying, 'Whom shall I send? Who will go for us?' And I said, 'Here am I; send me.'"[27]

In an incident that brings to mind the movie *Guess Who's Coming to Dinner,* after King moved back to Atlanta Rothschild invited him to his home for a meal. "You know it was all very strange and new, how to act," Greene quotes Janice Rothschild, the rabbi's wife, as saying. "I mean, when you had black guests, did you introduce them to your maid?" With her black housekeeper, she brought up her plan to serve the Kings Coquilles St. Jacques, a dish the rabbi's wife always prepared herself. But the housekeeper dissented. "'Mrs. Rothschild, *you* may know very well what your fancy friends like to eat, but *I* know what colored preachers like to eat—we are having barbecued chicken.' Mrs. Rothschild served both."[28]

The Kings arrived late, Janice Rothschild remembered. As far as the hosts were concerned, there was no need for explanation. Still, she continued, "Martin apologized anyhow and explained that they had been delayed trying to find our house." It seems the Kings were forced to knock on doors to get directions. "As Martin told us this, he quickly added, 'But we were careful not to embarrass you with your neighbors. I let Coretta go to the door so they'd think we were just coming to serve a party.'" Janice added, "I still get a lump in my throat when I think of it."[29]

The pressure to celebrate King after he won the Nobel Prize threw the reluctant elite of Atlanta into a tizzy. Rabbi Rothschild, along with Benjamin Mays and Cardinal Hallinan, served as co-chair of the memorial dinner. Coretta called Janice to consult on the dress she planned to wear to a function at the Dinkler Hotel, which had only recently allowed black people as patrons. Given King's sense of dignity in mixed settings, it was striking that he joked with Mayor Ivan Allen about his tardiness. "I forgot what time we were on," a grinning King told him.

"How's that?" Allen wanted to know. "Eastern Standard Time, CST, or CPT." A puzzled Allen replied, "CPT?" King answered back, "Colored People's Time. It always takes us longer to get where we're going." Despite the quipping, it was a big moment for the Kings and for Atlanta. After celebrating King, "You attest the truth that goodness and righteousness do reside in the human heart," Rabbi Rothschild presented him with a bowl from Tiffany's that Janice Rothschild had picked out.[30]

Many rabbis heeded King's call over the years and then found themselves engaged in all sorts of mutual crossings. During the Birmingham campaign, an exhausted King met with a delegation of rabbis who had come directly to King's headquarters in the Gaston Motel from the meeting of the Rabbinical Assembly of Conservative Judaism. Just as he used to cite his old pool-playing credentials in juke joints, King knew the equivalent overtures in this ecumenical setting. Reflecting on "his disappointment in so-called white liberals and their temporizing, . . . he quoted Martin Buber and the Hebrew Bible," Rabbi Andre Ungar recalled, "and when, at our request, he led us in a parting prayer, there was a sacred stillness in the air." The rabbis then joined a mass meeting at a black church where, according to Richard Rubenstein, "we were greeted as 'our rabbis,' as if we were a precious possession. We marched down the aisles amid standing and cheering congregants."[31]

None of these relationships were as close as the one King formed with Rabbi Abraham Joshua Heschel. King did not joke around with Heschel the way he did with Lowery and Abernathy. Other things drew them to-gether. Heschel's prose had an extraordinary poetic quality—it burned with intensity—that always appealed to King. They also shared a connec-tion to Niebuhr, beginning with Heschel citing Niebuhr at the conference at which he and King first met. Heschel taught at Jewish Theological Seminary in New York, which was across the street from Union Theologi-cal Seminary where Niebuhr taught. The two men were neighbors on Riverside Drive. In their later years, they walked the drive together, and Heschel often talked about his friendship with King. But what especially lingered in the memory of Ursula Niebuhr, Niebuhr's wife, was Heschel's repeated reminiscences about Selma. "He was shocked, deeply, to see white southern women spitting on and yelling at the Catholic nuns with whom he walked." Both King and Heschel would denounce the Vietnam War in prophetic terms from the pulpit of Riverside Church.[32]

King was cementing his ties to the circles of ecumenical liberalism at a 1963 conference on race and religion sponsored by the National Confer-ence of Christians and Jews when he first met Heschel. Like King and Rev. Joseph Lowery approaching each other at a black preaching conven-tion, King and Heschel did their own interfaith version of "preacheristic exaggerations" as they marveled at each other's oratory. Any discrepancies of code, race, or theology that separated a Southern Baptist preacher from an old-world sage descended from Hasidic royalty dissolved in the myriad parallels of prophecy, passion, and poetry.

In keeping with King's taste for Exodus, the always inventive Heschel observed that the main players at the first conference on race and religion were "Pharaoh and Moses. Moses' words were, 'Thus says the Lord, the God of Israel, Let My people go that they may celebrate a feast unto Me.' . . . The outcome of that summit meeting has not come to an end. Pha-raoh is not ready to capitulate. . . . In fact, it was easier for the children of Israel to cross the Red Sea than for a Negro to cross certain university campuses."[33]

If King affirmed "all God's children," Heschel asked the world "to re-member that humanity as a whole is God's beloved child. To act in the spirit of race is to sunder; to slash, to dismember the flesh of living com-munity." Racial prejudice, he said, was blasphemy, "a treacherous denial of the existence of God."

Echoing James Bevel in Birmingham a few months earlier ("the Bible is now"), King told the audience, "Religion deals not only with the hereafter but also with the here. Here—where the precious lives of men are still sadly disfigured by poverty and hatred. Here—where millions of God's children are being trampled by the iron feet of oppression." Heschel said at that same conference, "*We think of God in the past tense* and refuse to realize that *God is always present* and *never, never past;* that God may be more intimately *present in slums than in mansions.*"

Back in Georgia, did not Abernathy insist "this is God's Albany"? Heschel pronounced, "This is not a white man's world. This is not a colored man's world. It is God's world." King argued against resignation to the slights of the world. To those who thought action would be "too little and too late," that all we can do is weep, Heschel retorted that if Moses had followed that lesson, "I would still be in Egypt building pyramids."

Both men were capable of intense feelings that required a visceral language to express them adequately. Resorting in his speech to the same imagery of foul smell he had invoked in a Birmingham mass meeting, King said, "The oft-repeated cliches, 'The time is not ripe,' 'Negroes are not culturally ready,' are a stench in the nostrils of God." "My heart is sick," admitted Heschel, "when I think of the anguish and the sighs, of the quiet tears shed in the nights in the overcrowded dwellings in the slums of our great cities, of the pangs of despair, of the cup of humiliation that is running over."

To top it all off, both men cited King's favorite line from Amos, "Let justice roll down like waters, and righteousness like an everflowing stream."

The two men's friendship had a certain purity. It was forged by the spiritual audacity—the concept is Heschel's—that each man saw in the other. Such boldness also entailed a distinctive verbal practice. Like King, Heschel understood that the prophetic task entailed "speaking for those who are too weak to plead their own cause. Indeed, the major activity of the prophets was *interference,* remonstrating about wrongs inflicted on other people," which in turn entailed talking God into the world.[34]

When King was in need in Selma, he called on Heschel to come to his aid. At a service right before the march, Heschel read Psalm 27, "The Lord is my light and my salvation; whom shall I fear?" A famous photograph captured the two men walking over Pettus Bridge together. The marchers referred to the bearded sage as "Father Abraham." Back in New York, Heschel wrote King: "The day we marched together out of Selma was a day of sanctification. That day I hope will never be past to me—that day will continue to be this day." "For many of us," he later reflected, "the march from Selma to Montgomery was about protest and prayer. Legs are not lips and walking is not kneeling. And yet our legs uttered songs. Even without words, our march was worship. I felt my legs were praying."[35]

In his whole-hearted participation in the Selma march, Heschel was enacting his conception of the prophet as one who speaks for those who cannot. But he also saw that King's brand of black religion offered him, and Jews in general, something precious too: a road to revival for Judaism. In the midst of black churches, Heschel felt in the faith and fervor a vibration of Hasidic passion that he knew from Europe, something the modern spirit of "synagogue administration" had drained out of Judaism. So, if the *Jewish Forward* could translate lynchings into "pogroms," if one thousand rabbis could translate "We Shall Overcome" into Hebrew, why couldn't Heschel translate the Selma-to-Montgomery march into his own European Judaic terms? "I thought of my having walked with Hasidic rabbis on various occasions. I felt a sense of the Holy in what I was doing."[36]

A friendship built on spiritual audacity seems a bit rarefied. But that was never the totality of King and Heschel's relationship. As Susannah Heschel, the rabbi's daughter and a professor of Judaic Studies at Dartmouth, knows firsthand, there was also affection. It's not hard for her to remember what King meant to her father. The passion for King became a household project. She and her mother were there in spirit in Selma with her father—worried, but proud. "My father and King were deeply moved by each other," she says, clearly moved herself. Just as King made Stanley Levison his "honorary Christian," King called Heschel "my Rabbi." Both were ways of paying homage, one to a lawyer-accountant, the other to a prophet. The connection continued even in death. Heschel delivered a eulogy at King's funeral; Coretta spoke at Heschel's.

Susannah Heschel caught a glimpse of King's tender side in the service of the two men's mutual affection. She was a young teen in the front row at the Concord Hotel when the singing rabbis greeted King and her father introduced him as "a voice, a vision, and a way" and dubbed him "a modern-day prophet." King threw the prophetic compliment right back at Heschel. Afterwards, before King went off to huddle with the rabbis, he performed one of those acts of kindness to the least of these for which he was famous. It may seem odd to think of Heschel's daughter as the "least of these," but as a teenager in that setting, that's how she felt. Just as King would take time to chat with the janitor at Ebenezer Church even when he was late for a meeting, he took the time to say hello to Susannah and asked one of his aides to entertain her; the aide spirited her away to play with a mimeograph machine. As she understood, it was a gift from King, a gift from one father to another.[37]

It wouldn't be right to romanticize such race-mixing. We are catching high moments of culture sharing at their zenith, as they emerged out of the process of crossing borders. The crossover enterprise generated low moments too, the inevitable miscues and misunderstandings. There was an abrasive underside to mixing. One time in an Atlanta freedom house, the black activists forced Tom Houck and other white activists to take their showers last, sending them to the back of the line, if not the bus. Decades later, a minister apologized to Houck for his part in that less than Christian version of "the first shall be last."

But these were mainly the birth pangs of a new order, like the puzzlement over a dinner menu prompted by a simple invitation. There's a more important point here. As King carried out his crossover task, beloved community became more than a special state experienced only during speaking. In such moments, the oratory was not just enabled by existing relationships; it created them. In the process, beloved community was transfigured—from a dreamlike ideal into ordinary life.

SEVENTEEN

Validating the Movement

"To use the words of Martin Buber . . ."

It doesn't get much more sublime than exchanging high Protestant homily and prophetic compliments. Such lofty sentiments have had an ambivalent place in American life, however. If a preference for plain speaking and a hard-boiled mistrust of sentiment and sentimentality have flourished in a society that defined itself in part by repudiating European fanciness, the nation's social movements have often provided a righteous alternative to a politics of venal bargaining. The exalted language King spoke at the Chicago Sunday Club or the Rabbinical Assembly had precisely this quality of moral innocence, as high-minded people celebrated the spiritual meanings they shared together.

Yet King's appearances in such places were almost unique, at least to the extent that they were driven by spiritual passions at the core of his identity and somewhat independent of the movement. This is why Lawrence Reddick, King's friend, biographer, and companion on the trip to India, tried to wean him from these speaking engagements. As the editors of the King Papers relate, Reddick "had pressed King to cut back on speaking events that pulled him away from fund-raising for SCLC. King's petu-lant response, recalled Reddick, was that an artist should not 'be denied his means of expression. That he liked to preach and felt that he should do it.'"[1]

In truth, King did not always appear in the guise of the artist before white audiences. His white talk was not so innocent of larger purpose and political intent. It's not that the moral sentiments he spoke to white audi-ences were false, the ones he voiced to blacks genuine. It's rather that his voicing of them was keyed to the particular contingencies of the occasion, the specific audiences and expectations that composed it, and his precise aims in the setting. Typically, King sought to convince white audiences of the rightness of his cause, the virtues of nonviolent resistance, and the limits of patience. He was not trying to goad them into action but to per-suade them to support the movement, its goals of an integrated America, and its means of protest.

Even fair-minded whites who shared King's moral sensibility did not necessarily support black people's activism, any more than all blacks real-ized that "the acceptable year of the Lord is this year." Nor did all whites at the National Cathedral necessarily share the *racial* views of McCracken, Niebuhr, or King. Among Jews, many members of The Temple who dis-liked segregation still grumbled over Rabbi Rothschild's racial agenda. Its elder members, a vulnerable fragment, remembered the lynching of Leo Frank. Some southern Jews cringed when called upon to challenge the sta-tus quo. Such brashness about the South's peculiar customs could only draw dangerous attention to them. Even in these sympathetic settings, then, King's motive was never solely to celebrate shared values with like-minded souls. He had to work his high-toned beliefs to win over the reluctants. As King moved away from these affectionate communities into the more general white universe, the work of convincing was ever more urgent.

If the goal of mass meetings of blacks was mobilization, that of King's crossover appearances was primarily legitimation.[2] This was never an exer-cise in moral philosophy; it had a three-part structure of communion, edge, and elevation. Communion, part of opening up access to the rhetor-ical occasion, involved the search for shared premises, which King effected by deference to the prized vocabulary of his audience, recognition of their distinctive experience, and empathetic leaps into their world. "Edge" involved the subversive application of shared premises to the black struggle, even as King softened his prophetic chastisement of whites. Elevation healed the rift of any implied "correction" by lifting everyone into a glorious future.

As in the various versions of "The American Dream," King slid easily into the idiom of humanistic liberalism as the point of connection. Though he often invoked "the magnificent words of the Constitution and the Declaration of Independence," before local audiences he searched out specialized variants of universalism that resonated with the history and perspective of those he was addressing. At the annual convention of the AFL-CIO in 1961, he found the common premise in the language of moral work and equal rights, weaving together the working man's struggle for justice with the civil rights movement. "Negroes in the United States read this history of labor and find it mirrors their own experience." Even before he made the parallels explicit, King virtually recast workers as Negroes. "Less than a century ago the laborer had no rights, little or no respect, and led a life which was socially submerged and barren." Quoting Jack London, he went back in history to evoke that time when workers were "nobodies" before they attained a state of being somebody: "He did not walk like a man. He did not look like a man."[3]

As for the fight for collective rights, King recalled the brutal backlash against labor "fought mercilessly by those who blindly believed their right to uncontrolled profits was a law of the universe." And he congratulated labor for its "monumental struggle" in the 1930s when it secured the legal right to organize and exercised it against "stubborn, tenacious opposition." At that moment, "the day of economic democracy was born."[4]

The search for shared foundations was not confined to secular performances. Speaking at New York City's Episcopalian Cathedral of St. John the Divine and writing in *Strength to Love*, King found in Exodus an apt warrant for the principle that domination violates the sacred character of the universe. "When the children of Israel were held under the gripping yoke of Egyptian slavery, Egypt symbolized evil in the form of humiliating oppression, ungodly exploitation, and crushing domination."[5]

More often, it was passages from the roster of liberal Protestant preachers that helped King establish the high ground of irrefutable principle at Riverside Church, at the National Cathedral in Washington, at Yale's Battell Chapel, and countless other temples of high Protestantism. To buttress the idea of an obligation to care for others in "On Being a Good Neighbor," King took the contrast of tribal loyalty with care for mankind from George Buttrick's *The Parables of Jesus*. "And who is my neighbor?" King wanted to know.

The answer for King was not Max Weber's jaundiced view of neighborliness as "an unsentimental brotherhood" rooted in the mutual need arising from proximity. The whole point of King's use of the man left half dead by robbers on the Jericho road was to oppose self-interest as the basis for action. In a repeat of Dives' refusal to see, the priest and the Levite strode on by with barely a glance. They saw "only a bleeding body, not a human being like themselves." Before white and black audiences, King stressed the racial dimension of that inability to see. The Samaritan may have been a half-breed from an alien race, and the Jews did not have dealings with his kind, but he was no partisan of the "ethic of tribe," which, as King preached it, held that "thou shalt not kill" meant "thou shalt not kill a fellow Israelite, but for God's sake, kill a Philistine." This was the source of the Samaritan's special vision. He could see the beaten, bloody man "as a human being first, who was a Jew only by accident." The moral of the story, one that King would affirm in various idioms in his crossover oratory, was clear: To be a neighbor is a moral choice, not an ecological condition. The neighbor is "any needy man" on the "Jericho Roads of life."[6]

But King's conception of social obligation was much more expansive than the personal graciousness shown by the Samaritan in a fleeting encounter. Reminding his audience at the Noon Lenten series that Jesus never scoffed at the demands of the body, King preached, "We must forever be concerned about man's physical well-being. Jesus was concerned about that." King parsed Jesus' aphorism, "Man cannot live by bread alone," "but the mere fact that the 'alone' was added means that Jesus realized that man could not live without bread." Now King drew out its insurgent implication: "So as a minister of the gospel, I must not only preach to men and women to be good, but I must be concerned about the social conditions that often make them bad. . . . I must be concerned about the poverty in the world. . . . I must be concerned about the slums in the world. *(Amen)* It's all right to talk about the new Jerusalem, but I must be concerned about the new Detroit, the new New York, the new Atlanta *(Amen, Tell it)*."[7]

There was courtesy at work in King's effort to find the point of connection with his various audiences. But deference was only one step in creating legitimacy; quoting well-known sources was only one way King indicated belonging; and deference was never obsequiousness. Even when he borrowed sources from whites that presumably would resonate in a particular setting, King still drew on Howard Thurman and Benjamin Mays. Nor did he cease his appeals to secular arguments or diffuse Christian principles that did not belong to any single homiletic community. He invoked plain decency and cosmopolitan enlightenment that transcended black or white audiences. He cited the findings of social science. At other times, King pronounced the social gospel flat out with the same rhetoric of assertion he used to goad black people into action. "Christians are bound to recognize any passionate concern for social justice. . . . The Gospels abound with expressions of concern for the welfare of the poor. . . . Christians are also bound to recognize the ideal of a world unity in which all barriers of caste and color are abolished. Christianity repudiates racism."[8]

King's solicitousness extended to Jewish audiences as well. He showed an uncanny, if idealized, grasp of Milton Himmelfarb's definition of Jewish liberalism as that form of "Jewish particularism that likes to call itself universalism."[9] In his own wise-guy fashion, Himmelfarb was pointing to the stakes that a vulnerable pariah group had in pluralism and the insurance the group gained from protecting the rights of all minorities. In short, what goes around—in this case, rights—comes around.

King underscored the collective interest served by protecting every minority in his 1958 address to the American Jewish Congress. "My people were brought to America in chains. Your people were driven here to escape the chains fashioned for them in Europe. Our unity is born of our common struggle for centuries, not only to rid ourselves of bondage, but to make oppression of any people by others an impossibility."[10]

The American Jewish Committee audience broke into applause during a 1965 address whenever King affirmed universally compelling reasons for the black struggle. He aptly summarized the postwar Jewish wisdom when he said, "Any group struggling justly enlarges the right of all." The audience applauded again when King recalled the mix of rabbis, priests, and ministers swelling the streets of Selma.

Translating the larger moral principle of the obligation to aid strangers from a Christian parable into a secular, Jewish-inflected form, King summoned the words of Rabbi Joachim Prinz's speech at the March on Washington right before King delivered "I Have a Dream." King recalled the lesson Prinz took from the Holocaust. "'When I was a rabbi of the Jewish community in Berlin under the Hitler regime . . . the most important thing that I learned in my life and under those tragic circumstances is that bigotry and hatred are not the most urgent problems. The most urgent, the most disgraceful, the most shameful, and the most tragic problem is silence.' A great people which created a great civilization had become a nation of silent onlookers who remained silent in the face of hate, in the face of brutality, and in the face of mass murder."

As he had done in the context of labor history when he made workers black in some sense, King reinforced his arguments with displays of empathy. He reached across the divide of race and religion to urge people everywhere to adopt a technique of the Negro movement, nonviolent protest, on behalf of Soviet Jews. But King's identity flips were even more audacious. Imagining what might have been if Germans during the Nazi era had also tried nonviolence on behalf of Jews, he then extended the reach of German empathy further. King retroactively invited Germans to dress as Jews in a move that echoed reverse blackface. Perhaps, King speculated as he fell into a preacherly rhythm, "the brutal extermination of six million Jews . . . might have been averted . . . if Protestants and Catholics had engaged in nonviolent direct action and had made the oppression of the Jews their very own oppression and had come into the street beside the Jew to scrub the sidewalks. And had Gentiles worn the stigmatizing yellow armbands by the millions, a unique form of mass resistance to the Nazi regime might have developed."[11]

The dynamic of deference in King's efforts to justify was never more visible than in "Letter from Birmingham Jail." "To put it in the terms of St. Thomas Aquinas," King explained, "an unjust law is a human law that is not rooted in eternal and natural law. Any law that uplifts the human personality is just." Shifting religious communities, he pronounced, "As Reinhold Niebuhr has reminded us, groups are more immoral than individuals." Lest the lone rabbi among his clerical detractors be slighted, there were words from Martin Buber. King's intellectual name-dropping here was mainly the presentation of a scholarly self. His arguments were fragmentary and derivative, akin to bumper stickers. The array of sources suggests not so much a sustained theological encounter as an effort to make the rounds and pay homage to difference.

Communion eased entrance into the imaginative world of his white audience.[12] Once inside, the second phase of King's effort to validate the movement kicked in, the subversive application of the shared principles to the black plight. Edge was the slam behind the smile that turned the favored language into a weapon. It was the "correction," the force applied by moral consistency, that followed the "love" of communion. As King drew out the implications for his people's struggle, prophetic denunciation was channeled into cool, piercing logic.

It's not quite right to say that King was hoisting his audience by its own petard. But he was wielding shared premises for the leverage they gave him in gaining support for winning citizenship for blacks. Inevitably, this added an element of coercion to the purity of moral exhortation. Yet such a maneuver was more than a strategy. It followed naturally from King's realism—the hardheaded grasp of the recalcitrance of evil and what was required to vanquish it.

Having established a set of incontestable premises—God's indivisible love, his commitment to deliver the captives, the sinfulness of racism, the right to life, liberty, and happiness, the depraved indifference of the bystander—King put them to work on behalf of the movement. King's 1965 address to the American Jewish Committee epitomized the force of that drawing out. Invoking Rabbi Prinz's comments on the evil of silence repeated the move in "Letter from Birmingham Jail" when King heralded the moral obligation of third parties to care with a more personal slant that echoed his fantasy of Germans dressing up as Jews. "It was 'illegal' to aid and comfort a Jew in Hitler's Germany. But I am sure that if I had lived in Germany during that time I would have aided and comforted my Jewish brothers even though it was illegal."[13]

There was a price to be exacted for such generosity. Having established the shame of disengagement, King turned it around to compel the Jews to intervene on behalf of the Negro. He followed the sordid precedent—"They remained silent in the face of hate, in the face of brutality, and in the face of mass murder"—with a stirring principle: "America must not become a nation of onlookers. America must not remain silent" about black oppression.

In the case of the Phillips Brooks–inspired sermon that King preached to the Episcopalians at the Cathedral of St. John the Divine, the turnabout was less labyrinthine. King established the shared notion that God's purpose is the triumph of good over evil with the example of "when the children of Israel were held under the gripping yoke of Egyptian slavery." But then, armed with biblical story as authority, King put archetype aside, made his move back into history, and walked his white audience step-by-step through its racial implication, translating the black condition back into Brooks's terms: "The pharaohs of the South were determined to keep [the Negro] in slavery. Certainly the Emancipation Proclamation brought him nearer to the Red Sea, but it did not guarantee his passage through parted waters." Finally, "despite the patient cry of many a Moses, they refused to let the Negro people go."[14]

As the "cry of many a Moses" evoked, edge sometimes took on the resonance of prophetic rebuke. In the sermon "Paul's Letter to American Christians," King delegated the task of voicing criticism, which allowed him to rebuke his fellow Americans with all the weight carried by Paul's authority. Presumably the bitter medicine went down more easily coming from Paul than a black man. "There is another thing," said Paul/King, "that disturbs me to no end about the American church—You have a white church and you have a Negro church. You have allowed segregation to creep into the doors of the church. How can such a division exist in the true Body of Christ?" When Paul is startled by the discovery that Sunday church services are "the most segregated hour of Christian America," he shudders. "How appalling that is" (which was the same language that King jotted down in his copy of the Meek sermon, "Letter to American Christians"). Paul has even come to understand that some people "argue that the Negro is inferior by nature because of Noah's curse upon the children of Ham." Then, adopting King's sigh, Paul says, "Ohh, my friends, this is blasphemy," which provokes him to issue a policy declaration: "So Americans, I am impelled to urge you to get rid of every aspect of segregation."[15]

There seems to be no end to Paul's dismay, or to the care with which he has followed southern backlash. "There are some brothers among you who have risen up in open defiance. I hear that their legislative halls ring loud with such words as 'nullification' and 'interposition.'" Disavowing silence in the face of such evil, Paul urges his listeners to tell those brothers that they have revolted against not only "the noble precepts of your democracy, but also against the eternal edicts of God himself." Consecrating this prophetic role of Paul, King has him become King-quoting-Amos, "Yes America, there is still the need for an Amos to cry out to the nation: 'Let judgment roll down as waters, and righteousness as a mighty stream.'"

King cried out in his own voice at the National Cathedral in Washington a few weeks before his death as he was planning the Poor People's Campaign, the same occasion when he preached about the parable of Dives and Lazarus. To provoke the well-heeled audience out of complacency, he cycled from personal to general to ultimate. He began by declaring, "I have literally found myself crying," and told them about the haunting visit to Marks, Mississippi, that had occasioned the tears. "I tell you, I saw hundreds of little black boys and black girls walking the streets with no shoes to wear. I saw their mothers and fathers trying to carry on a little Head Start program, but they had no money. The federal government hadn't funded them, but they were trying to carry on. They raised a little money here and there; trying to get a little food to feed the children, trying to teach them a little something."[16]

Where direct experience and empathy might not win the day, King looked for other means of leverage. Jumping from Quitman County to biblical parable, King linked Dives' refusal to acknowledge a brother in need to America's shameful indifference. A few years earlier after a similar mention of Dives and Lazarus before a white audience, King had observed, "Surely it is un-Christian and unethical for some to wallow in the soft beds of luxury while others sink in the quicksands of poverty." Presumably the National Cathedral audience included some who knew the "soft beds of luxury," but King did not chastise them directly. Instead, he pointed at the larger nation: "Dives went to hell because he sought to be a conscientious objector in the war against poverty. . . . And this can happen to America, the richest nation in the world."

As King pressed this argument in different venues, the prophetic impulse blurred the difference between rally and church, mobilizing and preaching, black audience and white. Across settings, only the idiom and inflection varied, not the basic argument. At the National Cathedral, King dropped the folksy exclamations instead of his final consonants. And he drew out his account of the plight of the poor, as if he had to legitimate the possible chaos he was about to inflict on the capital. But the message—"Dives went to hell . . . and this can happen to America"—was the same one he delivered to a black audience in Greenwood, Mississippi: "America is on the way to hell. It may be that God has called us to save it." In both cases, parable gave way to jeremiad, and storytelling became righteous chastisement.

Having mustered the forces of experience and parable, King now enfolded both in a righteous burst. As King made God the Marks children, the Marks children became godly, and the appeal to empathy gave way to a more ominous warning. "It seems that I can hear the God of history saying, 'That was not enough! But I was hungry, and ye fed me not. I was naked, and ye clothed me not. I was deprived of a decent sanitary house to live in, and ye provided no shelter for me. And consequently, you cannot enter the kingdom of greatness. If ye do it unto the least of these, my brethren, ye do it unto me.' That's the question facing America today."[17]

The same blend of deference and edge entered King's civil religious argument with its vision of the American dream. On the face of it, the language of equality and the dignity of the individual is utterly in tune with the nation's dominant values, and the trope of American dreaming has served as nationalistic self-congratulation just as much as a critical brief for liberation. But King pushed civil religion talk in less than civil directions, transforming the platitudes of the inaugural ceremony into an instrument of judgment. In "I Have a Dream" King spoke the hallowed words of the Declaration of Independence, "The promise that all men, yes"—but almost immediately he interrupted himself, breaking in to add words and gain control over their framing with a sly rhetoric of assertion—"black men as well as white men"—"would be guaranteed the unalienable Rights of Life, Liberty, and the pursuit of Happiness."[18]

King also implemented edge in "I Have a Dream" through the contrasts of justice and transgression, possibility and fulfillment. The American dream, as King rendered it, was only potentiality. The phrase "one day will rise up and live out the true meaning of its creed" underscored its still-deferred status, just as the "still" in "I still have a dream" hinted at the effort faith required in the face of actual injustice. His insistence at the March on Washington, "Now is the time to make real the promises of democracy," pointedly separated dream from its realization. What the pieties seemed to offer, King took back by what he implied: An America that does not keep her promise has betrayed her promise.

The fact that "Negroes are still in the long night of captivity" one full century after the Emancipation Proclamation further heightened the gulf between the real and the ideal. The metaphors of bankruptcy and default in the early portion of "I Have a Dream" underlined moral failure. The sacred, irrefutable dicta, "life, liberty, and the pursuit of happiness," collided with the very necessity for the march, which King described prophetically: "We come here today to dramatize a shameful condition."

The search for critical corollaries was intense and studied in "Letter from Birmingham Jail." To turn consent to broad principles into a weapon of black deliverance, King spared no time on fine points. He invoked sources in an almost jittery fashion, plundering cultural authorities rather than parsing them. King followed the words of St. Augustine ("any law that degrades human personality is unjust") with the slam of syllogism: "All segregation statutes are unjust because segregation distorts the soul and damages the personality." For Rabbi Milton Grafman, King craftily slipped the word *segregation* into the mouth of a Jewish sage: "To use the words of Martin Buber, . . . segregation substitutes an 'I-it' relationship for the 'I-thou' relationship, and ends up relegating persons to the status of things. So segregation . . . is morally wrong and sinful." Then it was time for a Protestant aphorism, followed by an assertion disguised as a question. "Paul Tillich has said that sin is separation. Isn't segregation an existential expression of man's tragic separation, . . . his terrible sinfulness?"[19]

In "Letter," King took pains to justify not just integration but his entire repertoire of contention and its sense of urgency. Having already used Tillich to brand segregation sinful, King invoked him again by pivoting on the word "so." "So I can urge men to disobey segregation ordinances because they are morally wrong." To rebut the accusation of reckless timing, King let loose a barrage of "reasons"—a series of "I am here because"—which omitted the rationale he would trumpet in Selma ("I am here because my people are suffering"). King had come to Birmingham because he was "cognizant of the interrelatedness of all communities and states. . . . We are caught in an inescapable network of mutuality, tied in a single garment of destiny." But his occupational mandate and the Judeo-Christian mandate that bound King and his clerical detractors also obliged action. Juxtaposing the gospel of Jesus Christ and the gospel of freedom, King sought to endow his mission with the aura of incontrovertible duty, merging the eighth-century prophets who "left their little villages and carried their 'thus saith the Lord' far beyond the boundaries of their hometowns" with himself: "I too am compelled to carry the gospel of freedom beyond my particular hometown."

In validating insurgency and all its weapons, King showed the same eclecticism he did in revealing the sinfulness of racism. In "Death of Evil" he justified the need for protest by giving a prophetic twist to the sociological catechism he often invoked by itself—oppressors do not willingly give up power. In a sense, he was infusing his essentially inductive statement with a deductive flourish. "Pharaoh stubbornly refused to respond to the cry of Moses, even when plague after plague threatened his domain. This tells us something about evil that we must never forget, namely that evil is recalcitrant and determined, and never voluntarily relinquishes its hold short of a persistent, almost fanatical resistance."[20]

In operating with the weapons of premise and corollary, translation and metaphor, King was obeying an impeccable functionalist logic. Instead of separating a squirming audience from a wrathful King, his speeches spared white Americans the burden of personal blame. Instead, he released the force of logic to exert its influence. Yet this constituted pressure too, though of a highly cerebral sort, drawing its power from shared values and what King asserted followed naturally from them. Exposing the gap between formal principle and racist reality made for another sort of discomfort. Even if King did not accuse in a denunciatory tone, the diagnosis he handed down on countless occasions was devastating: "shameful conditions" and "sinful separation" and "distorted personality."

If King's version of prophetic correction was gentle, still it ran the risk of leaving the audience unsettled. So in the third phase of his moral witness, King elevated his audience, appealing to the higher selves of both whites and blacks and binding them together in a glorious moral community. In a sense, the beloved community King glimpsed in the first phase as shared moral premises was thwarted in the second by the reality of sinful separation, and finally achieved realization in the millennial anticipation of a just social order. Theology and performance achieved a perfect union here, as the precise sequence of King's rhetorical moves incarnated his larger faith.

It was in this final stage of his crossover talk that King sometimes reached into his Afro-Baptist repertoire to heighten expectancy of the

coming of freedom with prophetic intensity, rhythmic refrains, and crescendo. He reverted to his refined rendition of the prophetic preacher at
the American Jewish Committee, at the March on Washington, at a meeting of white civil rights workers, and at the National Cathedral. Nowhere
was this reversion as dissonant as at the annual meeting of the AFL-CIO.
If ever there was a community less receptive to sublime rhetoric, it was the
rough and tumble world of white ethnic working men and their spokes-
men. Such considerations did not deter King. As we have seen, he had
aligned the Negro struggle with that of the working man; he had chastised
unions for their treatment of black workers. King now found his rhythm
in a lingering finish that affirmed the "we" of blacks and labor.

If only they would fight discrimination in the unions and help the racial struggle in the South, King told the audience, "this convention will
have a glorious moral deed to add to an illustrious history." He imagined
the two partners as "architects of democracy" who "will extend the fron-
tiers of democracy for the whole nation." King's Fabian fantasy offered a
special version of his calling forth the future at the March on Washington
two years later, "the day when all who work for a living will be one with
no thought to their separateness as Negroes, Jews, Italians or any other
distinctions." That would also be the day when "the color of a man's skin"
will not trump "the content of his character," and "every man will respect
the dignity and worth of human personality."[21]

This was only part of the more elaborate prophecy of labor that King
was fashioning as he tailored a secular equivalent of the prophetic vision
to workmen's concerns, using old-fashioned social democratic language:
"A dream of equality of opportunity, of privilege and property widely distributed; a dream of a land where men will not take necessities from the
many to give luxuries to the few; . . . a dream of a nation where all our
gifts and resources are held not for ourselves alone but as instruments of
service for the rest of humanity."[22]

Now King vaulted to the skies, a shift preceded by a story. "There is a
little song that we sing in the movement," he told the AFL-CIO delegates.
"It goes like this, 'We shall overcome. We shall overcome.'" Rising above
the black perspective as he did before the American Jewish Committee, he
extended the "we shall overcome" to the entire democratic alliance, and
then went flying even higher, imagining the day "when all of God's children . . . join hands all over this nation and sing in the words of the old

Negro spiritual: 'Free At Last, Free At Last. Thank God Almighty, We Are Free At Last.'"[23]

Weaving in and out of various rhetorics, King constantly translated the black struggle into the moral and emotional terms of his audience. But he never played the translator role in its most familiar guise, as the objective mediator between two interested parties. King was an interested party too. His forays into the imaginative world of his white audiences always aimed to help them grasp the gulf between their professed values and the material facts of black oppression, and thus their own countenance of, if not complicity in, evil.

There was little in his retrievals that King could not find in some putative "black" tradition. King did not need Gandhi to instruct him in the theory of nonviolence; he had all his Christian teachings about turning the other cheek and loving one's enemies. He did not need "the magnificent texts" of the Declaration of Independence and the Constitution to affirm that we are all heirs to dignity; he had his own Afro-Baptist faith that "we are all God's children." He didn't need Phillips Brooks, Martin Buber, and Carlyle to justify his public ministry.

But if he didn't need these sources, neither did he hesitate to draw on "white" sources and traditions to reach his audience and frame his critique and defiant message. Nor did he necessarily think of them as "white." He also relied on them because he found them inherently compelling, which is why he used them before black audiences as well. King was not passive in his poaching; he always wove the sources seamlessly into his own voice. No captive of words, he owned them, made them work for him and for black people and for the nation at large.

None of this may seem radical. Tonally, the rebuke was gentle. It lacked the accusatory force of King's lamentation before black audiences, "America never showed the black man maternal care." The criticism was offhand, and often off to the side, left to reside in implication. And King always left the door wide open for whites to rejoin the beloved community they had mocked and violated.

Still, King was following the logic of much radicalism the world over. The oppressed have often found grounds for criticism in the official values of their society, even when they've had to turn them upside down to find their critical force. Put differently, King was a "connected critic" after the fashion that Michael Walzer describes: King's universalism was drenched in the specificity of the cultural traditions he drew from and the organic history from which he emerged. It did not come from an abstract notion of the ideal speech act or some philosopher's fantasy of a hypothetical starting line.[24] But that wasn't all. If King was connected, it was with a twist, with many twists. The connections were multistranded—to the dominant society, yes, in its generality, but also to a great variety of specialized white communities and organizations, and to his own black community. That King's web of connections was denser, more richly coiled, and extended further than most, that he was able to think through a host of idioms, gave his criticism greater reach and thus potential resonance. But the converse is also true, as King understood.

King practiced a particular kind of universalism in another sense. Just as the wounds of Jewish suffering produced respect for universal rights among Jews, the specificity of black suffering produced the question: "If God delivered Daniel from the lion's den and the Hebrew children in the fiery furnace . . . why not every man?" If other traditions besides one's own have often added to one's understanding, as the black use of Exodus attests, King also made clear that one can find in one's own experience the grounds for empathy for others.

There was still another side to this "conservative militance,"[25] having to do less with ideology than with "attitude," almost in the street sense of the word. Obviously, there was audacity, if not bragging, in the identities King claimed and the vast "I" that accompanied such equations as "Like Paul, I must constantly respond to the Macedonian call for aid." There was audacity in other ways too. When an outside group of rabbis descended on Birmingham to heed King's call, the local Jewish community was discomfited. Rabbi Milton Grafman later lashed out at sanctimonious northern Jews who judged their southern co-religionists from the privileged sanctuary of distance. But one Reform rabbi thought he caught another dynamic at work among southern Jews: "What seemed to stun them most agonizingly was the realization that we were at the call of the Negro leadership rather than vice versa. It appeared to outrage the natural order of things."[26]

In the end, King's gliding in and out of idioms anticipated in oratory the ideal of open borders that he sought to execute in reality. In rejecting the idea of the foreignness of white ideas by his embrace of them, King was claiming them as his own, insisting on his own right to enter the codes and the public realm of argument. His rhetorical act modeled a society built on mutual respect and recognition.

King's audacity extended further still, to an impudent claim of moral superiority implied by his role as teacher. For a black man of that time to establish the relationship of moral teacher to whites was an act of great boldness. Reversing established hierarchies of inferior and superior, King instructed whites through a confident rhetoric of assertion. "Let us turn to a more concrete example of just and unjust laws," King enlightened his detractors in "Letter from Birmingham Jail." "I am sure," he said, virtually patronizing the clergy, "that each of you would want to go beyond the superficial social analyst who looks merely at effects, and does not grapple with underlying causes." Were whites too clueless to note the "amazing universalism" of the Declaration of Independence? King spelled it out for them: "All men are created equal" did not mean some men or white men but included black men. Did Christians fail to grasp the racial relevance of "There is no East or West in Christ"? King made it plain for them. "In Christ there is neither Jew nor Gentile, bond nor free"—and King now added, "Negro nor white."[27] Here was a display of King's forte for translation at its acrobatic best. In the act of interpreting the black experience for his crossover audience, King was simultaneously interpreting for whites the true meaning of *their* professed creeds.

EIGHTEEN

The Allure of Rudeness

"The white man's personality is greatly distorted by segregation"

King couched his critique of segregation in reassuring language that seemed to say, "We will win you with our enticing vision and moral force." That same blend of solicitousness and bluntness appeared in another feature of King's universalism, the dance of manners and identities that accompanied his ideological critique. Such politesse can be seen in the delicate way King impugned whites, in his reliance on indirect logic to lay down judgment, in his chameleon gift for moving into others' worlds, and in the healing rituals through which he bound blacks and whites in beloved community. King seemed to argue, "We will win you with our capacity to suffer and our elegant style and splendid manners."

King's universalism was thus dramaturgical as much as ideological. He constantly translated his grand belief in redemptive love into verbal displays that dignified and reconciled difference. The other-directed character of King's addresses to whites was evident in his myriad efforts to reassure them about the character of blacks. The first of these, the strategy of refinement, aimed to depict King and black people in a positive light. The opening of "Letter from Birmingham Jail" provides a glimpse of King's decorous persona. His first words, "My dear Fellow Clergymen," embraced his audience as members of a professional brotherhood. The antiquarian, well-bred "my dear" offered a presumption of intimacy that ran in both directions even as it situated King in a genteel, almost precious community. The granting of grace that King conferred on them—"I feel that you are men of genuine good will" whose criticisms "are sincerely set forth"—reflected back as a sign of King's own graciousness. He held himself out as a responsible soul who posed no threat in what could be a touchy encounter. That he could hold back a moment and take the time for such niceties ratified his mannerly restraint. In *Stride toward Freedom*, King went as far as telling whites how he called a segregationist on the Montgomery negotiating committee to apologize for a churlish response in a meeting. When he was found guilty of violating the Alabama anti-boycott law, King evinced "sympathy" for the judge who issued the verdict.

The concern with presenting a pleasing black presence was a general feature of King's self-fashioning before white audiences. Consider the often remarked-upon vignette that King used to introduce himself to the American people in *Stride:* "On a cool Saturday afternoon in January 1954, I set out to drive from Atlanta, Georgia, to Montgomery, Alabama. It was a clear wintry day. The Metropolitan Opera was on the radio with a performance of one of my favorite operas—Donizetti's *Lucia di Lammermoor.* So with the beauty of the countryside, the inspiration of Donizetti's inimitable music, and the splendor of the skies, the usual monotony that accompanies a relatively long drive—especially when one is alone—was dispelled in pleasant diversions."[1]

The Donizetti vignette may seem gratuitous until one sees it as part of King's desire to cast himself as a man of sensibility and distinction. He is not listening to raspy gospel music or the wail of southern rhythm and blues. Like "my dear," the term "splendor" reinforced the point that King was a cultured cosmopolitan, whose aesthetic tastes tended toward the refined. In a typical move that King would later exploit in "Letter from Birmingham Jail," he took the time to comment on nature and architecture before launching into the topic of race.

What King edited out of that ride was as telling as what he included. He was not alone for the Atlanta-to-Montgomery leg of the trip and its immediate aftermath, both of which featured a good deal of less refined and racially barbed talk. King was accompanied by the maverick Reverend Vernon Johns, the former pastor of Dexter Avenue Baptist Church, a brilliant preacher whose "militant eccentricity," to use Richard Lischer's apt phrase, was accompanied by an indifference to white opinion. After a black man was murdered in Montgomery, Johns caused a stir by posting the title of his upcoming sermon outside the church: "It's Safe to Murder Negroes in Alabama." He also preached on "When the Rapist is White." He riled his black parishioners too. To their mortification, he sold watermelons and vegetables in front of Dexter. As Lischer recounts, "He not only insisted on singing spirituals in the worship service, which was strictly prohibited in the staid atmosphere of Dexter, but wondered out loud if his members were ashamed of their heritage."[2]

Johns had gotten a lift to Montgomery on his way to Ralph Abernathy's, and when King dropped him off, there was plenty of kidding about soul food and the enticing smells of Juanita Abernathy's cooking that were wafting from the kitchen. King had been invited to the house of one of the Dexter deacons for dinner, and when Abernathy suggested that King call and say he had been delayed, Johns added, "You better do it, boy. I've eaten at both houses, and there's no comparison. At the Brooks' house you will get white people's food. . . . Here you'll get the best meal you've ever had in your life." King responded, "Lord, that food is smelling so good." Before the talk turned to politics, Johns warned King, "If you take my church and a nigra named Randall is still there on the Board, you'd better be very careful." Such pastoral gossip only reinforced Daddy King's warning a few weeks earlier: "Martin, you don't want to go to that big nigger church."[3]

The sifting process that determined what King would share about his trip reflected his early attunement to the white audience. As Abernathy recalled, when he and King were weighing the two original candidates to head the Montgomery boycott organization, Abernathy was drawn to E. D. Nixon, prizing his authoritative, militant, and intimidating qualities. "A huge man with almost blue-black skin, he had a powerful voice that he used to great advantage, sweating prodigiously as he waved his arms or pounded the table. I thought he would be intimidating." But, Abernathy remembered, "Martin . . . objected to the fact that Nixon was uneducated and used poor grammar. He felt [Rufus] Lewis, an imposing brown-skinned man who was also polished in speech, could command more respect from the white community."[4]

The values of proper diction and decorum permeated King's crossover talk. At one point, in describing to his national white readership the techniques for rousing the blacks of Montgomery, King referred to the primacy of the "pep talk," but immediately noted "its rather undignified title." In such contexts, his constant appeals to blacks to conduct the struggle "on the high plane of dignity and discipline" were designed less for black ears than white ones, who were never privy to his chicken-eating preacher jokes.

The refinement King put on display implied a second feature of other-direction, the distance from emotion already encountered in King's preaching to whites and the sermons published in *Strength to Love*. At various points in *Stride toward Freedom*, King describes a struggle between unseemly feelings and the watchful self that observes, judges, and finally gains control of them. King is clearly a man of exquisite control, his eye always on himself. Even the bombing of his house that could have taken the lives of Coretta and Yolanda did not undermine his poise or belief in reason, as King informed the audience of *Stride toward Freedom;* he took the news "calmly" and rather than bolting to his family, he first reminded the church audience to "adhere strictly to our philosophy of nonviolence. I admonished them not to become panicky and lose their heads." Such disavowals were not sufficient to prevent the roiling inside, and later that night, unable to sleep, "I began to think of the viciousness of people who would bomb my home. I could feel the anger rising when I realized that my wife and baby could have been killed. . . . I was once more on the verge of corroding hatred." But the lapse, as chronicled for whites, was only fleeting: "And once more I caught myself and said: 'You must not allow yourself to become bitter.'"[5]

King's effort to demonstrate that blacks deserved full citizenship reached its height in a third gambit of other-direction, in his depiction of blacks not just as mannerly and reasonable but as exceptionally virtuous. This third guise, the cult of black nobility, followed directly from the virtues of reason and poise. King's effort not just to catch himself but to admonish himself as well was tied to the symbolic parallels with Christ and other exalted figures that King claimed for himself in his white talk no less than his black talk. Typically, King spread such Christ-like virtues across the race, putting forth the virtually masochistic notion that blacks had a special, heroic capacity for unearned suffering. His famous refrain, "We will win you with our capacity to suffer," dovetailed with more secular displays of King's ability to channel momentary twinges of bitterness into higher purpose.

In these ways, King countered stereotypes of black primitivism, highlighting his own worth and that of his people. But this message about black virtue was also a statement about black intentions toward whites. Other-direction unfolded in this fourth maneuver as sensitivity to whites' anxiety and the soothing pledge that King and his movement would not shame or savage them. With empathy, he entered the white racist mind and discerned a need to "mitigate" the terror that dwelled there. "A guilt-ridden white minority lives in fear that if the Negro should ever attain power, he would act without restraint or pity to revenge the injustices and brutality of the years." So, King prescribed, "The job of the Negro is to show them that they have nothing to fear, that the Negro understands and forgives and is ready to forget the past. He must convince the white man that all he seeks is justice, *for both himself and the white man.*"[6]

The force of doctrine (both Christianity and nonviolence) and manners converged in that effort. They both advised selfless concern for others and the sublimation of emotion. Nonviolence, King declared to the readers of *Stride toward Freedom,* "does not seek to defeat or humiliate the opponent, but to win his friendship and understanding." Non-cooperation and boycotts "are merely means to awaken a sense of moral shame in the opponent. The end is redemption and reconciliation." You can only awaken the moral shame of someone who is not shameless. As King put it in one of his sermons, "The evil deed of the enemy-neighbor, the thing that hurts, never quite expresses all that he is."[7]

King implemented such principles through a range of mannerly maneuvers. He always sought to step gingerly in the midst of touchy subjects. His penchant for abstraction, circumspection, and circumlocution softened the sting of criticism. In the same spirit, King generally dispensed with sarcasm or jeremiad; he tended to express anger in a cool register of disappointment. In addition, the term "white brothers" blunted the sharpness of antagonism. Even when King referred to "sick white brothers," the brothers endured, and "sick" suggested that whites were not inherently evil. Maybe a cure was possible.

Doctrine and manners alike disclosed an ability to rise above one's own wounds to enter the imagination of others, even racist others. Even in the throes of the Montgomery bus boycott, King reported, "I tried to put myself in the place of the three commissioners. I said to myself these men are not bad men. They are misguided." Reassuring whites that he had transmuted revenge into understanding, King further displaced and diminished blame. The officials, King observed reasonably, "are merely the children of their culture." This wasn't personal, King had assured his readers earlier in *Stride*. The attack on segregation "is directed against forces of evil rather than against the persons who happen to be doing the evil. . . . The tension in this city is not between white people and Negro people. The tension is, at bottom, between justice and injustice, between the forces of light and the forces of darkness."[8]

The tone here was cool, high-minded, and reflective. Still, at least occasionally in *Stride*, King's preacherly voice came through and the passion came with it. Not long after the bomb ripped through his house, King rushed home to check on his family and then addressed a gathering crowd of angry black people from his front porch. "Remember the words of Jesus: 'He who lives by the sword will perish by the sword.' I then urged them to leave peacefully. 'We must love our white brothers,' I said, no matter what they do to us. We must make them know that we love them. Jesus still cries out in words that echo across the centuries: 'Love your enemies; bless them that curse you; pray for them that despitefully use you.'"[9]

As a moment of black talk, King's urgings in that address to turn the other cheek aimed to restrain black passion that might hurt the movement, to maintain commitment to King's ideological faith in nonviolence, and to encourage the discipline that would lead to eventual victory. Recounted for a white audience in *Stride toward Freedom*, that lopsided exchange—prayer in return for spite—equally fulfilled a practical function, but this time the diplomatic one of reassuring whites that blacks were not dangerous primitives who could not be counted on to behave in a transracial democracy. As for trading a blessing for a curse, it was simply the verbal side of forswearing the negative reciprocity of tit-for-tat. Christianity thus served as a practical resource for managing insults and accusations that would challenge the equilibrium of encounters between the races.[10]

King also implemented this ban on racially mean words less biblically, relating for white readers how a minister, "after lashing out against the whites in distinctly untheological terms, ended by referring to the extremists of the white community as 'dirty crackers' . . . he was politely but firmly informed that his insulting phrases were out of place." The suggestions for good comportment on integrated buses in Montgomery included, "Do not boast! Do not brag!" and "Be . . . proud, but not arrogant; joyous, but not boisterous." The written pledge signed by demonstrators in Birmingham, which King also included in the Harper trade book *Why We Can't Wait*, involved refraining "from violence of fist, tongue and heart" and observing "with both friend and foe the ordinary rules of courtesy" as well as walking and talking "in the manner of love."[11]

King rescued and enhanced white dignity as well as preserved it. Victory would be no zero-sum game, no triumph of one group over the other, but victory for justice and light. Even if whites were guilty of mean-spirited conduct, they could rise up and overcome the sin of racism. In crediting them with a moral sense, no matter how latent, King held out the hope that racist whites could still become full-fledged members of the beloved community.[12]

King's recollection of the impromptu address after the bombing of his house reflected a fifth gambit of other-direction: retelling black conversations for the benefit of whites. He related a black man's comment to a policeman, "I ain't gonna move nowhere. That's the trouble now; you white folks is always pushin' us around. Now you got your .38 and I got mine; so let's battle it out." After going inside his home and finding Coretta and Yolanda safe, King returned to the porch to speak to the angry crowd. "In less than a moment there was complete silence. . . . 'Now let's not become panicky,' I continued. 'If you have weapons, take them home; if you do not have them, please do not seek to get them. We cannot solve this problem through retaliatory violence.'"[13]

That vignette repeated King's standard disavowal of vengeance. It also allowed whites access to filtered versions of black life, thereby announcing the irrelevance of racial secrecy and loyalty. By implication, King's ability to speak openly to whites indicated that understanding could flow across the chasm between the races. Beyond that, by unveiling for whites the hortatory role he played with blacks, King defined himself as providing a check on dangerous black emotion.

Running through those retellings was a tension not just between control and emotion but between black solidarity and the community of mankind. In *Where Do We Go From Here?*, the trade book he published in 1967, King divulged vivid details of his "private" row with Stokely Carmichael during the Meredith March. "For five long hours," King told his readers, "I pleaded with the group to abandon the Black Power slogan." King's didactic sketch of his theory of the speech act underscored his ability to take the position of others, even racist whites. Throughout, his arguments seemed to declare, "I care about how my words impinge on you."

As King retold the conversation, he warned the black nationalists that whites were quite susceptible to mistakes in fathoming the words that electrified blacks. "It was my contention that a leader has to be concerned about the problems of semantics." Ever the teacher, he instructed, "Each word . . . has a denotative meaning—its explicit and recognized sense—and a connotative meaning—its suggestive sense." Even if denotatively sound, the very phrase "Black Power" encouraged dangerous confusion. In mulling these complexities, King constantly took the position of whites to anticipate how they might experience black utterances. The phrase itself, King observed, was explosively "vulnerable." "The words 'black' and 'power' together," King warned, "give the impression that we are talking about black domination rather than black equality." It was possible that the slogan "would confuse our allies, isolate the Negro community and give many prejudiced whites, who might otherwise be ashamed of their anti-Negro feeling, a ready excuse for self-justification."[14]

As King portrayed it, even when no whites were present, he served as their surrogate, giving voice to their concerns. Just as he made himself Jewish or German as the occasion dictated, he entered the psyche of whites so he could anticipate their nervousness. This ability to remove himself from a parochial black standpoint, his willingness to step into the imaginative universe of others, and his concern with the impact of words on listeners reflected King's deeper belief that blacks and whites were members of a shared community whose equilibrium required vigilant attunement to other people's feelings.

A common theme of solicitousness runs through the previous chapter and this one so far. In the areas of demeanor and moral justification, King displayed a deference to whites that some race-proud blacks thought unseemly. Nationalists were convinced that King lived too nervously in the eyes of white others, bending needlessly to accommodate them. And it's true that King went out of his way to create moments of community based on mutual respect and recognition of difference. At the same time, one could point to the tension between the two forms of deference. To the extent that King worked the received ideology to condemn "shameful conditions," his acute sensitivity could be seen as a way to take the edge off strong criticism—healing after the rift.

But there is a third alternative that restores the symmetry. Powerful currents of rudeness lay just beneath the polite surface of King's crossover talk and often burst right through it. Just as playful with manners as he was with other kinds of talk, King had no problem blending reproach with decorousness. Indeed, ethnic boasting, oblique barbs, backhanded compliments, and implied insults were all elements of King's repertoire. Sometimes he even threw caution to the wind and succumbed to outright anger.

The rites of self-effacement could not expunge less-than-effacing content. King's portrait of noble, unthreatening, forbearing, Christian, dignified black people was balanced by his constant proclamations of black resolve. Where was the humility in King's insistence at the March on Washington when he recited the refrain, "We won't be satisfied"? Where was the decorousness in King's racially tinged warning in *Stride toward Freedom*: "The members of the opposition had also revealed that they did not know the Negroes with whom they were dealing. They thought they were dealing with a group who could be cajoled or forced to do whatever the white man wanted them to do. They were not aware that they were dealing with Negroes who had been freed from fear. . . . their methods were geared to the 'old Negro,' and they were dealing with a 'new Negro.'"[15] Even as King reassured whites on certain counts, he never stopped heralding this transformation of black consciousness, the fact that "we're not going to be turned around." If King's putting whites on notice sometimes had an earnest, even jejune quality in *Stride toward Freedom*, by the time of *Where Do We Go From Here?* it was infused with a streetwise steeliness, a greater emphasis on manhood, and warnings of God's wrath. But these were mainly shifts in tone. Neither the basic form nor its message had changed.

King's own version of ethnic trumpeting supplemented such insistence. A seemingly anxious desire to prove one's worthiness could slide into confident self-congratulation. The metaphoric equivalences that King used may have been taken for granted in the Afro-Baptist world accustomed to merging of voices by authoritative preachers, but it is less clear that whites were prepared for King's grand self-equating with Paul or Jesus. Moreover, the Christian identification with Jesus, "We will win you with our capacity to suffer," had a decidedly non-Christian aspect of pride. No matter how modestly put, it remained a boast: We are Christ-like. And it is not a stretch to hear another unspoken corollary in that claim—that whites lacked such virtues. It didn't take a genius to grasp the unstated implication of King's use of Booker T. Washington's admonition: "Never let a man pull you so low as to make you hate him." Countless whites had sunk that low.

King even insinuated the theme of black paternalism that he spelled out for black audiences: whites were in such a bad way, only blacks could rescue or redeem them. In *Stride* he did this through the almost patronizing notion of therapeutic redemption, whose racialist language defied his general cautions about mixing "some" and "all." "Since the white man's personality is greatly distorted by segregation, and his soul is greatly scarred, he needs the love of the Negro. The Negro must love the white man, because the white man needs his love to remove his tensions, insecurities, and fears." This reversal of the ordinary terms of racist paternalism reflected the belief in black spiritual power as the only solution for white moral incompetence. In a posthumously published essay, "Testament of Hope," King acknowledged the supremacism at work. America is doomed to moral disintegration, he preached, "unless, and here I admit to a bit of chauvinism, the black man in America can provide a new soul force for all Americans."[16]

Throwing over the moral hierarchy that elevated whites and devalued blacks was usually presented without resentment as a noble, even selfless endeavor: the black man will love the white man into health. But King's rudest moments came when he moved explicitly into reprimand. No matter how graciously put, chiding could not always restrain the anger that suffused it. In "Letter from Birmingham Jail," an indignant display of rhetoric if ever there was one, King injected anger through a series of running commentaries, a parallel subtext that sharply qualified the face-saving maneuvers.

At one point in "Letter," King used a parenthetical phrase to set up a counterpoint with the clause before, thereby splitting the coolness of the first assertion from the angry heat of the second: "One who breaks an unjust law must do it *openly, lovingly* (not hatefully as the white mothers did in New Orleans when they were seen on television screaming, 'nigger, nigger, nigger'), and with a willingness to accept the penalty."[17] It is almost as if King needed the spatial marker to keep his anger from spilling into the main body of the sentence.

In another place, anger flowed through a run-on series of phrases divided by semicolons. King first observed, "You warmly commended the Birmingham police force for keeping 'order' and 'preventing violence.'" Rather than criticizing the ministers outright, King relied on a tangled subjunctive: "I don't believe you would have so warmly commended the police force if you had seen its angry violent dogs literally biting six unarmed, nonviolent Negroes. I don't believe you would so quickly commend the policemen if you would observe their ugly and inhuman treatment of Negroes here in the city jail; if you would watch them push and curse old Negro women and young Negro girls; if you would see them slap and kick old Negro men and young boys; if you will observe them, as they did on two occasions, refuse to give us food because we wanted to sing our grace together."

If the phrase "I don't believe you would have" implied King's faith in the clergy (if only they had known the facts, of course they would not have commended the police behavior), everything in the passage belies his official professions of confidence. That same construction—sentences separated by semicolons, emphatic repetition, the shift to a personal voice of "you" and "us," the eventual compression of language as emotion flooded syntax—appeared elsewhere when King was irate. The injection of intensifiers like "warmly" and "quickly," their contrast with angry dogs and ugly treatment, the slapping of old Negroes and the allusion to King's own experience ("refused to give us food," denied us "our grace") reinforced the quiet fury of the sentence. Even then, the clincher had not come. It began with a stark assertion of difference: "I'm sorry that I can't join you in your praise for the police department." King's refusal set the stage for an escalation beyond "I don't think you would have commended" to a more straightforward rendering of the clergy's moral lapses. "I wish you had commended the Negro sit-inners and demonstrators of Birmingham for their sublime courage, their willingness to suffer and their amazing discipline in the midst of the most inhuman provocation."

As King moved toward the end of "Letter," he seemed to shift to a more humble stance. "I'm afraid that it is much too long to take your precious time." This restorative rite offered healing closure after the intense criticism he had heaped on his audience. King intensified the humility with an act of supplication: "If I have said anything in this letter that is an overstatement of the truth and is indicative of an unreasonable impatience, I beg you to forgive me." Like begging the white man, King's plea for forgiveness was charged in the context of the Birmingham insurgency and the movement generally. In countless black churches, King had proclaimed the gospel of now, all, and here. As a black man speaking to black men and women, he preached the urgency of action. Was King now retracting this in the interest of making nice? That odd qualification—"unreasonable impatience"—injected a note of ambiguity. All this attention to his audience's feelings, it turned out, was only a prelude to correction. Without abandoning the form of begging, King flipped its meaning: "If I have said anything in this letter that is an understatement of the truth and is indicative of my having a patience that makes me patient with anything less than brotherhood, I beg God to forgive me."

Despite its convolution, the accusation was clear: the clergy had an inverted sense of priorities. They praised vicious police who upheld a system of "immoral ends," but failed to praise abused black people who embodied moral ends and who did so with the exalted means of nonviolent spiritual discipline. King's second plea for forgiveness reestablished the moral dominion of God over the petty judgments of men, and trumped the clergy's moral authority with King's.

In each of the paired phrases, the sequence underscored the inequality between the two parts. The second half served not to qualify the first but to retract it. Discordant messages flowed through different channels. Form upheld the interactional order, its logic of equilibrium and remedial deference; content took back what deference only promised to offer. In the process, the struggle between manners and rudeness became the vehicle for a deeper ideological struggle between Christian forgiveness and prophetic criticism. In the end, denunciation of evil supplanted the equanimity of manners.

King's moral chiding, part of the hardheaded realism that stamped his theology and anthropology, was inseparable from the political chiding that was the end point of his agile maneuvering. The eight Birmingham clergymen were only proxies for larger political antagonists. "I have almost reached the regrettable conclusion," King reflected, "that the Negro's great stumbling block in the stride toward freedom is not the White Citizens Counciler or the Ku Klux Klanner, but the white moderate who is more devoted to 'order' than to justice." Given that King had identified the clergymen who provoked his reply as moderates, this was strong stuff, and it got stronger still. "I had hoped that the white moderate would see this. Maybe I was too optimistic. Maybe I expected too much."

The flattery of King's admission of error—"Maybe I expected too much of you"—was at once ambivalent and passive-aggressive. The character of the posited mistake—a cognitive inability to perceive correctly that flowed from his generosity—heightened the moral nature of the clergymen's failure. So did the dashed expectations of King's disappointment, which presumed the moral capacity of the ones who lapsed and thus their accountability. That moral verdict moved King into an extraordinary near-racial formulation that conflated the clergy with their whiteness: "I guess I should have realized that few members of a race that has oppressed another race can understand or appreciate the deep groans and passionate yearnings of those that have been oppressed and still fewer have the vision to see that injustice must be rooted out by strong, persistent and determined action." King had brought the tension between brotherhood and *brother*hood right into the heart of his crossover effort.

The ethnography of white spirituality gave King a perfect vehicle for venting his righteous indignation more baldly. The turnabout formed a stratagem of its own, which differed from King's effort to translate the justice of the black struggle into moral terms that whites could understand. It also differed from the times when King tried to increase white empathy by vividly evoking the black plight so that whites could feel what blacks experience. Rather, here King tried to translate the white experience into a form he could grasp and then turn against whites. King often played the role of tour guide, inviting whites into the black experience. Instead, now he invited himself into the white experience and tried to fathom what made whites tick. Whites were the opaque ones. They were the enigma in need of fathoming.

Traveling across the deep South, King recalled how "on sweltering summer days and crisp autumn mornings I have looked at her beautiful churches with their lofty spires pointing heavenward." That experience provoked questions in the reflective traveler. "Over and over again I have found myself asking: 'What kind of people worship here? Who is their God?'" These queries echoed the ones King raised at roughly the same time in a mass meeting after Bull Connor set the dogs loose. But that was a different King, a shaken man whose barely suppressed anger overflowed in the primordial imagery of "stench" and "nostrils." By contrast, in the context of a Pauline epistle to white clergy, King hewed to the fictional role of a musing observer of American life. Much as in the opening Donizetti vignette in *Stride toward Freedom,* his ability to note "lofty spires" seemed to mark a triumph over emotion. Yet this was artifice. The indirection of "Who is their God?" revealed the veneer of sublimation at work; after all, King might have asked, "Who is *your* God?" If that shift out of intimate direct address took the "my dear clergymen" out of the line of fire, the "their" signaled the emotional chasm separating King from the other clergy. King's contemplative distance from the lofty spires he had driven past echoed his remove from a white church defined by its less than prophetic stance.

In a version of "no room at the inn," SCLC's efforts to test their welcome in a number of Birmingham churches (some headed by signatories of the letter that provoked King's letter) gave *What kind of people worship there?* the charge of immediacy. In fact, the response was more mixed than King's depiction in "Letter from Birmingham Jail" indicated. At First Baptist Church, seventy whites walked out when Andrew Young and two black women were seated. Young later said that his offering was refused. But the minister, Earl Stallings, who wrote soon after that "we had no Christian justification for closing our doors," greeted Young "with a heartfelt smile and a warm handshake." The minister at First Methodist Church, Paul Hardin, "asked his flock to search their own hearts for racial bigotry, and he petitioned the congregation, as Christians, to treat blacks as Jesus would in every circumstance."[18]

A barrage of follow-up questions dissipated any doubt about King's answer to his previous question, "Who is their God?": "Where were their voices when the lips of [Mississippi] Governor Barnett dripped with words of interposition and nullification? Where were they when Governor Wallace gave a clarion call for defiance and hatred? Where were their voices of support when tired, bruised and weary Negro men and women decided to rise from the dark dungeons of complacency to the bright hills of creative protest?" The answer was clear. They were the sort of people, as King put it elsewhere in "Letter," who never called for integration as the expression of their moral faith but simply because it was the law.

Only after this shadow boxing did King drop the contrivance of the travelogue for a more personal stance. "In deep disappointment, I have wept over the laxity of the church. . . . The contemporary church is a weak vessel. Is organized religion too inextricably bound to the status quo to save our nation and the world? Maybe I must turn my faith to the inner spiritual church, the church within the church as the true ecclesia and the hope of the world."

Telling someone they lack the "true ecclesia" is not normally equated to "telling it like it is." But the difference in style cannot disguise the constancy of form and function. No matter how much it was draped in Pauline vestments, "Letter from Birmingham Jail" was an extension of the back talk that King practiced in his black talk in mass meetings. Instead of telling black men about white men, King was telling at least certain white men about themselves: they cooperated with evil, their silence made them complicit in the sin of racism, they were failures as Christians. Their lofty spires were empty forms.

King's decorous embrace of the troublemaker label, recalling Malcolm X's glad embrace of the demagogue label, defined the rude character of his life work, his "God-intoxicated" wish to be part of that "colony of heaven" of the early Christians. "I gradually gained a bit of satisfaction from being considered an extremist," he told the Birmingham clergymen and, through them, the nation. The staccato of King's questions and quotes was like the flurry of a boxer's jabs: "Was not Jesus an extremist in love—'Love your enemies, bless them that curse you, pray for them that despitefully use you.' Was not Amos an extremist for justice—'let Justice roll down like waters and righteousness like a mighty stream.' Was not Paul an extremist for the gospel of Jesus Christ—'I bear in my body the marks of the Lord Jesus.' Was not Martin Luther an extremist—'Here I stand; I can do none other so help me God.' Was not John Bunyan an extremist—'I will stay in jail to the end of my days before I make a butchery of my conscience.' Was not Abraham Lincoln an extremist—'this nation cannot survive half slave and half free.' Was not Thomas Jefferson an extremist—'We hold these truths to be self-evident, that all men are created equal.'"

NINETEEN

Black Interludes in the
Crossover Moment

"I guess it's easy for those who have never felt the sting of segregation
to say wait"

The rising anger of King's litany in "Letter from Birmingham Jail" con-
firms what was mostly hinted at earlier in the book: King revealed vulnerability, vented anger, and spoke as a black man before white audiences as
well as black ones. Even retellings of black conversations for the benefit of
whites that seemed to offer the privilege of intimate entrée could double
back with a counterpoint of black solidarity.

One can imagine white readers of King's account of his fight with
Stokely Carmichael over black power thinking, "This King is a fine fellow
who refuses to exclude us from a black moment." Yet that same vignette
in *Where Do We Go From Here?* revealed King's powerful sense of black
identity and his comfort with the strategy of black power, if not the
phrase (he offered "black equality" or "black consciousness" as substitutes). He presented the proponents of Black Power as reasonable and earnest people, not demonic extremists. Even when he described Carmichael
descending into racial bitterness, King showed to whites the same sympathy for nationalist anger that he displayed to black audiences. If in *Where*

do We Go From Here? King crossed from black to white perspective to imagine the impact of inflammatory words on whites, he crossed back again to explain why blacks had become bitter. Black Power, he wanted his readers to understand, "did not spring full grown from the head of some philosophical Zeus. It was born from the wounds of despair and disappointment. It is a cry of daily hurt and persistent pain." That empathetic reading reversed the charge of reverse racism, throwing it back where it belonged, onto whites. Entwined in "the tentacles of white power," King explained, "many Negroes have given up faith in the white majority because 'white power' with total control has left them empty-handed."[1]

In *Where Do We Go From Here?* King was explaining not just black hopelessness in general but the specific biographical journey of the younger generation of activists that Julius Lester called "the angry children of Malcolm X." To carry out that task, King adopted Lester's idiom as his own. As the nation fumed and puzzled over rising black stridency, King detailed all the white betrayals that had produced it. "If they are America's angry children today, this anger is not congenital." Bitterness was hard-won; it sprang from gritty experience. Elevating the militants for his white audience, King praised the "radiant faith in the future" they brought to the movement. "With idealism they accepted blows without retaliating; with dignity they allowed themselves to be plunged into filthy, stinking jail cells; with a majestic scorn for risk and danger they nonviolently confronted the Jim Clarks and the Bull Connors of the South."[2]

It was no coincidence, averred King, that the Black Power chant was born in Mississippi, "the state symbolizing the most blatant abuse of white power. In Mississippi the murder of civil rights workers is still a popular pastime." After more than forty murders and lynchings of movement workers in three years, "not a single man has been punished for these crimes. More than fifty Negro churches have been burned or bombed in Mississippi in the last two years, yet the bombers still walk the streets surrounded by the halo of adoration." King concluded, "This is white power in its most brutal, cold-blooded and vicious form."[3]

As King juxtaposed black feelings of hurt with the viciousness of white racists, one senses his anger building. "If Stokely Carmichael now says that nonviolence is irrelevant, it is because he, as a dedicated veteran of many battles, has seen with his own eyes the most brutal white violence."[4]

King was being circumspect. Privately, he and Andrew Young had worried about the traumatic impact on Carmichael of the death of Jonathan Daniels, a young seminarian who came to Selma in response to King's call to clergy and students. When the bullets of an assassin tore into Daniels, Carmichael was standing right next to him.

But there was a further, galling aspect to such murders of civil rights workers—"the fact that even when blacks and whites die together in the cause of justice, the death of the white person gets more attention and concern than the death of the black person." Still withholding his own feelings, King permitted more alienated SNCC members to express what he and his colleagues had said to one another. Just as King seemed to blend into the speech of the old slave shouter who told slaves, "You are not a nigger," King merged into Carmichael's physical presence before moving into his speaking presence too. "Stokely and his colleagues from SNCC were with us in Alabama when Jimmy Lee Jackson, a brave young Negro man, was killed and when James Reeb, a committed Unitarian white minister, was fatally clubbed to the ground."[5]

Still attributing ownership of both memory itself and the feelings it released to "the angry children," King continued to translate the sensibility of black resentment: "They remembered how President Johnson sent flowers to the gallant Mrs. Reeb, and in his eloquent 'We Shall Overcome' speech paused to mention that one person, James Reeb, had already died in the struggle." It was here that King seemed to drop the viewpoint and voice of the angry children for his own. "Somehow the president forgot to mention Jimmy, who died first. The parents and sister of Jimmy received no flowers from the president." That failure "only reinforced the impression that to white America the life of a Negro is insignificant and meaningless."[6]

King allowed the advocates of Black Power to articulate another cause of the disenchantment they shared: the hypocrisy of a militaristic America that praised blacks for their cheek-turning. Letting the "angry children" express the anger he had vented himself, King recounted, "These same black young men and women have watched as America sends black young men to burn Vietnamese with napalm, to slaughter men, women, and children; and they wonder what kind of nation it is that applauds nonviolence whenever Negroes face white people in the streets of the United States but then applauds violence and burning and death when these same

Negroes are sent to the fields of Vietnam."[7] If "they wonder" assigns the voice to the angry children, King authorized them to speak for him. It was King who had decried the fact that whites and blacks, as he would put it in settings as different as Greenwood, Mississippi and the National Cathedral, could kill "in brutal solidarity in Vietnam" but could not live on the same block once they returned.

Even the National Cathedral could not preempt the "blackening" of a King crossover appearance whose embittered notes were as striking as their modulation. Preaching the last sermon of his life on March 31, 1968, King found respite in the pulpit. It was "a rich and rewarding experience," he told them, to reflect with "concerned friends of good will." The refined beauty of the church's stained glass offered a contrast to the shacks of Marks and Eutau where King had been recently. Rip Van Winkle's long sleep, the vehicle for the theme of "Remaining Awake Through a Great Revolution," struck a further note of distance. The first fifteen minutes of King's sermon included his lament that the narrow world of neighborhood had yet to become a brotherhood, as well as a mix of King's standard images of universalism such as "single garment of destiny" and the old saw, "For some strange reason I can never be what I ought to be until you are what you ought to be."[8]

If this seemed like a long remove from the Black Belt barnstorming of the previous weeks, the overlap of content belied any differences of mood and tone. True, at the National Cathedral King did not exclaim, "We goin' to have a tiiime!" as he did in Montgomery, or wax poetical with the line "Countee Cullen came by here." Instead, John Donne alighted at the National Cathedral (he didn't "come by here"), along with his words, "no man is an island entire of itself." Yet King's harsh judgment—the "disease of racism" is "a way of life for the vast majority of white Americans" that "permeates and poisons a whole body politic"—prefigured the unvarnished message ahead.

Indeed, as we know already, King's telling of the parable of Dives and Lazarus was almost word for word what he said in the Black Belt. He did not waver in reaching the same apocalyptic judgment he had issued back in Greenwood: America was literally going to hell. A full five paragraphs echoed the Montgomery mass meeting of a few weeks earlier. The barbs King directed at the American past and present included the statement that "every court of jurisprudence would rise up against" the way whites treated blacks, and a bitter reference to the "cruel jest" of telling "a boot-less man that he ought to lift himself by his own bootstraps." Those espousing self-reliance and immigrant moxie as the answer, King contended, "never stop to realize that no other ethnic group has been a slave on American soil . . . [or] that the nation made the black man's color a stigma . . . [They] never stop to realize the debt that they owe a people who were kept in slavery two hundred and forty-four years."

King even brought the irrepressible presence of the primeval black nation in exile right into the cathedral as he let loose the entire chant: "we were here" before all the civil religious markers of Plymouth Rock, "the majestic words of the Declaration of Independence," and "the beautiful words of 'The Star Spangled Banner.'" It was one thing to issue that refrain at Ebenezer Baptist Church or a Mississippi rally, quite another to utter those same words to this high-toned congregation. Yet the tone at the sermon's end was not in-your-face resentment but pride in black people and their spirituality. As was typical of King's mixing, blackness did not oppose belonging but was its condition. The faith and fortitude of the ancestors set the stage for the faith and fortitude King would need to rejoin the American community.

King had already signaled that he was prepared to supplant the chronicle of black exile with a vision of a redeemed nation. The goal of America, King said revealingly, "still" is freedom. If the phrase "abused and scorned though we may be as a people" seemed to create distance, the "though" prepared for the belonging to come: "our destiny is tied up in the destiny of America." That spirit of reconciliation guided King as he pulled out of the "we were here" stanzas and began the work of binding the nation into a more sublime "we." Despite darkness, "angry feelings," and "explosions," King preached, "I can still sing 'We shall Overcome.'" This triggered a series of repetitions as each "we shall overcome" found its classical vindication: "because the arc of the moral universe is long, but it bends toward justice"; "because Carlyle is right: 'No lie can live forever'"; "because William Cullen Bryant is right: 'Truth, crushed to earth, will rise again.'"

By now King had moved a long way from his tear-filled time in Marks, Mississippi; he had moved beyond the "brutal solidarity" of blacks and whites killing in the napalm-covered jungle. At least for the rhetorical moment, he had returned to the fount of his theology of hope and all its mantras. "With this faith," King assured them, "we will be able to hew out of the mountain of despair the stone of hope" and "transform the jangling discords of our nation into a beautiful symphony of brotherhood. . . . And that day the morning stars will sing together and the sons of God will shout for joy. God bless you."

It might be tempting to read King's assertions of blackness before white audiences as another sign of Black Power's pressure on King's rhetoric or even on his ideological development. But as we have seen, while King's mood and tone evolved over the years, the continuities ran not just across black and white occasions but between the younger and the more seasoned King too. As early as *Stride toward Freedom,* King described a moment of black fellowship with ordinary black prisoners in the Montgomery jail. When they asked King to help them, he replied, "'I've got to get my ownself out.' At this they laughed." In the most byzantine retelling in *Stride,* King recounted for whites how Ralph Abernathy regaled a black audience with the tale of a white journalist who questioned the exotic religious customs of black people. "'Isn't it a little peculiar,'" King quoted Abernathy quoting the white man, "'for people to interrupt the Scripture in that way?'"[9]

King's revelations of blackness to whites were not confined to little moments of bemusing difference or consecration of the bonds of ancestors. Tellingly, *Stride toward Freedom,* written before the burdens of leadership had devoured King's private life, contained a number of such racially resonant moments. At one point he explained the smile he displayed when he left the Montgomery court and his pride in "my crime," which was bound up in his love for "my people." Transfiguring the meaning of his "crime" in the repetitive series he often used when shifting to a black angle of vision within his white talk, King entered the identity of "my people" as he insisted he was only guilty of "the crime of joining my people in a nonviolent protest against injustice. It was the crime of seeking to instill within my people a sense of dignity and self-respect. It was the crime of desiring for my people the unalienable rights of life, liberty, and the pursuit of happiness. It was above all the crime of seeking to convince my people that noncooperation with evil is just as much a moral duty as is cooperation with good."[10]

King also confessed in *Stride* that he had no immunity to racial bitterness. True, King used the episode of the bombing of his house to signal his exquisite control. He did "catch himself." But that confession had a flip side; in a moment of extremity, King felt his anger rising and was "on the verge of corroding hatred." This was a precise analogue to King's intimate disclosure to George Davis, his Crozer professor, in his "Autobiography of Religious Development," that he went through a phase of hating all white people.

None of these moments surpassed the intensity of King's two most powerful affirmations of blackness in his addresses to whites: the ones that came in "Letter from Birmingham Jail" and the "I Have a Dream" speech at the March on Washington. That's not to say those interludes triumphed over King's love of mankind, his embrace of the ideal of integration, and his Christian faith in all God's children. Despite King's "rudeness" toward his "dear colleagues," the key voice in "Letter" remained undeniably cosmopolitan. Still, "Letter" offered no unbroken progression toward beloved community. Waxing and waning, its dominant universalism was accompanied by feints, loops, and reversions that subverted it—none of them as fierce as the interval in which King abandoned the universal voice and revealed a fury that can only be described as racial.

Because that interlude in "Letter" is so complex and intense, it is worth taking a moment to summarize its key features. First, King notably shifted out of the identity of universal man, abstract ethicist, and movement leader to unabashed black man. Second, King conscripted whites into a King-led guided tour of the alien terrain of backstage black sentiment. Third, King's manifest anger—and the revelation of the master orator's momentary failure not just of composure but of language itself—qualified his efforts to present a collective definition of poise. Finally, King shifted the basis of legitimation of black demands from formal law and universal principles to feelings and experience distinct to black people.

The transition to this plunge into blackness began when King explained how he experienced the language of whites. "For years now I have heard the words 'wait!'" King's use of "I" signaled not just a move into personal experience but something more primal. In the concatenation about to explode, King will speak as a black man who shares in the fellowship of black suffering. That word *wait* "rings in the ear of every Negro with a piercing familiarity." It is as if the sensuous vexations of being a Negro—the hearing, the ringing—inexorably pushed King into the collective "we" of "every Negro."[11]

Freed to move in new directions, identity flowed not from particular to general or from black to white (translating black grievances into "universal"—i.e., white—moral terms that whites can grasp), but in a reverse direction, as King moved more deeply into the black state of mind. He began with an appraisal of the meaning of white words. In the Meredith March argument, King, eager to prevent interpretive mistakes, had worried that whites might get the wrong impression of a phrase like "Black Power." King now translated for whites how blacks interpreted the meaning of words that whites used, thereby underlining the lack of trust—his own included—in white words: "This 'Wait' has almost always meant 'Never.'"

After a few sentences, King shifted tone. "I guess it is easy for those who have never felt the stinging darts of segregation to say, 'Wait.'" The "I guess" barely took the edge off the rebuke, whose implication, the smugness of bystanders and the moral obtuseness of the clergymen, remained no less powerful for being unspoken. That sentence also repeated the complaint that members of a privileged race couldn't grasp the groans of an oppressed people. Again in his typical ventriloquist's way, King indirectly accused the disapproving Birmingham clergymen of saying "never" too, just like all the redneck racists with whom they would be shocked to be identified. One senses sarcasm in the "I guess," maybe even contempt—who can know? King recorded a spoken-word version of "Letter," in which the tone suggests as much, but it is not clear. In any case, the "moderate" clergy are just as clueless as any other white person. They lack the ability to stand in others' shoes that King exhibited constantly when he entered the mind of white racists. This is essentially the taunt that emerges from King's observation, "perhaps if you were Negro you'd understand." In the midst of a high-minded reassertion of beloved community, *brother*hood dominates: only black people can possibly understand.

This recognition of white moral insufficiency triggered the plunge into blackness that defines the confessional interlude proper. At least momentarily, King abandoned faith that the clergymen could possibly respond to the force of logic or appeals to shared morality. This giving up was the equivalent in one small rhetorical move of King's larger belief in the limits of moral appeal to bring about change unless fortified by social pressure. In short, more extreme measures were called for, rhetorical violence even.

So, in a wrenching moment of reverse crossover, King reached across the border of race, snatched up his readers by the neck, and dragged them back across the color line to experience what blacks experience. In the process, King skipped the reverse translation that would return them to their comfortable terrain. They will have to stand on the black side of the border for one gargantuan sentence, which takes the now-familiar form of the repetitive series King fell into when he was overcome with indignation.

"But when you have seen vicious mobs lynch your mothers and fathers at will and drown your sisters and brothers at whim; when you have seen hate-filled policemen curse, kick, brutalize and even kill your black brothers and sisters with impunity; when you see the vast majority of your twenty million Negro brothers and sisters smothering in an airtight cage of poverty in the midst of an affluent society; when you suddenly find your tongue twisted and your speech stammering as you seek to explain to your six-year-old daughter why she can't go to the public amusement park that has just been advertised on television, and see tears welling up in her little eyes when she is told that Funtown is closed to colored children, and see the depressing clouds of inferiority begin to form in her little mental sky, and see her begin to distort her little personality by unconsciously developing a bitterness toward white people; when you have to concoct an answer for a five-year-old son asking in agonizing pathos: 'Daddy, why do white people treat colored people so mean?'"

The torrent of indignation continued: "When you are humiliated day in and day out by nagging signs reading 'white' and 'colored'; when your first name becomes 'nigger' and your middle name becomes 'boy' (however old you are) . . . when you are harried by day and haunted by night by the fact that you are a Negro"—here King wove in a quote from W. E. B. Du Bois—"living constantly at tiptoe stance never quite knowing what to expect next, and plagued with inner fears and outer resentments."

Throughout, racial belonging was carried by the second person plural of "you" (as in "when you") that serves as a racially collective form of the personal, as well as the possessive "your" signaling racial belonging— "your black brothers and sisters," "your Negro brothers." In the midst of this series, the "your" in "your daughter," particularized by the six-year-old qualification and by the repetition of "little" that underscores vulnerability, was especially poignant, identifying its subject as Yolanda, not some generic black daughter. King's loss of poise, a compressed version of his use of Funtown in his black talk, reinforced his status as "every Negro." The wounds of racism were so insidious that even the most eloquent spokesman could be reduced to stammering. The emotions that cut through language when King was with Yolanda were the same ones that have blasted away all polish and poise in "Letter"—they derived from the fact of being black. Yet just as crossing over into Buber and Tillich did not entail a ceding of black perspective, here too King's blackness was not carried by code, source, or idiom. It was embedded in the perspective from which he addressed the white clergymen and the experience that was part of the meaning of being black.

King's slide into blackness was no more permanent than his slide into Buber or St. Augustine. Right after the run-on series, a sentence abruptly broke the frame of blackness. As King pulled out of his volatile state and returned to his address to the specific clergymen, he switched from the "you" of blackness to the personal, race-free "you" of the particular people he was addressing. He also reasserted the clergymen's capacity to empathize by noting, "then you will understand why we find it difficult to wait," which was followed by his shift from the ethnic "we" to the indirect and generalized mention of "there comes a time when the cup of endurance runs over, and men are no longer willing to be plunged into an abyss of injustice." As the restoration of transracial understanding ("you will understand") indicates, the confessional mode was not opposed to the task of legitimation. Rather, it was a form of legitimation by other means. If it justified the refusal to wait and did so through emotion, the emotions were moral ones like indignation.

Only recently made available, an extraordinary "black" version of "Letter" that King preached to a mass meeting underscores the constancy of that indignation and King's ability to voice it in different ways.[12] Fresh from the Birmingham jail, King was still churning as he orated many of the bits of what would eventually be published as "Letter": virtually the whole paragraph that included "Jesus was an extremist," the interpretation of the meaning of "wait," and a reflection on the illusion that "someone's going to give us our freedom." King included the prophetic rebuke he hurled at the Birmingham ministers, even as he translated it into a more vernacular and Afro-Baptist form. At one point, he even rendered Niebuhr this way: "Groups are a little more naughty than individuals."

Such shifts, no matter how stylistic, were not without their pleasures. At every turn, King sounded like a man who had been released from the restraint not just of prison but of politeness. His voice was quavering as he said, "We've got to let this nation know that we are through with segregation now, henceforth, and forever more." As the audience was calling and shouting, the labored nods to Buber and Tillich gave way to a fervent crescendo that included the ending King would use in "I Have a Dream" *(Let freedom ring, from every mountain side, from Stone Mountain of Georgia).* The gingerly search for common ground was replaced with the chant "Now is the time" and a reveling in the black presence—"Abused and scorned though we may be" and "we were here."

Most notably, the solicitousness vanished in a surrender to sarcasm. "My dear fellow clergymen" were demoted to "these preachers": "This worried me when I first read these preachers calling me an extremist." And then he called on all his powers of mimicry to capture the difference between such "moderates" and the rabble. The first group, King said, may be "a little more gentle and more articulate than Mr. Connor"—and here King enunciated precisely, calmly—"'I am a segregationist'—whereas Bull Connor says"—and here King rushed the words together in a snarl—"'I'm-a-segregationist' . . . But both of them are segregationists." Just as their ways of speaking did not hide the identity they shared, King's mass meeting performance did not differ in substance from what he would publish as the "Letter."

In its own idiosyncratic way, "Letter" offers a complex experiment in crossing boundaries in the mode of fiery madness. Yet before whites, King could get fiery-glad about his blackness too. As we move toward the end of our story, it may be in the less indignant moments that the full meaning of King's larger endeavor of crossing over comes most sharply into view. The famous "I Have a Dream" speech at the March on Washington shows the rich possibilities of this get-happier form of postethnic mixing.

As with "Letter from Birmingham Jail," King's performance of "I Have a Dream" at the March infused a civil religious occasion with aspects of blackness. Those dual elements permeated the double structure of "Dream": the two audiences of nation and "my people," the latter addressed through side conversation; the styles of fervent preaching and civil religious oratory; the contrast of prepared text and free-form improvising; and the thematic interplay of blackness and humanity, exile and belonging.

"Dream" earned its iconic status as an emblem of universalism. Its civil religious context was given in King's first sentences, which depicted the event as "the greatest demonstration for freedom in the history of our nation." With its "fivescore years ago" beginning, the next sentence presaged what soon became explicit: Abraham Lincoln's Emancipation Proclamation, another civil religious fixture in whose "symbolic shadow we stand today." The physical setting on the Mall gave resonance to King's celebration of the "magnificent words of the Constitution and Declaration of Independence." His chant toward the end—"Let freedom ring"—envisioned not simply the nation joined together, but the people for the first time making the nation whole by ringing the chimes of freedom together. And the very final words of course celebrated the beloved community of "all of God's children"—blacks and whites; Protestants, Catholics, and Jews.[13]

The vision of a redemptive national identity fit with the generic form of the march—petitioning the government for redress of grievances—and the strategic aim of gaining passage of the upcoming civil rights bill. This was the practical context of the soaring rhetoric. Still, this plunged the prophetic movement into the midst of hardheaded calculation. In a White House meeting at which civil rights leaders sought to get presidential support for the march, Vice President Lyndon Johnson offered this calculus: they needed 25 swing votes in the Senate to pull off a civil rights bill. President Kennedy, always in sway to realpolitik, focused on the practical imperatives as well. The political need to enlist support among the broader public and the march organizers' sensitivities to the upcoming vote on the civil rights bill framed the larger process of composing a majestic occasion.

These anxious estimations were built into the structure of the March, which was orchestrated to transform white opinion. The organizers had imposed a process of shaping and veto to filter out any disturbing notes and ensure maximum public relations payoff. There would be no "Black Power" chants or discomfiting challenges, no undignified talk that might roil mainstream opinion. Before Kennedy reluctantly came around to endorse the march, he insisted on many conditions. Meanwhile, John

Lewis's original draft of his speech, a militant critique of Kennedy and liberals, did not survive the sifting process. As King's urgings to Lewis make clear, he too brought caution to the drafting process, and he intended his own contribution to be directed at whites. As Taylor Branch put it, King's speech would call for his "clearest diction" and his "stateliest baritone."[14]

Given all this political trimming, it is not surprising that "I Have a Dream" would come to stand for a certain sentimentality about race. Such pressures may also explain the dichotomy that marked King's speech. In the minds of many seasoned King observers, the first half had a flat quality, and much in the prepared speech was inelegant. None of the final peroration, with its "I Have a Dream" refrain, appeared in the written version circulated to the press and key officials before the event. King had rejected the theme of the Dream as too complex to address in his allotted eight minutes.

So it is even more striking that King managed to break out of all the caution, offering up a run of prophetic oratory that did not overwhelm the civil religious format but commingled with it. In the end, if "Dream" did not unflaggingly adhere to the mode of universalism, it did not entirely repudiate that vision either. Imbuing classic images of redeemer nation and providential freedom with blackness, King ended up creating a novel "particular kind of universalism."

King himself had requested the black musical frame around his words. He brought the voice of the black ancestors into this white event, asking Mahalia Jackson to sing "I Been 'Buked and Scorned." The Afro-Christian character of the song and the nonstandard grammar of its title prefigured King's reading of the American experience in the light of a particular black experience of it. "Long night of their captivity" signaled the tension between that history and civil religious pieties, as did the gap between the promise of the dream and its fulfillment. King also insinuated a telling marker of separateness early on, a reference to "black exiles": "The Negro is still languished in the corners of American society and finds himself an exile in his own land." A subtle distinction—King's dream was "rooted in" but did not coincide with the American Dream—added distancing.

Beyond these signals, King inserted an intimate black voice in a critical turn away from his white audience. With President Kennedy following the advance text over in the White House and the entire nation listening in, King spoke directly to blacks as he adopted the frame of "my people."

"But there is something I must say to my people, who stand on the warm threshold which leads into the palace of justice."

Is this "private conversation" truly directed at King's people? Or is it a performance for white people to reassure them? Or both? Who can be sure? But whether King was using his warning about racial bitterness to pressure whites into accepting a moderate alternative or to confer virtue on the churched part of the movement, the message was clear: disavowal of bitterness yet a knowing empathy for its source. King was walking a tightrope here—between the black audience and the white one, between decrying bitterness and the danger of passivity. Despite the appeal to a biracial army, the admission that "we cannot walk alone," and the mention of our "white brothers," King immediately added a rousing invocation of the Negro's "marvelous new militancy." Remaining in the collective voice of an ethnic "we," King exhorted his people, "We must make the pledge that we shall always march ahead. We cannot turn back."

King returned from his aside to the nation within the nation, the black exiles languishing in America, to speak to the larger nation, ambiguously taking the edge off the black voice with an "us" defined as "devotees of civil rights." He conjured up a conversation with a generic white interlocutor who echoed the old Birmingham question, "There are those who are asking the devotees of civil rights, 'When will you be satisfied?'"

King's rhetoric of time here directly opposed the question of time posed in much of his black talk, where he heightened immediacy to galvanize action or raised the question "How long?" to buttress resolve, followed by the reassuring "not long" that will redeem all the sacrifice. Nor did King repeat the earlier phrase in "Dream" in which, in another echo of "Letter," he "remind[ed] America" of the fierce "urgency of now." The answer to the white questioner is neither justification for whites nor mobilization for blacks but something different: conveying black restiveness, frustration, and resolve to whites. Turning his voice into a collective instrument of his people, King let loose with the chant, "We can never be satisfied," whose rudeness was reinforced by its blatancy, by the repetition that displayed indomitable black will, and by the assertive attachment of conditions to the achievement of satisfaction.

This refusal to go along unless conditions were met picked up on his earlier implied threat ("Those who hope that the Negro needed to blow off steam" are in for "a rude awakening"). As King enumerated the conditions, he fell into a version of the most confessional series in "Letter," oscillating between "the Negro" and the more personal but still black "our" and "we" which subsumed King the black man: "As long as our bodies, heavy with the fatigue of travel, cannot gain lodging . . . as long as our children are stripped of their selfhood and robbed of their dignity by signs stating 'for whites only' [Applause]." Turning for a moment from the terms of future satisfaction to a blatant statement of the present black state of mind—"no, no, we are not satisfied"—King closed that with the ultimate condition, "We will not be satisfied until justice rolls like waters and righteousness like a mighty stream [Applause]." The repetition, the merging of his voice with that of the prophet Amos, and the sensuous imagery of justice rolling down like waters anticipated the Afro-Baptist run about to explode in the dream sequence.

But King was not yet ready to turn entirely to the nation, and he voiced a second aside not so much to blacks but to the specialized community of movement activists, the "veterans of creative suffering," who made the March on Washington possible. Once again, he adopted his knowing voice, but one more distanced than in his breakout to the veterans after the Selma to Montgomery march, in order to insert a bit of mobilization talk in the midst of a speech focused on legitimation: "I am not unmindful that some of you have come here out of excessive trials and tribulations. *(My Lord)* . . . fresh from narrow jail cells . . . from areas where your quest for freedom left you battered by the storms of persecution *(Yes)*." In a faint echo of the theology of hope that he used to respond to the classic mobilization question, he answered a version of "How long?" by urging, "Let us not wallow in the valley of despair."

Only after reassuring the movement cadres did King turn back to the nation. With that turn, he put aside once and for all the script vigilantly composed for the high-profile proceedings and fell into free-form preaching. Echoing his description in *Stride toward Freedom* of his preparation for the Holt Street meeting ("I thought of what the old black preachers said"), King explained later that "the dream just came to me." Perhaps the turn to the "veterans of creative suffering" touched something deep within him.

"The American Dream," of course, was ready to be called upon. As we have seen, it had long been part of King's repertoire. Most recently, King had given a longer version of the speech to thunderous applause in Detroit at the "Great March to Freedom." Befitting an overwhelmingly black urban audience of between one and two hundred thousand people, and with C. L. Franklin, Aretha Franklin, and Mahalia Jackson on the dais, King's version of "Dream" that day blackened the vision, even as it retained its essential imagery of glorious mankind. It was graced by a sustained appeal to black somebodyness and the "fleecy locks and black complexion" stanza, both of which were missing in the Washington setting. Along with his vision of little white and Negro children joining hands as brothers, King had a more ethnic dream that "my four little children will not come up in the same young days that I came up within" and that "one day right here in Detroit, Negroes will be able to buy a house or rent a house anywhere that their money will carry them and they will be able to get a job [Applause] (That's right)."[15]

King's unplanned swerve into "Dream" in Washington may have followed a rustling in the audience that served as encouragement. At a key point, others on the platform, realizing that King had wandered off the text, urged him on. Mahalia Jackson appears to have interceded from her place on the stage: "Tell them about the Dream, Martin."[16]

Whatever triggered the shift, what followed was a display of black preaching in all its glory for the larger nation to behold. More than the improvising itself, the call and shout that may have catalyzed it, or the spirituals that introduced it, the cutting loose of the finale marked "Dream" as a civic version of the black performed sermon. Merging his voice with that of Isaiah and Amos, King transported his audience to the biblical time of inspired prophecy, fusing the foretaste of the coming of the Lord with the savoring of freedom's coming. As he approached the run-up to his climax, King was bobbing and weaving, sampling from everywhere, blurring the boundaries between oration, sermon, and song. He moved from Isaiah's vision—"every valley shall be exalted"—to the "I have a dream" refrain, then suddenly sampled "My country 'tis of thee," was off to the chant of "Let freedom ring," and finally reached the crescendo of the slave spiritual, "Free at last, free at last, thank God almighty, we are free at last."

"I Have a Dream" was a breakthrough in American cultural life. It channeled the classic theme of American possibility into a hybrid form that was part political oration, part black sermon. It set a precedent for bringing black performance into mainstream venues. This wasn't just music in a metaphoric sense; it was singing almost literally as well. King had invented a kind of political soul music, steeped in Afro-Baptist intensities, yet modulated enough to transfer to the larger society. One can label "Dream" a typical piece of civil religious oratory only if one ignores its distinctive style. After his own fashion, King was declaring to the nation, "I'm black and I'm proud."

This mix of race, nation, and mankind was the culmination of a long process that had begun in obscure black churches and brought "Ain't gonna let nobody turn me 'round" and "I'm gonna let it shine" out into southern public life before arriving at the reflecting pool of the Lincoln Memorial. At the March on Washington, King was giving expressive form to the ambiguity of black identity that he would define more formally in the years ahead. "The old Hegelian synthesis," he would write in *Where Do We Go From Here?*, "still offers the best answer to many of life's dilemmas. The American Negro is neither totally African nor totally Western. He is Afro-American, a true hybrid, a combination of two cultures." Yet for King the dependence was mutual, the hybrid state shared. Still entangled in that "single garment of destiny," King argued, "the black man needs the white man and the white man needs the black man." For King, this was a fact of our shared cultural life as much as a moral ideal. So many things in America—the food, music, and language—"are an amalgam of black and white."[17]

It made sense that "Dream" gave voice to that notion through its musical means, even though realizing that ideal would prove much harder in life than in language. If King's hardheaded theology prepared him not to be shocked by the stubbornness of sin in the human soul, the sharpness of the white backlash that would only gather steam in the years after the March on Washington did surprise him. With the unfolding of the 1960s the surface of American life became more abrasive, and the sounds too became increasingly shrill and dissonant. As James Forman of SNCC observed after the killing of one of his colleagues, "They weren't singing no freedom songs. They were mad. People would try and strike up a freedom song, but it wouldn't work. All of a sudden you heard this, 'Black Power, Black Power.'"[18]

King would confront that musical reflection of the bitterness of a young generation of blacks at the Meredith March. "Once during the afternoon we stopped to sing 'We Shall Overcome.' The voices rang out with all the traditional fervor, the glad thunder and gentle strength." But some voices suddenly went mute when the song reached the verse, "black and white together," and when King asked about it, "The retort was: 'This is a new day, we don't sing those words any more. In fact, the whole song should be discarded. Not 'We Shall Overcome,' but 'We Shall Overrun.'" King reflected, "As I listened to all these comments, the words fell on my ears like strange music from a foreign land."[19]

In "America is Sick," an address he delivered in early 1968 to the California Democratic Party, King described another kind of cultural rejection that was the musical analogue to "No Room at the Inn." He had attended a program on "the music that made America great" at his children's integrated school and was eager to hear some "music that I knew was great, the most original music on American soil. . . . Sometimes it emerges in sorrow songs, but it has some gentle signs and glad thunders at times that can touch the soul. . . . And I will never forget as that concert came to an end and there was not the singing of one Negro spiritual, and none of the music that has come into being out of the black people, and out of the suffering and the agony of the black people of this country." Worse still, the evening concluded with the singing of "Dixie." Watching his son and daughter "having to end the program singing 'Dixie,' the music that made America great," King had a sinking feeling. "And I sat there and all but wept within. And I said to myself how can they ever feel they are somebody if they feel that they have no heritage, if they feel that they've done nothing or given nothing to the life of the world and history."[20]

Still, up there on the podium at the March on Washington, there was no better display of King's moral longing than the juxtaposition of two musical crossings in the finale of "I Have a Dream." Taken together, they perfectly captured King's hybrid vision. King did not just break into the exuberance of black performance as a prelude to citizenship; in an act of reciprocity, he invited the nation to cross into blackness as well.

The first bit of music in the songfest that closed the speech offered an elegy to citizenship in the secular equivalent of prophetic climax. King remained in the future tense, relishing the day "when all of God's children will be able to sing with new meaning—'my country 'tis of thee; sweet land of liberty; of thee I sing . . .'" In this civil religious rite, black exiles, reconciling musically with the land that had denied them maternal care, achieved membership through song. This ritual of inclusion repeated itself in the musical unison achieved by a nation united in the trumpeting of "let freedom ring" across an entire nation—the nation together ringing the chimes of freedom.

A second musical moment repeated the act of crossing but reversed direction. It defined even more powerfully the inventive, prescient character of King's vision. The final resting point of "Dream" was not with black voices entering the national anthem. The black ancestor whom King channeled in his black talk, the one he heard on the streets of Ghana and in the echoes of "Joshua Fit the Battle of Jericho," had the last word. In good civic fashion, all God's children—black men and white men, Protestants and Catholics and Jews—joined hands, but this time to blend their voices with "the words of that old Negro spiritual, and to sing out in joy, 'Free at last, free at last.'" Then, in a leap that ratified the communion at work, King made white people black and had them speak as Negroes in a universal black "we"—"thank God almighty we're free at last"—and made the slave ancestors their own.

NOTES

INDEX

Notes

1. The Artistry of Argument

1. Recording of the sermon "Remaining Awake Through a Great Revolution," the National Cathedral, Washington, D.C., March 31, 1968. Companion audio tape to Clayborne Carson and Peter Holloran, eds., *A Knock at Midnight: Inspiration from the Great Sermons of Reverend Martin Luther King, Jr.* (New York: Intellectual Properties Management in association with Warner Books, 2002). Hereafter, audio recordings of these sermons are cited as *Knock at Midnight*/IPM–Time Warner AudioBooks. The Johnson comment is cited in Andrew Young, *An Easy Burden: The Civil Rights Movement and the Transformation of America* (New York: HarperCollins, 1996), 434; "Letter from Birmingham Jail," in James M. Washington, ed., *A Testament of Hope: The Essential Writings and Speeches of Martin Luther King, Jr.* (New York: HarperCollins, 1991 [1986]), 290.

2. The three most important debts are as obvious as they are staggering: David Garrow's *Bearing the Cross;* Taylor Branch's trilogy (*Parting the Waters, Pillar of Fire,* and *At Canaan's Edge);* and the work of Clayborne Carson and

his associates at the Martin Luther King, Jr., Papers Project at Stanford University. The Acknowledgments provide a fuller listing of influential works.

3. Dell Hymes's approach to people's "ways of speaking" informs this entire book. His emphasis on such dimensions of talk as "language situations," communicative routines, speech communities, repertoires of idioms, and code shifting reflects an ethnographic pragmatism that focuses on the great variety of variables that shape people's talk at any particular moment. My book similarly seeks to grasp some of the "socially conditioned variations in speakers' natural performances," as John Gumperz put it. See John J. Gumperz, "Introduction," in John J. Gumperz and Dell Hymes, eds., *Directions in Sociolinguistics: The Ethnography of Communication* (New York: Holt, Rinehart and Winston, 1972), 24.

4. Recording of "I Have a Dream." Companion CD to Clayborne Carson and Kris Shepard, eds., *A Call to Conscience: The Landmark Speeches of Dr. Martin Luther King, Jr.* (New York: Intellectual Properties Management in association with Warner Books, 2001). Hereafter cited as *Call to Conscience*/IPM–Time Warner AudioBooks.

5. Newt Gingrich, "A Vision for America," videotape of address to GOPAC, Washington, D.C., Nov. 14, 1994.

6. "Address at the Conclusion of the Selma to Montgomery March," Montgomery, Alabama, March 25, 1965. *Call to Conscience*/IPM–Time Warner AudioBooks.

7. Hortense J. Spillers, "Martin Luther King and the Style of the Black Sermon," *The Black Scholar*, vol. 3, no. 9 (1971), 15.

8. David J. Garrow, *Bearing the Cross: Martin Luther King, Jr., and the Southern Christian Leadership Conference* (New York: William Morrow, 1986), 717.

9. That ideal "prefers voluntary to prescribed affiliations, appreciates multiple identities, pushes for communities of wide scope, recognizes the constructed character of ethno-racial groups, and accepts the formation of new groups as a part of the normal life of a democratic society." David A. Hollinger, *Postethnic America: Beyond Multiculturalism* (New York: Basic Books, 1995), 116.

10. Howie Becker's analysis of plastic artists applies no less to performing artists. Whatever King's personal talent or unique creativity may have been, he was part of a highly intricate "art world" of religious performance. Becker uses the term *art worlds* "to denote the network of people whose cooperative activity, organized via their joint knowledge of conventional means of doing things, produces the kind of art works that art world is noted for." See *Art*

Worlds (Berkeley: University of California Press, 1982), x. Such cooperative networks include the training institutions through which craft is acquired and institutions of aesthetic review, appreciation, and judgment that certify practitioners as competent members of the art community.

11. The Rev. Martin Luther King, Sr., with Clayton Riley, *Daddy King: An Autobiography* (New York: William Morrow, 1980), 27.

12. Lerone Bennett, Jr., *What Manner of Man: A Biography of Martin Luther King, Jr.* (Chicago: Johnson Publishing Co., 1968), 17; Stephen Oates, *Let the Trumpet Sound: A Life of Martin Luther King, Jr.* (New York: HarperCollins, 1982), 9–10.

13. King, Sr., *Daddy King,* 16–17; 21.

14. Ibid., 17; 19.

15. Bennett, Jr., *What Manner of Man,* 17.

16. Taylor Branch, *Parting the Waters: America in the King Years, 1954–63* (New York: Simon and Schuster, 1988), 63.

17. Audio tape of the sermon "Paul's Letter to American Christians," Dexter Avenue Baptist Church, Montgomery, Ala., Nov. 4, 1956. *Knock at Midnight*/IPM–Time Warner AudioBooks.

18. Audio tape of the sermon "Guidelines for a Constructive Church," Ebenezer Baptist Church, June 5, 1966. *Knock at Midnight*/IPM–Time Warner AudioBooks.

Part I. Inside the Circle of the Tribe

1. *Where Do We Go From Here: Chaos or Community?* (New York: Harper & Row, 1967). Reprinted in Washington, ed., *A Testament of Hope,* 632.

2. Audio tape of the sermon "Rediscovering Lost Values," Second Baptist Church, Detroit, Michigan, Feb. 28, 1954. *Knock at Midnight*/IPM–Time Warner AudioBooks.

3. "A Christmas Sermon on Peace," Ebenezer Baptist Church, Dec. 24, 1967. In Washington, ed., *A Testament of Hope,* 257.

2. The Geometry of Belonging

1. King, Sr., *Daddy King,* 31; 141.

2. Ibid., 130.

3. *The Papers of Martin Luther King, Jr.,* Volume I: *Called to Serve, January 1929–June 1951;* Senior Editor: Clayborne Carson; Volume Editors: Ralph E. Luker, Penny A. Russell; Advisory Editor: Louis R. Harlan (Berkeley:

University of California Press, 1992), 110–111. Hereafter cited as MLK Papers, Volume I.

4. Garrow, *Bearing the Cross*, 35.

5. Quoted in William E. Peters, "Our Weapon Is Love," *Redbook Magazine*, August 1956.

6. Ibid.

7. Russell Adams, "Memories of Morehouse," unpublished manuscript.

8. Qualifying Examinations Answers, History of Philosophy, Feb. 24, 1954, in *The Papers of Martin Luther King, Jr.*, Volume II: *Rediscovering Precious Values, July 1951–November 1955;* Senior Editor: Clayborne Carson; Volume Editors: Ralph E. Luker, Penny A. Russell, and Peter Holloran; Advisory Editor: Louis R. Harlan (Berkeley: University of California Press, 1994), 247. Hereafter cited as MLK Papers, Volume II.

9. "Rediscovering Lost Values." *Knock at Midnight*/IPM–Time Warner AudioBooks.

10. "From J. Pius Barbour," Oct. 3, 1957, *The Papers of Martin Luther King, Jr.*, Volume IV: *Symbol of the Movement, January 1957–December 1958;* Senior Editor: Clayborne Carson; Volume Editors: Susan Carson, Adrienne Clay, Virginia Shadron, and Kieran Taylor (Berkeley: University of California Press, 2000), 283. Hereafter cited as MLK Papers, Volume IV.

11. Richard Lischer, *The Preacher King: Martin Luther King, Jr. and the Word That Moved America* (New York: Oxford University Press, 1995), 70.

12. Lewis V. Baldwin, *There Is a Balm in Gilead: The Cultural Roots of Martin Luther King, Jr.* (Minneapolis: Fortress Press, 1991), 37; 38.

13. Branch, *Parting the Waters*, 77.

14. I am postponing the discussion of King's plagiarism on his Boston University dissertation until Chapter 15. Yet it does raise the issue of King's engagement in his doctoral studies. Indeed, as we will see, one approach views King's plagiarism as a form of resistance to the official abstractions of the white academic world. In this telling, he was engaging not in theft but in borrowing and thus affirming his membership in the lineage of the ancestors and the black folk pulpit that thought "intellectual property" belonged not to ministers but to the God who spoke through them. Thus was King affirming the Word over words. In short, he was really engaging in old-school sampling of the sort Jesus practiced when he took various Old Testament figures' words without attribution.

15. Branch, *Parting the Waters*, 87.

16. "An Autobiography of Religious Development," MLK Papers, Volume I, 362–363.

17. Garrow, *Bearing the Cross*, 41; 40–41.
18. Branch, *Parting the Waters*, 89.
19. Garrow, *Bearing the Cross*, 41.

3. Brotherhood and *Brother*hood

1. Pat Watters, *Down to Now: Reflections on the Southern Civil Rights Movement* (Athens, Ga.: University of Georgia Press, 1993 [1971]), 365. In a testimony to the coexistence of both of those forms of love, only moments after King declared his love for every single black person, he announced, "I am here because I love the white man" to the ratifying response of "Well" and "Yes." Ibid., 365.

2. "Keep Moving from This Mountain," address at Spelman College, April 10, 1960. *The Papers of Martin Luther King, Jr.*, Volume V: *Threshold of a New Decade, January 1959—December 1960;* Senior Editor: Clayborne Carson; Volume Editors: Tenisha Armstrong, Susan Carson, Adrienne Clay, and Kieran Taylor (Berkeley: University of California Press, 2005), 417. Hereafter cited as MLK Papers, Volume V.

3. Ibid., 417.

4. Ibid.

5. These subtleties help illuminate the distinctive functions of King's use of agape as a rhetorical instrument no less than a tenet of his faith: it validated racial bitterness without betraying the high-flown ideal of beloved community. It was precisely because feelings of vengeance and racial bitterness were so strong that one could not depend upon spontaneous feeling or split-second conversion to expunge the open wounds of living memory. Similarly, nonviolence in thought and action required normative constraint and social occasions to practice and ultimately internalize restraint. All the detailed role playing that nonviolent recruits had to undergo spoke precisely to the churched part of the movement's relationship to instinct, the importance of fashioning collective taboos to execute what, after all, was the unnaturalness of loving the enemy.

    King diverged some from the perfectionist take on beloved community offered by those who insisted that Christian love required not just refusing to strike back but extinguishing even the desire to strike back. His stress on the irrepressible nature of sin grasped that a certain amount of cultural labor was necessary to suppress violence. Just as King's "natural" sense of blackness coexisted with his moral faith in beloved community, his emotional and social experience coexisted—and even required—the moral forms that could temper it and ultimately transform it. Such recognition translated into those amazing experiments in crossover culture in which whites and blacks engaged in play acting and shifted racial roles, each taking on the psyche of the other. Andrew Young attested to the precariousness of restraint after being tear-gassed in Canton, Mississippi: "I completely lost my cool. I didn't say it, but I thought to myself, 'If I had a machine gun, I'd *show* those motherfuckers!'" Quoted in Adam Fairclough, *To Redeem the Soul of America: The Southern Christian Leadership Conference and Martin Luther King, Jr.* (Athens, Ga.: University of Georgia Press, 1987), 318.

6. Audio tape of mass meeting, "Lest We Forget 2: Birmingham, Alabama, 1963" (Folkways Records, The Smithsonian Institution, 1991).

7. "Conversation between Cornish Rogers and David Thelen," *The Journal of American History* (June 1991), 46; audio tape of the sermon "Mastering Our Fears," Ebenezer Baptist Church, Sept. 10, 1967, Howard University Divinity School Library, Tape Recording Collection, Washington, D.C. Hereafter cited as MLK-Howard.

8. "Mastering Our Fears."

9. Garrow, *Bearing the Cross*, 375.

10. "Kick Up Dust," Letter to the Editor, *Atlanta Constitution*, Aug. 6, 1946, in Clayborne Carson, ed., *The Autobiography of Martin Luther King, Jr.* (New York: Warner Books, 2001), 15; audio tape of the sermon "New Wine in New Bottles," Ebenezer Baptist Church, Jan. 2, 1966, MLK-Howard.

11. "Mastering Our Fears."

12. King-Levison telephone conversation, April 8, 1967, FBI wiretaps of Martin Luther King, Jr., U.S. Federal Bureau of Investigation, 100-111180, Stanley D. Levison, Sub-file 9, Vol. 8.

13. Taylor Branch, *At Canaan's Edge: America in the King Years, 1965–68* (New York: Simon and Schuster, 2006), 604.

14. Young, *An Easy Burden*, 436.

15. Stewart Burns, *To the Mountaintop: Martin Luther King Jr.'s Sacred Mission to Save America, 1955–1968* (San Francisco: HarperSanFrancisco, 2004), 377–378.

16. Peter Goldman, *The Death and Life of Malcolm X*, 2nd ed. (Urbana and Chicago: University of Illinois Press, 1979), 65; Taylor Branch, *Pillar of Fire: America in the King Years, 1963–65* (New York: Simon and Schuster, 1998), 250.

17. Branch, *Parting the Waters*, 672.

18. Young, *An Easy Burden*, 362.

19. CD recording of King appearance at Zion Baptist Church, Los Angeles,

June 17, 1966. "We Must Work," segment 4 of CD "Martin Luther King, Jr.: We Shall Overcome" (SoundWorks International, 2000); "A Christmas Sermon on Peace," Ebenezer Baptist Church, Dec. 24, 1967, in Washington, ed., *A Testament of Hope,* 257.

20. CD recording of King appearance at Zion Baptist Church, Los Angeles, June 17, 1966. "We Must Work," track 4 of "Martin Luther King, Jr.: We Shall Overcome" (SoundWorks International, 2000).

21. Watters, *Down to Now,* 214.

22. Ibid.

23. Clayborne Carson, *In Struggle: SNCC and the Black Awakening of the 1960s* (Cambridge, Mass.: Harvard University Press, 1981), 197; 219.

24. SCLC rally, July 10, 1966, Soldier Field, Chicago. Quoted in Nick Kotz, *Judgment Days: Lyndon Baines Johnson, Martin Luther King Jr., and the Laws That Changed America* (New York: Houghton Mifflin, 2005), 365; audio tape of the speech "Where Do We Go from Here?," address delivered to the Eleventh Annual Convention of the Southern Christian Leadership Conference, Aug. 16, 1967, *Call to Conscience*/IPM–Time Warner AudioBooks.

25. Audio tape of the speech "In Search of a Sense of Direction," Vermont Ave. Baptist Church, Washington, D.C., Feb. 7, 1968, MLK-Howard; "Some Things We Must Do," Address Delivered at the Second Annual Institute on Nonviolence and Social Change at Holt Street Baptist Church, Montgomery, Ala., Dec. 5, 1957, in *The Papers of Martin Luther King, Jr.,* Volume IV: *Symbol of the Movement, January 1957—December 1958,* Senior Editor: Clayborne Carson; Volume Editors: Susan Carson, Adrienne Clay, Virginia Shadron, and Kieran Taylor (Berkeley: University of California Press, 2000), 334.

26. Even the blunt preachment of his close adviser Clarence Jones—"There comes a time when you have to call a spade a spade, and you have to fight for the supremacy of your theory"—could not overcome King's reluctance. Fairclough, *To Redeem the Soul of America,* 320; Young, *An Easy Burden,* 404; Branch, *At Canaan's Edge,* 492.

27. Goldman, *The Death and Life of Malcolm X,* 75.

28. Ralph David Abernathy, *And the Walls Came Tumbling Down: An Autobiography* (New York: HarperPerennial, 1990 [1989]), 376.

29. Kotz, *Judgment Days,* 366.

30. David Halberstam, "The Second Coming of Martin Luther King," reprinted in *Reporting Civil Rights, Part Two, American Journalism 1963–1973* (New York: The Library of America, 2003), 577.

31. Fairclough, *To Redeem the Soul of America*, 353; audio tape of the sermon "Judging Others," Ebenezer Baptist Church, June 4, 1967, MLK-Howard.

32. Goldman, *The Death and Life of Malcolm X*, 65.

33. Dell Hymes, "Linguistic Aspects of Comparative Political Research," in R. T. Holt and J. E. Turner, eds., *The Methodology of Comparative Research* (New York: The Free Press, 1970), 322; Jonathan Rieder, *Canarsie: The Jews and Italians of Brooklyn Against Liberalism* (Cambridge, Mass.: Harvard University Press, 1985), 74. Hymes was concerned about the larger impact of "ignorance of communicative conventions." There is a danger of "communicative interference—misinterpretation of the import of features of communication by reading another system in terms of one's own." This simply states the more general interpretive dilemma posed by the task of deciphering the meaning of insults, which are embedded as much in tone and context as in content. As a result, we leap from word to meaning—for the speaker or the listener—only at great hazard. Ibid., 322.

34. *Where Do We Go From Here?*, in Washington, ed., *A Testament of Hope*, 571; Mark Zborowski and Elizabeth Herzog, *Life Is with People: The Jewish Little-Town of Eastern Europe* (New York: International Universities Press, 1952), 148.

35. One of Jesse Jackson's advisers in the 1984 Democratic primaries recalled, "He has words for everybody. . . . We'll be driving along and he'll see a black man who's been drinking, staggering along. And he'll say, 'Oh look, there goes Old Moz.' Or Old Mozella, if it's a woman." Quoted in Bob Faw and Nancy Skelton, *Thunder in America: The Improbable Presidential Campaign of Jesse Jackson* (Austen: University of Texas Press, 1986), 57; Al Vorspan, quoted in ibid., 52–53.

36. Jonathan Rieder, "Crackers and Other Interlopers—A Chat with Rev. Al Sharpton," *CommonQuest: The Magazine of Black-Jewish Relations*, Fall 1996, 4. In the public realm where democratic civility is constructed, such fine distinctions serve important ends. It does not even always matter if they are fictions. Public caution can be an effective way to manage the tensions of difference and protect the face of everyone in the larger public realm.

37. Audio tape of Summer Community Organization and Political Education (SCOPE) meeting, undated, The King Library and Archives, The King Center, Atlanta, Georgia. Hereafter cited as MLK-Atlanta.

38. "The State of the Movement," address at the SCLC staff retreat at Frogmore, South Carolina, Nov. 28, 1967, MLK-Atlanta; Garrow, *Bearing the Cross*, 535.

39. *Where Do We Go From Here?*, 575.

40. "Dr. King's Speech," address at the SCLC staff retreat, Frogmore, South Carolina, Nov. 14, 1966, MLK-Atlanta; audio tape of "In Search of a Sense of Direction."

41. "The State of the Movement."

4. Backstage and Blackstage

1. L. D. Reddick, *Crusader Without Violence: A Biography of Martin Luther King, Jr.* (New York: Harper & Brothers, 1959), 57; Bennett, *What Manner of Man,* 20; Reddick, *Crusader Without Violence,* 57.

2. This quote and all subsequent ones by Joseph Lowery are from author's interview with Lowery, May 11, 2005.

3. Young, *An Easy Burden,* 190; 23.

4. Fairclough, *To Redeem the Soul of America,* 31, 319; Rabbi Marc Schneier, *Shared Dreams: Martin Luther King, Jr. and the Jewish Community* (Woodstock, Vt.: Jewish Lights Publishing, 1999), 52; Fairclough, *To Redeem the Soul of America,* 319.

5. Audio tape of the sermon "No Room at the Inn," Ebenezer Baptist Church, Dec. 19, 1965, MLK-Atlanta.

6. Garrow, *Bearing the Cross,* 395; Branch, *At Canaan's Edge,* 641; author's interview with Andrew Young, May 10, 2005.

7. Branch, *At Canaan's Edge,* 678. After King had savaged staff members who were obstructing the Poor People's Campaign or the return to Memphis, the staff achieved harmony. "The Lord has been in this room this afternoon," Lowery said to the group. "I know he's been here because we could not have deliberated the way we did without the Holy Spirit being here. And the Holy Spirit is going to be with us in Memphis and Washington, and I know we're going to win." Branch, ibid., 744.

8. Ibid., 690; Garrow, *Bearing the Cross,* 455.

9. Interview with Stanley Levison, Ralph Bunch Oral History Archive, Moorland Spingarn Research Center, Howard University, Washington, D.C., 10.

10. Branch, *Pillar of Fire,* 207; 556–557.

11. Garrow, *Bearing the Cross,* 586.

12. Branch, *Parting the Waters,* 706.

13. Fred Shuttlesworth, Introduction, "Eulogy for the Young Victims of the Sixteenth Street Baptist Church Bombing," in Carson and Shepard, eds., *A Call to Conscience,* 91; interview with Walter McCall, MLK-Atlanta, Oral History Collection, 10–11.

14. Young, *An Easy Burden,* 311.

15. Audio tape of SCLC meeting for "Summer Community Organization and Political Education" (SCOPE), 1965, MLK-Atlanta; Branch, *At Canaan's Edge*, 653; audio tape of "What is Nonviolence?," SCLC staff discussion, Nov. 15, 1966, MLK-Atlanta; Young, *An Easy Burden*, 463.
16. Young, *An Easy Burden*, 332.
17. Branch, *Pillar of Fire*, 556–557.
18. Young, *An Easy Burden*, 311–312.
19. These quotes, and subsequent ones by Tom Houck, are from author's interview with Houck, May 12, 2005.
20. Yet more often than not the needling served more serious ends. For one thing, the banter provided a chance to vent political disagreements over the balance of militancy and compromise in a less than fatal fashion. The Williams-Young arguments almost always revolved around the struggle between caution and action. The quipping thus brought to the surface real boundary disputes about the relative merits of integration and desegregation, the airy ideals of "amazing brotherhood," and the resolve to free black people.
21. The backstage, then, has its own front stage. It is more precise to say that there was no single, shared backstage but something more like shifting, concentric circles of backstages, sometimes within the backstage, that were provisionally assembled by the occasion, participants, witnesses, and purposes.
22. Branch, *At Canaan's Edge*, 743.
23. "From Stanley Levison," Jan. 24, 1958, MLK Papers, Volume IV, 353; quotes in this chapter by Andrew Levison are from author's interview with Andrew Levison, June 21, 2005.
24. Branch, *At Canaan's Edge*, 739; quoted in Garrow, *Bearing the Cross*, 670, note 15.
25. Cited in Schneier, *Shared Dreams*, 55.
26. Branch, *Pillar of Fire*, 207.

5. Race Men and Real Men

1. John Lewis, *Walking with the Wind: A Memoir of the Movement* (New York: Harcourt Brace, 1998), 354.
2. Garrow, *Bearing the Cross*, 513.
3. Ibid., 512–513.
4. This quote and all subsequent ones by Rev. Bernard Lafayette are from author's interview with Lafayette, July 6, 2005.

5. Fairclough, *To Redeem the Soul of America,* 288–289.

6. This quote and all subsequent ones by Rev. Willie Bolden are from author's interview with Bolden, May 12, 2005.

7. This quote and all subsequent ones by Andrew Marrissett are from author's interview with Marrissett, June 28, 2005.

8. Lewis, *Walking with the Wind,* 319.

9. It's fair to say that the larger environment, which included a punitive local state, racist militias, and the variable skill of various sheriffs in reading the opposition, shaped the field staff. But adaptation was more than revelation; it took defeat in Albany, Georgia, for King and his colleagues to fully grasp their great need for organizational focus. SCLC's widening ambitions, its need to stage big spectacles to showcase King and gain the national spotlight, reinforced the folly of winging it.

10. Fairclough, *To Redeem the Nation,* 268–269.

11. Garrow, *Bearing the Cross,* 483.

12. Branch, *At Canaan's Edge,* 488.

13. This quote and all subsequent ones by J. T. Johnson are from author's interview with Johnson, May 11, 2005.

14. Young, *An Easy Burden,* 400.

15. CD recording of King appearance, Zion Baptist Church, Los Angeles, June 17, 1966; CD "Martin Luther King, Jr.: We Shall Overcome" (SoundWorks International, 2000).

16. "Dr. King's Speech," address at the SCLC staff retreat, Frogmore, South Carolina, address, Nov. 14, 1966. MLK-Atlanta.

6. The Prophetic Backstage

1. Howell Raines, *My Soul Is Rested: Movement Days in the Deep South Remembered* (New York: Penguin, 1983 [Putnam, 1977]), 449; David Garrow interview, Garrow Collection, Emory University, Box 8.2, 54; italics added.

2. Author's interview with J. T. Johnson, May 11, 2005.

3. Bennett, *What Manner of Man,* 105–106.

4. Branch, *At Canaan's Edge,* 641; Garrow, *Bearing the Cross,* 602.

5. Garrow, *Bearing the Cross,* 374.

6. Ibid., 602.

7. MLK Papers, Volume IV, 109.

8. Fairclough, *To Redeem the Soul of America,* 348.

9. Ralph Abernathy, *And the Walls Came Tumbling Down,* 428; Garrow, *Bearing the Cross,* 607; "I've Been to the Mountaintop."

10. Garrow, *Bearing the Cross,* 375.
11. David Garrow interview of Bernard Lee, Garrow Collection, Emory University, Box 8.2.
12. Georgia Davis Powers, *I Shared the Dream: The Pride, Passion and Politics of the First Black Woman Senator from Kentucky* (Far Hills, N.J.: New Horizon Press, 1995), 171–172; 173; 222; 227.
13. The subtext was the jealous maneuvering among the SCLC staff, the most egregious example of which was the egocentrism of Jesse Jackson, a relative newcomer, who, it would be claimed, took proximity to an unseemly level when after King's death he raced onto television with a white shirt soaked in the blood of the martyr, presumably a sign that he was with King when he was shot. Actually, Jackson dashed up the stairs after the shooting and, as Andrew Young observed, "Jesse put his hands in the blood and wiped it on the front of his shirt." Andrew Young interview, *Frontline,* "The Long Pilgrimage of Jesse Jackson," *www.pbs.org/wgbh/pages/frontline/Jesse/interviews/Young.*
14. Andrew Young interview, transcript of the film "Citizen King" (directed by Orlando Bagwell, 2004), *www.pbs.org/wgbh/amex/mlk/ filmmore/index.*
15. "Dr. King's Speech," address at the SCLC staff retreat, Frogmore, South Carolina, Nov. 14, 1966, MLK-Atlanta.
16. A time for such moral reminding was embedded in the official program. The November 1966 retreat at Frogmore allotted three hours for James Lawson's workshop on nonviolence. If many of the attendees had been inducted into the tender endeavor through King's suasive language, the retreats constituted a kind of refresher course in its basic grammar and vocabulary.
17. Audio tape of SCLC staff meeting, "What is Non-violence?" Nov. 15, 1966, MLK-Atlanta.
18. Author's interview with Rev. Joseph Lowery, May 11, 2005.
19. "The State of the Movement," address at the SCLC staff retreat, Frogmore, South Carolina, Nov. 28, 1967.
20. Author's interview with C. T. Vivian, May 11, 2005; audio tape of mass meeting, Montgomery, Ala., Feb. 17, 1968, MLK-Atlanta.
21. "Where Do We Go From Here?"
22. The quotes in this and the paragraphs that follow are from the audio tape of the speech "Why a Movement," address at the SCLC staff retreat, Frogmore, South Carolina, Nov. 28, 1967, MLK-Atlanta.
23. Young, *An Easy Burden,* 332.

24. King, *Why We Can't Wait* (New York: New American Library, 1964 [1963]), 62.

25. "Why a Movement."

Part II. Son of a (Black) Preacher Man

1. This quote and subsequent ones by Lowery are from author's interview with Rev. Joseph Lowery, May 11, 2005.

2. This quote and subsequent ones by Fauntroy are from author's interview with Rev. Walter Fauntroy, April 7, 2005.

7. Flight from the Folk?

1. Coretta Scott King, *My Life with Martin Luther King, Jr.* (New York: Holt, Rinehart and Winston, 1969), 59.

2. "Letter to Coretta," July 18, 1952, in Clayborne Carson, ed., *The Autobiography of Martin Luther King, Jr.* (New York: Warner Books, 1998), 36.

3. "Crozer Theological Seminary Field Work Department: Rating Sheet for Martin Luther King, Jr., by William E. Gardner," Fall 1950. In *The Papers of Martin Luther King, Jr.,* Volume I: *Called to Serve, January 1929–June 1951;* Senior Editor: Clayborne Carson; Volume Editors: Ralph E. Luker and Penny A. Russell; Advisory Editor: Louis R. Harlan (Berkeley: University of California Press, 1992), 381. Hereafter cited as MLK Papers, Volume I.

4. Branch, *Parting the Waters,* 267.

5. "Some Things We Must Do," address delivered at the Second Annual Institute on Nonviolence and Social Change at Holt Street Baptist Church, Montgomery, Alabama, Dec. 5, 1957. In *The Papers of Martin Luther King, Jr.,* Volume IV: *Symbol of the Movement, January 1957–December 1958;* Senior Editor: Clayborne Carson; Volume Editors: Susan Carson, Adrienne Clay, Virginia Shadron, and Kieran Taylor (Berkeley: University of California Press, 2000), 338. Hereafter cited as MLK Papers, Volume IV.

6. Coretta Scott King, *My Life with Martin Luther King, Jr.,* 86; cited in Lischer, *The Preacher King,* 46.

7. Abernathy, *And the Walls Came Tumbling Down,* 118; Keith D. Miller documents the extensiveness of King's borrowings from white liberal Protestant ministers in *Voice of Deliverance: The Language of Martin Luther King, Jr. and Its Sources* (New York: The Free Press, 1992). The King Papers have car-

ried out intensive detective work to refine our understanding of this fruitful exchange between King and the white liberal Protestant homiletic tradition in *The Papers of Martin Luther King, Jr.,* Volume VI: *Advocate of the Social Gospel, September 1948–March 1963;* Senior Editor: Clayborne Carson; Volume Editors: Susan Carson, Susan Englander, Troy Jackson, and Gerald L. Smith (Berkeley: University of California Press, 2007). Hereafter cited as MLK Papers, Volume VI. The King Papers' methods of documentation and citation make it easy to see the limits of the borrowing as well as its pervasiveness.

8. CD of "The Birth of a New Nation," Dexter Avenue Baptist Church, Montgomery, Alabama, April 7, 1957, in *Call to Conscience*/IPM–Time Warner AudioBooks.

9. "The Death of Evil Upon the Seashore," in Martin Luther King, Jr., *Strength to Love* (Philadelphia, Pa.: Fortress Press, 1981 [1963]), 76–77.

10. Abernathy, *And the Walls Came Tumbling Down,* 479–480.

11. "How Should a Christian View Communism," *Strength to Love,* 99; audio tape of the sermon "Loving Your Enemies," Dexter Avenue Baptist Church, Nov. 17, 1957, in *Knock at Midnight*/IPM–Time Warner AudioBooks; "From R. D. Crockett," February 8, 1954, *The Papers of Martin Luther King, Jr.,* Volume II: *Rediscovering Previous Values, July 1951–November 1955;* Senior Editor: Clayborne Carson; Volume Editors: Ralph E. Luker, Penny A. Russell, and Peter Holloran; Advisory Editor: Louis R. Harlan (Berkeley: University of California Press, 1994), 240. Hereafter cited as MLK Papers, Volume II.

12. *Strength to Love,* 123; "Antidotes for Fear," ibid., 122–123.

13. "Loving Your Enemies."

14. "Questions that Easter Answers," Dexter Avenue Baptist Church, April 21, 1957, MLK Papers, Volume VI, 289, 288; "Living Under the Tensions of Modern Life," Dexter Avenue Baptist Church, Sept. 1956, ibid., 269, 264.

15. "The Death of Evil Upon the Seashore," *Strength to Love,* 77.

16. James Cone, "Black Theology—Black Church," *Theology Today,* vol. 40, no. 4 (Jan. 1984), 409–420. I don't want to overstate the case, which is why I use the term "flirt." Cone recognized that "it is unquestionably true that these philosophers and theologians, as well as other writers and teachers whom King encountered in graduate school, had a profound effect upon the content, shape, and depth of his theological perspective."

17. Keith Miller employs this language of finding a genuine voice. Like Cone, Miller grasped the importance of the practical goal of persuasion in shaping

King's selections. In the process, both underlined the structural constraints of reception and legitimacy that guided King's linguistic selections. Yet Miller better grasped the racial dynamic when he pointed to the diversity of white voices, some of which were more entrancing to King than others. In a sense, Miller was controlling for race when he identified the influence not of the abstruse theologians but of the master white preachers. "King escaped the confines of his professors' strange, artificial tongue and their ivory-tower theological formalism. After leaving the academy, he sounded exactly like himself as he seized Fosdick's and others' sermons for the purpose of transferring black demands for freedom into an idiom acceptable to his main audience—white listeners." Miller, "Martin Luther King, Jr., and the Black Folk Pulpit," *The Journal of American History* (June 1991), 120. As much as Miller advanced the discussion of King, the limits of this rendering are considerable. Miller's notion that white listeners were King's main audience is hardly sustainable. Moreover, he did not pursue the explosive implications of his severing of genuine voice from race, missing the fact that King found in the white sources a powerful voice before black congregations, as I've noted already. In the process, he reproduced Cone's simplification of the rhetorical process; in a sense, they both assumed that King "talked white" when he addressed white audiences. They simply disagreed on which whites were influential. But both stressed the dominant rhetorical motive of deferring to the rhetorical and theological expectations of listeners, as if familiar words, phrases, and forms were the only source of resonance for an audience.

Despite the lack of empirical evidence for the dynamic of reception he imputed to white audiences, at least Miller offered a plausible if speculative account of King's borrowing in front of *white* audiences. Yet this dynamic cannot account for black audiences' responsiveness to some of these same sermons and quotations. More generally, the preoccupation with sources, authorities, and code risks devolving into a truism that, to put it in King's terms, Aunt Jane—and surely the average Baptist shouter—could grasp. Good orators tailor their language to the audience at hand. Yet in his urgent focus on tracing specific sources and the fixation on idiom that accompanied it, Miller tended to downplay the prevalence of King's white borrowings before *black* audiences. Maybe the members of Riverside Baptist Church and the National Cathedral had the cultural capital to respond, perhaps subliminally, to King's sampling of Buttrick and Hamilton. But how quotes from Buttrick and Hamilton would provoke "intertextuality" in the Dexter and Ebenezer congregations remains a mystery, to be sure.

18. James Weldon Johnson, *God's Trombones: Seven Negro Sermons in Verse* (New York: Viking Press, 1969 [1927]), 9.

19. Russell Adams, "Memories of Morehouse," unpublished manuscript.

20. Sandy Ray, *Journeying Through a Jungle* (Nashville, Tenn.: Broadman Press, 1979), 61; Gardner Taylor, "A President of Preaching," *The Words of Gardner Taylor, Vol. 4: Special Occasion and Expository Sermons,* compiled by Edward L. Taylor (Valley Forge, Pa.: Judson Press, 2001), 141.

21. Interview of Walter McCall, Mar. 31, 1970, MLK-Atlanta, Oral History Collection, 8–9.

22. Ibid., 9–10.

23. Author's interview with Rev. C. T. Vivian, May 11, 2005.

24. "Deacon John Fulgham," in Rev. Wally G. Vaughn, ed., *Reflections on Our Pastor: Dr. Martin Luther King, Jr. at Dexter Baptist Church, 1954–1960* (Dover, Mass.: The Majority Press, 1999), 40–41.

25. Cited in editorial notes, "From C. W. Kelly," *The Papers of Martin Luther King, Jr.,* Volume III: *Birth of a New Age, December 1955–December 1956;* Senior Editor: Clayborne Carson; Volume Editors: Stewart Burns, Susan Carson, Peter Holloran, and Dana L. H. Powell (Berkeley: University of California Press, 1997), 366. Hereafter cited as MLK Papers, Volume III.

26. "From C. W. Kelly," ibid., 366.

27. In Vaughn, *Reflections on Our Pastor,* 47.

28. "Loving Your Enemies."

29. Ibid.

30. Lischer, *The Preacher King,* 109–110. As he elaborates, "when King's whole sermons are read alongside the whole sermons of the influential preachers, it becomes clear that for the most part King used his peers—Fosdick, Buttrick, Thurman, Hamilton—the way preachers have always used the sermons of others: for an idea, a phrase, an outline."

31. "Paul's Letter to American Christians," MLK Papers, Volume III, 418.

32. Johnson, *God's Trombones,* 8.

8. Homilies of Black Liberation

1. Given my distinctive concerns, this is not the place to delve into the larger debate on King's relationship to black theology, which Lewis V. Baldwin has richly summarized in *To Make the Wounded Whole: The Cultural Legacy of Martin Luther King, Jr.* (Minneapolis: Fortress Press, 1992). The effort to assess influences from "inside" or "outside" the black vernacular tradition runs through his catalogue of the positions of various scholars. Baldwin cites the

work of Preston N. Williams, who grasped King's "reliance on a range of theological sources, black and white . . . [Williams] stops short of classifying King as a black theologian, mainly because of the universal implications of King's theological perspective." Baldwin also points to the work of Peter Paris, who "does not minimize the significance of King's dialogue with and indebtedness to sources outside the black community. He suggests that all of the key concepts pervading King's political and theological understanding . . . were either directly or indirectly influenced by Evangelical Liberalism, Social Gospelism, Personalism, and the thought of philosophers such as Marx and Hegel. In Paris' analysis, King emerges as a great synthesizer" (125). As Chapter 9 of this book will make powerfully clear, Williams's point applies homiletically no less than theologically.

2. Lewis, *Walking with the Wind*, 45.
3. Audio tape of the sermon "A Knock at Midnight," in *Knock at Midnight*/IPM–Time Warner AudioBooks.
4. "Some Things We Must Do," 332; 335–336.
5. Audio tape, "To the World It's Midnight," *The Wisdom of King*, side 2 (Collegedale, Tenn.: Black Label).
6. Audio tape of the sermon "Why Jesus Called a Man a Fool," Mount Pisgah Missionary Baptist Church, Chicago, Aug. 27, 1967, *Knock at Midnight*/IPM–Time Warner AudioBooks.
7. "Some Things We Must Do," 337; audio tape of the sermon "Making the Best of a Bad Mess," Ebenezer Baptist Church, April 24, 1966, MLK-Howard.
8. Audio tape of the sermon "To Serve the Present Age," undated, MLK-Howard; audio tape of the sermon "The American Dream," Ebenezer Baptist Church, July 4, 1965, *Knock at Midnight*/IPM–Time Warner AudioBooks.
9. Audio tape of the sermon "Judging Others," Ebenezer Baptist Church, June 4, 1967, MLK-Howard.
10. Audio tape of the sermon "Levels of Love," Ebenezer Baptist Church, May 21, 1967, MLK-Howard.
11. "Levels of Love," Ebenezer Baptist Church, Sept. 16, 1962, MLK Papers, Volume VI, 439.
12. Audio tape of the sermon "A Walk Through the Holy Land," Dexter Avenue Baptist Church, Mar. 29, 1959, MLK-Atlanta.
13. King's friend Archibald Carey, the Chicago minister, had first suggested this connection to King. Carey's address to the 1952 Republican National Convention provided King with some of the riffs and runs that King would use

at the end of "I Have a Dream" at the March on Washington, including the "Let freedom ring" series. See Miller, *Voice of Deliverance,* 146.

14. "The American Dream."

15. "From G. Ramachandran," Dec. 27, 1958, MLK Papers, Volume IV, 553. Blacks with Gandhian interests in King's orbit, no less than Gandhi himself and Nehru, had long observed the links between segregation and caste humiliation.

16. Mays, *Born to Rebel,* 158. The parallels between Mays's and King's narrations extend further. Mays too was attending a dinner with untouchables when he was introduced as an untouchable. "The headmaster told them that I had suffered at the hands of the white men in the United States every indignity that they suffered from the various castes in India." As King did, Mays then repeated a list of his experiences with racism that convinced him to embrace the untouchable label: "In my country, I was segregated almost everywhere I went. . . . I was not permitted to sleep or eat in white hotels and restaurants and was barred from worship in white churches. I had been slapped almost blind because I was black. . . . I—just as they—through the mere accident of birth, was indeed an untouchable!"

17. "The American Dream."

18. CD recording of King appearance at Zion Baptist Church, Los Angeles, June 17, 1966. "My Little Girl," track 2 of "Martin Luther King, Jr.: We Shall Overcome" (SoundWorks International, 2000).

19. "Why Jesus Called a Man a Fool."

20. Audio tape of the sermon "The Three Dimensions of a Complete Life," New Covenant Baptist Church, Chicago, April 9, 1967, *Knock at Midnight/* IPM–Time Warner AudioBooks.

21. Editorial notes and "Outline, Address to MIA Mass meeting at Bethel Baptist Church," Jan. 14, 1957, MLK Papers, Volume IV, 109–110.

22. *Stride toward Freedom: The Montgomery Story* (San Francisco: Harper & Row, 1958), 134; "Why Jesus Called a Man a Fool."

23. "Why Jesus Called a Man a Fool"; "The Three Dimensions of a Complete Life."

24. "The American Dream."

25. Audio tape of the sermon "Is the Universe Friendly?" Ebenezer Baptist Church, Dec. 1965, MLK-Howard.

26. "Some Things We Must Do," 330.

27. "Why Jesus Called a Man a Fool."

28. Audio tape of the sermon "The Interruptions of Life," Ebenezer Baptist Church, Jan. 21, 1968, MLK-Howard.

29. "A Knock at Midnight."
30. Audio tape of the sermon "Unfulfilled Dreams," Ebenezer Baptist Church, Mar. 3, 1968, *Knock at Midnight*/IPM–Time Warner AudioBooks.

9. Raw and Refined

1. "Mastering Our Fears."
2. Garrow, *Bearing the Cross,* 543.
3. Ibid., 550.
4. Audio tape of the sermon "The Drum Major Instinct," Ebenezer Baptist Church, Feb. 4, 1968, in *Knock at Midnight*/IPM–Time Warner AudioBooks.
5. Vaughn, *Our Pastor,* 97.
6. "Some Things We Must Do," 338.
7. Lewis, *Walking with the Wind,* 45.
8. "The Interruptions of Life."
9. "The Three Dimensions of a Complete Life."
10. "The Interruptions of Life."
11. "The Drum Major Instinct."
12. "Unfulfilled Dreams."
13. Ibid.; "Is the Universe Friendly?"
14. The social emphasis was evident early on. See MLK Papers, Volume VI, 1–44.
15. "A Knock at Midnight."
16. "A Walk Through the Holy Land."
17. "The Interruptions of Life."
18. Ibid.
19. "Why Jesus Called a Man a Fool." This was a riff King employed on a number of occasions. In "The Three Dimensions of a Complete Life," he preached, "Men through the ages have tried to talk about him. *(Yes)* Plato said that he was the Architectonic Good. Aristotle called him the Unmoved Mover. Hegel called him the Absolute Whole. Then there was a man named Paul Tillich, who called him Being-Itself."
20. "Why Jesus Called a Man a Fool"; "The Three Dimensions of a Complete Life."
21. "Making the Best of a Bad Mess."
22. Susannah Heschel, "Theological Affinities in the Writings of Abraham Joshua Heschel and Martin Luther King, Jr.," in Yvonne Chireau and Nathaniel Deutsch, eds., *Black Zion: African American Religious Encounters with Judaism* (New York: Oxford University Press, 2000), 168–169; Richard

L. Rubenstein, "The Rabbis Visit Birmingham," *The Reconstructionist,* May 31, 1963, 8.

23. James H. Smylie made a similar point in a somewhat different context in "On Jesus, Pharaohs, and the Chosen People: Martin Luther King as Biblical Interpreter and Humanist," *Interpretation,* vol. 24, no. 1 (1970), 74–91. "King defined the chosen people, oppression under this world's pharaohs, and the promised land in the light of his interpretation and acceptance of the radical demands of Jesus Christ upon his life" (75). Smylie also pointed out that King wanted to be like Jesus, not like Moses. Finally, he observed, "It is remarkable that King as a biblical interpreter alluded so infrequently in his formal writings to the Exodus narrative" (81). That infrequency offers a fitting parallel to the homiletic infrequency I have alluded to.

24. "Loving Your Enemies."

25. Audio tape of the sermon "New Wine in New Bottles," Ebenezer Baptist Church, Jan. 2, 1966, MLK-Howard.

26. Ibid.

27. "The Three Dimensions of a Complete Life."

28. Audio tape of the sermon "Guidelines for a Constructive Church," Ebenezer Baptist Church, June 5, 1966, in *Knock at Midnight*/IPM–Time Warner AudioBooks.

29. "The Three Dimensions of a Complete Life"; "On Being a Good Neighbor," *Strength to Love,* 27.

30. "The Drum Major Instinct."

31. Audio tape of the sermon "Is the Universe Friendly?," Ebenezer Baptist Church, Dec. 1965, MLK-Howard.

32. Author's interview with Rev. C. T. Vivian, May 11, 2005.

33. Abraham Joshua Heschel, *The Wisdom of Heschel* (New York: Farrar, Straus & Giroux, 1975), 279.

34. "Guidelines for a Constructive Church."

Part III. King in the Mass Meetings

1. "Address to the First Montgomery Improvement Association (MIA) Mass Meeting," Holt Street Baptist Church, Montgomery, Alabama, Dec. 5, 1955, in *Call to Conscience*/IPM–Time Warner AudioBooks.

2. The basic template of the mass meeting emerged from the powerful role that black ministers played in black life, the basic configuration of the church service, and the absence of alternative black-controlled spaces. "The black church filled a large part of the institutional void," writes sociologist

Aldon Morris, "by providing support and direction for the diverse activities of an oppressed group. It furnished outlets for social and artistic expression; a forum for the discussion of important issues; a social environment that developed, trained, and disciplined potential leaders from all walks of life; and meaningful symbols to engender hope, enthusiasm, and a resilient group spirit. The church was a place to observe, participate in, and experience the reality of owning and directing an institution free from the control of whites. The church was also an arena where group interests could be articulated and defended collectively." Morris, *The Origins of the Civil Rights Movement: Black Communities Organizing for Change* (New York: Free Press, 1986), 5.

3. Watters, *Down to Now*, 24.

4. Abernathy, *And the Walls Came Tumbling Down*, 152. "We would begin with scripture, prayer, and perhaps a hymn. Then Martin would talk about the abuses we were facing, the remedies we proposed, and the way in which nonviolent protest would accomplish our ends. . . . We closed the meeting that night with a rousing hymn, and the huge church trembled from the vibrations." Ibid., 153; "Address at the Conclusion of the Selma to Montgomery March," Montgomery, Alabama, March 25, 1965, in *Call to Conscience/*IPM–Time Warner AudioBooks.

5. King's comments on intermarriage in his preaching ("I don't want to be the white man's brother-in-law") likely were filched from Abernathy's comments in Albany, Georgia, about white fears that black men wanted to sleep with white women.

6. Quoted in Branch, *Parting the Waters*, 363; *The Papers of Martin Luther King, Jr.,* Volume III: *Birth of a New Age, December 1955–December 1956;* Senior Editor: Clayborne Carson; Volume Editors: Stewart Burns, Susan Carson, Peter Holloran, and Dana L. H. Powell (Berkeley: University of California Press, 1997), 199. Hereafter cited as MLK Papers, Volume III. Birmingham Civil Rights Institute, Mass Meeting Tapes, Society for the Advancement of American Philosophy Collection, recordings made by Rev. C. Herbert Oliver in 1963, CD V, side 1. Hereafter referred to as BCRI-Meetings.

7. These elements of translation may explain a key aspect of the reception of King's oratory: they provided clues that allowed unlettered listeners to get the gist of King's more obscure distinctions. Maybe the crowd at Holt Street Baptist Church did not quite get it when King snuck in a capsule summary of Niebuhr's distinction between love and correction, yet how many educated white professionals would have caught the rarefied reference either?

But when he followed up similarly obscure distinctions with the more familiar idiom of jeremiad and warned, "America, you got a lot of repentin' to do," King could not have been more clear. Who could miss his message that there was evil in the world that required chastisement, that the civil rights movement was on the side of righteousness, that God, as King relayed his inner state, "was not pleased with the way some of his children are being treated"?

8. Watters, *Down to Now,* 190.
9. Audio tape of mass meeting, "Lest We Forget 2: Birmingham, Alabama, 1963," Folkway Records, the Smithsonian Institution, 1991.
10. Watters, *Down to Now,* 195–196.

10. Beloved Black Community

1. Branch, *Parting the Waters,* 545; Watters, *Down to Now,* 12.
2. Watters, *Down to Now,* 12.
3. Branch, *Parting the Waters,* 545.
4. Watters, *Down to Now,* 14.
5. Max Atkinson, *Our Masters' Voices: The Language and Body Language of Politics* (London and New York: Methuen, 1984), 110.
6. Ibid., 110–111. That same mutuality was evident in the apparent ability of competent speakers to convey an array of meanings that various inflections of a single word can signal and of competent listeners to scan them and recognize the situationally correct one. As Pat Watters reported (*Down to Now,* 22): "All different meanings put into the saying of 'Well' by the tone, the manner of speaking, sometimes bitten off, almost harsh, sometimes almost crooned, and by inflection. 'Well' (quietly) in affirmation. 'WELL' (crackling out) in strong affirmation. 'Well?' urging the speaker to continue, to tell more, helping him build interest and to reach his own heights of eloquence. 'Well' in sorrow over something cruel or outrageous told. 'Well' in joy. And 'WELL' in righteous anger. 'WELL' most often of all in affirmation, agreement, support: 'WELL. . . . Well.'

   "A convention of Negro religious services, this responsive 'Well,' and in the mass meetings an important part of the musical, poetic effect, of the impromptu eloquence and the attainment of so much unity and communion . . ."
7. Recording of Selma mass meeting, Birmingham Public Library Archives, CD "Tapes 6 & 7." Hereafter cited as BPL-Selma.

8. "Address to the First Montgomery Improvement Association (MIA) Mass Meeting."

9. Recording of Selma mass meeting, BPL-Selma, CD "MLK Tapes 6 & 7."

10. Ibid., CD "MLK Tape 1."

11. Ibid.

12. BPL-Selma, CD "MLK Tapes 6 & 7."

13. Ibid. The "my body took a back seat" vignette was likely inspired by Benjamin Mays. As Noel E. Burtenshaw writes about the gatherings the Morehouse president held for his students, "Sedition was planned at Mays's home also. 'Your mind does not have to sit in the back of the bus,' he would say." See Burtenshaw, "Seeds of Revolution," in Carter, ed., *Walking Integrity*, 341. As Mays described his mission, "I spent half of my life demonstrating to myself I was not inferior. I spent the rest carrying that message to the students at Morehouse."

14. Cleveland Sellers, *The River of No Return: The Autobiography of a Black Militant and the Life and Death of SNCC* (Jackson, Miss.: University Press of Mississippi, 1990), 164–165.

15. Recording of Birmingham mass meeting, Birmingham Civil Rights Institute, Mass Meeting Tapes, Rev. Herbert Oliver Collection, CD VI, side 1. Hereafter cited as BCRI-Meetings.

16. BPL-Selma, CD "MLK Tape 1"; ibid., "MLK Tapes 4 & 5."

17. BCRI-Meetings, CD "King, Abernathy, Shuttlesworth, May 3, 1963 mass mtg. Sixteenth St. Bapt."

18. These quotes and those in the following paragraphs are from audio tape of mass meeting, Greenwood, Mississippi, March 19, 1968, MLK-Atlanta.

19. Audio tape of mass meeting, Montgomery, Ala., Feb. 17, 1968, MLK-Atlanta. These notes of wounding rejection marked a shift in King's use of maternal imagery. The mother's solicitousness that King had mentioned in a late 1950s Spelman College address stood for the virtues of caring. Even as the refusal to welcome the baby Jesus in King's 1965 Christmas sermon, "No Room at the Inn," mocked the ideal of nurturing, "No Room" had a paradoxically optimistic twist: the people who turned Mary and Joseph away were not evil people, King preached; "They didn't mean to reject Christ." By contrast, speaking in a Birmingham mass meeting, James Bevel targeted the malevolent whites in rural Alabama who rejected him, his wife Diane Nash, and their child: "You can't go around preaching one thing and doing something else," Bevel bristled. "I was at a conference, some white preachers came in a preaching, you know, they're great preachers"—and

361

then in typical Bevel fashion he slipped in, "They're great liars too"—"[and the white preacher] was a preaching, he said, 'Yeah, Jesus went to the inn, and Mary was pregnant, you know, he got to the inn, and the folks in the inn wouldn't let 'em because they said they didn't have any room.'" As the Birmingham audience registered its disapproval, Bevel calmed it, saying, "at least that man had a legitimate excuse. But I was traveling over Alabama with my wife in the car, and I drove up to a motel that had empty rooms, and the man came out who was a deacon of a Baptist church and said, 'You cannot come in.' That wasn't back in the backwoods of yesteryear. That was in nineteen hundred and sixty two . . . my wife was pregnant just like sister Mary and here in Alabama that white man came out and told me that 'I have room in my inn and yes, you can't come in.'" BCRI-meetings, CD 1, side 1, 2.

While King held to the "didn't mean to" frame in his rendition of "No Room," it worked awkwardly when he transitioned from the general tendency to reject what was new—Jesus, King observed, was a new kind of king—to the short interlude in which he considered the specific rejection of black people. The emotive language King used to describe the situation of no room in the inns of Rhodesia, South Africa, and the American South, where the people who had been turned away because of "shameful" segregation were "crying out for freedom," pointed to a moral deficiency, not inattention. No lapse of attention, the failure to nourish was malign intention.

20. "The State of the Movement," address at the SCLC staff retreat, Frogmore, South Carolina, Nov. 14, 1966, MLK-Atlanta.

21. "The African Revolution and Its Impact on the American Negro," address to the Harvard Law School forum, Dec. 16, 1964, *www. law.harvard.edu/students/orgs/forum.*

22. "Address at the Conclusion of the Selma to Montgomery March."

23. BPL-Selma, CD "MLK Tapes 4 & 5."

24. BPL-Selma, CD "MLK Tapes 2 & 3."

25. Audio tape of mass meeting, Greenwood, Mississippi, March 19, 1968, MLK-Atlanta; Garrow, *Bearing the Cross,* 607.

26. Audio tape of mass meeting, Montgomery, Alabama, Feb. 17, 1968, MLK-Atlanta.

27. Abernathy, *And the Walls Came Tumbling Down,* 413.

28. Audio tape of mass meeting, Greenwood, Mississippi, March 19, 1968, MLK-Atlanta.

29. Audio tape of "I've Been to the Mountaintop," Memphis, Tennessee, April 3, 1968, in *Call to Conscience*/IPM–Time Warner AudioBooks.

30. Recording of Birmingham mass meeting, BCRI-Meetings, CD V, side 1. "Race traitor" was not typical King palaver. Nor did King use the word "Uncle Tom" in the indiscriminate fashion of nationalist agitators who later honed the phrase into a weapon to coerce ersatz community. Still, the lingo of racial treachery marked the evolution of a captive black nation into a black community aroused in struggle.

31. "Address to the First Montgomery Improvement Association (MIA) Mass Meeting."

32. Branch, *At Canaan's Edge,* 719; audio tape of mass meeting, Greenwood, Mississippi, March 19, 1968, MLK-Atlanta.

33. "Address to the First Montgomery Improvement Association (MIA) Mass Meeting."

11. The Physics of Deliverance

1. *Why We Can't Wait,* in Washington, ed., *A Testament of Hope,* 535; italics added.

2. Watters, *Down to Now,* 183–184.

3. Young, *An Easy Burden,* 183.

4. Ibid., 223.

5. Ibid., 261–262.

6. Watters, *Down to Now,* 327.

7. Ibid., 290; 186.

8. By turning to the dynamic functions and specific purposes of King's religious idiom, we diminish one aspect of the model of the rational speaker— the one that focuses on the "maintenance" motives of gaining entrée to the rhetorical occasion, conforming to the dictates of the setting, and maintaining validity as a competent member of the speech community—and highlight another: the intentions of the speaker and the goals he hopes to accomplish with his ways of speaking. In the midst of that shift, our guiding principle inverts Erving Goffman's aphorism, "moments and their men," which obscures the larger uses to which King put his prophetic faith, replacing it with a focus on "men and their moments."

9. Michael Walzer, *Exodus and Revolution* (New York: Basic Books, 1986 [1985]), x.

10. "I've Been to the Mountaintop."

11. Watters, *Down to Now,* 154; 197.

12. Abernathy, *And the Walls Came Tumbling Down,* 153.

13. Watters, *Down to Now,* 206.

14. Garrow, *Bearing the Cross,* 229.
15. Quoted in Glenn T. Eskew, *But for Birmingham: The Local and National Movements in the Civil Rights Struggle* (Chapel Hill, N.C.: University of North Carolina Press, 1997), 230.
16. Ibid., 227–228.
17. During the Albany movement of 1962, Pat Watters spotted a man who seemingly averted his eyes, embarrassed by his last-minute self-removal to the sidelines. Then again in Selma, there was that moment when the teachers led by Frederick Reece, vulnerable employees of the racist state, finally shook off their hesitancy and moved out of Brown Chapel, thereby summoning the courage the children had already been showing.
18. Young, *An Easy Burden,* 232; author's interview with Willie Bolden, May 12, 2005; Recording of Rev. Lawrence Campbell, "Sermon," *Voices of the Civil Rights Movement: Black American Freedom Songs 1960–1966,* record side 6, The Smithsonian Institution, Program in Black American Culture.
19. "Lest We Forget 2: Birmingham, Alabama, 1963."
20. Of course, this division of queries is merely heuristic. As an empirical matter, none of these questions nor the responses to them were neatly separable in reality. The more allies one could call on, the more powerful one's sense of self, then the greater was the likelihood of success, which fortified the estimation of the rationality of defiance. Across speeches, or within a particular moment of a particular oration, the precise emphasis on one of these functions varied. In this sense, King's talk tracked the dynamics of a song like "We Shall Overcome," whose "we" declared solidarity, whose "overcome" summoned a sense of agency, whose "shall" evoked plausibility.
21. For a further analysis of the dynamic quality of political culture, see my "Doing Political Culture: Interpretive Practice and the Earnest Heuristic," *Research on Democracy and Society,* vol. 2 (1994), 117–151.
22. Benjamin E. Mays and Joseph W. Nicholson, *The Negro's Church* (New York: Institute of Social and Religious Research, 1933).
23. Lewis, *Walking with the Wind,* 65.
24. Jerry Falwell, *Strength for the Journey: An Autobiography* (New York: Pocketbooks, 1998 [1987]), 276. A similar disapproval drove the recoil of many churched black people from what they viewed as an execration—the way rhythm and blues cut through the division behind sacred and profane, this time in the realm of the erotic and romantic rather than the political, as when Ray Charles and the Raylets made call-and-shout an instrument of erotic moaning in "What'd I Say." Much like Ralph Abernathy's casual

equation of civil rights struggle with being in the fiery furnace, King's rein-
terpretation of Christian witness in the mass meeting context—"Get ready
for a witness"—flirted with blasphemy in a way not so different from
Marvin Gaye's plea, "Can I get a Witness?"

25. C. L. Franklin, "Moses at the Red Sea," in Reverend C. L. Franklin, *Give
Me This Mountain: Life Story and Selected Sermons,* ed. Jeff Todd Titon
(Champaign, Ill.: University of Illinois Press, 1989), 107; 112–113.

26. Aldon Morris aptly described this task as "refocusing." Movement leaders
"were activating a religious view latent in the church." They were accom-
plishing that end with "a familiar religious doctrine that had been sig-
nificantly altered to encourage protest." *Origins of the Civil Rights Movement,* 98–99. As Charles Payne observes, in retrieving the deliverance
themes that were prominent in slave religion, movement organizers were
"bending Afro-American Christianity toward emancipatory ends." Charles
M. Payne, *I've Got the Light of Freedom: The Organizing Tradition and the
Mississippi Freedom Struggle* (Berkeley, Calif.: University of California Press,
1996 [1995]), 257. The reemergence of the spirituals suggests the enhanced
value of the deliverance theme in the political context of mobilization. My
discussion identifies the intricate means and maneuvers through which
bending and refocusing were achieved, and the broad array of specific tasks
that were involved in preparing Christians for insurgency.

27. Eskew, *But for Birmingham,* 229.

28. Ibid., 230–231.

29. Audio tape of the sermon "Guidelines for a Constructive Church,"
Ebenezer Baptist Church, June 5, 1966, in *Knock at Midnight*/IPM–Time
Warner AudioBooks.

30. "Why Jesus Called a Man a Fool."

31. Recording of Birmingham mass meetings, BCRI-Meetings, CD "King, Abernathy, Shuttlesworth, May 3, 1963 mass mtg. Sixteenth St. Bapt."

32. "Guidelines For a Constructive Church."

33. "Letter from Birmingham Jail," in Washington, ed., *A Testament of Hope,*
290–302.

34. Similar substitutionary logic was at work in the Frogmore parable that featured the effort of Jesus to convince Peter to troll not for fish but for souls.
That was the same metaphor Malcolm X used to describe his mobilization
effort for the Nation of Islam, exhorting potential recruits on the street corners of Detroit and Harlem. King was Jesus in the narrative, the SCLC
staffers were his disciples, and he was commanding them to mobilize 3,000
souls to go to Washington.

35. "Address to the First Montgomery Improvement Association (MIA) Mass Meeting."
36. Recording of Birmingham mass meeting, BCRI-Meetings, CD VII, side 2.
37. Audio tape of mass meeting, "Lest We Forget 2: Birmingham, Alabama, 1963."
38. Recording of Birmingham mass meeting, BCRI-Meetings, CD I, side l.
39. Quoted in Morris, *Origins of the Civil Rights Movement,* 98. In line with the additional role of King's metaphoric language in shaping perceptions of likely success, which will be explored in the next chapter, Morris goes on to comment, "Mrs. Clark maintained that King's speeches made people feel that if they worked hard enough, they really could make justice roll down like water, and righteousness like a mighty stream."
40. Author's interview with Congressman John Lewis, April 6, 2005.
41. "Address at the Conclusion of the Selma to Montgomery March."
42. BCRI-Meetings, CD VI, side 2. My main claim and concern here does not involve the effects of King's rhetoric on his audience. Clearly, a good deal of caution is in order in appraising the effect of the vivid biblical present on listeners. Still, the logic of this rhetoric of evocation and intimation is clear. Moreover, there is a wealth of personal testimonies of the impact of such evocative and emotional language and the mass meetings more generally.
43. Richard Wright, *12 Million Black Voices* (New York: Viking Press, 1941), 68.
44. Watters, *Down to Now,* 143.
45. Ibid., 203.
46. This entire interpretive endeavor falls under the sociological rubric of "framing," to which scholars of collective action have drawn considerable attention. For our purposes here, the important point is that King's religious casting was not simply an opportunistic framing to achieve secular ends. Of course, as Doug McAdam puts it, "King and his SCLC lieutenants' genius as 'master framers'" was undeniable, and "the SCLC brain trust displayed what can only be described as a genius for strategic dramaturgy." Surely there was opportunism involved, as will emerge throughout this chapter. Just as surely, the religious appeals were means—or more precisely they were also means—to an end. But, paradoxically, the religious appeals could only be effective to the extent that there was genuine fervency of belief and broad membership in a spiritual community that fortified it. See McAdam, "The framing function of movement tactics: Strategic dramaturgy in the American civil rights movement," in Doug McAdam, John D. McCarthy, and Mayer N. Zald, eds., *Comparative Perspectives on Social Movements: Political*

Opportunities, Mobilizing Structures, and Cultural Framings (New York: Cambridge University Press, 1996), 348.

47. "Guidelines For a Constructive Church"; italics added.

12. The Rationality of Defiance

1. "Address at the Conclusion of the Selma to Montgomery March."
2. Stewart Burns, *To the Mountaintop*, 270–271.
3. One is hard-pressed to find a King performance that approaches the biblical detail of Abernathy's remarkable analogy between the movement and the stages of the cross in a Birmingham mass meeting that echoed the gospel song "Were You There When They Crucified My Lord" (BCRI-Meetings, CD VI, side 2; in a few places the words are difficult to decipher). "I'm feeling better tonight because tomorrow I'm goin' to jail," Abernathy announced to the gathering, "tell Bull Connor to get the cell ready." Having established the context, Abernathy was ready to shift gears for the witness ahead. "We don't care what comes our way, it's not gonna stop us cause tomorrow is Good Friday." Then Abernathy continued with a declaration, "And I'm thinkin' about a man," which alerted the audience to a preaching frame. As he found his rhythm, each of Abernathy's gently rocking, wave-like phrases was met by the sound of the audience's assent:

> Somebody here ought to know what I'm talking about.
> Thinkin' about a man one day
> who stooped down at the foot of the mountain
> and took a cross on his shoulder
> and tuggle it up the rugged brow of God's
>   [undecipherable word] hills.
> And it got heavy,
> and sweat-like drops of blood ran down,
> but he never said a mumblin' word.
> Went on up the hill with the cross on his shoulder,
> And when he got up on top of the hill,
> they drove spikes in his hands,
> they drove nails in his feet,
> they pierced him in the side,
> they spat in his face,
> they placed a thorny crown on his head.
> And it got so dark
> that at 3 o'clock in the afternoon,

the chickens went to the roostin' pole.
The world reeled and rocked like a guilty man
And he cried out,
"My God, my God,
why hath thou forsaken me?"
And had not a tomb to be buried in
But somebody always cares,
For Joseph begged his body,
and laid it in the tomb,
to put the seal of the government on the tomb
and he stayed there all Friday night.
It was dark and lonely Friday night.

Abernathy chronicled how Peter and James and John wandered off, he took the audience through the darkness of Saturday, the wrestling in hell with the devil, took them right on through to Sunday when "my God got up" and the stone rolled away. "When God gets ready to move, no man can stop him. When God gets ready to move, the dogs can't stop him. And said, 'All power in heaven and earth is in my hands.'"

Go tell my disciples,
Go tell Martin Luther King,
Go tell Ralph Abernathy,
To meet us in Galilee,
I'll be there on tomorrow morning
Will you be there?

4. As Eugene Genovese observed, in the slave's mind "Moses had become Jesus, and Jesus, Moses; and with their union the two aspects of the slaves' religious quest—collective deliverance as a people and redemption from their terrible personal sufferings—had become one through the mediation of the imaginative power so beautifully manifested in the spirituals." Eugene D. Genovese, *Roll, Jordan, Roll: The World the Slaves Made* (New York: Vintage, 1976 [1972]), 253.

5. "A Challenge to the Churches and Synagogues," revised published version of King's address at the National Conference on Religion and Race, Chicago, Jan. 17, 1963, in Mathew Ahmann, ed., *Race: Challenge to Religion; Original Essays and An Appeal to the Conscience from the National Conference on Religion and Race* (Chicago: Henry Regnery, 1963), 155–170.

6. Miller, *Voice of Deliverance,* 175.

7. "Address at the Conclusion of the Selma to Montgomery March."
8. *Watters, Down to Now,* 198. It's fair to glimpse in the salt march and biblical "miracles" the common logic of rare but sensational events that trumpet the possibility of victory against all odds. From Daniel in the Lion's Den to the Hebrew children in the fiery furnace, a vast store of biblical precedents of deliverance offered empirical instances of the triumph of the weak over the strong and reversals like "the last shall be first."

   This dynamic clearly resembles the one social psychologists call the availability heuristic, in which rational individuals mistake rare but riveting events as signs of larger trends. Movement speakers had to compensate for the failure of listeners to discern those rare precedents. Framing here took the form of highlighting the existence of such precedents, suggesting their relevance to contemporary struggle, and thereby making them more "available." In the context of cajoling people to protest, such distorted, imperfect, and hardly representative information might prove functional.

   If attribution errors like blaming one's woes on oneself rather than the system often discourage collective action, focusing on miraculous or implausible precedents encouraged the belief in political opportunities. No matter how much opportunities were shaped by larger structural forces, ordinary people had to perceive those opportunities, and perceive them as realistic, for opportunity to play its mobilizing role. In this respect, the master frame of biblical stories provided the resonance that shaped responsiveness to King's more specific efforts to frame reward and punishment, risk and likely success. See William Gamson and David S. Meyer, "Framing Political Opportunity," in McAdam, McCarthy, and Zald, eds., *Comparative Perspectives on Social Movements,* 285.
9. "Address at the Conclusion of the Selma to Montgomery March."
10. Ibid.
11. "Lest We Forget 2: Birmingham, Alabama, 1963."
12. Audio tape of mass meeting, Montgomery, Alabama, Feb. 17, 1968, MLK-Atlanta.
13. Again, it is worth mentioning that my main concern is not with the reception of King's language. Although the precise impact of such language, as well as something as mysterious as "extraverbal thrust," on those who heard it is hard to gauge, it is also hard to resist the testimony of countless people who experienced the electrifying impact of the vividness of King's performance and the added emotional kick his appeals gave them.
14. As many studies of social movements have stressed, people's hunches about

payoff play a key role in spurring social movement participation. The point here is that King supplemented such estimations of risk and reward with intimations of them too.

15. Watters, *Down to Now,* 279.
16. Ibid., 199–200.
17. Audio tape of sermon "Judges 16:23–25," Rev. Johnny Ray Youngblood, Saint Paul Community Baptist Church, Brooklyn, New York, May 3, 1992, 8 A.M.
18. Watters, *Down to Now,* 199; "Address at the Conclusion of the Selma to Montgomery March."
19. Charles E. Fager, *Selma, 1965* (New York: Charles Scribner, 1974), 83.
20. Ibid., 85; cited in Branch, *At Canaan's Edge,* 24. The quote is from the *New York Times.*
21. Branch, *At Canaan's Edge,* 24; Fager, *Selma,* 85.
22. Garrow, *Bearing the Cross,* 394.
23. "Address at the Conclusion of the Selma to Montgomery March."
24. BPL-Selma, CD "MLK Tapes 2 & 3."
25. Ibid.
26. "I've Been to the Mountaintop."

13. The Courage to Be

1. Doug McAdam, *Political Process and the Development of Black Insurgency, 1930–1970* (Chicago: University of Chicago Press, 1982), 48–51.
2. Charles Payne's fine account of local organizing efforts in Mississippi also underscores this emotive dimension, as well as others. See his analysis of the range of dynamics beyond the cognitive at work in the mass meetings: Payne, *I've Got the Light of Freedom,* 256–264.
3. MLK Papers, Volume IV, 332–333; *Stride toward Freedom,* 211–212.
4. BCRI-Meetings, CD V, side 1.
5. Ibid., CD VI, side 1.
6. Watters, *Down to Now,* 198.
7. Ibid., 198–199.
8. Samuel G. Freedman provides a powerful glimpse into this Christian appropriation of the idiom of therapeutic recovery in *Upon This Rock: The Miracles of a Black Church* (New York: HarperCollins, 1993).
9. BPL-Selma, CD "Tapes 6 & 7."
10. Ibid.
11. "Lest We Forget 2: Birmingham, Ala., 1963."

12. *Stride toward Freedom,* 161.

13. BCRI-Meetings, CD IV, side 1.

14. BPL-Selma, CD "MLK Tapes 2 & 3"; Fager, *Selma,* 44–45.

15. Watters, *Down to Now,* 287.

16. Quoted in Fager, *Selma, 1965,* 103.

17. Jack Katz, *Seductions of Crime: Moral and Sensual Attractions in Doing Evil* (New York: Basic Books, 1988), 80–113. Katz's description of the moral logic of the badass might be applied to King if one simply changes the word "violence" to "nonviolence." The badass "must seem prepared to use violence, not only in a utilitarian, instrumental fashion but as a means to ensure the predominance of his meaning, . . . To make clear that 'he means it,' the badass celebrates a commitment to violence beyond any reason comprehensible to others" (100); author's interview with Rev. C. T. Vivian, May 11, 2005.

18. Branch, *At Canaan's Edge,* 719; audio tape of "Where Do We Go From Here?" address to the eleventh annual convention of SCLC, Atlanta, Georgia, Aug. 16, 1967, in *Call to Conscience*/IPM–Time Warner AudioBooks.

19. "Address at the Conclusion of the Selma to Montgomery March."

20. Watters, *Down to Now,* 197–200.

21. "Address at the Conclusion of the Selma to Montgomery March."

22. Author's interview with Rev. Willie Bolden, May 12, 2005.

23. BCRI-Meetings, CD VII, side 1.

24. BPL-Selma, CD "MLK tapes 2 & 3."

25. The parallel with rhythm and blues is again striking. Once more, common generic forms like imploring could be applied to religious, political, or romantic contexts. "I'm so weak, help me somebody," is James Brown's lacerating cry on "Lost Someone" when his love interest rejects him.

26. Audio tape, "Story of Greenwood, Mississippi," Smithsonian Folkways Records, 1965.

27. As Jon Michael Spencer observes, the oral tradition reworked the Charles Tindley gospel hymn "I'll Overcome Someday" in a number of ways. Most critical was the shift from first person singular to first person plural. "Traditionally 'I' had a communal aspect in black musical culture. . . . The collective language of the freedom songs, a trait of abolitionist and Social Gospel hymnody as well, fostered the needed sense of community." At the same time, freedom singing effected an even more fundamental change on gospel music that brought it into alignment with the this-worldly emphasis of the spirituals. "No longer are Christians enjoined to turn heavenward from hatred, sadness, madness, and confusion. . . . Rather than being the Ultimate

Alternative to the world, the Lord is the Ultimate Source of its transformation." In this way, freedom singing falls under Spencer's rubric of "the conversionist or 'Christ the Transformer of Culture' type." *Protest and Praise,* 84–85; 218–219.

28. Watters, *Down to Now,* 55.
29. "The Three Dimensions of a Complete Life"; "Why Jesus Called a Man a Fool."
30. BPL-Selma, CD "Tapes 2 & 3."
31. Audio tape of "Address to the First Mass Meeting of the Montgomery Improvement Association (MIA) Mass Meeting."
32. Cited in Lischer, *The Preacher King,* 183.
33. Andrew Young, *A Way Out of No Way: The Spiritual Memoirs of Andrew Young* (Nashville: Thomas Nelson, 1994), 92–94.

14. Free Riders and Freedom Riders

1. As shrewd as they may be, free riders thus raise charged ethical questions of distributive justice, for they do not shoulder a fair share of collective burdens even as they consume unfair helpings of collective goods.
2. Albert O. Hirschman, *Shifting Involvements: Private Interest and Public Action* (Princeton, N.J.: Princeton University Press, 1982), 9–14.
3. Abernathy, *And the Walls Came Tumbling Down,* 152; Lewis, *Walking with the Wind,* 362.
4. David L. Chappell, *A Stone of Hope: Prophetic Religion and the Death of Jim Crow* (Chapel Hill, N.C.: University of North Carolina Press, 2004).
5. Eskew, *But for Birmingham,* 228.
6. Walter Kaufmann, *Nietzsche: Philosopher, Psychologist, Antichrist* (New York: Random House, 1968), 371.
7. James Farmer, *Lay Bare the Heart: An Autobiography of the Civil Rights Movement* (Fort Worth, Tex.: Texas Christian University Press, 1986 [1985]), 203; 7; 21.
8. Glenn T. Eskew, "The Alabama Christian Movement for Human Rights and the Birmingham Struggle for Civil Rights, 1956–1963," in David J. Garrow, ed., *Martin Luther King, Jr. and the Civil Rights Movement* (Brooklyn, N.Y.: Carlson, 1989), 60.
9. Farmer, *Lay Bare the Heart,* 205.
10. Morris, *Origins of the Civil Rights Movement,* 72.
11. Lewis, *Walking with the Wind,* 122.
12. In Hirschman's terms, all of King's efforts to spiritualize the material may be

seen as efforts not just to change desire or preference but to change people's meta-preferences, their desires about their own desires. Hirschman's premise is that "people's critical appraisals of their own experiences and choices . . . [are] . . . important determinants of new and different choices. In this manner, human perception, self-perception, and interpretation should be accorded their proper weight in the unfolding of events." The emotional intensity of King's preachments about scarred souls and lives not worth living cannot disguise their philosophical content, and his audience's philosophical capacity which they presupposed, even if he translated that debate about the good and the true into commonsense terms. Hirschman notes the parallels between the pleasurable experiences of eating and drinking and the way people often speak about their efforts to fight for the common good—as when they are "thirsting for justice" or "craving for liberty." Hirschman, *Shifting Involvements,* 6; 90–91. As James Coleman might put it, free riders find a counterfoil in all those people who are graced with "excess zeal."

13. Watters, *Down to Now,* 287.
14. BPL-Selma, CD "MLK Tapes 6 & 7."
15. BCRI-Meetings, CD "King, Abernathy, Shuttlesworth, May 3, 1963 mass mtg. Sixteenth St. Bapt."; "Lest We Forget 2: Birmingham, Alabama, 1963."
16. Audio tape of mass meeting, Montgomery, Alabama, February 17, 1968, MLK-Atlanta.

Part IV. Crossing Over into Beloved Community

1. David Levering Lewis, *King: A Biography* (Urbana: University of Illinois Press, 1978), 252.
2. Young, *An Easy Burden,* 228.
3. Garrow, *Bearing the Cross,* 496–497.

15. Artifice and Authenticity

1. James Cone, "Black Theology—Black Church," *Theology Today,* vol. 40, no. 4 (Jan. 1984), 409–420; Keith D. Miller, "Martin Luther King, Jr., and the Black Folk Pulpit," *The Journal of American History* (June 1991), 121. There's an ironic convergence here between Cone and Miller: despite their rival takes on the link between race and authentic voice, both view King's borrowing from white sources as governed by the motive of pleasing or deferring to whites.
2. "From Marcus Garvey Wood," Feb. 16, 1956, *The Papers of Martin Luther*

King, Jr., Volume III: *Birth of a New Age, December 1955–December 1956;* Senior Editor: Clayborne Carson; Volume Editors: Stewart Burns, Susan Carson, Peter Holloran, and Dana L. H. Powell (Berkeley: University of California Press, 1997), 130. Hereafter cited as MLK Papers, Volume III.

3. As Miller put it, "King consistently rejected white Protestants' deep and unresolved ambivalence about homiletic borrowing." In contrast to the print-based notion that views "language as private property to be copyrighted, packaged, and sold as a commodity," King affirmed the folk pulpit's oral conventions and "resisted academic commandments about language." Miller, "Martin Luther King, Jr., and the Black Folk Pulpit," 121; Wyatt Tee Walker, quoted in Lischer, *The Preacher King,* 75.

4. David Levering Lewis, "Failing to Know Martin Luther King, Jr.," *The Journal of American History* (June 1991), 82, 85.

5. David Garrow, "King's Plagiarism: Imitation, Insecurity, and Transformation," *The Journal of American History* (June 1991), 89–90.

6. "From Melvin Arnold," May 5, 1958, *The Papers of Martin Luther King, Jr.,* Volume IV: *Symbol of the Movement, January 1957–December 1958;* Senior Editor: Clayborne Carson; Volume Editors: Susan Carson, Adrienne Clay, Virginia Shadron, and Kieran Taylor (Berkeley: University of California Press, 2000), 405. Hereafter cited as MLK Papers, Volume IV.

7. *The Papers of Martin Luther King, Jr.,* Volume VI: *Advocate of the Social Gospel, September 1948–March 1963;* Senior Editor: Clayborne Carson; Volume Editors: Susan Carson, Susan Englander, Troy Jackson, and Gerald L. Smith (Berkeley: University of California Press, 2007), 41. Hereafter cited as MLK Papers, Volume VI.

8. S. Jonathan Bass, *Blessed are the Peacemakers: Martin Luther King Jr., Eight White Religious Leaders and the "Letter from Birmingham Jail"* (Baton Rouge: Louisiana State University Press, 2001), 136.

9. *Stride toward Freedom,* 97.

10. Garrow, *Bearing the Cross,* 41.

11. "From George D. Kelsey," April 4, 1958, MLK Papers, Volume IV, 395.

12. "From Hilda Proctor," May 22, 1959, *The Papers of Martin Luther King, Jr.,* Volume V: *Threshold of a New Decade, January 1959–December 1960;* Senior Editor: Clayborne Carson; Volume Editors: Tenisha Armstrong, Susan Carson, Adrienne Clay, and Kieran Taylor (Berkeley: University of California Press, 2005), 213. Hereafter cited as MLK Papers, Volume V. Aldon Morris points to a more complex reality that at once credits Smiley and vindicates Proctor's point.

13. Fairclough, *To Redeem the Soul of America,* 25; quoted in John D'Emilio, *Lost Prophet: The Life and Times of Bayard Rustin* (New York: Free Press, 2003), 230.

14. Burns, *To the Mountaintop,* 82; MLK Papers, Volume III, 125.

15. The same mix of spontaneity and guile characterized King's books and speeches directed at whites. King's voice was so powerful that it managed to break through the self-conscious and deadly passages. Signature phrases from his most heartfelt preaching and exhorting before black audiences find their way into the trade books. Every so often, King's prose falls into the identifiable rhythm of his oral performance.

16. At one point, the FBI agents wiretapped King warning Levison, "I would just check on that thing about a majority and bout that thing where you talked about France and where you said 'Total Victory'; maybe you should say 'Total Military Victory.' Levison answers back, "Right." King-Levison phone discussion, April 13, 1967, Federal Government Freedom of Information Act Releases, U.S. Federal Bureau of Investigation, 100-111180 Stanley Levison, sub-file 9, vol. 8; Drew D. Hansen, *The Dream: Martin Luther King, Jr., and the Speech that Inspired a Nation* (New York: HarperCollins, 2003), 68.

17. Nick Kotz, *Judgment Days,* 373.

18. CD recording of "Beyond Vietnam," delivered at Riverside Church, New York City, April 4, 1967, in *Call to Conscience*/IPM–Time Warner AudioBooks.

19. Ibid.

20. Nick Kotz, *Judgment Days,* 375. Even Stanley Levison told King that the speech was "intemperate."

21. Jervis Anderson, *Bayard Rustin: Troubles I've Seen* (New York: HarperCollins, 1997), 206–207.

22. King-Levison phone discussion, April 13, 1967. Such trading places could also work in reverse. One can't always be sure in King's appearances before Jewish audiences if the amanuensis Levison was speaking through him, or even Clarence Jones, a lawyer who worked with Levison on early drafts of the March on Washington speech, knew the Jewish community, and scripted some of King's Jewish speeches. At the same time, it will be clear, over time King's leaps into the Jewish imagination moved from studied to seamless.

23. Garrow, *Bearing the Cross,* 649, note 2.

24. Lewis, *King,* 96.

25. Bennett, *What Manner of Man,* 101, 104.

26. We return once more to the same methodological dilemma we have confronted in so many different aspects of King's life. To ignore the power of "outside" ideas, experiences, and idioms requires a single-minded reduction of all interesting questions to the racial one of whether the black or the white influences were greater. At a certain point, the straining to diminish such rival influences becomes as strained and suspect as King's borrowings were alleged to be.

27. "Palm Sunday Sermon on Mohandas K. Gandhi," Dexter Avenue Baptist Church, March 22, 1959, MLK Papers, Volume V, 145–157.

16. Practicing What You Preach

1. The observation was made by Atlantic Records producer Jerry Wexler. Quoted in Peter Guralnick, *Sweet Soul Music: Rhythm and Blues and the Southern Dream of Freedom* (Boston: Little, Brown, 1999 [1986]), 214.

2. Garrow, *Bearing the Cross,* 707, note 11.

3. Watters, *Down to Now,* 176; James Brown, with Bruce Tucker, *James Brown: The Godfather of Soul* (New York: Thunder's Mouth Press, 1997 [1986]), 64; Mel Watkins, "The Way it Was," *CommonQuest: The Magazine of Black-Jewish Relations,* vol. 3, no.3/vol.4/no.1, 25.

4. Etta James with David Ritz, *Rage to Survive: The Etta James Story* (Cambridge, Mass.: Da Capo Press, 2003 [1995]), 47; Brown, *James Brown,* 12.

5. Birmingham Police Department report, Feb. 27, 1962, Birmingham Public Library, Birmingham, Alabama, Eugene "Bull" Connor Papers, Alabama Christian Movement for Human Rights, 13.1.

6. Branch, *Pillar of Fire,* 354.

7. Lewis, *Walking with the Wind,* 91.

8. This was the practical foundation of the crossover endeavor. Just as *brotherhood* was rooted in King's black relations, brotherhood was equally grounded in the concrete relationships King developed with whites and white organizations.

9. This paragraph and the next one owe much to Miller, *Voice of Deliverance.*

10. MLK Papers, Volume VI, 411–415; 425.

11. Miller, *Voice of Deliverance,* 191–192.

12. MLK Papers, Volume VI, 342, note 20; 177; 371. King, who once described his compositional priority as first choosing the "landing strip" of a sermon, noted in his copy of Fosdick's *Riverside Sermons,* "Close by showing that religion does not clear up all the answers. At the heart of our religion is

the deepest mystery of all, the cross, where love was nailed to a tree by hate." Ibid., 348.

13. Miller, *Voice of Deliverance*, 191.

14. Peter Guralnick, *Last Train to Memphis: The Rise of Elvis Presley* (Boston: Little, Brown, 1994), 75; 60.

15. Gardner Taylor, "There is Power in That Cross," delivered at the annual convention of American Baptists, Denver, Colorado, May 1953, in Taylor, *The Words of Gardner Taylor, Volume 4*, 31, 32–33; Benjamin Mays, quoted in Mark Chapman, "'Of One Blood': Mays and the Theology of Race Relations," in Lawrence Edward Carter Sr., ed., *Walking Integrity: Benjamin Elijah Mays, Mentor to Martin Luther King, Jr.* (Macon, Ga.: Mercer University Press, 1998), 248.

16. "We are tied together": quoted in Chapman, "'Of One Blood'"; "The chief sin": MLK Papers, Volume VI, 323. According to Ralph Abernathy, Benjamin Mays's wife was annoyed that King didn't credit her husband for all the ideas King had imbibed from him. "It wasn't exactly plagiarism, she said, but it wasn't quite honest either. 'That was Benny's idea,' she would say. 'Why won't Martin just say so.'" *And the Walls Came Tumbling Down*, 480.

17. Benjamin Mays, *Born to Rebel: An Autobiography* (Athens, Ga.: University of Georgia Press, 2003 [1971]), 14.

18. Randall M. Jelks, "Mays's Academic Formation, 1917–1936," in Carter, ed., *Walking Integrity*, 118.

19. These markers only hint at the full range of metaphysical and practical connections that fashioned this theological alliance, as Miller has shown. They included Buttrick's biweekly lunches with Harlem preachers when he was ensconced in a Madison Avenue pulpit and, when he was at Harvard, his annual swapping of pulpits with Howard Thurman, who was across the river at Boston University's Marsh Chapel.

20. The phrase is from John Cuddihy's classic *No Offense: Civil Religion and Protestant Taste* (New York: Seabury Press, 1978).

21. Howard Thurman, *Jesus and the Disinherited* (Boston: Beacon Press, 1996 [1949]), 90–91. Once again, the boundaries of race blurred in complex ways here. If King owed much to George Buttrick's formulation of the Samaritan in *The Parables of Jesus*, Thurman also saw the Samaritan's grace in racial terms as a direct response "to human need across the barriers of class, race, and condition."

22. Ibid., 50.

23. "The Christian Doctrine of Man," Sermon Delivered at the Detroit Council of Churches' Noon Lenten Services, Detroit, March 12, 1958, MLK Papers, Volume VI, 337.
24. Ibid., 337.
25. *Strength to Love* (Philadelphia: Fortress Press, 1988 [1963]), 91; 92; 92; 95.
26. Hasia Diner, "Trading Faces," *CommonQuest,* vol. 2, no. 1 (Summer 1997), 43.
27. Melissa Fay Greene, "Civil Rights and the Pulpit," *CommonQuest: The Magazine of Black-Jewish Relations* (Spring 1996), 47, 49.
28. Melissa Fay Greene, *The Temple Bombing* (Reading, Mass.: Addison-Wesley, 1996), 382–383.
29. Ibid., 383.
30. Ibid., 422.
31. Andre Ungar, "To Birmingham and Back," quoted in Schneier, *Shared Dreams,* 89; Richard L. Rubenstein, "The Rabbis Visit Birmingham," *The Reconstructionist,* May 31, 1963.
32. Ursula M. Niebuhr, "Notes on a Friendship: Abraham Joshua Heschel and Reinhold Niebuhr," in John C. Merkle, ed., *Abraham Joshua Heschel: Exploring His Life and Thought* (New York: MacMillan, 1985), 37.
33. The speeches of Heschel and King at this conference were published as the essays from which the quotes are derived. Dr. Abraham J. Heschel, "The Religious Basis of Equality of Opportunity—The Segregation of God," in Ahmann, ed., *Race: Challenge to Religion,* 55–72. King's remarks were published in the same volume as "A Challenge to the Churches and Synagogues," ibid., 155–170.
34. Heschel, *The Wisdom of Heschel,* 296.
35. Quoted in Susannah Heschel, "Praying with their Feet: Remembering Abraham Joshua Heschel and Martin Luther King," *www.peaceworkmagazine.org/node/393.* One Saturday night at the end of the Sabbath ceremony, Heschel apparently answered his doorbell only to discover King and the minister William Sloane Coffin outside. Before long, King and Coffin were taking part in *havdalah,* the candle lighting that concludes the Sabbath. Afterwards, Heschel told an allegory about human growth, reflecting on Moses after he assumed the leadership of his people. "The reference could not be lost on anyone in that room—they were in the presence of a new Moses, one who had come from Georgia, not from the wilderness of Sinai." Schneier, *Shared Dreams,* 140–141.
36. MLK Papers, Volume VI, 33.
37. Author's interview with Susannah Heschel, April 20, 2007.

17. Validating the Movement

1. MLK Papers, Volume VI, 33.

2. James Cone grasped this practical impulse at work in guiding King's choice of code in his crossover addresses. Although I've already pointed to flaws in Cone's larger argument, he did understand well the critical impact of the occasion-defined purposes on King's rhetoric. In addition to the problems I identified earlier, it is relevant to mention additional ones in this context. Cone radically overstated the generic white appetite for fancy theological language, missing the extent to which King relied on substantive arguments, everyday notions of fairness, appeals to shared sentiments, displays of empathy, and voyages into the imaginative universe of his target audience, as well as invocations of black experience and sources.

3. "If the Negro Wins, Labor Wins." Address to the Fourth Constitutional Convention of the American Federation of Labor–Congress of Industrial Organizations, Bal Harbour, Florida, Dec. 11, 1961. In Washington, *A Testament of Hope,* 201–202.

4. Ibid., 202.

5. "The Death of Evil Upon the Seashore," in Martin Luther King, Jr., *Strength to Love* (Philadelphia: Fortress Press, 1981 [1963]), 77.

6. "On Being a Good Neighbor," in *Strength to Love,* 26–35. This rejection of the ethic of clan and tribe was equally a rejection of the classical stuff of one version of American political culture, with its defense of property and the lone individual. Heralding instead the fullness of the individual in a context of Christian love, King put forth an essentially "feminine" political culture of connection and care.

7. MLK Papers, Volume VI, 332.

8. King, *Strength to Love,* 100.

9. Milton Himmelfarb, "Jewish Class Conflict," in *Overcoming Middle-Class Rage,* ed. Murray Friedman (Philadelphia: Westminster Press, 1971), 205.

10. Address to the American Jewish Congress National Biennial Convention, Miami Beach, Florida, May 14, 1958. MLK Papers, Volume IV, 406–410.

11. Recording of King's address to the American Jewish Committee (AJC), May 20, 1965, on the occasion of accepting the AJC American Liberties Medallion. CD, "The Rev. Dr. Martin Luther King, Jr.: In Search of Freedom" (New York: PolyGram Records, 1995).

12. This is why the tracing of King's sources, as valuable as it may be, at a certain point devolves into obsessive fussing. King always cared more about content than code, and he never wavered on the principled clarity of his

goal: to free his people. Homing in on common phrases, identities, metaphors, lyrics, and formulas and lifting them out of the entire process of legitimation obscures their context-laden meaning in a glut of detail.

13. "Letter from Birmingham Jail," in Washington, ed., *Testament of Hope*, 289–302. Hereafter, all references are to this source.

14. "The Death of Evil Upon the Seashore."

15. "Paul's Letter to American Christians," delivered to the Commission on Ecumenical Missions and Relations, United Presbyterian Church, U.S.A., June 3, 1958, in MLK Papers, Volume VI, 342–343.

16. Audio tape of the sermon "Remaining Awake Through a Great Revolution," the National Cathedral, Washington, D.C., March 31, 1968, in *Knock at Midnight*/IPM–Time Warner AudioBooks.

17. Ibid.

18. Audio tape of the speech "I Have a Dream," in *Call to Conscience*/IPM–Time Warner AudioBooks.

19. "Letter from Birmingham Jail."

20. "The Death of Evil Upon the Seashore."

21. "If the Negro Wins, Labor Wins," in Washington, ed., *Testament of Hope*, 206.

22. Ibid.

23. Ibid., 206–207.

24. Michael Walzer, *Interpretation and Social Criticism* (Cambridge, Mass.: Harvard University Press, 1987).

25. The fine phrase is August Meier's. See his "The Conservative Militant," in C. Eric Lincoln, ed., *Martin Luther King, Jr.: A Profile* (New York: Hill and Wang, 1984).

26. Quoted in Schneier, *Shared Dreams*, 90.

27. "Letter from Birmingham Jail."

18. The Allure of Rudeness

1. *Stride toward Freedom*, 15.

2. Lischer, *The Preacher King*, 74–75.

3. Abernathy, *And the Walls Came Tumbling Down*, 125; "Lord, that food": Branch, *Parting the Waters*, 106; "Martin, you don't want to go": quoted in Vaughn, ed., *Reflections on Our Pastor*, 3.

4. Abernathy, *And the Walls Came Tumbling Down*, 143.

5. *Stride toward Freedom*, 136, 139.

6. Ibid., 215.

7. *Stride toward Freedom,* 102; "Loving Your Enemies," in *Strength to Love,* 49. As we saw in earlier chapters, King's ability to rise above immediate emotion through forgiveness and understanding reflected a broader strategy of sublimation. Reflecting the parallel functions of secular psychology and Christian theology in face-to-face interaction, King entwined the two in a Dexter sermon that explained the concept of sublimation, which he linked directly to Christ's ethos of forgiveness. "But all of the psychologists tell us that it's dangerous to repress our emotions, that we must always keep them on the forefront of consciousness. And we must do something else—not repress but sublimate. . . . But religion gives you the art of sublimation, and so you don't repress your emotions, you substitute the positive for the negative of repression." King goes on to quote Jesus telling a woman, "Don't get bogged down in the path and worry because you've committed adultery. Everybody has committed it, but turn around into the future and move on out, and you will become somebody because you have accepted my grace and my forgiving power." "Living under the Tensions of Modern Life," Dexter Baptist Church, Montgomery, Alabama, Sept. 1956, MLK Papers, Volume VI, 267.
8. Ibid., 139; 102–103.
9. Ibid., 137–138.
10. Most of the maneuvers we have been considering thus conform to the logic behind what Erving Goffman calls "face work" and the corrective actions that uphold the ritual order of face-to-face interaction. Yet if that was all King was doing, his larger ideological insistence on justice would seem paradoxically at odds with his micro-practice, in which he appeared to trade fairness for face.
11. *Stride toward Freedom,* 87, 164; *Why We Can't Wait,* 537. The formalization of taboos on rude language, like the broader set of guidelines for correct behavior, again signified movement tough-mindedness. Far from ethereal idealism, King's stance was a hardheaded recognition of the difficulty of sublimation. To love those who have spitefully used you was easier in theory than in practice, even for ministers of the Gospel. Movement training exercises reinforced such edicts with practical dicta and anticipatory rehearsal.
12. King's musings implied a particular stance toward racial exchange. A violation of the dire "tit-for-tat" of revenge, trading love for a racist epithet might seem one-sided, even perverse. To love thugs who killed little black children pushed to their limit the ideals of mercy or "walking the extra mile," commonly sanctioned departures from reciprocity. Still, King knew that his less than conventional idea of sublime exchange required ideological work, both to enact in practice and to convince others to try it.

13. *Stride toward Freedom,* 136–137.
14. *Where Do We Go From Here?,* 573–574.
15. *Stride toward Freedom,* 150.
16. Ibid., 105; "Testament of Hope," in Washington, ed., *A Testament of Hope,* 323. To the extent that boastful claims transgress the rules of etiquette that restrain self-exaltation, the entire meaning system of black Christian exceptionalism could be placed under the larger category of rudeness.
17. This and the following quotes are from "Letter from Birmingham Jail."
18. Bass, *Blessed Are the Peacemakers,* 76–77.

19. Black Interludes in the Crossover Moment

1. *Where Do We Go From Here?,* in Washington, ed., *A Testament of Hope,* 575.
2. Ibid., 575.
3. Ibid.
4. Ibid.
5. Ibid., 576.
6. Ibid.
7. Ibid., 577.
8. "Remaining Awake Through a Great Revolution."
9. *Stride toward Freedom,* 129; 161.
10. Ibid., 149.
11. "Letter from Birmingham Jail," in Washington, ed., *A Testament of Hope.* Subsequent quotes are from this source.
12. BCRI-Meetings, CD III, side 1.
13. Audio tape of the speech "I Have a Dream," in *Call to Conscience*/IPM– Time Warner AudioBooks. Subsequent quotes are from this source.
14. Branch, *Parting the Waters,* 881.
15. Audio tape of "Address at the Freedom Rally in Cobo Hall," Detroit, Michigan, June 23, 1963, in *Call to Conscience*/IPM–Time Warner AudioBooks.
16. John Lewis told me this story, which he reported in his autobiography. Taylor Branch also mentions it.
17. *Where Do We Go From Here?,* 588.
18. Quoted in Spencer, *Protest and Praise,* 99.
19. *Where Do We Go From Here?,* 570.
20. Audio tape of the speech "America is Sick," Address to the California Democratic Party, 1968. MLK-Howard.

Index

Abernathy, Juanita, 304

Abernathy, Rev. Ralph, 35, 40, 77, 93, 97; back talk and, 230; burlesque in speeches of, 221; on Clark's police brutality, 240; confrontations with racist hatred, 65; on Dexter Avenue congregation, 94; Exodus invoked by, 200–201; FBI tapes of King and, 55; on God's movement, 196–197; in jail with King, 194, 210; in King's inner circle, 51; King's joking and teasing with, 56, 58, 282; on King's Nobel Prize, 165; King's speech in Memphis and, 216; at mass meetings with King, 155–156; Montgomery bus boycott and, 153, 154, 158–159, 214, 304–305; on nonviolence, 43–44; on Poor People's Campaign, 174; preaching and singing, 227–228; on rationalism in the pulpit, 146; on risks of action, 239; Selma protest and, 171; sermons rehearsed with King, 82; on sources for King's sermons, 96; on "Uncle Toms," 188–189

Abolitionists, nineteenth-century, 42

Adams, Russell, 24–25, 100, 101

Africa, 106, 110, 170; Algeria, 227; Ghana, 94, 95, 105–107, 112, 336; humanitarian aid to, 117; return to, 113, 230

Agape (spiritualized love), 9, 32–33, 96, 103, 157, 273; Jesus and, 191; King as apostle of, 1; levels of love and, 116; manly defiance and, 225

Alpha Phi Alpha, 18

"America is Sick" (King speech), 335

American Dream, 129–130, 295, 330

American Indians, 5, 148, 168, 170, 172, 230

American Jewish Committee, 290, 292, 297

American Jewish Congress, 25, 280

Amos (biblical prophet), 80, 154, 203, 333; as extremist for justice, 316; on justice and righteousness, 283, 294, 332

Anderson, Marian, 22, 100, 125

Anthropology, 96, 239, 314

Anti-Semitism, 47, 59, 275

Apocalyptic visions, 124

Atkinson, Max, 160, 161

Atlanta, 13, 24, 27, 63, 285; *Atlanta Constitution,* 35; Auburn Avenue neighborhood, 18; Ebenezer Baptist Church, 76, 99; elite of, 281; Jewish temple bombed in, 280; King's departure from, 18, 21; King's home in, 61; SCLC in, 55

Augustine, Saint, 139, 296, 327

Authenticity, 7, 8, 250, 251

"Autobiography of Religious Development" (King), 30, 324

Back talk, 230

Baggett, James, 271

Baptists, 11, 68, 134, 170, 245, 275

Barbour, Rev. J. Pius, 26–27, 28, 31, 102, 103

Barnett, Gov. Ross, 37, 315–316

"Battle Hymn of the Republic," 137

Belafonte, Harry, 55–56, 58

Bennett, Lerone, 11, 76, 264

Bevel, Rev. James, 9, 48, 282–283; Children's Crusade and, 240; on confession of infidelities, 54; in King's inner circle, 51; King's opinion of, 61; mobilization of street-wise volunteers, 67; at Nashville sit-ins, 243–244; shock therapy style of preaching, 220–221; on social gospel, 198; street sensibility and, 66–67; on struggle against evil, 191–192; task of reassurance and, 210–211; use of "nigger" epithet, 57; womanizing of, 59

"Beyond Vietnam: A Time to Break Silence" (King), 261–262

Bible, 81, 84, 96, 230, 281; Acts, 210; Amos, 10; biblical stories in King's sermons, 137–138, 192; Corinthians, 204; Daniel, 244; Esther, 210; Hebrews, 144; Isaiah, 10; Judges, 209; Matthew, 144; Psalms, 283; Revelation, 84. *See also* Exodus

Billups, Rev. Charles, 271

Birmingham, Ala., 67, 189; boycott campaign in, 176, 184; Children's Crusade, 239–240; four little girls blown up in, 5, 211, 241; Six-teenth Street Baptist Church, 134, 152, 191, 224; white clergy of, 315, 325, 328; white racist police of, 36, 68, 312

Bitterness, 3, 6, 65, 331; Black Power and, 34, 318–319; channeled into higher purpose, 306; children and, 326; King's empathetic response to, 112; King tempted by, 305, 323–324; racial divide of Christian church and, 111; temptation of black rage and, 39

Black audiences, 7, 25, 30, 110, 177, 299; "black talk" and, 20; consoled and provoked, 251; cosmopolitan enlightenment and, 290; delight in erudite preaching, 102; idiom and, 9; immediacy of performance and, 91; King's constancy before, 89; King's self-disclosure reserved for, 120; sermons delivered to, 94, 96; on urban streets, 43–44

Black Belt, 9, 85, 163, 195, 321; King's tours through, 10, 78; Poor People's Campaign in, 166, 204; poverty in, 174

"Black is beautiful" slogan, 125

Black nationalism, 2, 6; Christian, 110; King criticized by, 32, 239; King in competition with, 239; rejection of King's "beloved community," 39; white audiences and, 8

Blackness, 3, 110, 266; authenticity and, 7, 8; "black talk" and, 18, 20; as *brother*hood, 124–125; as condition for belonging, 322; exclusion from, 238; high jinks and "cracking," 58; King as totemic exemplar of, 125; in King's speeches and writings, 112, 324–335; martial imagery and, 75; mass meetings and, 153, 157, 170; pariah identity and, 132; physical characteristics of, 42, 177–178, 190; primal bonds of, 32; racial pride and, 51, 92; racism as ancestral truth, 120; stereotype and, 135; universalism and, 18, 251; whites admitted to status of, 62–63

Black Power, 8, 41, 334; Jesse Jackson and, 222; King's criticism of, 309, 318–319, 325; March on Washington and, 329; multiple meanings of, 48–49; white interpretation of, 48, 116, 325

Blacks: Afro-American as hybrid identity, 334; black identity, 2, 20, 45, 118; "black" issues, 1, 36; labor of, 113–114; in poverty, 326; as soldiers in Vietnam, 320–321; suffering of, 300; theatrics of defiance, 51; as untouchables, 132

Blackstone Rangers (Chicago gang), 44, 65, 66

Bloody Sunday, in Selma, 64, 68, 153, 187, 210; encounter with pain in struggle and, 212; fortieth anniversary (2005), 193; media coverage of, 240; protesters and power of God during, 234

Blues (musical idiom), 12, 99, 102, 108, 268, 270, 274, 279, 303

Bolden, Willie, 66, 67–68, 69, 242; crowds prepared for King appearance, 229–230, 277; first meeting with King, 73–74; on King as athlete, 75; on morale of freedom songs, 185;

police violence against, 72–73; in St. Augustine, 235; violence suffered by, 210; vocation of suffering and, 71–72

Borders, Rev. William, 13, 94–95

Boston University Divinity School, 12, 25, 146; "Dialectical Society" at, 28–29, 34, 92; King's classmates at, 256

Branch, Ben, 231

Branch, Taylor, 27–28, 55, 62, 330

Brando, Marlon, 153

Brooks, Phillips, 8, 94, 293, 299

Brotherhood, 111, 266, 323; music and, 269; tension with *brother*hood, 20, 314; whites and, 19–20, 34, 47, 306

Brown, James, 43, 269, 270

Brown Chapel AME Church (Selma), 5, 152, 180

Bryant, William Cullen, 96, 322

Buber, Martin, 93, 133, 281, 291, 299, 327; on "I-thou" and "I-it" relationships, 118, 296; King's crossover talk and, 45; "Letter from Birmingham Jail" and, 189

Bunch (King's mother), 22

Burns, Stewart, 37

Buttrick, George, 10, 95, 99, 147, 272, 275; King's sermons and, 105; *Parables of Jesus,* 96, 273, 289

Call-and-shout, 231

Calvary Baptist Church (Chester, Pa.), 26, 27

Campbell, Rev. Lawrence, 185

Capitalism, 256, 257, 262

Carlyle, Thomas, 10, 155, 299, 322

Carmichael, Stokely, 41, 63, 309, 318, 319–320

Carson, Clayborne, 139

Cathedral of St. John the Divine (New York), 288, 293

Catholics, 4, 291, 329, 336

Chaney, James, 65, 69

Chappell, David, 239

Charles, Ray, 233, 268

Chess Records, 94

Chicago, 43–44, 48; gangs of, 65–66; Mount Pisgah Missionary Church, 125; New Covenant Baptist Church, 114; Sunday Evening Club, 272, 273, 275, 276, 286; white ethnic neighborhoods, 65

Children, racism and, 119–120, 326

Children's Crusade, 239–240

Christian Century (journal), 272

Christianity, 80, 98, 182–183; Afro-Baptist tradition, 7–8, 9; Afro-Christianity as religion of the oppressed, 206; black identity and, 50–51, 52–53; creed versus practice, 51; nonviolence and, 6; racism repudiated by, 290; soulless white Christianity, 273; stoicism and, 217; universal message of, 110. *See also* Catholics; Protestants; *specific churches*

Christianity Today (journal), 275

Christology, 96, 139, 144, 279

Civil religion, 2, 4, 168, 170, 201, 295

Civil Rights Act (1964), 181

Civil rights movement, 10, 40, 92, 176; Bloody Sunday in Selma and, 5; Exodus story and, 144; free riders and, 238; God's interest in, 125; labor unions and, 288; murders of civil rights workers, 65, 198, 245, 320; secular wing of, 146; "We Shall Overcome" anthem, 232, 234, 271; white appreciation of black culture and, 269

Clark, Ben, 133

Clark, Sheriff Jim, 36, 68, 171, 224–225, 229; black defiance of, 230, 319; interaction with protesters, 181; as pharaoh, 193, 196; restraint abandoned by, 240; violence by, 196, 210

Clark, Septima, 193

Class system, 115, 171, 298

Cobras (Chicago gang), 44, 66

Colonialism, 257

"Come by Here My Lord," 162, 163

Communism, 96, 262, 273

Community, beloved, 18, 19, 30, 50; as *brother*hood, 325; crossover task and, 285; race man sentiments and, 172; rejection of, 39, 43; whites and, 299, 308

Cone, James, 98–99, 102, 254

Confessions (Augustine), 139

Congregational Church, 52

Connor, Bull, 36, 67, 181, 188, 220, 315; black defiance of, 166, 230, 319; Children's Crusade and, 240; detectives sent to penetrate meetings, 153, 270–271; nonviolence as spiritual force against, 245–246; as pharaoh, 229, 231; police rampage in Birmingham and, 165; white clergy of Birmingham and, 328

Constitution, U.S., 288, 299

Cooper, Annie Lee, 171, 196, 224–225

Cotton, Dorothy, 67, 77, 240

Cowper, William, 42, 102, 125, 178

Crozer Theological Seminary, 12, 18, 23, 146; Barbour coterie at, 26; King's classmates, 56, 254–255; professors, 28, 30, 324

Cullen, Countee, 167, 321

"Daddy King." *See* King, Martin Luther, Sr. ("Daddy King")

Daniels, Jonathan, 320

Davis, George, 30, 324

Declaration of Independence, 168, 288, 299, 301, 322; "I Have a Dream" speech and, 295–296; Jefferson and, 113, 167

Deep River (Thurman), 277

Democracy, 192, 288, 294, 295, 298

Democratic Party, 251, 272, 335

DeWolfe, Harold, 29

Dexter Avenue Baptist Church (Montgomery), 14, 76, 304; congregation, 94, 103, 106, 107; King's preaching, 100, 104, 106, 107, 134, 265; King's sermons at, 98, 99, 117

"Dialectical Society," 28–29, 34, 92

Dialect speech, 2, 108, 127, 226; black folk preachers and, 100; of slaves, 154, 194

Dirty hands, dilemma of, 66, 69

Diwakar, Ranganath, 264

Dothard, William "Meatball," 224

"Dozens" ritual insults, 6, 60, 156

Dream, The (Hansen), 261

Dresner, Rabbi Israel, 271, 280

Du Bois, W. E. B., 326

Ebenezer Baptist Church (Atlanta), 7, 18, 34, 143, 322; congregation, 114; King as co-pastor, 76; King's training as preacher and, 11, 25, 30, 259; sermons at, 20, 79, 110

"Egyptians Dead Upon the Seashore" (Brooks sermon), 95

Eisendrath, Maurice, 280

Emancipation Proclamation, 169, 293, 296, 329

Episcopalians, 245, 288, 293

Eros ("aesthetic love"), 32, 33, 96, 103, 156, 273

Eschatology, 154, 201

Eskew, Glenn, 184–185, 240

Eskridge, Chauncey, 53, 54, 55

Eulogies, 3, 101–102, 284

Evans, Ahmed, 44–45

Evers, Medgar, 245

Evil, problem of, 206

Exile, black, 4, 170, 173, 322, 330, 335–336

Existential psychology and theology, 97, 141

Exodus (biblical narrative), 5, 8, 105, 107, 200–202, 288; conference on race and religion and, 282; Daddy King's preaching and, 94–95; deliverance as rational goal and, 200; empathy for suffering of others and, 300; faith in moral cosmos and, 207; freedom songs and, 196; invoked at mass meetings, 154; King's blackness and, 7; sacred and secular history in, 183; "Wade in the Water" spiritual, 181

Fager, Charles, 210–211, 224–225

Fairclough, Adam, 52, 66

Falwell, Jerry, 11, 187

Farmer, James, 242–243

Fauntroy, Rev. Walter, 51, 53, 54, 61, 89

FBI (Federal Bureau of Investigation), 45, 135, 256, 260–261; monitoring of mass rallies, 153; rumors about King's promiscuity, 77; telephone calls monitored by, 263; Willard Hotel tryst tapes, 62, 80

Fellowship of Reconciliation (FOR), 259

Forgiveness, 126, 171, 313

Forman, James, 240, 334

Fosdick, Harry Emerson, 2, 30, 99, 272, 275; King's sermons and, 105; on racism as denial of God, 276; sermons by, 13, 273

Franklin, Aretha, 333

Franklin, Reverend C. L., 12, 26, 88, 94, 188, 333

Freedom riders, 67, 77, 183, 221, 241, 242

Freedom songs, 162, 179, 185, 334; chorus of resolve, 228; "Oh Mary Don't You Weep, Don't You Moan," 200; "Over My Head I See Freedom," 196; powers of the self and, 219; "Wade in the Water," 200; white audiences and, 269. *See also* Spirituals

Freedom Summer, 69

Free riders, 237–238, 241

Frist, Sen. Bill, 5

Fulgham, John, 102–103

Gandhi, Mohandas K., 29, 39, 74; asceticism of, 264–265; caste system and, 119, 265; Howard University lecture on, 258–259; Jesus compared with, 260, 266–267; March to the Sea, 202, 222, 258; mission to free India, 170; themes of suffering and sacrifice, 263–264

Gangs, 44, 65

Garrow, David, 54, 75, 256, 268; on FBI campaign against King, 77; on King and Poor People's Campaign, 172; on "oratorical illusion," 241

Garvey, Marcus, 177

Genovese, Eugene, 126

George, Nelson, 269

Ghana (former Gold Coast), 94, 95, 105–107, 112, 336

Gingrich, Newt, 5

"Give Us the Ballot" (King speech), 262–263

God's Trombones (Johnson), 108

Goldman, Peter, 37

Goodman, Andrew, 65, 69

Good Samaritan, parable of, 147–148, 173, 289

Gordy, Berry, 50, 268

Gospel music, 12, 94, 187, 231, 303

Graetz, Rev. Robert, 224

Grafman, Rabbi Milton, 296, 300

Greene, Melissa Fay, 280

Guilt feelings, 97, 172, 238

Guralnick, Peter, 274

Habacca (biblical prophet), 208, 209, 212

"Hallelujah Chorus" (Handel), 141

Hamer, Fanny Lou, 196

Hamilton, J. Wallace, 272, 274

Hankerson, Lester, 66, 71, 72, 74

Hansen, Drew, 261

Hardin, Rev. Paul, 315

Harding, Vincent, 4

Harris, Rutha, 159

Healing, 140, 278, 313; "beloved community" and, 302; racial, 126, 131, 222; spiritual, 139–140

Hegel, G. W. F., 90, 118, 142, 256

Henley, William, 100

Heschel, Rabbi Abraham Joshua, 144–145, 149, 153, 260, 281–284

Heschel, Susannah, 284–285

Himmelfarb, Milton, 290

Hinduism, 98, 265

Hip-hop nation, 4, 6, 9, 269

Hirschman, Albert, 238

Holocaust, 291

Holt Street Church (Montgomery), 112, 154, 203

Homilies, 118, 131, 286; blackness and, 148; on tension between hope and despair, 140; transition to song, 137

Hooping, 88, 89, 99, 104, 145

Horns and Halos in Human Nature (Hamilton), 274

Houck, Tom, 58–59, 60, 63, 285

Howard University, 24, 52, 99, 258–259, 275

Hughes, Langston, 167, 261

Humanism, 4, 45, 57, 125, 157

Humor, 3, 50, 79, 144

Hymes, Dell, 3, 46

Hymns, 10, 12, 19, 162, 196

"I am Somebody" (Borders sermon), 13

Identity, racial, 4, 19, 41, 104, 178

Identity politics, 4, 277

Idiom, 3, 8, 108, 268; blackness and, 20; blend of styles and, 105; folk idiom in King's sermons, 95; Malcolm X and, 11; southern black, 56–57; switching of, 9

"I Have a Dream" (March on Washington) speech, 14, 22, 250, 261, 291, 310; African ancestors and, 107; blackness in, 9, 324–335; crossover talk and, 132; Declaration of Independence and, 295–296; dream transformed into nightmare, 20; homiletic reprise of, 118; Rabbi Prinz and, 291; veteran activists and, 332; vision of future in, 298; as "white" talk, 7

Imperialism, 83, 95

India, 2, 18, 264; homeless people of Calcutta, 148; struggle of American blacks and, 119; untouchable caste, 118, 132

Integration, racial, 6, 48, 250

Intermarriage, 34–35, 125

Isaiah (biblical prophet), 109, 255, 333

"I-thou" relationship, 108, 118, 296

"I've Been to the Mountaintop" speech, 79, 106, 160–161, 216–217, 245

Jackson, Jesse, 5, 11; "black talk" and, 19; "Hymie Town" remarks, 19, 47; King's opinion of, 61; street-wise persona, 222

Jackson, Jimmie Lee, 5, 38, 210, 320; funeral of, 211–212, 230; shooting of, 72, 73

Jackson, Mahalia, 12, 79, 330, 333

James, C. L. R., 8

Jefferson, Thomas, 10, 45, 113, 167, 168, 317

Jelks, Randall, 276

Jeremiads, 3, 133

Jeremiah (biblical prophet), 128, 176, 215

Jesus, 33, 80, 83, 115, 141, 172; apostles and, 84; commitment to justice and, 138; ethic of revenge rejected by, 258; as extremist, 327;

Jesus *(continued)*
"feminine" ethic of care, 64; as fighter, 191; Gandhi compared with, 258, 260, 264; God's love for humanity and, 147; gospel of freedom and, 296; Isaiah and, 255; King's Christmas sermon (1965) on, 145–146; language and message of, 96; levels of love and, 116; Moses commingled with, 201; nonviolence and, 39, 70; parables of, 95, 289; as prophet, 21, 28, 86; redemptive powers of, 140; Resurrection of, 107; suffering of, 98; universal God and, 148–149, 301; way to Calvary, 117

Jesus and the Disinherited (Thurman), 277–278

Jewish Theological Seminary, 282

Jews, 4, 10, 250, 267, 329, 336; Exodus narrative and, 7; Hebrew language, 279; Jackson's "Hymie Town" remarks and, 47; Jewish organizations, 2, 25; King's appeals to Jewish audiences, 256, 290–292; King's networks and, 272; Kol Nidre prayer, 279; Marx (Karl), 80; power as ethnic group, 42; rabbis, 144–145, 271, 280–285; southern, 287, 300; Soviet, 158, 291; suffering of, 300; tribal consciousness and, 117–118; Yiddish language, 46–47, 271, 279

Jim Crow system, 171, 194, 265, 269

Johns, Rev. Vernon, 13, 101, 255, 276, 304

Johnson, J. T., 66, 69, 74, 210, 277; on acceptance of nonviolence, 71; on King's playfulness, 70; violence suffered by, 242

Johnson, James Weldon, 2, 99–100, 108, 155, 202

Johnson, Lyndon, 1, 72, 211; civil rights bill and, 329; King's public rebuke of Vietnam War and, 261, 262; on telephone with King, 82; "We Shall Overcome" speech, 37–38, 64, 240, 320

Johnson, Mordecai, 13, 101, 108, 258

Jokes, 3, 6, 137, 239, 281–282, 305; ethnic humor and prejudice, 47; racial joshing within SCLC, 57, 58, 80

Jones, Charles, 40, 261

Jones, Clarence, 53, 54

Jones, E. Stanley, 272

Jordan, Richard, 134

Joshua (biblical), 2, 10, 194, 200, 204, 227

Judaism, 98, 125, 284; Conservative, 144, 260, 281; Reform, 271, 280

Juke joints, 40

Kaplan, Kivie, 52

Katz, Jack, 226, 242

Kaufmann, Walter, 241

"Keep Your Hand on the Gospel Plow" (hymn), 196

Keighton, Robert, 28

Kelly, Reverend C. W., 103

Kelsey, George, 30, 100, 259

Kennedy, John F., 37, 56, 241, 329–330

Kennedy, Robert, 234

King, Coretta Scott, 27, 55, 59, 76, 281; bombing of King house and, 305, 308; at Heschel's funeral, 284; Martin's courtship of, 92, 129; Martin's jailhouse letters to, 96, 154; on Martin's preaching, 91–92, 93–94

King, Martin Luther, Jr.: Afro-Baptist tradition and, 103, 265, 266; assassination, 1, 61, 216; back talk and, 230–231; biblical narratives used by, 193; biographers of, 27–28; Birmingham actions and, 184; black critics of, 36–37, 44, 62, 121; black nationalists and, 43–44; "Black Power" slogan criticized by, 41, 309; "black talk" and, 18–20, 99, 267, 307; at Boston University, 25, 28–29, 256; as bridge between blacks and whites, 251–253; on brotherhood with whites, 47; call for America's repentance, 83; chameleon-like qualities of, 1–2, 302; charisma, 10; civil religion and, 295; confrontations with racist hatred, 65, 69, 70; "courage to be" fortified by, 221–222; "crossover" talk and, 45, 65, 74, 108, 132, 260, 271, 287–288, 310; at Crozer Theological Seminary, 23, 25, 26, 258; as cultured cosmopolitan, 303; death, preoccupation with, 77–78, 138, 212, 244–245; death threats against, 92, 122–123; on deliverance as rational goal, 199–200; despondency of, 62, 84, 97, 138, 211, 213, 233, 240–241; diverse audiences appealed to, 9; dress style, 22, 100, 176; early encounters with white racism, 21–24, 30; erudition of, 103; Exodus invoked by, 5, 200–202, 220; as father, 119–120, 123, 285; FBI spying on, 45, 55, 62, 260–261, 263; field staff of SCLC and, 69, 70–71; C. L. Franklin as influence on, 88; funeral of, 284; at funeral of Jimmie Jackson, 211–212, 220; Gandhian legacy and, 263–266; in Ghana, 94, 106–107, 112; God as depicted by, 143–144, 146–147, 265; idioms of, 8, 9, 268, 300–301; imaginative universe of others and, 132,

292, 299, 309; in India, 118–119, 132, 260, 264–265; inner circle of, 50–51, 54; institutional education, 10–12, 18; intellectual influences, 25, 29, 30, 80, 82, 96, 101, 104, 117, 275–276, 321; on intermarriage, 34–36; in jail, 56, 62, 96, 184, 194, 206, 220, 257, 264; Jewish audiences and, 290–292; language facility of, 13, 14, 96–97, 118, 135, 143, 204–206, 278; legitimacy talk, 250; on love and justice, 155; on loving enemies, 33–34; mainstream views of, 6; manly action called for, 223–226, 231; mass rally speeches, 152–157, 160, 164–165, 207; millennial triumphalism of, 200; mobilization talk, 233, 237, 270; Montgomery bus boycott and, 158–159, 201, 213–216, 233, 251, 307; at Morehouse, 11, 12, 14, 23, 28, 100; Mosaic identification of, 1, 2, 10, 68, 72, 194, 232; multiple aspects of identity, 4; Nation of Islam and, 45–46; "Negro emotionality" and, 93–94; Nobel Prize and, 14, 72, 105, 138, 164–165, 251, 281; optimism against despair and, 206–207; pacifism and, 40, 258–260, 308; perceived as an "Uncle Tom," 2, 37, 44; performances, 2, 8, 91, 135–137, 195, 256, 288; playful aspect of, 69–70, 75, 105; Poor People's Campaign and, 172, 173, 174–175, 204, 294; as "postethnic" man, 9; as pragmatist, 239; preaching of, 82–84, 88, 90, 94–109, 126; presidents of United States and, 14, 37, 56, 72, 82, 251; prophetic voice, 108, 136; on psychology of racism, 171–172; on race and poverty, 166–167; racial elevation and, 223; retreats from public persona and pressures, 79–80; ribald company in SCLC and, 55–59; "rudeness" of, 251, 310; secular authorities and, 97, 146; slave ancestors and, 222, 227; SNCC and, 41–43; social gospel and, 98, 99, 189, 290; southern black culture and, 54, 56, 57–58; spirituals and, 226–229; stressful life of, 75–76; on suffering, 241, 244; on temptation of black rage, 38–39; trivialization of legacy of, 5; universalism and, 38, 299–300, 302, 321, 330; vernacular sources, 8; Vietnam War denounced by, 1, 36, 77; violence directed toward, 65, 73, 77, 78, 101, 305, 307, 308, 323–324; on Watts rioters, 38; "white talk" and, 99, 255, 256–257, 287; women and, 26, 27, 30–31, 34, 62, 64, 78. See also Sermons (by MLK); see under individual titles for speeches and writings

King, Martin Luther, Sr. ("Daddy King"), 6–7, 63; attitudes toward whites, 51, 59; in Ebenezer pulpit, 76, 99; Exodus preaching, 94–95; friends and colleagues, 26, 88; gospel singers as friends of, 12; at Morehouse, 14; as old-school Baptist preacher, 11; as race man, 21–22

King, Yolanda (daughter of MLK), 119–120, 305, 308, 327

King birthday holiday, 4, 133

Ku Klux Klan, 157, 182, 188, 210, 226, 314; manly resistance to, 232; nonviolence in face of brutality of, 74; plot to kill King, 212, 225; Selma marchers attacked by, 72

Labor unions, 2, 27, 54, 114, 288, 298

Lafayette, Rev. Bernard, 51, 65–67, 210

Language, 49, 100; "crying out," 278; King's love of, 13–14, 80, 96; range in King's preaching, 103–104; rhetoric of menace, 41; "ugly words," 47; vernacular, 105, 113, 114–115, 134; working-class speech, 46–47. See also Dialect speech

Lawson, Rev. James, 54, 187

Lazarus (biblical), 173, 174, 175, 294, 321

Lee, Rev. Bernard, 37, 61, 78; FBI tapes of King and, 55; in King's inner circle, 51; on King's outrage over Vietnam War, 132–133

Lester, Julius, 319

"Letter from Birmingham Jail," 108, 257–258, 332; anger in, 311–313, 318; blackness in, 324–328; clergy addressed in, 303; dynamic of deference in, 291; humble stance in, 313–316; on moral obligation of third parties, 292; as reply to white critics, 260, 301; use of cultural authorities in, 296–297

"Letter to American Christians, A" (Meek sermon), 273

Levison, Stanley, 36, 44, 77, 118, 272; antiwar oratory of King and, 133; friendship with King, 44, 53, 61–62; King's rebuke of Vietnam War and, 263; on King's relations with whites, 54–55; March on Washington speech and, 261; objection to radio sermons, 268; secular leftism of, 279–280; seriousness of, 60

Lewis, David Levering, 252, 255, 264

Lewis, John, 5, 13, 271; critique of Kennedy liberals, 330; on Exodus metaphor, 193–194; freedom riders and, 238; as head of SNCC, 64; on King's "cracking" banter, 59; King's

Lewis, John (continued)
  sermons and, 111, 135; Nashville actions
  and, 187, 243; on oratorical power of King,
  193; violence suffered by, 210, 239
Lewis, Rufus, 304
Liberalism, 96, 250, 267; deep roots of preju-
  dice and, 62; ecumenical, 282; humanistic,
  288; Jewish, 52, 250, 267, 290; Protestant, 7,
  250, 277; secular, 146
Lincoln, Abraham, 317, 329
Lingo, Al, 240
Lischer, Richard, 26, 105, 304
Liuzza, Viola, 210
Longfellow, Henry Wadsworth, 154
Lopez Tijerina, Reies, 172
Los Angeles: churches, 36, 38, 119, 260; riots
  (1992), 208
Love. See Agape; Eros; Philea
Lowery, Rev. Joseph, 61, 81, 88, 103; on black
  audiences, 102; FBI tapes of King and, 55; in
  King's inner circle, 51; King's joking with,
  282; on playing the dozens, 60; as race-man
  preacher, 88–89
Luther, Martin, 316
Lynchings, 22, 38, 68, 279, 284, 287, 326

MacDonald, Dora, 62
Maddox, Lester, 81, 147
Maimonides (Moses ben Maimon), 100
Malcolm X, 6, 37, 182; assassination of, 212;
  audience expectations and, 8; demagogue la-
  bel embraced by, 316; denunciations of
  whites, 170; in jail, 129; King in parallel to,
  168; as master of idioms, 11; on nonviolence
  as cowardice, 241; "white devils" doctrine,
  23, 43; young activists and, 319
March on Washington speech. See "I Have a
  Dream" (March on Washington) speech
Marriage, interracial, 30–31
Marrissett, Andrew, 67, 68, 74, 181, 196
Martyrdom, 85, 200
Masculinity, 6, 59; gang culture and, 67; King's
  appeals to manhood, 223–226, 231; SCLC
  field staff culture and, 64
Mays, Benjamin, 12–13, 24, 100, 101, 290; in
  India, 119; liberal Protestantism and, 30; The
  Negro's Church, 187; social gospel liberalism
  and, 276; at Sunday Evening Club, 275
McAdam, Doug, 219
McCall, Walter, 27–28, 56, 102
McCracken, Robert, 273, 274, 275, 287

Mead, Margaret, 275
Media, 41, 240, 262
Meek, Frederick, 103, 273, 293
Memphis, 10, 177; King's assassination in, 61,
  216; sanitation workers' strike, 226; Sun Re-
  cords, 274; violent protest in, 62, 77
Meredith, James, 29, 40
Meredith March, 40, 42, 69, 164, 309, 325,
  334
Miller, Keith, 201, 273, 274
"Ministers and Marches" (Falwell sermon), 187
Montgomery, Ala., 5, 193, 245; Holt Street
  Church, 112, 154, 203; march from Selma,
  211, 284, 332. See also Dexter Avenue Baptist Church
Montgomery bus boycott, 14, 18, 76, 88, 122,
  223; bombing of King's house and, 77; described in Stride toward Freedom, 256; Exodus narrative and, 201; Gandhi as influence,
  258; King's appeals to white audiences and,
  251; King's primal encounter with God and,
  92; oratory at start of, 153–154; racist officials and, 307; Supreme Court ruling, 214;
  whooping and, 158–159
Montgomery Improvement Association, 152,
  184, 234–235
Moral Man and Immoral Society (Niebuhr), 274
Morehouse College, 23, 99; King's classmates,
  11, 56; Mays as president, 276; social gospel
  tradition at, 100; Spelman as sister school to,
  33
Morris, Aldon, 243
Moses (biblical), 1, 2, 193, 200, 282; black-
  Jewish ecumenical encounters and, 144–145;
  Canaan and, 106; Exodus narrative and, 220;
  Jesus commingled with, 201; King identified
  with, 1, 2, 10, 68, 72, 194, 232; plagues of
  Egypt and, 297; Promised Land and, 217
"Moses at the Red Sea" (C. L. Franklin), 94,
  188
Muhammad, Elijah, 45–46, 48
Music, 132, 141, 268–269, 274–275; gospel,
  12, 94, 187, 231, 303; hymns, 10, 12, 19,
  162, 196; at mass meetings, 153, 156; opera,
  96, 102, 129, 303. See also Blues (musical id-
  iom); Freedom songs; Spirituals

NAACP (National Association for the Advance-
  ment of Colored People), 18, 43, 52, 262
Nash, Diane, 242
National Baptist Convention, 18, 26, 103

National Cathedral (Washington, D.C.), 25, 173, 287, 288, 294, 321

Nation of Islam (NOI), 45, 222

"Negro and the Constitution, The" (King), 22

Negro's Church, The (Mays), 187

Nehru, Jawaharlal, 264

"Never Alone" (gospel hymn), 124, 137, 144

"New Negro," 177

New York City, 43, 47; Cathedral of St. John the Divine, 288, 293; Harlem, 43, 101; Jesse Jackson in, 47; Jewish liberals and leftists, 53

Niebuhr, Reinhold, 155, 256, 263, 272, 282, 287; on evil of racism, 276; on groups and individuals, 291, 328; *Moral Man and Immoral Society,* 274; social gospel and, 29

Niebuhr, Ursula, 282

Nietzsche, Friedrich, 104, 241

"Nigger" epithet, 32, 60, 271, 304, 312, 326; ambiguity in meaning of, 46; "crazy nigger" syndrome, 243; in death threats against King, 122–123, 233; racial bitterness produced by, 33; used in King's inner circle, 57

Nixon, E. D., 304

Nkrumah, Kwame, 94, 95, 106, 108, 110

Nonviolence, 6, 81, 241; gangs and, 65–66; King's mannerly restraint and, 305; suffering and, 71. *See also* Pacifism

Noon Lenten series, 273, 278, 289

"On Being Fit to Live With" (Fosdick sermon), 273

Opera, King's love of, 96, 102, 129, 303

Orange, James, 66, 67, 252; violence suffered by, 210

Oratory, King's, 2, 7, 154–155, 244, 250; "biting into" applause, 160; at mass meetings, 179, 182, 186, 191, 192; rhythm of, 161; white audiences and, 267

Otis, Johnny, 270

Pacifism, 29, 40, 258–260, 308. *See also* Nonviolence

Parables of Jesus, The (Buttrick), 96, 289

Parks, Rosa, 152, 176–177, 245

Paul, Apostle, 19, 190, 204, 316

"Paul's Letter to American Christians" (King sermon), 15, 103, 108, 273, 278; King as Paul, 293–294; radio broadcast of, 111

Peace of Mind (Liebman), 125

Performance, 3, 181; ecstasy as means of mobilization, 195; immediacy of, 91; rational ex-

pectations and, 218; substance and, 89; synthesis with theology, 27, 297

Personalism, 143, 256

Pettus Bridge (Selma, Ala.), 5, 68, 180, 193, 234

Philea (friendship), 103, 139, 273; levels of love and, 116

Phillips, Sam, 274–275

Pollard, Sister, 114, 121, 127, 131, 177, 243

Poor People's Campaign, 83, 133, 166, 172, 204, 294

Popper, Hermine I., 257

Poverty, 5, 16, 20, 119, 174, 326

Powell, Adam Clayton, 78, 106, 252

Powers, Georgia Davis, 78–79

Prayer Pilgrimage for Freedom, 262

Preachers, black folk, 7, 124, 255; language and, 100; "walking the benches," 93; white preachers and mutual influence, 269

Preachers, white, 12, 13, 29, 94, 96; of Birmingham, 315, 325, 328; New England (nineteenth century), 8, 94

"Precious Lord, Take My Hand" (gospel song), 231

Presley, Elvis, 274–275

Price, Sheriff Cecil Ray, 69

Pride, racial, 51, 52, 125, 309

Prinz, Rabbi Joachim, 291, 292

Pritchett, Sheriff Laurie, 184, 199, 228, 234, 240

Prophets, 1, 149, 208, 215, 279

Protestants, white, 4, 7, 10, 267, 279, 329; King's presence in networks of, 272; mainstream, 2; in Nazi Germany, 291; preachers, 12, 13, 29, 94, 96; temples of high Protestantism, 288

Rabbinical Assembly, 286

Race, 2, 6; anthropologists on, 275; brotherhood and, 19–20; cosmopolitan downplaying of, 97–98; King's crossover rhetoric and, 30; race mixing and eroticism, 30; speech and, 8, 15

Race man, figure of, 6, 21–22, 50, 52, 144

Racism, 2, 20, 30, 116, 275; black racism, 45; Christian repudiation of, 290; cultural voyeurism and, 270–271; as denial of God, 282; depth of, 166; in northern white working class, 65; psychology, 125, 172; racist imagery turned around, 34; as sickness, 207, 220;

Racism *(continued)*
  sinfulness of, 207, 292, 297, 316; strength of, 4; unconscious, 35
Ramachandran, G., 119
Rauschenbusch, Walter, 6, 256, 276
Ray, Sandy, 13, 101
Reddick, Lawrence, 61, 286–287
Reeb, Rev. James, 38, 320
Reece, Carlton, 228
Resurrection, 107, 201, 207
Ricks, Willie, 41, 43
Riverside Church, 261, 272, 282, 288
Robeson, Paul, 279
Rogers, Cornish, 34, 256
Rothschild, Rabbi Jacob, 280–281, 287
Rothschild, Janice, 280–281
Rubenstein, Richard, 281
Rustin, Bayard, 32–33, 52, 81, 259, 280; on King's talk of death, 77; as philo-Semite, 279; Southern Baptist culture and, 54; spat with King over speech, 262–263
Rutherford, William, 54, 55, 57

St. Augustine, Fla., 152, 206, 226; desegregation of beaches, 226; Ku Klux Klan in, 182, 225; nonviolent tactics in, 71; plot on King's life in, 244; rabbis in, 271; Young beaten in, 235–236
Schwerner, Michael, 65, 69
Scott, Coretta. *See* King, Coretta Scott
Segregation, 152, 171, 176, 190, 199, 328; as distortion of human personality, 276; as new slavery, 223; sickness and, 220; sinfulness of, 296; as "ugly practice" of United States, 257
Sellers, Cleveland, 164
Selma, Ala., 5, 14, 122, 180; battle of Jericho invoked in, 10; Brown Chapel AME Church, 152, 211; march to Montgomery, 162, 209, 211, 284, 332; Marrissett as hero in, 68; white minister killed in, 38. *See also* Bloody Sunday, in Selma
Separatism, 20, 44, 45
Sermons (by MLK): "American Dream," 118, 288; "Antidotes for Fear," 96, 97; "Birth of a New Nation," 94, 95, 97, 105–109, 110; "Christian Doctrine of Man," 278; "Death of Evil Upon the Seashore," 95–96, 98; "Dimensions of a Complete Life," 94, 105; "Drum Major Instinct," 138, 148; "Guidelines for a Constructive Church," 149; "Interruptions of Life," 141; "Is the Universe

Friendly?" 139, 148; "Judging Others," 115; "Knock at Midnight," 111, 122, 140; "Levels of Love," 115–117; "Loving Your Enemies," 97, 104, 105, 145, 273; "Making the Best of a Bad Mess," 144; "Mastering Our Fears," 132; "On Being a Good Neighbor," 289; oral gospel tradition and, 7; ordination sermon at Ebenezer Baptist Church, 12, 30; "Paul's Letter to American Christians," 15, 103, 108, 111, 273, 278, 293–294; "Questions that Easter Answers," 97–98; on radio, 268; rawness and refinement in, 90, 92; "Rediscovering Lost Values," 192; "Remaining Awake Through a Great Revolution," 321; "Shattered Dreams," 278–279; "Three Dimensions," 125, 134, 146–147, 273; "Unfulfilled Dreams," 36, 139; "What Is Man?" 274; "Why Jesus Called a Man a Fool," 113, 122–123, 124, 142, 273. *See also Strength to Love*
Sexuality, 92, 112; Gandhian asceticism, 265; interracial, 57, 59, 60, 279; marital infidelities, 55; stress of King's life and, 78; Willard Hotel tryst, 62, 80
Shuttlesworth, Rev. Fred, 51, 164, 184, 242–243, 252
Sixteenth Street Baptist Church (Birmingham), 152, 191, 224, 246
Slaves and slavery, 4, 83, 129, 141, 154, 222, 322; ancestors, 2, 154, 222, 336; anticipation of freedom, 107; Exodus story and, 94, 201; legacy of, 168; quest for recognition and, 126; reparations for, 169; slave preachers, 126–127, 148, 175; songs of slaves, 125, 128, 130, 179; spiritual fortitude of slaves, 128, 142, 167, 277; suffering and, 98, 279; "utilitarian love" and, 117
Smiley, Glenn, 243
Smith, Rev. Kelly, 187, 243
Social gospel, 187, 189, 197–198, 290
Socialism, 8, 256, 257
Somebodyness, 125–126, 163, 222, 333
Soul food, 6, 27, 78, 258, 304
Southern Christian Leadership Conference (SCLC), 40, 43, 48, 84, 226; as apostolic vanguard, 85; backstage ribaldry, 55–59, 64; black Christian identity and, 50–51; executive directors, 53, 54, 55; field staff, 59, 66; fundraising, 287; internal tensions, 172; King as head of, 5, 76; mass meetings and, 153; Operation Bread Basket, 52–53; retreats, 80–

81, 170, 191, 232; spectacles of suffering
and, 180; tension between tough and tender,
157; Vietnam War and, 133; white churches
of Birmingham and, 315; whites excluded
from, 52; Young teased within, 252
Spelman College, 33, 99
Spillers, Hortense, 7
Spirituals, 6, 10, 99, 102, 154, 304; deliverance
theme, 187; Exodus narrative and, 181; "Go
Down Moses," 229; "I Have a Dream"
speech and, 107; "Joshua Fit the Battle of Jericho," 226, 227, 336; King's love of black
culture and, 129. See also Freedom songs
Stallings, Rev. Earl, 315
Stewart, Francis, 258
Strange Career of Jim Crow, The (Woodward),
171
Strength to Love (book of King sermons), 108,
173, 273, 275, 288; distance from emotion
in, 305; socialism edited out of, 257; targeted
to white audience, 94, 278
Stride toward Freedom (King), 122, 123–124,
131, 223, 256, 315; on black fellowship,
323; diplomatic reassuring of whites and,
307; "I Have a Dream" speech and, 332; insurgent role as deliberate process, 258;
Kelsey's critique of, 259; King's mannerly restraint in, 303, 305; on nonviolence, 306; on
old and new Negro, 310; Reddick and, 61;
on sin of segregation, 275–276
Student Nonviolent Coordinating Committee
(SNCC), 40–41, 64, 163, 200; Black Power
slogan and, 334; on media spectacle of police
brutality, 240; murders of civil rights workers
and, 320
Student sit-in movement, 184
Suffering, redemptive, 239, 243, 244
Sunday Evening Club (Chicago), 272, 273,
275, 276, 286
Sun Records, 274–275
Supreme Court, U.S., 214, 267
"Symmetry of Life, The" (Brooks sermon), 94

Taylor, Gardner, 13, 26, 101–102, 275, 276
"Testament of Hope" (King), 311
Theologians, 10, 29, 95, 98, 254
Theology, 7, 93, 142, 314; "black theology,"
110, 131; communism's lack of, 96; deliver-
ance and, 188; existential, 141; of hope, 140;
performance and, 297; personalist, 143
Thomas Aquinas, Saint, 96, 291

Thoreau, Henry David, 96, 260, 265
"Three Words" (King), 190
Thurman, Howard, 10, 13, 101, 276, 290;
books by, 277–278; on Jeremiah, 128, 215–
216
Tillich, Paul, 10, 12, 89, 189, 272; abstract theology of, 143; on "courage to be," 141; Dialectical Society debates on, 92; existentialism
of, 256; King's sermons and, 96; on sin as
separation, 296
Twelfth Street Baptist Church (Boston), 25, 27

"Uncle Tom," 2, 37, 44, 188, 226; exclusion
from blackness and, 238; King wounded by
charges of, 252
Ungar, Rabbi Andre, 281
Universalism, 2, 4, 6, 18; black fellowship as
countercurrent to, 50; hypocrisy of whites
and, 36; "I Have a Dream" speech and, 330;
King's immersion in blackness and, 18; language and, 104; race-blind, 60; rooted, 9;
somebodyness and, 126; specialized variants
of, 288
Untouchable caste (India), 2, 118, 265

Vietnam War, 1, 5, 18, 82, 211, 282; American
racism and, 168; children burned with napalm, 132, 148; Democratic coalition fractured by, 251; King criticized for denouncing, 36, 77, 261–262; King disturbed by,
132–133; peace movement, 272
Vivian, Reverend C. T., 5, 48, 187; Exodus invoked by, 200–201; in jail, 242; in King's inner circle, 51; King's opinion of, 61; on
King's preaching, 82; on New Testament influence in King, 149; on substance of King's
preaching, 89; violence suffered by, 196, 210,
226
Vorspan, Al, 47, 271
Vote, right to, 35, 38, 210; Exodus in support
of, 200–201; free riders and, 237; mass rallies
for, 152
Voting Rights Act, 5, 211, 240

Wachtel, Harry, 53
"Wade in the Water" (spiritual), 7, 181, 200
Walker, Rev. Wyatt Tee, 53, 55; delegation of
forbidden acts, 67; in King's inner circle, 51;
on martyrdom, 220; at mass meetings, 153;
on media spectacle of police brutality, 240;
oral tradition and, 255; on substance of

Walker, Rev. Wyatt Tee *(continued)*
King's preaching, 89; on young people in jail, 191
Wallace, George, 4, 11, 36, 147, 229; black defiance of, 231, 234; as Pharaoh, 193; state police of, 180, 240
Walzer, Michael, 183, 299–300
Warren, Robert Penn, 252
Watters, Pat, 156, 232
Weber, Max, 289
"We Shall Overcome" (hymn), 158, 182, 232, 234, 271, 322; Black Power and, 334–335; sung in Hebrew, 279, 284
Wheat Street Baptist Church (Atlanta), 13, 95
Where Do We Go From Here? (King), 256, 309, 310, 318–319, 334
Whitaker, Ed, 31
White audiences, 7, 25, 30, 89, 110, 250; black nationalist rhetoric and, 8; blackness of King and, 318; blackness mixed with universalism and, 251; "black talk" and, 20; communion and, 292; confronted with complicity in evil, 299; cosmopolitan enlightenment and, 290; crossover talk and, 257–258, 287; Exodus narrative and, 293; idiom and, 9; "I Have a Dream" speech and, 330; King's fancy language and, 80; King's self-presentation to, 303; sermons delivered to, 96, 98; slave songs and, 131; vision of community and, 18
Whites, 96, 99, 250, 267; backlash of, 18, 172, 241, 251; black music and, 268–270; at Boston University, 29; brotherhood and, 19–20, 34, 47, 306; in civil rights movement, 210; deep roots of prejudice and, 62; as "devils," 46–48; ethnic working class, 298; hypocrisy of, 65; Jews, 250, 267; in King's inner

circle, 58–59; King's messages to, 2–3, 4; northern working class, 65; peasant immigrants to America, 169; police, 153; poor, 148, 172; sinfulness of slavery and, 167–168; women, 35, 57, 59, 60, 312
Whooping, 136, 159, 234; black popular music and, 268; of Reverend Franklin, 88, 94; Jewish, 271, 280; of King, 92, 135
Why We Can't Wait (King), 256, 257, 308
Willard Hotel tryst, 62, 80
Williams, Reverend A. D., 13
Williams, Rev. Hosea, 41, 48, 59, 73, 85; Exodus invoked by, 200–201; King's opinion of, 61, 67, 69; "nigger" epithet used by, 57; opposition to Vietnam War and, 133; street sensibility and, 66; violence suffered by, 210
Wood, Marcus Garvey, 254–255
Working class, 46, 58–59, 65, 67
World Baptist Convention, 275
Wright, Richard, 195

Young, Rev. Andrew, 6, 9, 37, 77; appeals to manhood, 226; assassination of King and, 61; blackness and, 51–52; Black Power militants and, 320; confrontations with racist hatred, 65; FBI tapes of King and, 55; on folk oratory, 185; integration of Birmingham churches and, 315; on King and "Black Power" militants, 43; King's inner circle and, 51; King's opinion of, 61; mobilization of street-wise volunteers, 67; racial joshing in SCLC and, 57, 58, 80; on racist murders, 38; on sainthood, 85; on Selma protest, 181; as "Uncle Tom," 252; violence suffered by, 235–236
Youngblood, Rev. Johnny, 208–209